The Borzoi Handbook for Writers

Frederick Crews
University of California at Berkeley

Sandra Schor
Queens College
The City University of New York

Alfred A. Knopf   New York

Acknowledgments

Page 152: Bashō, from *The Narrrow Road to the Deep North and Other Travel Sketches*. Reprinted by permission of Penguin Books Ltd.

Page 254: Edith Iglauer, from "The Strangers Next Door," *Atlantic*, July 1973, p. 90. Copyright © 1973 Edith Iglauer as first published in *The Atlantic*. Reprinted with permission.

Page 274: Steven J. Marcus, "How to Court a Cat," *Newsweek*, 22 March 1982, p. 13. Copyright © 1982 by Newsweek, Inc. All Rights Reserved. Reprinted by permission.

Page 299: Susanne K. Langer, "The Lord of Creation," *Fortune*, Jan. 1944, p. 140. Courtesy of *Fortune* Magazine.

Page 301: Nora Ephron, "Seagram's with Moxie," *New York Times Book Review*, 11 March 1979, p. 13. Copyright © 1979 by The New York Times Company. Reprinted by permission.

Page 310: H. W. Fowler, from *A Dictionary of Modern English Usage*, 1937. Reprinted by permission of Oxford University Press.

Page 314: From *The Random House College Dictionary*, Revised Edition. Copyright © 1982 by Random House, Inc. Reprinted by permission.

Page 337: Saul Bellow, from *Herzog*. Copyright © 1961, 1963, 1964 by Saul Bellow. Reprinted by permission of Viking Penguin Inc.

Page 338: Clifton Daniel, from "Presidents I Have Known," *New York Times*, 3 June 1984, sec. 6, 84. Copyright © 1984 by The New York Times Company. Reprinted by permission.

Page 409: Gerald Nachman, "Your Home Guide to Energy Divestiture," *San Francisco Chronicle*, 25 March 1984, Sunday Punch, p. 2. Copyright © San Francisco Chronicle, 1984. Reprinted by permission.

Page 454: Excerpt from *Reader's Guide to Periodical Literature*. Copyright © 1978, 1979 by The H. W. Wilson Company. Material reproduced by permission of the publisher.

Page 456: Excerpt from *Book Review Digest*. Copyright © 1975, 1976 by the H. W. Wilson Company. Material reproduced by permission of the publisher.

Page 465: Paul Johnson, from *Modern Times: The World from the Twenties to the Eighties*. Copyright © 1983 by Paul Johnson. Reprinted by permission of Harper & Row, Publishers, Inc. and Wiedenfeld and Nicholson, Ltd., London.

First Edition

987

Library of Congress Cataloging in Publication Data

Crews, Frederick C.
   The Borzoi handbook for writers.
   Includes index.
   1. English language—Rhetoric. 2. English
language—Grammar—1950- . I. Schor, Sandra.
II. Title.
PE1408.C7145 1984   808'.042   84-21814
ISBN 0-394-33201-6

Manufactured in the United States of America

Cover design: Lawrence R. Didona

Preface

The Borzoi Handbook for Writers is a positive, comprehensive, and flexible guide to prose composition. It combines a reference work's systematic treatment of usage and punctuation with detailed advice about rhetorical strategies. Many examples of student and professional writing illustrate points of both technical correctness and persuasive style. As a result, students should find our chapters useful in every phase of composing, from searching for ideas to drafting, revising, and preparing an appropriate copy for submission.

The following features deserve special mention:

1. Unlike most handbooks, this one does not require a student to memorize grammatical distinctions for their own sake. We treat grammar only insofar as it bears on usage.

2. Our Glossary of Terms, however, supplies fuller grammatical information for those who seek it, and the book's thorough cross-referencing enables a reader to locate concise explanations as needed.

3. Though we amply treat the college essay, students will find that most of our advice applies to any prose they may need to write, from term papers and laboratory reports to memoranda and business letters.

4. This book is above all a guide to drafting and revising. We consistently urge writers to improve their work by stages instead of allowing anxiety over correctness to interfere with the flow of ideas. As for "the rules," we cover them in full measure—but we also show how to keep from being tyrannized by them. Where the strictest "good English" would lead to awkwardness, we offer ways of recasting the entire sentence more idiomatically.

5. Following the advice of Francis Christensen and Mina Shaughnessy, we treat key principles of punctuation under the relevant syntactic structures—modifiers, independent clauses, parallel constructions, and so on. A reader can master both the

placement and the punctuation of, say, nonrestrictive modifiers without having to consult widely separated parts of the book. At the same time, we recognize that an instructor may ask a student to "review the uses of the semicolon" or "learn the difference between parentheses and brackets." Accordingly, we also treat punctuation as a topic in its own right. This double coverage of many rules makes them uniquely easy to locate and apply.

6. We include two sample research papers, showing both the traditional MLA documentation style, with endnotes and a bibliography, and the newer reference list style as explained in the 1984 edition of the *MLA Handbook for Writers of Research Papers.*

Instructors who find exercises helpful should consider adding Michael J. Hennessy's *Borzoi Practice Book for Writers,* an exceptionally full and innovative text that has been prepared expressly to accompany this *Handbook.* Knopf will provide instructors, on request, with an Instructor's Kit containing a manual and answer key for the *Practice Book,* ditto masters and explanations of Robert Atwan's two *Borzoi Diagnostic Tests of Composition,* and sample course syllabuses prepared by four experienced teachers of composition.

As the authors of prior textbooks—*The Random House Guide to Writing* (Schor, with Judith Fishman) and *The Random House Handbook* (Crews)—we remain grateful to many colleagues, students, and editors whose advice endures in the present book. Some readers will notice that we are also specifically indebted to the fourth edition of *The Random House Handbook* itself; we have drawn on many of its precepts and examples without attempting to reproduce its tone. Student writers represented in this book include, among others, Jaime Baczkowski, Angela Day, Carol Dougherty, John Higgins, Louise Hope, George McCoy, Alex Melvin, Avi Miller, and Stefani Pont. Within Random House/Knopf, June Smith, Steve

Pensinger, Seibert Adams, David Follmer, Elisa Turner, and especially Jennifer Sutherland have afforded us their devoted work and sound judgment. And the following experts on composition provided invaluable criticisms that influenced the final shape of our book: Kathleen Dubs, University of San Francisco; Ruth Foreman, South Dakota State University; Roy Fox, Boise State University; Richard Hannaford, University of Idaho; Michael Hennessy, Southwest Texas State University; James Kinney, Virginia Commonwealth University; Linda Peterson, Yale University; Katherine Stone, Georgia State University; Ralph Voss, University of Alabama; and Jean Wyrick, Colorado State University.

Frederick Crews
Sandra Schor

To the Student Writer

The *Borzoi Handbook* is organized as a reference work that you can consult whenever you meet a problem in your writing. Much of its advice deals with relatively small matters such as where to place a punctuation mark or which tense to choose. But the book is also a resource for writing in a wider sense. If you are a college student facing a composition course, we suggest that you begin by reading Chapters 30–35, which will give you a sense of the true "basics"—finding a good idea, developing an appropriate structure, and progressing from draft to draft until you are sure you have made your point clearly and effectively. It is only toward the end of that process that you need concern yourself with the rules and conventions that are often taken to be the heart of acceptable prose.

To get answers to questions you may already have in mind, you need not wait for an instructor to assign specific chapters. Any part of the book can be understood independently of the others, and you will find cross references to any unknown terms. But you should also have a general sense of the *Handbook*'s features. You can get acquainted with those features by glancing at the following parts of the book.

1. The **inside front cover** provides an abbreviated table of contents and a guide to key lists within the text. The Checklist for Revision (p. 420), can be especially useful when you are trying to improve your drafts.

2. The **Table of Contents** (p. xi) shows how the whole book is organized into parts and chapters.

3. The **inside back cover** provides a list of Symbols for Comment and Revision that your instructor may use in marking your papers. Note that problems such as a comma splice can be marked either by a symbol (*cs*) or by a section number (*2b*). Since section numbers accompany the symbols on the inside back cover, you can always find the relevant discussion by locating its *thumb index*—the red box in the margin.

4. The **index** (p. 564) is your surest means of locating any point you need to look up.

5. The **Index of Diction** (p. 341) is a handy alphabetical list which can help you resolve common problems of word choice—for example, *affect* versus *effect*.

6. The **Glossary of Terms** (p. 538) provides definitions of grammatical and rhetorical terms and indicates where you can find a fuller treatment of each term.

Once you grasp the various ways in which this book can be consulted, you should find it of lasting use to your writing in college and beyond.

Contents

I COHERENCE

A USAGE

Usage

Whatever you have to say in your writing, you will want to say it within the rules of **standard written English**—*the "good English" that readers generally expect to find in papers, reports, articles, and books. Fortunately, you already follow most of those rules without having to think about them. In fact, if you did think about them while composing, you would have trouble concentrating on your ideas. The time to worry about correctness is after you have finished at least one draft. Then you can begin making certain that your points will come across without such distractions as incomplete sentences, spelling errors, and subjects and verbs that are incorrectly related.*

Problems with standard written English are usually divided into those of **usage** *and those of* **punctuation**—*that is, between rules for the choice and order of words (usage) and rules for the insertion of marks to bring out a sentence's meaning (punctuation). But usage and punctuation work together toward the same end of making sentences coherent, or fitting together in an easily understood way. Certain classic "usage" problems, such as the sentence fragment and the run-on sentence, are punctuation problems as well. Therefore, though we review the punctuation marks and their functions separately (Chapters 9–13), we also deal with punctuation in the present set of chapters. For example, if you are having trouble with modifiers or parallel constructions, you will find those topics treated as whole units, without artificial postponement of the relevant comma rules.*

1 Complete Sentences

Since a sentence is the basic unit of written discourse, you must be able to recognize complete and incomplete sentences in your drafts. An incomplete sentence—a sentence fragment (1d, p. 11)—will annoy and possibly confuse your reader unless it creates an intended emphatic effect (1e, p. 15).

A sentence begins with a capital letter and customarily ends with a period, question mark, or exclamation point. Unfortunately, unacceptable (unintentional) sentence fragments show these same features. You need to know, then, that a grammatically **complete sentence** normally requires a verb and its subject within an independent clause.

1a Recognize a Verb.

A **verb** is a word or group of words telling the state of its subject or an action that the subject performs. The verb either

1. transmits the action of the subject to a **direct object** (*transitive verb*):

   V   D OBJ
   - The doctor *solved* the *problem*.

   V   D OBJ
   - The technician *took* an *x-ray*.

frag

1a

2. in itself expresses the whole action (*intransitive verb*):

  V
* The patient *recovered.*

  V
* Dr. McGill *lectures* often.

or

3. connects the subject to a **complement,** an element that helps to identify or describe the subject (*linking verb*):

  V   COMP
* Her training *has been scientific.*

  V   COMP
* She *is* a recognized *professional.*

The verb plus all the words belonging with it make up the **predicate.**

Verb Position

In normal word order for statements, the verb follows its subject:

  S   V
* The *committee is meeting.*

  S   V
* The *lawyers argued.*

  S   V
* The *law will remain* on the books.

But in some questions the verb comes before the subject:

  V   S
* *Are you* sure?

And in most questions the verb has two parts that surround the subject:

          ⌐—V—⌐
* *Is* the guitarist *playing* tonight?
      S

          ⌐—V—⌐
* When *does* Claude *speak* Japanese?
          S

          ⌐—V—⌐
* *Have* scientists *been consulted?*
         S

Change of Verb Form

Verbs show **inflection,** or changes of form, to indicate tense or time. Note the following examples.

PRESENT TENSE	PAST TENSE	FUTURE TENSE
They *iron* their jeans.	They *ironed* their jeans.	They *will iron* their jeans.
He *fights* hard.	He *fought* hard.	He *will fight* hard.

Verb versus Verbal

Certain words resemble verbs and can even change their form to show different times. Yet these **verbals**—infinitives, participles, and gerunds—function like nouns or modifiers instead of like verbs. Thus they do *not* supply a key element for sentence completeness. Compare the sentences and fragments below.

COMPLETE SENTENCE	FRAGMENT
$\overset{\text{V}}{\text{We }\textit{will break}}$ our record.	INF (=NOUN) *To break* our record.
$\overset{\text{V}}{\text{Eve }\textit{was laughing}}$ out loud.	PART (=MOD) *Laughing* out loud.
$\overset{\text{V}}{\text{Are they }\textit{winning}}$ the championship?	GER (=NOUN) *Winning* the championship.

Note how you can tell that the three verbals in the right column are not functioning as verbs:

1. One kind of verbal, an infinitive, is often preceded by *to (to break)*. A true verb in a sentence stands alone.

2. A verbal ending in *-ing* is one word. When a true verb ends in *-ing,* it is always preceded by a word or words that count as part of the verb *(was laughing, have been winning).*

You can write complete sentences that include verbals, but only by supplying true subject-verb combinations:

- $\overbrace{\textit{To break our record}}^{\text{S}}\ \overset{\text{V}}{\textit{will be}}$ difficult.

- Laughing out loud, *Eve ran* a victory lap.
  S V

- *Winning the championship is* not easy.
  S V

1b Recognize a Subject.

A **subject** is the person, thing, or idea about which something is said or asked. Locating a subject therefore involves locating its accompanying verb.

Most subjects are nouns—words like *car, philosophy,* and *Herbert.* Some subjects are pronouns, such as *she* or *they* or *someone.* And others, which we will call *nounlike elements,* are whole groups of words that function together as single nouns: *to run fast, winning the championship,* etc. Thus you cannot spot a subject simply by its form. You must find the verb and then ask who or what performs the action of that verb or is in the state expressed by it:

- My car   } V
- Whatever you see } *is* for sale.

> What is for sale? *My car, Whatever you see.*
> These two elements are the subjects.

- That law *affects* all drivers.
  V

> What affects all drivers? *That law.*
> The subject is *That law.*

- *Does* anyone *speak* Japanese?
  V

> Does who speak Japanese? The subject is *anyone.*

Implied Subject

You cannot write a grammatically complete sentence without a verb, but in commands the subject *you* typically disappears:

- [You] Watch out!

This example would not be considered a fragment, since the implied subject *You* is regarded as part of the sentence.

1c Distinguish an Independent Clause from a Subordinate One.

A **clause** is a cluster of words containing a subject and a predicate—that is, something written about (the subject) and the verb plus all the words that go with it (the predicate):

      S   PRED
- *Mike sells chickens.*

            S   PRED
- Although *Mike sells chickens, . . .*

As you can see, there is an important difference between these two examples. The first clause is **independent;** it can stand alone as a sentence. The second is **subordinate** (or dependent); other elements must accompany it to make a complete sentence. Again:

INDEPENDENT CLAUSES	SUBORDINATE CLAUSES
The poster was badly printed.	Although the poster was badly printed, . . .
Dogs were running wild.	Because dogs were running wild, . . .
It rained on Tuesday.	After it rained on Tuesday, . . .

Subordinate clauses serve important functions, but by themselves they are sentence fragments. You can learn to recognize most of them by the way they begin. A subordinate clause is usually introduced by either

1. a **subordinating conjunction,** a word like *although, as, because,* or *when,* which subordinates (makes dependent) the following subject and predicate,

or

2. a **relative pronoun,** a word like *who, which,* or *that,* which begins a relative clause.

A **relative clause** is a subordinate clause that relates its statement to an earlier or *antecedent* part of the sentence.

ANT   REL CLAUSE
- She is the *one who ran the race.*

Sometimes you will find that an independent clause, like many subordinate ones, follows a conjunction. But that word will always be one of the seven **coordinating conjunctions.** If you keep those seven words distinct in your mind from subordinating conjunctions and relative pronouns, you will have a head start toward distinguishing between independent and subordinate clauses.

COORDINATING CONJUNCTIONS
(may precede independent clauses)

and	for	or	yet
but	nor	so	

SUBORDINATING CONJUNCTIONS
(begin some subordinate clauses)

after	because	than	whenever
although	before	that	where
as	if	though	wherever
as if	in order that	till	while
as long as	provided (that)	unless	why
as soon as	since	until	
as though	so (that)	when	

RELATIVE PRONOUNS (begin relative subordinate clauses)

who	whom	which	that

Remember, then, that each of your sentences should normally contain at least one independent clause—a construction which, like *Mike sells chickens,* contains a subject and predicate but is not introduced by a subordinating conjunction or relative pronoun:

IND CLAUSE
- Acting on a hunch, *I removed the book from the shelf.*

IND CLAUSE
- As I opened the book, *twenty-dollar bills fluttered to the carpet.*

IND CLAUSE   IND CLAUSE
- *I stared intently,* and *my palms began to sweat.*

IND CLAUSE
- Although I am tempted to keep it, *this money will have to be turned over to the police.*

1d Eliminate an Unacceptable Sentence Fragment.

A **sentence fragment** is a word or set of words beginning with a capital letter and punctuated as a sentence but lacking an independent clause (1c). Typically, a fragment is either a subordinate clause (1c) or a **phrase**—a cluster of words lacking a subject-predicate combination:

SUBORDINATE CLAUSES:

x Because milk and eggs are still a bargain.

x Unless winning at chess is important to you.

x Which makes my uncle nervous.

PHRASES:

x Such as milk and eggs.

x Winning at chess.

x My uncle being nervous.

Most unacceptable fragments are detached parts of a preceding sentence. They may be difficult to spot, for your mind supplies connections that are hidden from your reader. The handiest way to correct most fragments is to add them to that earlier sentence:

frag
1d

UNACCEPTABLE FRAGMENTS (italicized):

- Local agencies will become overcrowded and ineffective. x *Unless the number of mental health services is increased.*
- Alex and Dolores played tennis in the park. x *Instead of at school.*
- They stood back and watched the crows. x *Wheeling and cawing over the splattered melon.*
- It is still productive. x *The tobacco farm which has been in use since the Civil War.*

COMPLETE SENTENCES:

- Unless the number of mental health services is increased, local agencies will become overcrowded and ineffective.
- Alex and Dolores played tennis in the park instead of at school.
- They stood back and watched the crows wheeling and cawing over the splattered melon.
- The tobacco farm, which has been in use since the Civil War, is still productive.

Again, the italicized parts of the following passage are unacceptable fragments.

CONTAINING FRAGMENTS:

On Thursday we reported the numbers of our missing traveler's checks. *Which were lost during our arrival in New Orleans that morning.* We sat down outside the American Express office and watched other tourists. *Who were sunning themselves on the levee.* We were feeling low because we thought we had missed our chance to hear some Dixieland jazz. We were overjoyed, though, when a group of musicians ambled by and set up their instruments. *Right there on the levee.* We spent the rest of the afternoon listening to their music. *The best open-air jazz concert in town.*

REVISED:

On Thursday we reported the numbers of our missing traveler's checks, which we had lost during our arrival in New Orleans that morning. We sat down outside the American Express office and watched other tourists sunning themselves on the levee. We were feeling low because we thought we had missed our chance to hear some Dixieland jazz. We were overjoyed, though, when a group of musicians ambled by and set up their instruments right there on the levee. We spent the rest of the afternoon listening to their music—the best open-air jazz concert in town.

How to Spot a Fragment

You can recognize many fragments by the words that introduce them—subordinating terms such as *although, because, especially, even, except, for example, including, instead of, so that, such as, that, which, who,* and *when.* Some fragments lack such tipoff words, but when you see a draft "sentence" beginning with one of those terms, check to see if you have included a full independent clause (1c, p. 9).

DRAFT (fragments italicized):

I always helped my brother. *Especially with his car.* I assisted him in many chores. *Such as washing the car and vacuuming the interior.* He let me do whatever I wanted. *Except start the engine.* Now I drive my own car. *Which is a 1974 Chevy.* I am thinking of possible jobs to help pay the cost of upkeep. *Including driving a cab. Because maintaining a car these days can be expensive.*

REVISED:

I always helped my brother, especially with his car. I assisted him in many chores, such as washing the car and vacuuming the interior. He let me do whatever I wanted except start the engine. Now I drive my own car, a 1974 Chevy. I am thinking of possible jobs, including driving a cab, to help pay the cost of upkeep. Maintaining a car these days can be expensive.

Learn to recognize the following five types of fragments.

1. A subordinate clause posing as a whole sentence.

DRAFT:

Living in the city is more dangerous than ever. *Especially if you are wearing a gold chain.* During the past several weeks gold snatchers have been on a crime spree. *Although the police have tried to track down the thieves.* Nobody with a chain is safe. *Because the victims range from drivers stalled in traffic jams to students in gym classes.*

REVISED:

Living in the city is more dangerous than ever, especially if you are wearing a gold chain. Although the police have tried to track down the thieves, during the past several weeks gold snatchers have been on a crime spree. Nobody with a chain is safe; the victims range from drivers stalled in traffic jams to students in gym classes.

2. A verbal (1a, p. 7) unaccompanied by an independent clause.

DRAFT:

Before the start of the race, the drivers sat in their cars. *Revving up their engines.* They all had the same dream. *To see that checkered flag waving when they crossed the finish line.*

REVISED:

Before the start of the race, the drivers sat in their cars, revving up their engines. They all had the same dream: to see that checkered flag waving when they crossed the finish line.

3. An appositive (4l, p. 62) standing alone.

DRAFT:

I love to read about the Roaring Twenties. *A decade that had its own personality.* For a while at least, people seemed to forget about the terrors of the twentieth century. *War, economic collapse, widespread hunger.*

REVISED:

I love to read about the Roaring Twenties, a decade that had its own personality. For a while at least, people seemed to forget about the terrors of the twentieth century—war, economic collapse, widespread hunger.

4. A disconnected second verb governed by a subject in the sentence before.

DRAFT:

The speech for my radio course took a long time to prepare. *And then turned out poorly.* I needed a live audience. *But didn't have one for the test.*

REVISED:

The speech for my radio course took a long time to prepare and then turned out poorly. I needed a live audience but didn't have one for the test.

5. A "sentence" lacking a main verb.

DRAFT:

If there are no more malpractice suits, the hospital to win its license renewal. But no one can be sure. *Because patients these days are very quick to go to court.*

REVISED:

If there are no more malpractice suits, the hospital will win its license renewal. But no one can be sure, because patients these days are very quick to go to court.

Sentence Beginning with a Coordinating Conjunction

Note that there is nothing wrong with beginning a sentence with a coordinating conjunction (1c, p. 10) such as *and* or *but,* provided you want the effect to be informal or conversational.

ACCEPTABLE:

- I said farewell to my friends in high school. *And in September I began a completely new life.*

1e If You Have Overcome the Unacceptable Sentence Fragment, Note the Uses of the Intentional One.

Some composition instructors advise against any use of fragments in submitted work. They feel, understandably, that students should eliminate habitual mistakes before trying flourishes of style. But you should know that practiced writers do resort to an occasional **intentional fragment** when they want to reply to a question in the previous sentence or make a point concisely and emphatically. When you are sure you have the unacceptable fragment under control, you may want to try your hand at the intentional one.

ACCEPTABLE:

- He sets him up with jabs, he works to the body, he corners him
  INTENTIONAL FRAG
  on the ropes. *Then the finish, a left hook to the jaw that brings him down.*

- Many secretaries were outraged by the shift to a later working
  INTENTIONAL FRAG
  day. *But not quite all of them.*

                                      INTENTIONAL FRAG
- And now for the dessert. *Pecan pie and ice cream!*

You will see from your reading of published authors that intentional fragments usually possess a certain "shock value." Whereas an unacceptable fragment looks like a missing part of a neighboring sentence, an intentional fragment is a condensed means of lending punch to a new statement.

2 Joining Independent Clauses

2a Join Two Independent Clauses Either with a Comma and a Coordinating Conjunction or with a Semicolon.

An **independent clause** is a grammatically complete statement, question, or exclamation—one that could stand alone as a full sentence, whether or not it actually does stand alone (1c, p. 9).

INDEPENDENT CLAUSES:

- I need a rest.   [statement]
- Have I ever been this tired before?   [question]
- Leave me alone!   [exclamation]

Comma and Coordinating Conjunction

There are two usual ways of joining independent clauses within a single sentence. The first way is to put a comma after the first independent clause and to follow the comma with a **coordinating conjunction**—that is, one of the following seven connectives: *and, but, for, or, nor, so, yet.*

IND CLAUSE   COORD CONJ   IND CLAUSE

- Many students took this course, *but* few have kept up with the work.

IND CLAUSE   COORD CONJ   IND CLAUSE

- I am not prepared, *and* I dread seeing the questions.

IND CLAUSE   COORD CONJ   IND CLAUSE

- Am I going crazy, *or* do I just need a good night's sleep?

IND CLAUSE   COORD CONJ   IND CLAUSE

- Stop talking, *and* turn that radio down!

Semicolon

Alternatively, you can join independent clauses with a semicolon alone if they are closely related in meaning and spirit or show a striking, pointed contrast:

IND CLAUSE   IND CLAUSE

- I am not prepared; I dread seeing the questions.

IND CLAUSE   IND CLAUSE

- Many students took this course; few have kept up with the work.

When using a semicolon, test to see if what comes before it could make a complete sentence and if what comes after it could also make a complete sentence. If either test fails, your draft sentence is faulty.

DON'T:

x She said she was sorry I was leaving; especially because it would not be easy to find a replacement.

x My wife thought I should have apologized; since I was the one who had left the directions at home.

x Only five of us; however, had been to the previous meeting.

x My grandparents said that they were too tired to see me; but that they would phone me later.

x He strode into the room; while flicking the light switch on.

If you decide to keep the semicolon, reword the sentence to make sure you have independent clauses on both sides.

DO:

* She said she was sorry I was leaving; it would not be easy, she added, to find a replacement.
* My wife thought I should have apologized; after all, I was the one who had left the directions at home.

In some cases you will find it easier simply to eliminate the semicolon or replace it with a comma.

DO:

* Only five of us, however, had been to the previous meeting.
* My grandparents said that they were too tired to see me, but that they would phone me later.
* He strode into the room while flicking the light switch on.

2b Avoid a Run-on Sentence.

If you remember how to join independent clauses, you will be able to spot and correct a **run-on sentence**—that is, a sentence in which two or more independent clauses are joined with no punctuation or with only a comma between them.

RUN-ON SENTENCES:

x I need a rest, I must keep studying for the exam.

x I am not prepared I dread seeing the questions.

We will see that these sentences illustrate the two most common kinds of run-on, the comma splice and the fused sentence.

There are other ways to correct a run-on besides inserting a semicolon or a comma and a coordinating conjunction—for example, by changing one of the independent clauses to a subordinate clause or a phrase (2d, p. 26). But if you decide to keep your two independent clauses, remember the rules for joining them correctly (2a).

COMMA AND COORDINATING CONJUNCTION:

• I need a rest, *but* I must keep studying for the exam.

SEMICOLON:

• I am not prepared; I dread seeing the questions.

Comma Splice

A run-on sentence in which a comma alone joins two independent clauses is known as a **comma splice.** Such a construction does not seriously garble the statement being made, but it fails to indicate how its two clauses are related in meaning.

DON'T:

| FIRST IND CLAUSE | SECOND IND CLAUSE |

x Faulkner's novel is psychologically deep, they wanted to explore it further.

| FIRST IND CLAUSE | SECOND IND CLAUSE |

x They discussed Faulkner's novel, the class hour ended all too soon.

If you find a comma splice in one of your drafts, you can revise it in a number of ways, including the subordinating of one element to another.

COMMA AND COORDINATING CONJUNCTION (2a, p. 17):

• Faulkner's novel is psychologically deep, *and* they wanted to explore it further.

SEMICOLON (2a, p. 18):

• Faulkner's novel is psychologically deep; they wanted to explore it further.

SUBORDINATE CLAUSE (1c, p. 9):

• *Although they discussed Faulkner's novel,* the class hour ended all too soon.

PHRASE (1d, p. 11):

- The class hour came to an end, *leaving them unable to finish their discussion of Faulkner's novel.*

Exception: Note that a tag such as *she thought* or *he said* can be joined to a quotation by a comma alone, even if the quotation is another independent clause.

```
             IND CLAUSE              IND CLAUSE
```
- "That is a matter of opinion," Emily replied.

For further ways of joining independent clauses, including another exception to the rule against comma splices, see 2d and 2e, pages 25–27.

Fused Sentence

A run-on sentence in which independent clauses are merged with no sign of their separateness—neither a comma nor a coordinating conjunction—is called a **fused sentence.**

DON'T:

```
              IND CLAUSE                 IND CLAUSE
```
x Some people can hide their nervous habits I envy them.

```
            IND CLAUSE                 IND CLAUSE
```
x Sometimes I have to stand up in front of other students it makes me sick.

Revise by choosing from the same options given above for correcting a comma splice.

COMMA AND COORDINATING CONJUNCTION:
- Some people can hide their nervous habits, *and* I envy them.

SEMICOLON:
- Some people can hide their nervous habits; I envy them.

SUBORDINATE CLAUSE:
- I feel sick *whenever I have to stand up in front of other students.*

PHRASE:
- I feel sick *standing up in front of other students.*

2c Do Not Mistake a Sentence Adverb or Transitional Phrase for a Conjunction.

Look through the following terms, which often lead a writer to commit a comma splice (2b, p. 20):

SENTENCE ADVERBS		
again	hence	nonetheless
also	however	otherwise
besides	indeed	similarly
consequently	likewise	then
further	moreover	therefore
furthermore	nevertheless	thus *(etc.)*

TRANSITIONAL PHRASES		
after all	for example	in reality
as a result	in addition	in truth
at the same time	in fact	on the contrary
even so	in other words	on the other hand *(etc.)*

A **sentence adverb** (also called a *conjunctive adverb*) is a word that modifies a whole previous statement. Note how such a term differs from an ordinary adverb.

ORDINARY ADVERB:
- She applied for the job *again* in March.
- *Then* she made arrangements to have her furniture stored.

run-on
2c

SENTENCE ADVERB:
- *Again,* there is still another reason to delay a decision.
- We see, *then,* that precautions are in order.

An ordinary adverb modifies part of the statement in which it appears: she applied *again;* she stored her furniture *then.* But a sentence adverb modifies the whole statement by showing its logical relation to the preceding statement: after the already stated reason to delay, here *(again)* is another one; because of the preceding statement, we therefore *(then)* see that precautions are in order. A **transitional phrase** is a multiword expression that functions like a sentence adverb.

What makes these modifiers tricky is that they "feel like" conjunctions such as *and, but, although, so,* and *yet.* If you treat a sentence adverb or transitional phrase as if it were a conjunction, the result will be a comma splice.

DON'T:

    SENT ADV
x We planted a garden, *however* nothing grew.

         SENT ADV
x Severe rains washed away our seeds, *furthermore,* a late freeze occurred in April.

       TRANS PHRASE
x Our garden was a disappointment, *in fact* it was a disaster.

       TRANS PHRASE
x We had no vegetables of our own, *as a result* we had to rely on the grocery store.

You can revise such sentences in any of the ways previously discussed, either by properly joining the independent clauses (2a, p. 17) or by changing the whole construction.

DO:

- We planted a garden, but nothing grew.
- Severe rains washed away our seeds; furthermore, a late freeze occurred in April.
- Our garden was not just a disappointment but a disaster.
- We had no vegetables of our own, and as a result we had to rely on the grocery store.

If you are not sure whether a certain word is a sentence adverb, test to see whether it could be moved without loss of meaning. A conjunction must stay put, but a sentence adverb can always be moved to at least one other position:

- We planted a garden; *however,* nothing grew.
- We planted a garden; nothing, *however,* grew.
- We planted a garden; nothing grew, *however.*

When you are sure of the difference between conjunctions and sentence adverbs, you will be able to avoid putting an unneeded comma after a conjunction.

DON'T:

             CONJ
x He swam for the island, *but,* the swim exhausted him.

             CONJ
x Take one pill every six hours, *or,* take two pills at bedtime.

             CONJ
x The strike ended quickly, *since,* both management and labor were eager to return to work.

             CONJ
x The threat is serious, *yet,* I think we have grounds for hope.

DO:

- He swam for the island, but the swim exhausted him.
- Take one pill every six hours, or take two pills at bedtime.

- The strike ended quickly, since both management and labor were eager to return to work.
- The threat is serious, yet I think we have grounds for hope.

Setting Off Sentence Adverbs and Transitional Phrases

Since these expressions modify a whole previous statement, they are usually set apart by punctuation on both sides. Do not allow a sentence adverb or transitional phrase to "leak" at one end or the other.

DON'T:

x John, *however* was nowhere to be seen.

x Guatemala *in contrast,* has a troubled history.

DO:

- John, however, was nowhere to be seen.
- Guatemala, in contrast, has a troubled history.

In some cases you can omit commas or other punctuation around a sentence adverb *(And thus it is clear that . . .)*. But if you supply punctuation at one end, be sure to supply it at the other end as well. (See 4k, p. 61.)

2d Correct a Run-on Sentence by Bringing Out Logical Relations.

If you habitually write run-on sentences, you may think you can solve your problem by keeping to safe, short sentences that scarcely combine clauses at all. But that can only be a stopgap measure; before long you will want to aim for more variety and logical development. Begin thinking, then, not of stripping down your sentences but of developing them by showing just how one element relates to another. Note the following options.

1. **semicolon** (2a, p. 18). Use a semicolon to show that two independent clauses are closely related in meaning:

- The seed company recently went bankrupt; apparently the other customers were as unhappy as we had been.

2. **comma and coordinating conjunction** (2a, p. 17). Show the roughly equal importance of two independent clauses by means of a comma and a coordinating conjunction:

- The garden was a failure, *but* at least we got some fresh air and exercise.

3. **subordinate clause** (1c, p. 9). Use a subordinate clause—one that cannot stand alone—to show that one element is logically dependent on the other, more important one:

- *Although the garden was a failure*, at least we got some fresh air and exercise.

4. **phrase** (1d, p. 11). Use a phrase—a cluster of words lacking a subject-predicate combination—to reduce your sentence to one statement accompanied by a modifier:

- *After bruising our hands in the garden*, we were ready for a new form of recreation.

For further options in sentence variety see Chapter 26, especially pp. 306–309.

2e Recognize Exceptional Ways of Joining Independent Clauses.

Optional Comma after Brief Independent Clause

If your first independent clause is brief, consider the comma optional:

- *I was late* and it was already growing dark.

  But a comma after *late* would also be correct. When in doubt, retain the comma.

Optional Conjunctions in Series of Independent Clauses

When you are presenting several brief, tightly related independent clauses in a series (7j, p. 100), you can gain a dramatic effect by doing without a coordinating conjunction:

**run-on
2e**

- He saw the train, he fell to the tracks, he covered his head with his arms.

 By omitting *and* before the last clause, the writer brings out the rapidity and urgency of the three actions. This is a rare case of an acceptable comma splice.

Reversal of Negative Emphasis

If a second independent clause reverses the negative emphasis of the first, consider joining them only with a comma:

- That summer Thoreau did not read books, he hoed beans.

 The *not* clause leaves us anticipating a second clause that will say what Thoreau did do. The absence of a conjunction brings out the tight, necessary relation between the two statements.

Compare:

 x Thoreau hoed beans all summer, he did not read books.

 Lacking a "reversal of negative emphasis," this sentence shows a classic *unacceptable* comma splice.

3 Subject-Verb Relations

3a Avoid a Mixed Construction.

If your subjects and verbs (1a and 1b, pp. 5–9) are to work efficiently together, you cannot leave your reader wondering which part of a sentence is the subject. Do not begin a sentence with one subject and then change your mind.

DON'T:

     SUBJ?   SUBJ?

x The *old gentleman, he* should watch his step in the bathtub.

> Here the reader has every reason to think that *old gentleman* will be the subject of the verb *watch*. But after the comma the writer serves up a new subject, *he,* leaving the *old gentleman* grammatically stranded. *He* is a redundant (extra) subject.

DO:

• The old gentleman should watch his step in the bathtub.

The first "old gentleman" sentence illustrates **mixed construction**, whereby a sentence sprouts a new element that does not fit into its apparent structure. This problem of incoherence extends beyond subjects and verbs.

DON'T:

x In doing the workbook problems was extremely useful.

> The sentence begins with a prepositional phrase (p. 555) that can only serve as a modifier (4a, p. 46)—as it would, for ex-

28

ample, in this sentence: *In doing the workbook problems I had trouble with quadratic equations.* But the writer has tried unsuccessfully to turn *In doing the workbook problems* into a subject.

When you suspect that a draft sentence suffers from mixed construction, first isolate the predicate (1a, p. 6); then ask yourself what *one* thing makes that predicate meaningful. Thus, *what* was extremely useful? *Doing the workbook problems.* That phrase should become the subject.

DO:

* Doing the workbook problems was extremely useful.

DON'T:
>   D OBJ?   D OBJ?

x They gave *it* to her for Christmas *what* she had been asking for.

Here *it* and *what* are competing to be the direct object (1a, p. 5) of the verb *gave.* The solution is to choose one or the other and make a consistent pattern.

DO:

* For Christmas they gave her what she had been asking for.

If your prose contains mixed constructions, review the essential sentence elements: subject, verb, direct object, complement (1a, pp. 5–6). And be aware that in written prose you cannot make your meaning clear by changing your voice or by abandoning a sentence in the middle and starting over. The first element in a written sentence usually commits it to a certain structure that you must then follow. If you run into trouble, recast the sentence from the beginning.

3b Make a Verb Agree with Its Subject in Number and Person.

In standard written English the ending of a verb often shows the **number** of the subject —that is, whether the subject is **singular** (one

agr
3b

item) or **plural** (more than one item). A singular subject requires a singular verb; a plural subject requires a plural verb.

SUBJ   V
● The *river flows* south.

> Here the *-s* ending on the verb *flows* indicates that the verb is in the third person, is singular, and is in the present tense.

In grammar we refer to three **persons**:

	EXAMPLE	IDENTITY
First Person	I pull	the speaker or writer
	we pull	the speakers or writers
Second Person	you pull	the person or persons addressed
Third Person	he, she, it pulls the mother speaks the signal changes	the person or thing spoken or written about
	they pull the mothers speak the signals change	the persons or things spoken or written about

We also refer to the *time* of a verb as its **tense** —present, past, future, etc.

The grammatical correspondence of subjects and verbs is called **agreement.** In *The river flows south* the verb *flows* is said to agree with its singular, third-person subject *river*. Note that the singular subject usually has no *-s* ending but that a singular, third-person verb in the present tense does have an *-s* ending: *flows*. Compare:

SUBJ   V
● The *rivers flow* south.

> The lack of an *-s* ending on the verb *flow* indicates that the verb is plural, in agreement with its plural subject *rivers*. Notice that the *-s* on *rivers* marks it as a plural noun.

SINGULAR:
- The river flows.

PLURAL:
- The rivers flow.

Many native speakers of English use the same forms for both the singular and plural of certain verbs in the present tense: *she don't, they don't; he is, we is.* In standard written English, however, it is important to observe the difference: *she does not, she doesn't, they do not, they don't; he is, we are.*

DON'T:

x They *is* having a party.

x He *don't* expect to rent a car.

DO:

- They *are* having a party.
- He *does not* expect to rent a car.
- He *doesn't* expect to rent a car.

For further verb forms in various tenses, see 15b and 15c, pp. 171, 179.

3c Do Not Allow an Intervening Clause or Phrase to Disguise the True Subject.

It is easy to lose track of your subject if it is followed by a phrase or clause instead of by the verb. The last word of the phrase or clause can get mistaken for the subject, and the result is subject-verb disagreement.

DON'T:

SUBJ INTERVENING CLAUSE

x The *highway* that runs through these isolated mountain towns
V
are steep and narrow.

agr
3d

SUBJ INTERVENING PHRASE V
x The *pleasures* of a motorcyclist *includes* repairing the bike.

DO:

SUBJ   V
● The *highway* . . . *is* steep and narrow.

SUBJ   V
● The *pleasures* . . . *include* repairing the bike.

Testing for a Singular or Plural Subject

Learn to locate the true subject by asking who or what performs the action of the verb or is in the state indicated by the verb. Test for singular or plural by these steps:

1. Locate the verb and its subject.

2. Put the phrase between them into imaginary parentheses:

    The pleasures (of a motorcyclist) $\dfrac{\text{include}}{\text{includes}}$ . . . .

3. Then say aloud:

    "The pleasures include"

and

    "The pleasures includes."

The form of the verb that is correct without the element "in parentheses" is also correct with it: *The pleasures of a motorcyclist include*. . . .

3d Do Not Count an Additive Phrase as Part of the Subject.

An **additive phrase** is an expression that begins with a term like *accompanied by, along with, as well as, in addition to, including,* or *together with.* Though it is typically set off by commas (4j, p. 60), it can "feel like" part of the subject. For example, if you say *Joan, together with her friends,* you certainly have more than one person in mind. But grammatically, additive phrases do *not* add anything to the subject. Disregard the additive phrase, just as you would any other intervening element (3c). If the subject apart from the additive phrase is singular, make the verb singular as well.

DON'T:

SUBJ ⎯⎯⎯⎯⎯ ADDITIVE PHRASE ⎯⎯⎯⎯⎯ V

x *Jill,* along with her two karate instructors, *are* highly disciplined.

SUBJ ⎯⎯⎯⎯⎯ ADDITIVE PHRASE ⎯⎯⎯⎯⎯

x *Practical knowledge,* in addition to statistics and market theory,

V

enter into the training of an economist.

DO:

- Jill, along with her two karate instructors, *is* highly disciplined.

- Practical knowledge, in addition to statistics and market theory, *enters* into the training of an economist.

3e When a Subject Follows a Verb, Do Not Allow an Earlier Noun to Control the Number of the Verb.

DON'T:

V   SUBJ

x Beside the blue waters *lie Claire,* waiting for Henry to bring the towels.

To find the true subject, mentally rearrange the sentence into normal subject-verb word order: *Claire lies beside. . . .*

DO:

- Beside the blue waters *lies* Claire, waiting for Henry to bring the towels.

Expressions Like *There Is*, *Here Comes*

Watch especially for agreement problems when the subject is delayed by an expression like *There is* or *Here comes.* By the time such a sentence is finished it may have acquired a plural subject.

DON'T:

         V   SUBJ
x There *is* pay-as-you-write *typewriters* in the library.

       V   SUBJ
x Here *comes a clown and three elephants.*

DO:

- There *are* pay-as-you-write typewriters in the library.
- Here *come* a clown and three elephants.

Or, since this example sounds strained:

- Here *comes* a clown leading three elephants.

3f When Your Subject Is a Phrase or Clause, Make the Verb Singular.

A phrase or clause acting as a subject takes a singular verb, even if it contains plural items. Do not be misled by a plural word at the end of the phrase or clause. The following sentences are correct:

      PHRASE AS SUBJ   V
- *Having a robot with eight arms is* quite a convenience.

      CLAUSE AS SUBJ   V
- *Whenever you have time to test these skates is* a good time for me.

3g Usually Treat a Collective Noun as Singular.

A **collective noun** is one having a singular form but referring to a group of members: *administration, army, audience, class, crowd, orchestra, team,* etc. This conflict between form and meaning can lead to agreement problems. But in general you should think of a collective noun as singular and thus make the verb singular, too:

- The faculty *has* voted against allowing musicians to perform outside classroom windows.
- The audience *is* on its feet and applauding wildly.
- The orchestra *returns* and *takes* another bow.

Once in a while, however, you may want to emphasize the individual members of the group. Then you should make the verb plural:

- The faculty *have* come to their assignments from all over the world.

Plural *Of* Construction

A plural verb is especially common when a collective noun is followed by a plural *of* construction:

SUBJ   V
- *A team of experts are* arriving by plane tomorrow.

   In this sentence *is* would also be correct, but it would put emphasis on the collective *team* instead of on the individual *experts.*

3h When the Subject Is Compound, Usually Treat It as Plural.

A compound subject, such as *a clown and three elephants,* is made up of more than one unit. With three exceptions (3i, 3j, 3k) such a subject calls for a plural verb.

SUBJ   V
- *A teller and a guard operate* the drive-in window at the bank.

SUBJ   V   COMPL
- *A bouquet and a box of candy are* no substitute for a fair wage.

   Note that *substitute* is singular even though the subject and verb are plural. Agreement does not extend to complements (1a, p. 6)—words in the predicate that identify or modify the subject.

3i If Your Subject Contains *Or, Either . . . Or,* or *Neither . . . Nor,* Make the Verb Agree Only with the Nearest Part of the Subject.

Compound subjects (3h) joined by *or, either . . . or,* or *neither . . . nor* are called **disjunctive.** They ask the reader to choose between two or more parts. Consequently, the verb should agree with only one of those parts—the one nearest the verb.

DON'T:

          DISJUNCTIVE SUBJ   V

x *Either his children or his cat are* responsible for the dead goldfish.

BETTER:

          NEAREST PART OF
          DISJUNCTIVE SUBJ
                V

- Either his children or *his cat is* responsible for the dead goldfish.

  But such conflicts of number are awkward. Rewrite to avoid the problem.

PREFERABLE:

        SUBJ   V

- Either *his children are* responsible for the dead goldfish or

  SUBJ V
  his cat is.

or

     SUBJ   V

- *No one* but his children or his cat *could have killed* the goldfish.

Some disjunctive subjects "feel plural" even though each item within them is singular, for the writer is thinking about two or more things. But so long as the individual disjunctive items are singular, the verb must be singular, too.

DON'T:

          DISJUNCTIVE SUBJ   V

x *Neither WNCN nor WQXR carry* the country-Western sing-off.

DO:

NEAREST PART OF
DISJUNCTIVE SUBJ
V
● Neither WNCN nor *WQXR carries* the country-Western sing-off.

agr
3k

3j If Both Parts of a Compound Subject Refer to the Same Thing or Person, Consider the Subject Singular.

Even when the parts of a compound subject (3h) are joined by *and,* common sense will sometimes tell you that only one thing or person is being discussed. Make the verb singular in such a case:

● My best friend and severest critic has moved to Atlanta.

> One person is both friend and critic. By changing the verb to *have* the writer would be saying that two people, not one, have moved to Atlanta. Both sentences could be correct but their meanings would differ.

3k If You Have Placed *Each* or *Every* before a Compound Subject, Treat the Subject as Singular.

Each or *every,* if it comes before the subject, guarantees that the subject will be singular even if it contains multiple parts:

SUBJ   V
● *Every linebacker and tackle in the league was pleased* with the settlement.

SUBJ   V
● Before being put away for the summer, *each coat and sweater is* to be mothproofed.

But note that when *each* comes *after* a subject it has no effect on the number of the verb:

SUBJ   V
● *They* each *have* their own reasons for protesting.

agr
31

31 If the Subject Is a Numerical Word or a Plural Term of Quantity, Choose a Singular or Plural Verb according to Your Meaning.

Numerical words (*majority, minority, number, plurality,* etc.) and plural terms of quantity (*three dollars, fifty years,* etc.) can take either a singular or a plural verb. If you have in mind the *totality* of items, make the verb singular:

SUBJ   V

* The Democratic *majority favors* the bill.

But if you mean the separate items that make up that totality, make the verb plural:

SUBJ   V

* *The majority of Democrats* on the North Shore *are opposed* to building a bridge.

The Word Number

When the word *number* is preceded by *the,* it is always singular:

SUBJ   V

* The *number* of unhappy voters *is growing.*

But when *number* is preceded by *a,* you must look to see whether it refers to the total unit (singular) or to individual parts (plural).

TOTAL UNIT (SINGULAR):

SUBJ   V

* A *number* like ten billion *is* hard to comprehend.

INDIVIDUAL PARTS (PLURAL):

SUBJ   V

* *A number of voters have arrived* at their choice.

> Note that although *of voters* looks like a modifier of the subject *number,* we read *a number of* as if it said *many.*

When your subject contains an actual number, decide once again whether you mean the total unit or the individual parts.

TOTAL UNIT (SINGULAR):

    SUBJ   V

- *Twenty-six miles is* the length of the race.

INDIVIDUAL PARTS (PLURAL):

      SUBJ   V

- *Twenty-six difficult miles lie* ahead of her.

3m Usually Consider a "Borderline" Indefinite Pronoun Singular.

An **indefinite pronoun** leaves unspecified the person or thing it refers to.

INDEFINITE PRONOUNS		
all	everybody	no one
another	everyone	nothing
any	everything	one
anybody	few	others
anyone	many	several
anything	most	some
both	much	somebody
each	neither	someone
each one	nobody	something
either	none	such

Some of these words serve other functions, too; they are indefinite pronouns only when they stand alone without modifying another term.

ADJECTIVE:
- *All* leopards are fast.

INDEFINITE PRONOUN:
- *All* have spots.

Some indefinite pronouns, such as *another,* are obviously singular, and some others, such as *several,* are obviously plural. But there is also a "borderline" class: *each, each one, either, everybody, everyone, everything, neither, nobody, none, no one.* These terms have a singular form, yet they call to mind plural things or persons. According to convention you should generally treat them as singular:

      SUBJ   V
* *Everyone seems* to be late tonight.

      SUBJ   V
* *Neither has brought* the music for the duet.

Keep to a singular verb even when the indefinite pronoun is followed by a plural construction such as *of them:*

      SUBJ   V
* *Neither* of them *has* the music for the duet.

      SUBJ   V
* *Each* of those cordless phones *has* a touch-tone dial.

None

None is usually treated as singular:

      SUBJ   V
* *None* of us *is* ready yet.

    But some writers recognize an option here. If you mean *all of us are not ready* rather than *not one of us is ready,* you can make the verb plural:

* None of us are ready yet.

    Since some writers would consider this sentence mistaken, keep to the singular wherever it does not sound forced.

3n Make a Verb in a Relative Clause Agree with the Antecedent of the Relative Pronoun.

Consider the following correctly formed sentence:

                   REL CLAUSE
* The telephone bills *that are overdue* include a charge for a lengthy call to Paris.

Here *that are overdue* is a **relative clause**—a subordinate clause (1c, p. 9) that functions like an adjective. A relative clause usually begins with a word like *who, whom, whose, that,* or *which.* The relative clause modifies an **antecedent,** a noun or nounlike element in the previous clause. In this case the antecedent is *telephone bills.*

agr
3n

Relative clauses can make for tricky agreement problems. You will avoid trouble, however, if you remember that the verb in a relative clause agrees in number with its antecedent. Thus, in the example above, *are* agrees with the plural antecedent *telephone bills.* Again:

>   ANT   V
> - There have been complaints about *service* that *is* painfully slow.

Note that you cannot automatically assume that the antecedent is the last term before the relative clause.

>   ANT   V
> - There have been *complaints* about service that *were* entirely justified.
>   ANT   V
> - The *oceans* of the world, which *have become* a dumping ground, may never be completely unpolluted again.

Ask yourself what the verb in the relative clause refers to:

> What is painfully slow? Service.
> What was entirely justified? Complaints.
> What has become a dumping ground? Oceans.

Once you have an answer, a singular or plural term, you also have the right number for the verb in your relative clause.

Singular Complement in Relative Clause

Look at the following mistaken but typical sentence.

DON'T:

>   PLURAL ANT   V   SING COMPL
> x *Math problems,* which *is* her *specialty,* cause her no concern.

A singular complement (1a, p. 6) in a *who, which,* or *that* clause can trick you into making the verb in that clause singular when the antecedent is actually plural. Here the complement *specialty* has wrongly influenced the number of the verb *is*. That verb, like any other verb in a relative clause, must agree with its antecedent.

DO:
  • Math problems, which are her specialty, cause her no concern.

One of Those Who

Consider the following sentences, both of which are correct:

             ANT   V
  • Joe is one of those *chemists* who *believe* that science is an art.
             ANT   V
  • Joe is the only *one* of those chemists who *believes* that science is an art.

The expression *one of those who* contains both a singular and a plural term— *one* and *those*. To avoid confusion, be careful to decide which of the two is the antecedent. In most cases it will be the plural *those* (or *those chemists,* etc.), but to be sure you must isolate the relative clause and ask yourself what it modifies.

3o Watch for a Subject with Plural Form but Singular Meaning.

Some nouns have an *-s* ending but take a singular verb: *economics, mathematics, mumps, news, physics,* etc.:

  • *Physics* has made enormous strides in this century.

Some other nouns ending in *-s* can be singular in one meaning and plural in another. When they refer to a body of knowledge, they are singular.

AS BODY OF KNOWLEDGE:
     SUBJ V
  • *Politics is* an important study for many historians.
     SUBJ   V
  • *Acoustics requires* an understanding of mathematics.

But when the same words are used in a more particular sense—not politics as a field but somebody's politics—they are considered plural.

IN PARTICULAR SENSE:

>   SUBJ   V
- Gloria's *politics are* left of center.

>   V   SUBJ
- How *are* the *acoustics* in the new auditorium?

3p Observe the Agreement Rules for Mathematical Operations.

Adding or Multiplying

When adding or multiplying, you can choose either a singular or a plural verb:

- One and one *is* two.
- One and one *are* two.
- Eleven times three *is* thirty-three.
- Eleven times three *are* thirty-three.

Subtracting or Dividing

When subtracting or dividing, keep to the singular:

- Sixty minus forty *is* twenty.
- Sixty minus forty *leaves* twenty.
- Eight divided by two *is* four.

3q Prefer a Singular Verb with the Title of a Work.

Titles of works are generally treated as singular even when they have a plural form, because only one work is being discussed:

> SUBJ   V
- Joyce's *Dubliners has justified* the author's faith in its importance.

> SUBJ   V
- Camus's *Lyrical and Critical Essays was* required reading in Comparative Literature 102 last term.

  The plural verb *were* would misleadingly refer to the individual essays rather than the whole book.

3r Do Not Put an Unnecessary Comma between a Subject and Its Verb.

An element that comes between a subject and its verb may need to be set off by commas, as in the sentence *Teenage suicide, which has become common in recent years, is a matter of urgent public concern* (4j, p. 60). But beware of inserting commas simply to draw a breath, for the demands of grammar and of easy breathing do not always match up. You want to show your reader that a subject is connected to its verb. If the modifier following a subject is not a *grammatical* interruption, do not set it off with commas.

DON'T:

> SUBJ   V
x *Ishi* alone, *remained* to tell the story of his tribe.

DO:

- Ishi alone remained to tell the story of his tribe.

Even when you have a lengthy subject, itself made up of parts separated by commas, you should try to connect it to its verb without interruption.

DON'T:

> SUBJ   V
x *A pair of scissors, a pot of glue, and a stapler, are* still essential to a writer who does not use a word processor.

DO:

*   A pair of scissors, a pot of glue, and a stapler are still essential to a writer who does not use a word processor.

agr
3r

DON'T:

SUBJ

x *Those construction workers who had collected unemployment*

V

checks in the slump of December through March, were delighted that spring had finally arrived.

DO:

*   Those construction workers who had collected unemployment checks in the slump of December through March were delighted that spring had finally arrived.

4 Modifiers

4a Recognize Modifiers and Their Functions.

A **modifier** is an expression that limits or describes another element:

- *tall* boy
- the *tall* boy *with blond hair*
- the *tall* boy *with blond hair who is locking his bicycle*
- The *tall* boy *with blond hair who is locking his bicycle* is *from Finland.*

A modifier can consist of a single word, a phrase, or a subordinate clause.

1. a single word:

- The *tall* boy is from Finland.
- A *new* star appeared in the *darkening* sky.
- They did it *gladly.*
- *That* proposal, *however,* was *soundly* defeated.

2. a **phrase,** or cluster of words lacking a subject-verb combination (1d, p. 11):

- The boy *with blond hair* is *from Finland.*
- *At ten o'clock* she gave up hope.
- *In view of the fuel shortage,* they remained *at home.*

3. a **subordinate clause,** or cluster of words that does contain a subject-verb combination but does not form an independent statement (1c, p. 9):

- The boy *who is locking his bicycle* is from Finland.
- The telephone company, *which has enjoyed a near monopoly on phone appliances,* is now being challenged in the open marketplace.
- My old friends from the block always play a game of stickball *when they come home for the holidays.*

A single-word modifier is usually either an adjective or an adverb. An **adjective** modifies a noun, pronoun, or other element that functions as a noun. An **adverb** can modify not only a verb but also an adjective, another adverb, a preposition, an infinitive, a participle, a phrase, a clause, or a whole sentence.

All modifiers are subordinate, or grammatically dependent on another element. But there is nothing minor about the benefit that a careful and imaginative use of modifiers can bring to your style. Some modifiers lend vividness and precision to descriptions, stories, and ideas, while others establish logical relationships, allowing a sentence to convey more shadings of thought and complexity of structure.

For the comparison of adjectives and adverbs, see Chapter 17, pages 195–197.

PLACING MODIFIERS

4b Place a Modifier Where It Will Bring Out Your Meaning.

Adjective and Adverb

The position you assign a modifier can significantly affect the meaning of your sentence. Most adjectives and adverbs occupy a position just before the modified term.

ADJ
- It was a *beautiful* moon.

ADV
- We *hastily* adjusted the telescope.

A **predicate adjective,** however, follows the verb:

PRED ADJ
- The moon was *beautiful.*

Adverbs such as *only, just,* and *merely* often control the way an entire statement is interpreted. In order to avoid ambiguity, or double meaning, you should place them just before the modified element. Compare:

- *Only* I can understand your argument. [No one else can.]
- I can *only* understand your argument. [I cannot agree with it.]
- I can understand *only* your argument. [But not your motives; *or* The arguments of others mystify me.]
- She had *just* eaten the sandwich. [A moment ago.]
- She had eaten *just* the sandwich. [Not the rest of the food.]

Sentence Adverb

Unlike other adverbs, a **sentence adverb** (2c, p. 22) such as *however, nevertheless,* or *furthermore* puts a whole statement into logical relation to the preceding statement:

- Much of the world is threatened with famine in the next twenty years. *Nevertheless,* the populations of the most threatened areas continue to increase at a reckless pace.

The placement of a sentence adverb is especially flexible, but different positions suggest different emphases. In general, a sentence adverb puts stress on the word that precedes it:

- I, *however,* refuse to comply. [I contrast myself with others.]
- I refuse, *however,* to comply. [My refusal is absolute.]

In the first and last positions of a sentence, where a sentence adverb cannot be set off on both sides by commas, it makes a less pointed effect:

- *However,* I refuse to comply. ⎫ No single element within the
- I refuse to comply, *however.* ⎭ main statement is highlighted.

The final position is the weakest—the one that gets least stress from the logical force of the sentence adverb. In some sentences, however, this may be just the effect you are seeking.

mod
4c

Transitional Phrase

The same principles of emphatic placement apply to **transitional phrases** like *in fact, on the contrary,* and *as a result,* which are really multiword sentence adverbs. Note how meaning as well as emphasis can sometimes be affected by different placement of the same transitional phrase:

- *In fact,* Marie was overjoyed. [Marie was not unhappy. No, indeed. . . .]
- Marie, *in fact,* was overjoyed. [Others were happy, but one person—singled out here—was more so.]

For fuller lists of sentence adverbs and transitional phrases, see 2c, p. 22.

4c Avoid a Dangling Modifier.

When you use a modifier, it is not enough for you to know what thing or idea you are modifying; you must openly supply that modified term within your sentence. Otherwise you have written a **dangling modifier**—one that either modifies nothing at all or that wrongly appears to modify a nearby term.

Missing Modified Term

DON'T:

DANGL MOD
x *Pinning one mugger to the ground,* the other escaped.

The person doing the pinning is left unmentioned. Readers will go through a two-step process of frustration. First they will take *the other* to be the modified term. Then, realizing their mistake, they will become annoyed with the writer for having given them a false lead.

DO:

MOD   MODIFIED
                              TERM

- *Pinning one mugger to the ground,* the *victim* helplessly watched the other escape.

DON'T:

DANGL MOD

x *Once considered a culturally backward country,* Australian film-makers have surprised the world's most demanding audiences.

The writer, criticized for a dangling modifier, might protest, "Can't you see I was referring to Australia in the first phrase?" But where is *Australia* in the sentence? Since *Australian film-makers* can hardly be called a *country,* the modifier does dangle.

DO:

MOD   MODIFIED
                              TERM

- *Once considered a culturally backward country,* Australia has surprised the world's most demanding audiences with its excellent filmmakers.

DON'T:

DANGL MOD

x *To win in court,* an attorney's witnesses must convince the jury.

Precisely because it makes perfect grammatical sense, this is a dangerously misleading sentence. Readers must do a double take to realize that it is the attorney, not the witnesses, who wants to win in court.

DO:

MOD   MODIFIED
                   TERM

- *To win in court,* an attorney must choose witnesses who can convince a jury.

DONT:

DANGL MOD

x *By x-raying multiple layers of tissue,* abnormal cells can be detected at an early stage.

There is little danger of misunderstanding here, and some competent writers would let this sentence pass. But the best policy is to include the modified term every time.

mod
4c

DO:

MOD   MODIFIED TERM
- *By x-raying multiple layers of tissue, the CAT scanner* can detect abnormal cells at an early stage.

Mistaken Modified Term

Merely including the modified term is not enough; you must also place it where a reader will immediately identify it as such. Any noun or nounlike element just preceding or following a modifier will look like the modified term. When it is not, chaos or comedy results.

DON'T:

DANGL MOD   APPARENT MODIFIED TERM
x *Stolen out of the garage the night before, my grandmother* spotted

MODIFIED TERM
my station wagon on Jefferson Street.

The reader must reassess the sentence to get over the impression that it was the grandmother who was stolen from the garage.

DO:

MOD   MODIFIED TERM
- *Stolen out of the garage the night before, my station wagon* was on Jefferson Street when my grandmother spotted it.

DON'T:

DANGL MOD   APPARENT MODIFIED TERM
x *Towering across the African plain, it* seemed impossible to pho-

MODIFIED TERM
tograph *the giraffes.*

Here *it* is merely an anticipatory word, not a thing that could be towering across the plain. Unfortunately, readers are put to the trouble of reaching that conclusion for themselves after momentary confusion.

DO:

$$\underbrace{\qquad\qquad\text{MOD}\qquad\qquad}$$ MODIFIED TERM

* *Towering across the African plain, the giraffes* appeared impossible to photograph.

4d Avoid a Squinting Modifier.

You may find that in a draft sentence you have surrounded a modifier with two elements, either of which might be the modified term. Such a modifier is called **squinting** because it does not "look directly at" the real modified term.

DON'T:

SQ MOD

x How the mechanic silenced the transmission *completely* amazed me.

Did the mechanic do a complete job of silencing, or was the writer completely amazed? Readers should never be left with such puzzles to solve.

DO:

MOD   MODIFIED TERM

* How the mechanic *completely silenced* the transmission amazed me.

or

MOD   MODIFIED TERM

* I was *completely amazed* by the way the mechanic silenced the transmission.

DON'T:

SQ MOD

x They were sure *by August* they would be freed.

Were they sure by August, or would they be freed by August?

DO:

MODIFIED TERM   MOD

* They were *sure by August* that they would be freed.

or

MOD   MODIFIED
                                                 TERM
• They were sure that *by August* they *would be freed.*

Notice how the insertion of *that* either before or after the modifier clarifies the writer's meaning.

4e Avoid a Split Infinitive If You Can Do So without Awkwardness.

Some readers object to every **split infinitive,** a modifier placed between *to* and the base verb form: *to thoroughly understand.* To avoid offending such readers you would do well to eliminate most split infinitives.

DON'T:
                          SPLIT INF
x It is important *to clearly see* the problem.

DO:
                    INF   ADV
• It is important *to see* the problem *clearly.*

But when you correct a split infinitive, beware of creating an awkward construction that announces in effect, "Here is the result of my struggle not to split an infinitive."

DON'T:
x It is important *clearly to see* the problem.

The writer has avoided a split infinitive but has created a pretzel. The "split" version, *It is important to clearly see the problem,* would be preferable. But *It is important to see the problem clearly* would satisfy everyone.

Even readers who do not mind an inconspicuous, natural-sounding split infinitive are bothered by *lengthy* modifiers in the split-infinitive position.

DON'T: SPLIT INF
x We are going *to soberly and patiently analyze* the problem.

DO:
- We are going to analyze the problem soberly and patiently.

or

- We are going to make a sober and patient analysis of the problem.

4f Do Not Hesitate to Make Use of an Absolute Phrase.

Fear of the dangling modifier (4c, p. 49) leads some writers to shun the **absolute phrase,** a group of words that acts as a modifier to the whole statement. (Compare *transitional phrase*, 2c, p. 22.) But a well-managed absolute phrase can be an effective resource.

DO:
                                              ABS PHRASE
- He rose from the negotiating table, *his stooped shoulders a sign of discouragement.*

Far from causing a usage problem, such added phrases enable you to write a graceful cumulative sentence (26i, p. 308)— one that sharpens or elaborates an initial main statement.

A classic absolute phrase differs from a dangling modifier by containing its own "subject," such as *his stooped shoulders* in the example above. Again:

    "SUBJECT"
- *All struggle* over, the troops lay down their arms.
    ABS PHRASE

                                                 "SUBJECT"
- The quarterback called three plays in one huddle, *the clock* having stopped after the incomplete pass.
    ABS PHRASE

Some other absolute phrases do look exactly like dangling modifiers, but they are accepted as idioms—that is, as fixed expressions that everyone considers normal:

mod
4g

ABS PHRASE
* *Generally speaking,* the economy is sluggish.

ABS PHRASE
* *To summarize,* most of your energy is still untapped.

4g Avoid a Double Negative.

In written English the modifier *not* does all the work of denial that a negative statement needs. A **double negative,** though common in some people's speech, is considered a mistake rather than an especially strong negation.

DON'T:

x She *didn't* say *nothing.*

The sentence could mean either *She said nothing at all* or *What she said was more than nothing.*

DO:
* She *didn't* say *anything.*
or
* She said *nothing.*

Cumbersome Negative Formulas

Avoid certain negative constructions which are roundabout or confusing:

1. negatives following *shouldn't wonder, wouldn't be surprised,* etc.

DON'T:
x I shouldn't wonder if it *didn't* rain.

DO:
* I shouldn't wonder if it *rained.*

2. *cannot help but*

DON'T:

x They *cannot help but* think sadly about John Lennon.

DO:

• They *cannot help thinking* sadly about John Lennon.

3. *can't hardly, can't scarcely,* etc.

DON'T:

x We *can't hardly* wait to visit Mexico City.

DO:

• We *can hardly* wait to visit Mexico City.

4. *no doubt but what, no doubt but that*

DON'T:

x She does not *doubt but what* dreams foretell the future.
x There is *no doubt but that* writing assists the memory.

DO:

• She *does not doubt that* dreams foretell the future.
• There *is no doubt that* writing assists the memory.

PUNCTUATING MODIFIERS

4h Include a Comma after an Initial Modifier That Is More than a Few Words Long.

If a modifier preceding your main clause takes up more than a few words, automatically follow it with a comma:

SUBSTANTIAL PHRASE
- *Instead of having the chocolate mousse,* Walter ordered an apple for dessert.

mod
4i

SUBSTANTIAL SUB CLAUSE
- *When they learned that the Metroliner had been derailed,* they spent the night at the "Y."

4i Consider a Comma Optional after a Brief Initial Modifier.

If a modifier preceding your main clause is no more than a few words long, you can choose whether or not to end it with a comma. A comma marks a more formal separation between the modifier and the main clause.

ACCEPTABLE:
BRIEF PHRASE
- *Until this week,* I had kept up with my assignments.

BRIEF SUB CLAUSE
- *When the pizza arrived,* they sang "Happy Birthday."

or
- Until this week I had kept up with my assignments.
- When the pizza arrived they sang "Happy Birthday."

Avoiding Ambiguity

Note, however, that you must include the comma if your sentence would be ambiguous—double in meaning—without it.

DON'T:
x After Stephanie left Andrew wrote her a long letter.

  Here the reader at first sees the misleading unit *After Stephanie left Andrew.*

DO:
- After Stephanie left, Andrew wrote her a long letter.

4j Master the Punctuation of Restrictive and Nonrestrictive Elements.

To punctuate modifiers in every position except the initial one (4h, 4i), you must recognize a sometimes tricky distinction between two kinds of modifiers—restrictive and nonrestrictive.

RESTRICTIVE	NONRESTRICTIVE
This is the lamp *we bought yesterday.*	This lamp, *which we bought yesterday,* is defective.
Suzanne is a woman *who minds her own business.*	Suzanne, *who minds her own business,* is a strong woman.
The coffee *that comes from Brazilian mountainsides* is the best.	The best coffee, *which comes from Brazilian mountainsides,* is also the most expensive.

Restrictive Element

A **restrictive element** is essential to the identification of the term it modifies. It restricts or narrows down the scope of that term, identifying precisely *which* lamp, woman, or coffee the writer has in mind. Study the two columns above and you will see that only the left-hand sentences contain modifiers of this kind. In the right-hand sentences the lamp, woman, and coffee under discussion do not need to be identified by restrictive modifiers; presumably the reader already knows which person or thing the writer intends.

Note also how the absence or use of commas marks the difference of function. A restrictive modifier can do its job of narrowing only if it is *not* isolated by commas.

DON'T:

x Women, *who are over thirty-five,* tend to show reduced fertility.

Here the commas, which isolate the italicized element from the (misleading) statement *Women tend to show reduced fer-*

tility, keep that element from properly restricting the subject to women over thirty-five. The commas absurdly suggest that all women are over thirty-five.

DO:

RESTR EL
• Women *who are over thirty-five* tend to show reduced fertility.

With the commas gone, the sentence says what the writer originally wanted to say; the restrictive element is free to do its narrowing work.

DON'T:

x I admire bus drivers, *who announce the streets as they come up.*

The comma suggests that all bus drivers announce the streets as they come up and that the writer therefore admires all of them. This is not what was meant.

DO:

RESTR EL
• I admire bus drivers *who announce the streets as they come up.*

Without a comma, the modifier restricts those bus drivers who are admired to just one kind, those who announce the streets.

DON'T:

x Many junk food addicts change their diet, *when they develop a vitamin deficiency.*

The comma after *diet* tells us that the main statement ends there. But the writer is trying to say that junk food addicts change their diet only at a certain point. The intended meaning becomes clear when the comma is removed.

DO:

RESTR EL
• Many junk food addicts change their diet *when they develop a vitamin deficiency.*

DON'T:

x I had a dream, *in which I finally got to the end of the tightrope.*

The comma after *dream* wrongly tells a reader that the main statement ends there. The writer wanted the restrictive element to identify a *particular* dream.

DO:
                                                    RESTR EL
• I had a dream *in which I finally got to the end of the tightrope.*

Nonrestrictive Element

A **nonrestrictive element** is not essential to the identification of the term it modifies. Instead of narrowing that term, a nonrestrictive element adds some further information about it. To perform this function it must be set off by punctuation, usually commas.

DON'T:

x The reference librarian *who is a writer's best resource* is often acknowledged in the preface to a book.

The absence of commas after *librarian* and *resource* implies that the italicized element is restrictive, telling us which reference librarian is meant. Notice that when the modifier is left out altogether, there is nothing misleading about the statement: *The reference librarian is often acknowledged in the preface to a book.* That is a sure sign that the modifier is nonrestrictive and that it therefore deserves to be set off.

DO:
                                                    NONR EL
• The reference librarian, *who is a writer's best resource,* is often acknowledged in the preface to a book.

DON'T:

x They snack on trail mix *which is a wholesome blend of nuts, seeds, raisins, and other dried fruit.*

The absence of a comma after *mix* implies that one particular kind of trail mix is being identified. By adding a comma the writer can make it clear that trail mix in general is intended.

mod
4k

DO:

NONR EL

• They snack on trail mix, *which is a wholesome blend of nuts, seeds, raisins, and other dried fruit.*

DON'T:

x Powerful people *who never walk aimlessly* appear to glide across a room.

Without commas after *people* and *aimlessly* the sentence appears to isolate one group of powerful people, those who never walk aimlessly. But clearly the writer is not trying to distinguish that group from those powerful people who do walk aimlessly. A comma, making it plain that the modifier is nonrestrictive, brings out the intended reference to *all* powerful people.

DO:

NONR EL

• Powerful people, *who never walk aimlessly,* appear to glide across a room.

4k Set Off a Sentence Adverb or a Transitional Phrase with Commas.

Sentence adverbs and transitional phrases (2c, p. 22) can never be restrictive (4j). Instead of narrowing the meaning of one element in a statement, they show a relationship between the whole statement and the one before it. To bring out this function, be sure your sentence adverbs and transitional phrases are "stopped" at both ends, either by two commas, by a semicolon and a comma, or by a comma and the beginning or end of the sentence:

SENT ADV

• A circus, *furthermore,* lifts the spirits of young and old alike.

> SENT ADV
- Laughter is good for the soul; *moreover,* it reduces bodily tension.

  TRANS PHRASE
- *On the contrary,* she intends to stay where she is.

  > TRANS PHRASE
- The deficit has continued to grow, *as a matter of fact.*

Exception: Some Brief Sentence Adverbs

Even though they are nonrestrictive, certain brief sentence adverbs such as *thus* and *hence* are often seen without commas:

- We can *thus* discount the immediate threat of war.
- *Hence* there is no need to call up the reserves.

For the important distinction between sentence adverbs and conjunctions, see 2c, p. 23.

4l In Punctuating an Appositive, Observe the Restrictive/Nonrestrictive Rule.

An **appositive** is a word or group of words that identifies or restates an immediately preceding noun or noun substitute:

> APP
- Teresa, *an old friend of mine,* has scarcely changed through the years.

  > APP
- What they saw, *a black bear approaching the baby's cradle,* riveted them with fear.

  > APP
- The horn gave three blasts, *signals that we had to say our final good-byes.*

Most appositives, like those above, are set off by commas, but you should not automatically make that choice. Instead, ask whether the appositive narrows down ("restricts") the term it follows or merely restates that term. To see why some appositives should appear without commas, compare these sentences:

NONR APP
- My sister, *Diane,* studied Portuguese in the Navy.

mod
4m

RESTR APP   RESTR APP
- My brother *Bert* played baseball in college, but my brother *Jack* was not athletic at all.

The commas in the first sentence tell us that the writer has only one sister—namely, Diane. The appositive does not restrict our understanding of *sister;* it merely supplies the sister's name. In contrast, the absence of commas in the second example reflects the fact that the writer has at least two brothers. *Bert* and *Jack* are restrictive appositives, since each name tells us *which* brother is meant.

The distinction here is a fine one, and few readers would object if the commas were dropped from the "Diane" example. But whenever you use an appositive to narrow the meaning of a term (which brother, which friend, etc.), you should omit the commas.

4m Set Off an Interrupting Element at Both Ends.

Study the following sentences:

INT EL
- Our leading advocate of clean streets, *you understand,* is the Mayor.

INT EL
- The City Council, *however,* has no funds for a clean-up squad.

INT EL
- You, *Frank,* will sweep the sidewalk at 7 A.M.

INT EL
- The Mayor's televised plea, *which is rebroadcast every evening on the 6 o'clock news,* reaches everyone in town.

In each instance the italicized words are an **interrupting element** (also known as a *parenthetical element*). An interrupting element can be a phrase, a clause, a sentence adverb like *however,* a transitional phrase like *in fact,* an appositive (4l), a name in direct address (you, *Frank*), or an inserted question or exclamation. Since an interrupting element comes between parts of the sentence that belong together in meaning, you must set it off by punctuation at both ends. Note the commas in all four examples above.

The main risk in punctuating an interrupting element is that you may forget to close it off before resuming the main statement. The risk increases if the last words of the interrupting element happen to fit grammatically with the words that follow.

DON'T:

x The Mayor's televised plea, which is rebroadcast every evening on the 6 o'clock news reaches everyone in town.

You can expect to come across such "unstopped" interrupting elements in your first drafts. When in doubt as to whether the element is truly an interruption, reread the sentence without it: *The Mayor's televised plea reaches everyone in town.* Since that statement makes complete sense, you know that the omitted part *is* interruptive and must be set off at both ends.

Other Punctuation

Commas are the most usual but not the only means of setting off an interrupting element. Extreme breaks such as whole statements, questions, or exclamations are often better served by parentheses or dashes:

INT EL
• The sky in New Mexico *(have you ever been there?)* is the most dramatic I have seen.

INT EL
• Our recent weather—*what snow storms we have had!*—makes me long to be back in California.

When you need to interrupt quoted material to insert words of your own, enclose your insertion in brackets (13p, p. 159).

4n Use Commas with Coordinate Modifiers.

If a draft sentence contains two or more modifiers in a row, should you put commas between them? The answer depends on whether the modifiers all modify the same term. Usually they do; such modifiers are **coordinate**, or serving the same grammatical function. You should separate coordinate modifiers from each other by commas:

                                                    MODIFIED
                                          MOD   MOD TERM
* I arrived at my new school on a *sunlit, windy day.*

> Since *sunlit* and *windy* both modify the same term, *day,* they are separated from each other by a comma.

But sometimes you will find that an apparent modifier is actually part of the term being modified. In that case, omit a comma after the modifier that comes before the whole modified term.

DON'T:

x She never forgave them for the way they insulted her on that
                 MODIFIED
        MOD   TERM
infamous, first day of school.

> Does *infamous* modify *day?* No, it modifies *first day.* The comma after *infamous* thus violates rule 4o below: do not place a comma between the last (or only) modifier and the whole modified term.

DO:

* She never forgave them for the way they insulted her on that infamous first day of school.

> The absence of commas shows that there are no coordinate modifiers in the sentence. Note, in the following example, how the punctuation changes when genuine coordinate modifiers are added.

DO:

* She never forgave them for the way they insulted her on that
                                        MODIFIED
        MOD   MOD   MOD   TERM
infamous, outrageous, unforgettable first day of school.

> Now the sentence contains three coordinate modifiers, properly separated by commas. A comma after *unforgettable* would still be wrong, for *first day* continues to be the whole modified term.

To test whether you are dealing with coordinate modifiers, try shifting the order of the words. Truly coordinate terms can be reversed without a change of meaning: *a sunlit, windy day; a windy, sunlit day.* Noncoordinate terms change their meaning *(a blue racing car; a racing blue car)* or become nonsensical *(an eager fire brigade; a fire eager brigade).*

4o Do Not Place a Comma between the Final (or Only) Modifier and the Modified Term.

When a modifier comes just before the modified term, no punctuation should separate them. Thus, however many coordinate modifiers you supply, be sure to omit a comma after the final one.

DON'T:

FINAL MOD
x O'Keeffe produced an intense, starkly simple, *radiantly glowing,*
MODIFIED
TERM
painting of a flower.

The comma after *glowing* must be removed so that the whole set of coordinate modifiers—*intense, starkly simple, radiantly glowing*—can stand in proper relation to the modified term, *painting.*

For an exception to this rule, keep reading.

4p Consider Enclosing a "Contrary" Modifier in Commas.

In some sentences one modifier opposes another:

MOD   CONTRARY MOD   MODIFIED
TERM
• She told a *fascinating but not altogether believable story.*

You can, if you choose, emphasize the opposition by enclosing the contrary modifier in commas.

ACCEPTABLE:

- She told a fascinating, but not altogether believable, story.

If you set off the contrary modifier at one end, be sure to supply a second comma at the other end.

DON'T:

x She told a fascinating, but not altogether believable story.

For the handling of commas and conjunctions in a *series* of coordinate modifiers (more than two terms), see 71, p. 102.

5 Cases of Nouns and Pronouns

5a Recognize the Case Forms and Their Functions.

Nouns and pronouns change their form to show certain grammatical relations to other words within a sentence. These forms are called **cases**. They show whether a term is a subject of discussion or performer of action (**subjective case**), a receiver of action or an object of a preposition (**objective case**), or a "possessor" of another term (**possessive case**):

1. subjective case: *I, we, they, who, Bill, cars,* etc.

2. objective case: *me, us, them, whom,* etc.

3. possessive case: *my, mine; our, ours; their, theirs; whose, Bill's, cars',* etc.

Most personal pronouns (*I, she,* etc.) show changes of form for all three cases, and so does the relative pronoun *who.* Nouns, however, do not change for the objective case.

	SUBJECTIVE	OBJECTIVE	POSSESSIVE
Personal Pronouns	I	me	my, mine
	you	you	your, yours
	he	him	his
	she	her	her, hers
	it	it	its
	we	us	our, ours
	they	them	their, theirs
Who	who	whom	whose
Nouns	car	car	car's
	mountains	mountains	mountains'
	Janice	Janice	Janice's
	Soviet Union	Soviet Union	Soviet Union's

A change in form helps to show which sentence function a word is performing. For example:

SUBJECTIVE CASE

1. Subject of verb:
   - *He* went home.
   - *They* went home.
   - The one *who* went home was disappointed.

2. Complement:
   - It was *she* who was guilty.
   - The victims are *we* ourselves.

OBJECTIVE CASE

1. Direct object of verb:
   - They praised *him*.
   - We fed the child *whom* the agency had entrusted to us.

2. Indirect object of verb:
   - They taught *him* a lesson.
   - The fine cost *them* a pretty penny.

3. Object of preposition:
   - She told it to *us*.
   - For *whom* did you work last year?

4. Subject of infinitive:
   - They wanted *her* to stay.
   - She expected *them* to give her a raise.

POSSESSIVE CASE

1. With nouns:
   - *Our* hats were all squashed.
   - *Jim's* case was the worst of all.
   - The *Beatles'* music still keeps its freshness.
   - *Whose* pen is this?

2. With gerunds:
   - *His* departing left us sad.
   - *Their* training every day made them too tired for fun.
   - *Jane's* humming all day drove everyone wild.

In general, case forms must match sentence functions: subjective case for subjects of clauses, objective case for objects of several kinds, and possessive case for a possessing relation to the governed term.

We will see that in practice the choice of case can become tricky. Note at the outset that the "subject" of an infinitive takes the objective case and that the "subject" of a gerund usually takes the possessive case. The names are unfortunate, but most writers intuitively choose case by function, not by name.

5b Keep the Subject of a Clause in the Subjective Case.

Standard usage requires that you avoid using objective-case pronouns for subjects of clauses.

DON'T:

      /SUBJ\   V
x *Him* and *me* were good friends.

DO:
* *He* and *I* were good friends.

See 5g, p. 75, for a pronoun subject in a subordinate clause.

5c Avoid an Awkwardly "Correct" Subjective Pronoun Complement.

Note the following sentences.

DON'T:
               COMPL
x The one I had in mind is *him*.

AVOID:
               COMPL
x The one I had in mind is *he*.

The first example violates standard written English; pronoun complements (1a, p. 6) should not appear in the objective case. Yet the "correction" to *he* sounds pompous and awkward. Try, then, to avoid sentences that call for a prissy "good English" at the expense of naturalness. Think of a new way of conveying the same point.

PREFER:

SUBJ
* *He* is the one I had in mind.

    Shifted from a complement to a subject, *he* now sounds unstrained.

case
5d

5d Keep a Pronoun Object in the Objective Case.

The rule for pronoun objects of all kinds is simple: put them in the objective case.

DIRECT OBJECT OF VERB:
- Many differences separate *us*.

INDIRECT OBJECT OF VERB:
- She gave *me* cause for worry.

OBJECT OF PREPOSITION:
- Toward *whom* is your anger directed?

SUBJECT OF INFINITIVE:
- They asked *her* to serve a second term.

Choice of a correct objective form becomes harder when the object is *compound,* or made up of more than one term. Knowing that it is wrong to write *Him and me were good friends,* some writers "overcorrect" and put the subjective forms where they do not belong.

DON'T:
                 V   D OBJS
x They appointed *she* and *I* to a subcommittee.

                         OBJS OF
                PREP   PREP
x That will be a dilemma for *you* and *I*.

DO:
- They appointed *her* and *me* to a subcommittee.
- That will be a dilemma for you and *me*.

When in doubt, test for case by disregarding one of the two objects. Since you would never write x *They appointed she* or x *That will be a dilemma for I,* you know that both of the objects must be objective in case.

The danger of choosing the wrong case seems to increase when a noun and a pronoun are paired as objects.

DON'T:

OBJS OF
PREP ⟋PREP⟍
x As for *Jack* and *I*, we will take the bus.

Would you write *As for I?* No; therefore keep to the objective case.

DO:

• As for Jack and *me,* we will take the bus.

Who versus Whom

In informal speech and writing, *whom* has become a rare form even where grammar strictly requires it. When the pronoun appears first in a clause, the subjective *who* automatically comes to mind.

COLLOQUIAL:

• *Who* did he marry?
• *Who* will you play against?

In standard written English, however, the question of *who* versus *whom* is still determined by grammatical function, not by speech habits. Note the reason for choosing *whom* in each of the following revisions.

DO:

D OBJ ⟋V⟍
• *Whom* did he marry?

Whom is the direct object of the verb *did marry.*

OBJ OF
PREP   PREP
• *Whom* will you play against?

or

OBJ OF
PREP   PREP
• Against *whom* will you play?

Whom is the object of the preposition *against.*

case
5f

5e Avoid an Awkward Choice of Pronoun Case after *Than* or *As*.

Many writers agonize over the case of a pronoun following *than* or *as*. Should one write *Alex is taller than I* or *Alex is taller than me?* Technically, the answer is that both versions are correct. In the first instance *than* serves as a subordinating conjunction: *Alex is taller than I [am]*. In the second, *than* has become a preposition with the object *me*.

In other sentences, however, one choice is clearly incorrect. Consider:

- The cows chased Margaret farther than $\left\{ \begin{array}{c} \text{I} \\ \text{me} \end{array} \right\}$

Here *I* would indicate that Margaret was chased by both the cows and the writer: *The cows chased Margaret farther than I did*. Since that is not the intended meaning, the right choice is *me*.

When in doubt, consider your intended meaning and mentally supply any missing part of the clause:

- The cows chased Margaret farther than ⟨they chased⟩ me.

The added words will tell you which case to use for the pronoun.

Wherever both choices sound awkward, as in the "Alex" example above, look for an alternative construction:

SUB CLAUSE
- Alex is taller *than I am*.

   By supplying the whole subordinate clause, you can avoid any hesitation between *I* and *me*.

5f Ignore the Influence of a Following Appositive on Pronoun Case.

When an appositive (4l, p. 62) follows a pronoun, many writers automatically put the pronoun in the subjective case. As often as not the result is a usage error.

DON'T:

                   PRO   APP

x Inflation is a problem for *we* pensioners.

Test the prepositional phrase without the appositive. Since *for we* is obviously wrong, so is *for we pensioners*. Ignore the appositive and give the pronoun its proper case.

DO:

• Inflation is a problem for *us* pensioners.

5g Choose a Pronoun's Case by Its Function within Its Own Clause.

One of the hardest choices of case involves a pronoun that seems to have rival functions in two clauses.

DON'T:

x He will read his poems to *whomever* will listen.

> The writer has made *whomever* objective because it looks like the object of the preposition *to*: *to whomever*. But the real object of *to* is the whole subordinate clause that follows it.

DO:

                             SUBJ   V

• He will read his poems to <u>whoever will listen</u>.

                               SUB CLAUSE

> The subject of the subordinate clause *whoever will listen* belongs in the subjective case.

Whenever a subordinate clause is embedded within a larger structure, you can settle problems of case by mentally eliminating everything but the subordinate clause.

DON'T:

x Josh had no doubt about *whom* would plan the geriatric meeting.

The test for case shows that *whom would plan the geriatric meeting* is ungrammatical. The object of *about* is the whole subordinate clause, which requires a subject in the subjective case.

DO:

- Josh had no doubt about *who* would plan the geriatric meeting.

When a choice of pronoun case is difficult, the air of difficulty may remain even after you have chosen correctly. Your reader may be distracted by the same doubt that you have just resolved. It is therefore a good idea to dodge the whole problem.

DO:

- He will read his poems to *anyone* who will listen.
- Josh was sure that *he* would be the planner of the geriatric meeting.

5h Use the Possessive Case for Most Subjects of Gerunds.

A **gerund** is a verbal (1a, p. 7) that functions as a noun. Most gerunds end in *-ing,* but there is also a two-word past form.

PRESENT GERUND:

GER
- There is less *swooning* in Hollywood movies than there used to be.

PAST GERUND:

GER
- *Having swum* across the lake made him generally less fearful.

A gerund can be preceded not only by a word like *a, the,* or *this,* but also by a governing noun or pronoun known as the **subject of the gerund**: *Wilson's achieving unity, his having achieved unity.* (A gerund can also take an object; see p. 548.) The name *subject* is misleading, for most subjects of gerunds, like words that "possess" nouns, belong in the possessive case.

POSSESSION OF NOUN	POSSESSION OF GERUND
his achievement	his achieving
our departure	our departing
Marian's reliance	Marian's relying
Edgar's loss	Edgar's having lost

In general, then, put subjects of gerunds into the possessive case.

DON'T:

SUBJ
OF GER   GER
x *Esther* commuting to Boston ended with her graduation.

DO:

• *Esther's* commuting to Boston ended with her graduation.

If the subject of a gerund feels like an object, you should nevertheless keep to the possessive form.

DON'T: OBJ OF
PREP PREP?
x Harold wondered why people laughed at *him* wearing that hat.

Here the writer has made *him* objective because it "feels like" the object of the preposition *at*. In fact, the object of that preposition is the whole gerund phrase *his wearing that hat*.

DO: SUBJ   OBJ
OF GER GER   OF GER
• Harold wondered why people laughed at *his* wearing that hat.
                                    OBJ OF PREP

Note how the possessive *his* directs a reader's attention to the next word, *wearing.* It is the activity, not the person, that inspired laughter.

Exceptions

When the subject of a gerund is an abstract or inanimate noun—one like *physics* or *chaos*—it can appear in a nonpossessive form.

ACCEPTABLE:
                           SUBJ
                          OF GER   GER

- We cannot ignore the danger of *catastrophe striking* again.

But *catastrophe's* would also be acceptable here. Rather than choose, however, why not recast the sentence?

PREFERABLE:

- We cannot ignore the danger that catastrophe will strike again.

When a gerund's subject is separated from the gerund by other words, the gerund tends to change into a modifier (a participle). In such a sentence the possessive form is not used:

          D OBJ   PART

- They admired *him,* a Canadian, *enduring* the heat of Kenya.

Without the intervening appositive (41, p. 62), *a Canadian,* we would recognize *enduring* as a gerund: *They admired his enduring. . . .* But in the sentence as it stands, *him* is a direct object modified by the whole phrase *enduring the heat of Kenya.*

5i Use a Double Possessive When It Is Needed for Clarity.

The possessive relation for nouns is usually indicated either by an *-'s* or *-s'* form *(Henry's, the three cats')* or by an *of* construction *(of Henry, of the three cats).* But sometimes you can combine the two forms to avoid confusion. Compare:

- He remained unmoved by any thought of Barbara.
- He remained unmoved by any thought of Barbara's.

Both sentences are handled correctly, but their meanings differ. The first sentence deals with a thought *about* Barbara, the second with a thought *proposed by* Barbara.

    Some writers worry that the double possessive, like the double negative (4g, p. 55), is a usage error. But everyone uses the double possessive with pronouns: *a peculiarity of hers, that nasty habit of his,* etc. Feel free to use nouns in exactly the same way: *a peculiarity of Nancy's, that nasty habit of Ralph's.*

case
5i

6 Pronoun Reference

Pronouns offer you relief from the monotony of needlessly repeating a term or name when your reader already knows what or whom you mean. But precisely because many pronouns are substitutes for other words, they raise a variety of usage problems, including subject-verb agreement (Chapter 3) and choice of the correct case (Chapter 5). Here we consider **pronoun reference** —that is, the relation between a pronoun and its **antecedent**, the term it refers to. Those pronouns that require antecedents are the personal pronouns (*I, they,* etc.), the relative pronouns (*who, which,* etc.), and the demonstrative pronouns (*this, that, these, those*).

For the choice of a governing pronoun for a whole piece of writing, see 32d, p. 407.

6a Avoid an Abrupt Pronoun Shift.

Your choice of a noun or pronoun in one sentence or part of a sentence establishes a certain person and number.

	SINGULAR NUMBER	PLURAL NUMBER	
First Person	I	we	
Second Person	you	you	
Third Person	he, she, one, it	they	
	this	these	
	that	those	
and all other singular nouns	{ car { Jones { Canadian	cars Joneses Canadians	} and all other } plural } nouns

When you refer again to the same individual(s) or thing(s), do not shift unexpectedly between persons and numbers—for example, from the singular *someone* to the plural *they*, from the third-person *students* or *they* to the second-person *you*, or from the third-person plural *people* to the second-person singular *you*. Keep to one person and number.

DON'T:

                        THIRD   SECOND
                        PERSON   PERSON

x A good song stays with *someone,* making *you* feel less alone.

    Having committed the sentence to a third-person pronoun, the writer jars us by switching to the second-person *you.*

DO:

                        PLURAL   PLURAL
                        ANT   PRO

• A good song stays with *people,* making *them* feel less alone.

Or, more informally:

                        SAME PRO

• A good song stays with *you,* making *you* feel less alone.

Or, more personally:

                        SAME PRO

• A good song stays with *me,* making *me* feel less alone.

Still another solution is grammatically correct but offensive to many readers.

DON'T:

x A good song stays with a *person,* making *him* feel less alone.

Both *person* and *him* are third-person singular; the sentence is not guilty of a pronoun shift. But it implies that all the "real" representatives of the human race are male. You would do well to avoid such constructions, which are widely considered to be sexist language (27e, p. 321).

6b Supply an Explicit Antecedent.

In informal conversation, pronouns often go without antecedents, since both parties know who or what is being discussed: *He wants me to phone home at least once a week.* In writing, however, you want your antecedents to be explicitly (openly) stated.

DON'T:

x *They* say we are in for another cold winter.

Who is *They?*

x *It* explains here that the access road will be closed for repairs.

If the previous sentence has no antecedent for *It,* revision is called for.

DO:

　　　　　　ANT　　　　　　　　　　　　　　　　PRO
• *The weather forecasters* have more bad news for us. *They* say we are in for another cold winter.

　　　　ANT　　　　　　　　　　　　　　　　　　　PRO
• *This bulletin* tells why the backpacking trip was postponed. *It* explains that the access road will be closed for repairs.

Of course you can also do without the pronoun altogether: *The weather forecasters say. . . . This bulletin explains. . . .*

6c Eliminate Competition for the Role of Antecedent.

If you allow a pronoun and its antecedent to stand too far apart, another element in your sentence may look like the real antecedent. This confusion is usually temporary, but you should work to avoid confusing your reader even momentarily.

DON'T:

ANT?   ANT? PRO

x Keats sat under a huge *tree* to write his *ode*. *It* was dense and kept him from the Hampstead mist.

The nearness of *ode* to *It* makes *ode* a likely candidate for antecedent, especially since an ode might be described as dense. With a little extra thought the reader can identify *tree* as the real antecedent—but a good revision can make that fact immediately clear.

DO:

ANT PRO

* Keats wrote his ode while sitting under a huge *tree, which* was dense and kept him from the Hampstead mist.

or

ANT PRO

* Keats wrote his ode while sitting under a huge *tree, whose* dense foliage kept him from the Hampstead mist.

DON'T:

ANT?   ANT?

x Before I sold *cosmetics,* I used to walk by all the *salespersons* in

PRO

the cosmetics department, amazed by *their* variety.

What was various, the cosmetics or the salespersons?

DO:

* Before I sold cosmetics, I used to walk by all the salespersons in the cosmetics department, amazed by the variety of make-up on display.

DON'T:

ANT? ANT? PRO
x The *priest* sitting next to the *conductor* was reading *his* newspaper.

Whose newspaper was the priest reading? The antecedent of
his is uncertain.

DO:

ANT PRO
• The *priest,* reading *his* newspaper, was sitting next to the conductor.

DON'T:

ANT?
x During World War I, Germany had a continuing *dispute* with
Great Britain over freedom of the seas. Merchant ships were

ANT? PRO
attacked and Germany declared a submarine *blockade. It* finally
enmeshed the United States as well.

The intended antecedent, *dispute,* is so far from the pronoun
It that the reader mistakenly takes the antecedent to be *blockade.*

DO:

• During World War I, Germany had a continuing dispute with
Great Britain over freedom of the seas. Merchant ships were
attacked and Germany declared a submarine blockade. The dispute finally enmeshed the United States as well.

When an antecedent is hopelessly distant, you can get out of
trouble by simply repeating it instead of using a pronoun.

6d Make Sure the Antecedent Is a Whole Term, Not Part of One.

The antecedent of a pronoun should not be a modifier or a piece of a
larger term.

DON'T:

ANT   PRO
x Alexander waited at the *train* station until *it* came.

ref
6e

Here the word *train* is part of a larger noun, *train station*. The sentence contains no reference to a train, and thus *it* has no distinct antecedent. The pronoun "dangles" like a dangling modifier (4c, p. 49).

DO:

ANT   PRO
• Alexander waited at the station for the *train* until *it* came.

DON'T:

ANT
x He was opposed to *gun* control because he thought the Consti-

PRO
tution guaranteed every citizen the right to own *one.*

DO:

ANT
• He was opposed to the control of *guns* because he thought the

PRO
Constitution guaranteed all citizens the right to own *them.*

or

• He was opposed to gun control because he thought the Constitution guaranteed every citizen's right to own a gun.

6e Beware of Vagueness in Using *This* and *That*.

Study the following unclear passage.

DON'T:

x The town board voted to eliminate school crossing guards, even though a serious accident had recently occurred at the corner of Jefferson and Truman. *This* brought the parents out in protest.

Does *This* refer to the elimination of the crossing guards, to the accident, or to the whole preceding statement?

When *this, that, these,* or *those* is used alone, without modifying another word, it is known as a **demonstrative pronoun**. Inexperienced writers sometimes use the singular forms *this* and *that* imprecisely, hoping to refer to a whole previous idea rather than to a specific antecedent. The problem is that nearby terms may also look like antecedents. While all writers use an occasional demonstrative pronoun, you should check each *this* or *that* to make sure its antecedent is clear. The remedy for vagueness is to make *this* or *that* modify another term or to rephrase the statement.

DO:

• The town board voted to eliminate school crossing guards, even though a serious accident had recently occurred at the corner of
                MOD   MODIFIED TERM
Jefferson and Truman. *This dangerous economy* brought the parents out in protest.

The writer has gone from *This* to *This dangerous economy,* turning a vague demonstrative pronoun *(this)* into a precise modifier—a **demonstrative adjective**.

DON'T:

x The cat shed great quantities of fur on the chair. *That* made Mary Ann extremely anxious.

Though the antecedent of *that* (the whole previous sentence) is reasonably clear, the second sentence is not very informative. What was Mary Ann anxious about, the cat's health or the condition of the chair?

DO:

• The cat shed great quantities of fur on the chair. Mary Ann worried that when her mother saw the chair, the cat would be banished from the house.

or

• The cat shed great quantities of fur on the chair. The possibility that he was ill made Mary Ann extremely anxious.

6f Beware of Vagueness in Using *Which.*

When you find a clause beginning with the relative pronoun *which,* check to see whether that word refers to a single preceding term or to a whole statement. If the antecedent is a whole statement, you risk unclarity.

DON'T:

x In the subfreezing weather we could not start the car, *which* interfered with our plans.

> Although a reader can see on a "double take" that the antecedent of *which* is not *car* but the whole preceding statement, writers should not put readers to such pains.

DO:

• The subfreezing weather interfered with our plans, especially when the car would not start.

or

• Since the car would not start in the subfreezing weather, we had to change our plans.

DON'T:

x We skate on the frozen pond, *which* I enjoy.

> What is enjoyed, the activity or the pond?

DO:

• I enjoy skating on the frozen pond.

DON'T:

x The improving weather allowed her to fly home, *which* is what she had been hoping for.

> Had she been hoping that the weather would improve or that she could fly home? Even though the two facts are connected, a reader needs to know which one is meant.

ref
6g

DO:

or

- The improving weather allowed her to fly home, as she had hoped to do.

- The improving weather, which she had been hoping for, allowed her to fly home.

6g Avoid Using Rival Senses of *It* within a Sentence.

It can serve as both a personal pronoun *(It is mine)* and an indefinite indicator *(It is raining),* but your reader will be momentarily baffled if you combine those two uses within a sentence.

DON'T:

| INDEFINITE INDICATOR | PERSONAL PRO |

x Although *it* is a ten-minute walk to the bus, *it* comes frequently.

DO:

- Although it is a ten-minute walk to the bus stop, *buses* come frequently.

7 Parallelism

When two or more parts of a sentence are governed by a single grammatical device, they are said to be structurally **parallel**.

PATTERN	EXAMPLE
either *x* or *y*	either *boxing* or *wrestling*
neither *x* nor *y*	neither *tennis* nor *racquetball*
not only *x* but also *y*	He not only *sleeps soundly* but also *snores loudly.*
Let me *x* and *y*.	Let me *smile with the wise,* and *feed with the rich.* (Samuel Johnson)
It matters not *x* but *y*.	It matters not *how a man dies,* but *how he lives.* (Samuel Johnson)
The *x*'s are wiser than the *y*'s.	*The tigers of wrath* are wiser than *the horses of instruction.* (William Blake)
It is more blessed to *x* than to *y*.	It is more blessed *to give* than *to receive.*
Do you promise to *x*, *y*, and *z*?	Do you promise to *love, honor,* and *cherish*?
I write entirely to find out *w*, *x*, *y* and *z*.	I write entirely to find out *what I'm thinking, what I'm looking at, what I see* and *what it means.* (Joan Didion)

//

7a

Note from these examples that parallelism can include both **comparisons** (more *x* than *y*) and **series,** or the alignment of three or more elements (to *x, y,* and *z*). In general, parallelism entails matching the grammar, punctuation, and logic of two or more elements in a sentence.

As Chapter 26 shows in detail, the matching of parallel elements can lend your prose clarity, conciseness, and emphasis. But under the pressure of composing a draft, it is sometimes hard to keep track of all the parts of a parallel construction. In this chapter we will focus on the typical problems of faulty parallelism you should look for when revising.

7a Use Like Elements within a Parallel Construction.

However many terms you are making parallel, the first of them establishes what kind of element the others must be. If the first term is a verb, the others must be verbs as well. Align a noun with other nouns or nounlike elements, a participle (1a, p. 7) with other participles, a whole clause (1c, p. 9) with other clauses, and so forth.

DON'T:

x His black leather jacket was both *snug* and *looked wet.*
              x   y

> Since the parallel formula here is *both x and y,* the first term within it is the adjective *snug.* Thus the *y* term should also be an adjective. Instead, we find the unwelcome verb *looked.* Revise to get the two adjectives *snug* and *wet* into parallelism.

DO:

• His black leather jacket looked both *snug* and *wet.*
                                    x   y

DON'T:

x He enjoyed *rocking his torso* and *to flail his arms.*
                   x   y

> The *x* element is a gerund phrase (p. 555), requiring the *y* element to be a gerund or gerund phrase as well. The infinitive phrase (p. 555) *to flail his arms* breaks the parallelism.

DO:

- He enjoyed *rocking his torso* and *flailing his arms*.

DON'T:

x She likes to *wear designer clothes, listen to classical music,* and *gourmet food is essential.*

> The series begins with the completion of an infinitive: *to wear.*
> At this point the writer has two good options: either to keep
> repeating the *to* or to supply further verb forms to be governed
> by the original *to*.

DO:

- She likes *to wear designer clothes, to listen to classical music,* and *to eat gourmet food.*

or

- She likes to *wear designer clothes, listen to classical music,* and *eat gourmet food.*

> Either version adequately corrects the earlier one, in which a
> whole clause, *gourmet food is essential,* was forced into par-
> allelism with two infinitive constructions. A further option,
> one that keeps the emphasis of the original statement, is to
> end the parallelism early.

DO:

- She likes to *wear designer clothes* and *listen to classical music,* and she finds gourmet food essential.

Comparing Comparable Things

The problem of mismatched parallel elements arises most frequently
in comparisons. The writer knows what is being compared with what,
but the words on the page say something else.

//
7a

DON'T:

x *The office in Boston* was better equipped than *New York.*

The sentence appears to compare an office to a city. The writer must add *the one in* to show that one office is being compared to another.

DO:

- *The office in Boston* was better equipped than *the one in New York.*

DON'T:

x The twins swore that *their lives* would be different from *their parents.*

The writer means to compare one set of lives to another, but the actual wording compares lives to people.

DO:

- The twins swore that *their lives* would be different from *those of their parents.*

or

- The twins swore that *their lives* would be different from *their parents'.*

The apostrophe after *parents* makes that word possessive (16i, p. 187), allowing us to understand that the parents' *lives* are being compared with the twins' lives.

DON'T:

x *Solar heating for a large office building* is technically different from *a single-family home.*

The writer is trying to compare one kind of solar heating to another, but the sentence actually compares one kind of solar heating to a single-family home.

//
7b

DO:

x

• *Solar heating for a large office building* is technically different
y

from *that for a single-family home.*

7b Make the Second Half of a Parallel Construction As Grammatically Complete As the First.

When you are aligning two elements *x* and *y*, be careful not to omit parts of your *y* element that are necessary to make it grammatically parallel with your *x* element. The problem tends to arise when the parallelism comes at the beginning of the sentence, especially if the formula being used is *not only x but also y.*

DON'T:

x

x Not only *did Mendel study the color of the peas,* but also *the*
y

shapes of the seeds.

Some good writers would find this sentence adequate; after all, its meaning is clear. But other writers would want to make a better match between *x* and *y*. Since the *x* element contains a subject *(Mendel)* and a verb *(did study),* the *y* element should follow suit.

IMPROVED:

V   SUBJ
• Not only *did Mendel study* the color of the peas, but *he* also
V   SUBJ

studied the shapes of the seeds.

But this revision is wordy. Such a construction can be made more concise by shifting the *not only* to a later position.

PREFER:

• Mendel studied not only $\overbrace{the\ color\ of\ the\ peas}^{x}$ but also $\overbrace{the\ shapes}$ $\underbrace{of\ the\ seeds}_{y}$.

7c Be Sure to Complete the Expected Parts of an Anticipatory Pattern.

Many parallel constructions are governed by **anticipatory patterns** (26b, p. 300)—formulas that demand to be completed in a certain predictable way. If you begin the formula but then change or abandon it, your sentence falls out of parallelism.

Neither . . . Nor

A *neither* demands a *nor,* not an *or.*

DON'T:

x Banging his fist on the table, he insisted that he had *neither* a drinking problem *or* a problem with his temper.

Change *or* to *nor.*

More Like x Than y

Do not sabotage this formula by adding the word *rather.*

DON'T:

x He seemed *more like* a Marine sergeant *rather than* a social worker.

Delete *rather.*

No Sooner x Than y

Here the common error is to change *than* to *when.*

DON'T:

x *No sooner* had I left *when* my typewriter was stolen.

When must be changed to *than* if the anticipatory formula is to complete its work.

Not So Much x As y

Be sure that the necessary *as* is not replaced by an unwelcome *but rather*.

DON'T:

x She was *not so much* selfish, *but rather* impulsive.

DO:

• She was *not so much* selfish *as* impulsive.

or

• She was *not so much* selfish *as she was* impulsive.

Note the absence of a comma in the two satisfactory versions (7i, p. 99).

7d In a *Not . . . Neither* Construction, Make Sure the First Negation Does Not Warp the Meaning of the Second One.

DON'T:

x   y

x The Marquis de Sade was *not an agreeable man,* and *neither are his novels.*

The complement *man* in the x element makes the sentence appear to say that the novels were not an agreeable man.

DO:

x   y

• The Marquis de Sade was *not agreeable,* and *neither are his novels.*

7e Beware of a Suspended Verb or a Suspended Comparison.

Suspended Verb

Watch out for a parallel construction involving a **suspended verb** — one using a single verb form to complete two thoughts *(the plan should*

//
7e

and will succeed). Sometimes that form is appropriate to only one of the two expressions.

DON'T:

x They *can,* and indeed *have been, making* progress on the case.

The way to check such sentences is to read them without the interruption: *They can making . . . ?* Once you spot a problem, decide whether you want to repair the construction or get rid of it. As a rule you will find it easier to do without the double statement.

DO:

● They can make, and indeed have been making, progress on the case.

or

● They have been making progress on the case.

Suspended Comparison

Like those with a suspended verb, parallel constructions involving a **suspended** (delayed) **comparison** sometimes end in a tangle.

DON'T:

x Wendy likes jazz *as much,* if not *more than, folk music.*

Check the sentence by reading it without the interruption. *Wendy likes jazz as much folk music?* Recognizing that this is nonsense, you can either repair or discard the suspended comparison.

DO:

● Wendy likes jazz as much as, if not more than, folk music.

or

● Wendy likes jazz at least as much as she does folk music.

7f If You Begin a Parallelism with a *That* Clause, Be Sure to Repeat *That* in Introducing Other Clauses in the Parallelism.

//
7g

It is all too easy, when placing whole clauses into parallelism, to allow the parallel effect to lapse after the first clause. The danger is greatest when the *x* element is a *that* clause.

DON'T:

x Sue wrote *that she hated her job,* but *she was glad to be working.*

$\overbrace{\hspace{4cm}}^{x}$ $\overbrace{\hspace{4cm}}^{y}$

As worded, this sentence allows the *y* element to become a direct statement about how Sue felt. But the writer's intention was to reveal two things that Sue *wrote.* A second *that* brings out that meaning.

DO:

• Sue wrote *that* she hated her job but *that* she was glad to be working.

Some good writers would not have removed the comma after *job.* The case for doing so is stated at 7i, p. 99.

7g Do Not Introduce *And Who* or *And Which* without a Prior *Who* or *Which*.

DON'T:

x She is a woman of action, *and who* cares about the public good.

DO:

• She is a woman *who* takes strong action *and who* cares about the public good.

Alternatively, you can rewrite the sentence without the *and:*
She is a woman of action who cares about the public good.

//
7h

DON'T:

x That is a questionable idea, *and which* has been opposed for many years.

DO:

• That is a questionable idea which has been opposed for many years.

7h Once You Have Begun a Parallel Construction, Do Not Repeat a Term That Came before the First Element.

Remember that elements already in place before a parallelism begins should not be repeated *inside* it.

Either . . . Or, Neither . . . Nor

A parallelism involving one of these formulas may be grammatically dependent on an immediately preceding word or sentence element *(he wants either sausage or bacon)*. Be sure to keep the preceding expression from reappearing inside the parallel construction itself.

DON'T:

x They serve *as* either guidance counselors or *as* soccer coaches.

To check for a problem, isolate the whole parallelism—*either guidance counselors or as soccer coaches*—and then see if it repeats the word that came just before it. Yes: the second *as* must go.

DO:

• They serve as either guidance counselors or soccer coaches.

or

• They serve either as guidance counselors or as soccer coaches.

Here *as* is repeated *within* the parallelism in order to make the *x* and *y* elements, *guidance counselors* and *soccer coaches*, fully parallel. Note how the two allowable versions differ from the faulty one:

//
7i

either *x* or as *y*	wrongly repeats an earlier element, *as*
either *x* or *y*	fully parallel
either as *x* or as *y*	fully parallel

Not Only x But Also y

This formula, useful when it works, can be easily misaligned. Once again you must see where the parallelism begins and avoid repeating an earlier element.

DON'T:

x She remembered not only $\overbrace{\text{her maps}}^{\text{x}}$ but $\overbrace{\text{she also remembered}}^{\text{y}}$ her tire repair kit.

> The first *remembered* comes just before the parallel construction and governs both of its parts. The second *remembered* thus breaks the parallel effect.

DO:

• She remembered not only $\overbrace{\text{her maps}}^{\text{x}}$ but also $\overbrace{\text{her tire repair kit.}}^{\text{y}}$

> Now *x* and *y* are parallel; they are the two things that were remembered. The sentence lines up like this:

She remembered $\left\{ \begin{array}{l} \textit{not only} \text{ her maps} \\ \textit{but also} \text{ her tire repair kit.} \end{array} \right.$
(not only *x* but also *y*)

7i Join Most Paired Elements without an Intervening Comma.

To show that two elements are meant to be parallel, omit a comma after the first one.

DON'T:

x Last night's storm blew out $\overbrace{\textit{my electric blanket,}}^{\text{x}}$ and $\overbrace{\textit{my clock}}^{\text{y}}$ radio.

//
7j

The comma implies that the only direct object (1a, p. 5) of *blew out* has already been given and that the main statement is over. By removing the comma the writer can show that the *x* and *y* elements are parallel objects.

DON'T:

$$\overbrace{\hphantom{a \; blessing \; by \; some,}}^{x} \qquad \overbrace{\hphantom{a \; dangerous \; drug}}^{y}$$

x Aspirin has been called *a blessing by some,* and *a dangerous drug by others.*

Aspirin has been called *x* and *y*; remove the comma to show that *x* and *y* are tightly related.

Pairing Independent Clauses

The no-comma rule above need not apply when the *x* element is an independent clause (1c, p. 9), as in *Not only did they adjust the fan belt, but they also adjusted the brakes.* But in *either . . . or* constructions you should omit the comma to keep the *y* statement from escaping the controlling effect of the parallelism.

DON'T:

$$\overbrace{\hphantom{you \; are \; wrong \; about \; the \; guitar \; strings,}}^{x}$$

x Either *you are wrong about the guitar strings,* or *I have forgotten*

$$\overbrace{\hphantom{everything \; I \; knew.}}^{y}$$

everything I knew.

Remove the comma and notice how the two statements then fit more tightly together.

7j Use Commas and a Coordinating Conjunction to Separate Items in a Series.

The normal way to present a **series** (three or more parallel items) is to separate the items with commas, adding a coordinating conjunction such as *and* or *or* before the last one:

- I used to sprinkle my writing with *commas,* *semicolons,* and *periods* as though they were salt and pepper.

Optional Final Comma

Many writers, especially journalists, omit the final comma in a series. So can you if you are consistent about it throughout a given piece of writing.

//
7k

ACCEPTABLE:

x   y   z
• *Football, baseball* and *basketball* were his only concerns.

Note, however, that the *x, y and z* formula may not always allow your meaning to come through clearly. Consider the following sentences, which are identical except for the comma or its absence after *friends.*

ACCEPTABLE:

x
• When Alex joins the Air Force, he will leave behind *a loving*

y   y
family, friends and *a room that he has had all to himself.*

Has Alex had the friends to himself as well as the room? This is not the writer's intention, but the reader may wonder about it for a moment.

PREFERABLE:

• When Alex joins the Air Force, he will leave behind a loving family, friends, and a room that he has had all to himself.

Now there is no chance of misunderstanding. You can see why many good writers always use a final comma in a series.

7k Carry Through with Any Repeated Modifier in a Series.

If you begin repeating any modifier within a series, be sure to keep doing so for all the remaining items.

DON'T:

w   x   y
x He can never find *his textbooks, his tapes,* calculator, and

z
homework.

The modifier *his* in the *x* element commits the writer to using the word again in *y* and *z*. Note the options for revision.

DO:

- He can never find $\overbrace{\textit{his textbooks,}}^{w}$ $\overbrace{\textit{his tapes,}}^{x}$ $\overbrace{\textit{his calculator,}}^{y}$ and $\overbrace{\textit{his homework.}}^{z}$

or

- He can never find his $\underset{w}{\textit{textbooks,}}$ $\underset{x}{\textit{tapes,}}$ $\underset{y}{\textit{calculator,}}$ and $\underset{z}{\textit{homework.}}$

71 If an Item in a Series Contains a Comma, Use Semicolons to Show Where the Items End.

Once you have begun a series, you may find yourself using commas for two quite different purposes: to separate the *x, y,* and *z* elements and to punctuate *within* one or more of those elements. If so, your reader may have trouble seeing where each item ends. To show the important breaks between the main parallel items, separate *x, y,* and *z* with semicolons:

- The Director of Food Services said that during the renovation the students would have priority in the dining halls; that faculty members should plan to cook at home, eat elsewhere, or bring bag lunches to their offices; and that the college's neighbors, including several retired professors living nearby, would be barred from the student halls until the work had been completed.

For other options in the ordering and punctuation of series, see 26d, p. 303.

8 Relations between Tenses

Every time you use a verb, you are expressing a **tense** or time frame. (For tense forms see 15b–15c, pp. 170–179. Some tenses are obviously appropriate to certain functions—the present for statements of opinion, the past for storytelling, the future for prediction. But choice of tense becomes trickier when you need to combine two or more time frames within a sentence (*He said he would have been ready if the plane had not been late; She will have finished by the day we get home;* etc.). When revising your work, check to see that your combinations of tenses observe the following rules.

8a Choose One Governing Tense for a Piece of Writing.

Stating Facts and Ideas

The normal way to state facts or offer your ideas about any general or current topic is to use the present tense.

For example:

- Water boils at 100° Celsius.
- Does the new divorce law protect the rights of children?

Note how the following passage establishes a present time frame, departing from it only to narrate events that occurred previously:

- The great debate *continues* between heredity and environment.

  PRES

  PRES

  Some observers *believe* that accidents of our circumstances *act*

  PRES

  PRES

  upon us and *make* us who we are. Others *believe* that our genes

  PRES

  seal our destiny.

  PRES

  Both sides have strong arguments, but I *am convinced* that

  PRES

  PAST

  technology *adjusts* our fate. My grandfather, for example, *was* dead at thirty-six from diabetes, a disease that my father

  PRES PERF

  has lived with for sixty years, thanks to this century's advances in medical research.

If you are stating ideas about the past, many of your verbs will be in the past tense. Even so, the present is appropriate for conveying your current reflections about past events:

  PRES

  PRES

  PAST

- I *believe* we *can prove* that the Etruscans *had* much more influ-

  PRES

  ence on Roman civilization than most people *realize*.

Narrating Events

The usual tense for narrating events is the past:

  PAST

  PAST

- She *arrived* home in a fury, and she *was* still upset when the

  PAST

  phone *rang*.

  PAST

- The solution *was allowed* to stand for three minutes, after which

  PAST

  200 cc of nitrogen *were added*.

In this second example the past verbs are in the passive voice (15c, p. 178).

Sometimes, to get a special effect of immediacy, you may even want to use the present for narration:

      PRES   PRES

• When he *phones* her, she *tells* him to leave her alone.

But note that once you adopt this present-tense convention for storytelling, you have committed yourself to it throughout the piece of writing. Do not try to switch back to the more usual past.

DON'T:

           PRES   PRES

x When he *phones* her, she *tells* him to leave her alone. But he

PAST   PAST PERF

acted as if he *hadn't understood* her point.

For consistency the verbs in the second sentence should be *acts* and *hasn't* (or *has not*) *understood*.

8b Relate Your Other Tenses to the Governing Tense.

Once you have established a controlling time frame, or **governing tense**, shift into other tenses as logic requires.

Present Time Frame

A present frame, established by a present governing tense, allows you to use a variety of other tenses to indicate the times of actions or states. Suppose, for example, you are writing a sentence that begins *He meditates every day, and . . .* The following are ways of completing that sentence.

He meditates every day, and . . .

COMPLETION OF SENTENCE	TENSE
he *is meditating* right now.	present progressive (action ongoing in the present)

COMPLETION OF SENTENCE	**TENSE**
he *has meditated* five thousand times.	present perfect (past action completed thus far)
he *has been meditating* since dawn.	present perfect progressive (action begun in the past and continuing in the present)
he *meditated* again yesterday.	past (completed action)
he *was meditating* before I was born.	past progressive (action that was ongoing in a previous time)
he *had meditated* for years before hearing about the popularity of meditation.	past perfect (action completed before another past time)
he *had been meditating* for three hours before the interview.	past perfect progressive (ongoing action completed before another past time)
he *will meditate* tomorrow.	future (action to occur later)
he *will be meditating* for the rest of his life.	future progressive (ongoing action to occur later)
he *will have meditated* for more hours than anyone ever has.	future perfect (action regarded as completed at a later time)
he *will have been meditating* for ten years by the time he is thirty.	future perfect progressive (ongoing action regarded as having begun before a later time)

Past Time Frame

If your time frame is the past and you want to mention an action completed at a still earlier time, put the verb expressing that earlier action not in the past but the past perfect tense.

DON'T:

      PAST   PAST

x There *were* rumors around school that the Dean *was* a sergeant in the Army in the Korean War.

tense
8b

DO:

      PAST   PAST PERF

• There *were* rumors around school that the Dean *had been* a sergeant in the Army in the Korean War.

DON'T:

      PAST   PAST

x She *asked* us if we *saw* the Super Bowl.

DO:

      PAST   PAST PERF

• She *asked* us if we *had seen* the Super Bowl.

But if the "still earlier" action was a continuing one, use the past perfect progressive.

DON'T:

    PAST PROGR   PAST

x We *were driving* for quite some time when we *came* to a diner.

DO:

    PAST PERF PROGR   PAST

• We *had been driving* for quite some time when we *came* to a diner.

If your time frame is the past and you want to look forward from that time to a subsequent one, use the auxiliary *would* plus the base (infinitive) form of the verb.

DON'T:

      PAST   FUTURE

x I *knew* that I *will remember* this trip for a long time.

DO:
    PAST   WOULD + BASE V
• I *knew* that I *would remember* this trip for a long time.

DON'T:
        PAST   FUTURE
x The officer *said* that he *will lift* the motorcycle into the back of the paddy wagon.

DO:
        PAST   WOULD + BASE V
• The officer *said* that he *would lift* the motorcycle into the back of the paddy wagon.

Hypothetical Condition

Certain sentences containing *if* clauses set forth **hypothetical conditions.** That is, they tell what would be true or would have been true in certain imagined circumstances. Note that such sentences differ in both form and meaning from sentences proposing likely conditions.

LIKELY CONDITION:
• I *will dance* if you *clear* a space on the floor.
• If she *studies* now, she *will pass.*

HYPOTHETICAL CONDITION:
• I *would dance* if you *cleared* a space on the floor.
• If she *studied* now, she *would pass.*

The "likely condition" sentences anticipate that the condition may be met, but the "hypothetical condition" sentences are sheer speculation: what would happen if . . . ? These require use of the **subjunctive mood** (15d, p. 180) in the *if* clause. And in the "consequence" clause they require a **conditional** form, either present or past:

CONDITIONAL FORMS			
Present	*would* *could* }	+ base verb	would go could go
Past	*would* *could* }	+ *have* + past participle	would have gone could have gone

Thus:

IF CLAUSE	CONSEQUENCE CLAUSE
PAST SUBJN If you *worked* overtime,	PRES CONDL you *would have* more spending money.
PAST SUBJN If she *had concentrated,*	PAST CONDL she *could have written* a perfect translation.
PRES SUBJN If they *won* a million dollars,	PRES CONDL what *would* they *do* with the money?
PAST SUBJN If you *had been* old enough,	PAST CONDL *would* you *have married* Barbara?

Sometimes the consequence clause precedes the *if* clause:

CONSEQUENCE CLAUSE	IF CLAUSE
You would have more spending money	if you worked overtime.
She could have written a perfect translation	if she had concentrated.
What would they do with the money	if they won a million dollars?
Would you have married Barbara	if you had been old enough?

**tense
8c**

The most common mistake in combining tenses is to use *would* in both parts of a conditional statement. Remember that *would* goes only in the consequence clause, not in the *if* clause.

DON'T:

x If they *would* try harder, they would succeed.

x If they *would have* tried harder, they would have succeeded.

DO:

• If they *tried* harder, they would succeed.

• If they *had tried* harder, they would have succeeded.

8c Do Not Shift between Quotation and Indirect Discourse within a Sentence.

Once you have begun to quote someone's speech or writing, do not suddenly move into **indirect discourse**, or the use of your own language to report what was said. Similarly, do not leap from indirect discourse to quotation.

DON'T:

QUOTATION

x She said, *"I love science fiction movies,"* and *had I seen the one*
INDIRECT DISCOURSE

about the teenage Martians on a rampage?

DO:

QUOTATION

• She said, *"I love science fiction movies,"* and asked me, *"Have you*
QUOTATION

seen the one about the teenage Martians on a rampage?"

DON'T:

INDIRECT DISCOURSE   QUOTATION

x My boss said *the key was missing* and *are you the one who took*
it?

DO:

| | INDIRECT DISCOURSE | INDIRECT DISCOURSE | tense 8d |

* My boss said *the key was missing* and asked *if I was the one who*

had taken it.

8d Learn How Tenses Differ between Quotation and Indirect Discourse.

In the following chart, notice what happens to tenses when you shift from what was actually said (quotation) to a report of what was said (indirect discourse).

	QUOTATION	**INDIRECT DISCOURSE**
present verb in quotation	"I *want* to join the Navy after graduation," he said.	He said that he *wanted* to join the Navy after graduation.
past verb in quotation	"I *wanted* to join the Navy after my graduation," he revealed.	He revealed that he *had wanted* to join the Navy after his graduation.
present perfect verb in quotation	He protested, "I *have* never *wanted* to join the Air Force."	He protested that he *had* never *wanted* to join the Air Force.
past perfect verb in quotation	"Until then," he reminded us, "I *had* always *planned* to study photography."	He reminded us that until then he *had* always *planned* to study photography.
future verb in quotation	"I *will look* into photographic training in the military," he said.	He said that he *would look* into photographic training in the military.

tense
8e

To summarize these changes of tense, indirect discourse:

	QUOTATION	INDIRECT DISCOURSE
makes a present verb past	want ⟶	wanted
makes a past or present perfect verb past perfect	wanted have wanted ⟶	had wanted
leaves a past perfect verb past perfect	had wanted ⟶	had wanted
turns a future verb into *would* + a base (infinitive) form	will want ⟶	would want

You can deduce other tense changes in indirect discourse from these basic ones: *will have wanted* becomes *would have wanted, has been wanting* becomes *had been wanting,* etc.

8e Use the Present Tense to Discuss an Author's Ideas within a Particular Work or to Convey the Unfolding Action of a Plot.

Discussing Ideas within a Work

No matter how long ago a book or other publication was written, use the present tense to characterize the ideas it expresses:

- In *The Republic* Plato *maintains* that artists are a menace to the ideal state.
- Thoreau *says* in *Walden* that we can find peace by staying exactly where we are.

The present-tense verbs are appropriate because any book "speaks to" its readers in a continuing present time.

If, on the other hand, you want to refer to a noncontemporary author's ideas without reference to a particular work, use the past:

- Plato *believed* that artists were a menace to the ideal republic.
- Thoreau *was convinced* that people could find peace by staying exactly where they were.

Discussing Actions within a Plot

Unlike a real event, a scene within a work of art does not happen once and for all. It is always ready to be experienced afresh by a new reader, viewer, or listener. Consequently, the time frame for discussing such a scene is the present. Though you should use the past tense to write about the historical creating of the art work, you should use the present tense to convey what the work "says to us." This function of the present tense is called the **literary present**.

HISTORICAL PAST:

- Shakespeare *was* probably familiar with the plays of Kyd and Marlowe when he *wrote* his great tragedies. He *expressed* his deepest feelings in those plays.

LITERARY PRESENT:

- Shakespeare *reveals* Hamlet's mind through soliloquy.
- Hamlet's unrelenting psychological dilemma *drives* him toward catastrophe.
- The Misfit, in Flannery O'Connor's story "A Good Man Is Hard to Find," *murders* an entire family.
- In the 1949 film version of *Oliver Twist,* Alec Guinness *plays* Fagin.

    If the verb in this last example were *played,* the sentence would be making a statement not about the movie but about an event in Alec Guinness's acting career.

8f In Discussing a Plot, Relate Other Tenses to the Literary Present.

When an event in a plot follows certain developments or anticipates others that you want to mention, use the literary present (8e) for the action being immediately discussed and the past or future (and related tenses) for the earlier or later actions:

> PAST   PAST
> • When Hamlet's suspicions *were* confirmed by the ghost, he *vowed*
>
>   PRES   PRES PERF
> revenge. But by Act Two he *fears* that his self-doubts *have dulled*
>
>   PRES
> his purpose. He *engages* a troupe of players to reenact the murder
>
>   PRES   FUTURE
> and *swears* that the play *will* "*catch* the conscience of the King. . . ."

> Notice how the writer has chosen a point of focus in Act Two of *Hamlet*. The use of the literary present for that time determines which tenses are appropriate for the other described actions.

8g Do Not Allow the Past Form of a Quoted Verb to Influence Your Own Choice of Tense.

It is hard to keep to the literary present (8e) when you have just quoted a passage containing verbs in the past tense. The tendency is to allow your own verbs to slip into the past. Keep to the rule, however: use the present tense for actions or states under immediate discussion.

DON'T:

>   PAST
> x D. H. Lawrence *describes* Cecilia as "a big dark-complexioned,
>
>   PAST
> pug-faced young woman who very rarely *spoke*. . . ." When
>
>   PAST   PAST
> she *did speak,* however, her words *were* sharp enough to kill her aunt Pauline.

Here *did speak* and *were,* influenced by the quoted verb *spoke,* wrongly depart from the literary present.

DO:

- D. H. Lawrence *describes* Cecilia as "a big dark-complexioned, pug-faced young woman who very rarely spoke...." When she *does speak,* however, her words *are* sharp enough to kill her aunt Pauline.

8h Change the Tense of a Verbal to Show a Different Relation to the Indicated Time of Action.

When you use a **verbal** (1a, p. 7)—an infinitive, a participle, or a gerund—ask yourself how it relates in time to the rest of your statement. Verbals change their form only if they characterize an *earlier* action or state than the main one.

Same or Later Time: Present Form

Use the present form of a verbal if it conveys an action or state no earlier than the time established in the rest of the sentence.

SAME TIME:

PRES
PRES INF
- We *try to ski* every day.

PRES
PAST INF
- We *tried to ski* every day.

PRES
PAST GER
- We *tried skiing* every day.

PRES
PART   PAST
- *Skiing* every day, we greatly *improved* our technique.

LATER TIME:

PRES
PRES INF
- We *intend to ski* every day next winter.

PRES   PRES GER

- We *anticipate* months of *skiing*.

PRES   PRES PART

- We *hope* to become stronger, *skiing* every day.

Earlier Time: Past Form

In the rare case when your verbal is placed into relation with a later time, put it into a past form:

PAST INF

- We expect *to have improved* our skiing by next season.

PAST INF

- We wanted *to have made* a breakthrough before the new season began.

PRES GER

- Our goal will be *to have made* a breakthrough by then.

PAST PART

- *Having improved* so much the year before, we had good reason to feel hopeful.

B PUNCTUATION

Punctuation

Marks of punctuation are essential for clear meaning in written prose. Beyond showing where pauses or stops would occur in speech, they indicate logical relations that would otherwise be hard for a reader to make out. For example, parentheses, brackets, dashes, and commas all signal a pause, but they suggest different relations between main and subordinate material. The only way to be sure that your punctuation marks are working with your meaning, not against it, is to master the rules.

Part A above, "Usage," covers a good many punctuation rules for handling such grammatical features as independent clauses, modifying elements, and parallel constructions. This part repeats those rules (giving cross references to the fuller discussions), adds other rules, and shows how you can choose between punctuation marks that are closely related in function.

Note that standard practices of quotation are handled in Chapter 13 and that problems with apostrophes and hyphens are treated under spelling, Chapter 18. To see how punctuation marks are formed and spaced on the page, consult Chapter 14.

9 Period, Question Mark, Exclamation Point

PERIOD

9a Place a Period at the End of a Sentence Making a Statement, a Polite Command, or a Mild Exclamation.

STATEMENT:
- I think the Olympic Games have become too politicized.
- Art historians are showing new respect for nineteenth-century narrative painting.

POLITE COMMAND:
- Tell me why you think the Olympic Games have become too politicized.
- Consider the new respect that art historians are showing toward nineteenth-century narrative painting.

MILD EXCLAMATION:
- What a pity that the Olympic Games have become so politicized.

- How remarkable it is to see the art historians reversing their former scorn for nineteenth-century narrative painting.

    Exclamation points at the end of these two sentences would have made them more emphatic; see 9j, p. 124.

9c

9b End an Indirect Question with a Period.

An **indirect question,** instead of taking a question form, reports that a question is or was asked. Thus an indirect question is a *declarative sentence*—one that makes a statement. As such, it should be completed by a period, not a question mark.

DON'T:

x Ted asked me whether I was good at boardsailing?

DO:

- Ted asked me whether I was good at boardsailing.

9c Consider a Period Optional after a Courtesy Question.

Some questions in business letters (Chapter 39) are really requests or mild commands. You can end such a sentence with either a period or a question mark.

DO:

- Would you be kind enough to reply within thirty days.

or

- Would you be kind enough to reply within thirty days?

The period makes a more impersonal and routine effect. If you want to express actual courtesy toward a reader you know, keep to the question mark.

9d Eliminate an Unacceptable Sentence Fragment [1d, p. 11].

DON'T:

x They stood back and watched the crows. *Wheeling and cawing*
FRAG
over the splattered melon.

9e

DO:

• They stood back and watched the crows wheeling and cawing over the splattered melon.

DON'T:

x Most Americans should study recent changes in the tax laws.
FRAG
Such as those affecting deductions for medical expenses, child care, and IRAs.

DO:

• Most Americans should study recent changes in the tax laws, such as those affecting deductions for medical expenses, child care, and IRAs.

For the intentional sentence fragment, see 1e, p. 15.

9e If a Sentence Ends with an Abbreviation, Do Not Add a Second Period.

DON'T:
x She made many sacrifices to complete her Ph.D. .

DO:
• She made many sacrifices to complete her Ph.D.

QUESTION MARK

9f Place a Question Mark after a Direct Question.

?

9g

Most questions are complete sentences, but now and then you may want to add a question to a statement or insert a question within a statement. In every instance, put a question mark immediately after the question:

- Do you like to write?
- Many people are proud of their written work, but *does anyone really like to write?*
- *"Can you imagine someone finding it easier to write,"* I asked, *"than to call?"*
- You and I—*is it possible?*—may yet learn to enjoy writing.

But if your sentence poses a question that is then modified by other language, place the question mark at the end:

- How could he treat me like that, after all the consideration I showed him?

9g Use a Question Mark within Parentheses to Express Doubt.

- Saint Thomas Aquinas, 1225(?)–1274, considered faith more important than reason.

  If the dates here were in parentheses, the question mark would go inside brackets: *(1225[?]–1274).*

Sarcastic Question Mark

No grammatical rule prevents you from getting a sarcastic effect from the "doubting" question mark. But if you are determined to be sarcastic, quotation marks will do a better job of conveying your attitude.

AVOID:

x The President expects to make four nonpolitical (?) speeches in the month before the election.

PREFER:

• The President expects to make four "nonpolitical" speeches in the month before the election.

?
9i

9h If a Sentence Asking a Question Contains a Question at the End, Use Only One Question Mark.

DON'T:

x Are you the skeptic who asked, "Why write?"?

DO:

• Are you the skeptic who asked, "Why write?"

9i As a General Practice, Do Not Use a Comma or a Period after a Question Mark.

DON'T:

x Now I know the answer to the question, "Why study?".

DO:

• Now I know the answer to the question, "Why study?"

DON'T:

x "Where is my journal?", she asked.

DO:

• "Where is my journal?" she asked.

An exception is made for material inserted within parentheses. See 12i, p. 145.

EXCLAMATION POINT

9j Use Exclamation Points Sparingly to Show Intensity.

!
9j

When you quote an outburst or want to express extremely strong feeling, end the sentence or intentional sentence fragment (1e, p. 15) with an exclamation point:

- Excellent!
- Call a doctor!
- My wallet, my glasses, my notes—all gone!
- And this is the result of their so-called peace offensive!

Frequent use of exclamation points, however, dulls their effect. And though an exclamation point, like a question mark, can be inserted parenthetically to convey sarcasm (9g), the effect is usually weak.

AVOID:

x Warren thought that a black-and-white photocopy (!) of the Rembrandt painting would give him everything he needed to write his art history paper.

10 Comma

10a Join Two Independent Clauses Either with a Comma and a Coordinating Conjunction or with a Semicolon [2a, p. 17].

* Many students took this course, *but* few have kept up with the work.
* Many students took this course; few have kept up with the work.
* Every blink is like fire, *and* tears well up constantly.
* Every blink is like fire; tears well up constantly.

10b Avoid a Run-on Sentence [2b, p. 19].

DON'T:

x They discussed Faulkner's novel, the class hour ended all too soon. [comma splice]

x I hate having a brainy sister it makes me feel stupid. [fused sentence]

DO:

* They discussed Faulkner's novel, *but* the class hour ended before they could get very far.
* I hate having a brainy sister, *since* it makes me feel stupid.

DON'T:

x Some people know how to hide their nervous habits, I do not.

x I get nervous in front of the class I start to stutter.

125

DO:
- Some people know how to hide their nervous habits, *but* I do not.
- I get nervous in front of the class; I start to stutter.

For other ways of correcting a run-on, see 2d, p. 26.

10c Do Not Put a Comma between Sentence Elements That Belong Together.

Subject and Verb (3r, p. 44)

DON'T:
SUBJ   V.
x *Ishi* alone, *remained* to tell the story.

DO:
- Ishi alone remained to tell the story.

Verb and Direct Object (1a, p. 5)

DON'T:
V   D.OBJ
x Ralph *saw* in a dream, the *running shoes* that would enable him to win the 5000 meters.

DO:
- Ralph saw in a dream the running shoes that would enable him to win the 5000 meters.

Verb and Complement (1a, p. 6)

DON'T:
V   COMPL
x The laws against drug use *were* not always, so *strict* as they are today.

DO:
- The laws against drug use were not always so strict as they are today.

Subordinating Conjunction and the Rest of Its Clause (1c, p. 10)

DON'T:

SUBORD CONJ   REST OF CLAUSE

ˣ Another reason for delay is *that, the market may improve.*

DO:

• Another reason for delay is that the market may improve.

Preposition and Its Object (p. 553)

DON'T:

PREP   OBJ OF PREP

ˣ My worries keep returning *to, inflation, unemployment, and natural disasters.*

DO:

• My worries keep returning to inflation, unemployment, and natural disasters.

Exceptions: Comma Allowed

When a direct object precedes the subject and verb, you can follow it with a comma to indicate that it is not the subject:

D OBJ   SUBJ   V

• *That we are here on earth merely to pass along our DNA, I cannot believe.*

The same rule applies to an initial **objective complement**—that is, a complement of a direct object:

OBJ COMPL   SUBJ V D OBJ

• *What she calls happiness, I call slavery.*

10d   Include a Comma after an Initial Modifier That Is More than a Few Words Long [4h, p. 56].

• Instead of having the chocolate mousse, Walter ordered an apple for dessert.

- Since we ate lunch after three o'clock, we are not interested in dinner now.

10e Consider a Comma Optional after a Brief Initial Modifier [4i, p. 57].

ACCEPTABLE:
- Until this week, I had kept up with my assignments.
- In 1912, the *Titanic* sank in icy waters off the coast of Newfoundland.

or

- Until this week I had kept up with my assignments.
- In 1912 the *Titanic* sank in icy waters off the coast of Newfoundland.

10f Master the Punctuation Of Restrictive and Nonrestrictive Elements [4j, p. 58].

RESTRICTIVE:
        RESTR EL
- Women *who are over thirty-five* tend to show reduced fertility.

                        RESTR EL
- Some women *who have taken up running in their thirties and forties* have proved to be world-class marathoners.

NONRESTRICTIVE:
        NONRESTR EL
- Women, *who have rarely been treated equally in the job market,* still tend to be relatively underpaid.

                        NONRESTR EL
- Women, *whose adaptability to long-distance running was not appreciated until recently,* seem better able to manage fatigue than their male counterparts.

10g Set Off a Sentence Adverb or a Transitional Phrase with Commas [4k, p. 61].

SENT ADV
- A circus, *furthermore*, lifts the spirits of young and old alike.

TRANS PHRASE
- The deficit has continued to grow, *as a matter of fact*.

For exceptions, see 4k, p. 62.

10h

10h In Punctuating an Appositive, Observe the Restrictive/Nonrestrictive Rule [4l, p. 62].

RESTRICTIVE APPOSITIVE:

RESTR APP   RESTR APP
- My brother *Bert* played baseball in college, but my brother *Jack* was not athletic at all.

    Bert and *Jack* are restrictive appositives, telling in each case which brother is meant.

NONRESTRICTIVE APPOSITIVE:

NONRESTR APP
- My sister, *Diane*, studied Portuguese in the Navy.

    The commas tell us that the writer has only one sister, Diane. Thus the appositive does not restrict the meaning of the preceding term, *sister*.

RESTRICTIVE APPOSITIVE:

RESTR APP
- In her poem *"The bustle in a house"* Emily Dickinson uses ordinary domestic images to express the emotional aftermath of a death in the family.

    Dickinson wrote many poems; the lack of commas before and after the appositive shows that it is restrictive, narrowing the reference to just one of those poems.

NONRESTRICTIVE APPOSITIVE:

NONRESTR APP
- In writing his play, *Otho the Great,* Keats collaborated with Charles Brown.

    Otho the Great is the only play Keats is known to have written. The commas indicate this fact; the nonrestrictive appositive names the play but does not single it out from others.

10j

10i Set Off an Interrupting Element at Both Ends [4m, p. 63].

INT EL
- Our leading advocate of clean streets, *you understand,* is the Mayor.

INT EL
- Every morning at nine certain students—*always the wrong ones*—hear Professor Fry's advice about habits of punctuality.

10j Use Commas with Coordinate Modifiers [4n, p. 64].

COORDINATE MODIFIERS:
- I arrived at my new school on a *sunlit, windy* day.
- The show included the work of a *small, innovative* group of local artists.

    The group is both small and innovative; the two coordinate adjectives modify the same term, as the comma shows.

NONCOORDINATE MODIFIERS:
- She never forgave them for the way they insulted her on that *infamous first* day of school.
- A *small support* group of battered wives meets at the high school on Wednesday evenings.

What is *small* is not a group but a *support group;* thus *small* and *support* are not coordinate, and no comma is called for.

10k Do Not Place a Comma between the Final (or Only) Modifier and the Modified Term [4o, p. 66].

FINAL MOD
- O'Keeffe produced an intense, starkly simple, *radiantly glowing*

MODIFIED TERM
painting of a flower.

- Flemish artists of the seventeenth century painted merry, sen-

FINAL MOD   MODIFIED TERM
sual, *ironic scenes* of peasant life.

10l Consider Enclosing a "Contrary" Modifier in Commas [4p, p. 66].

ACCEPTABLE:
- She told a fascinating, but not altogether believable, story.
- The Senator's speech was a bitter, though carefully worded, reply to his opponents.

or
- She told a fascinating but not altogether believable story.
- The Senator's speech was a bitter though carefully worded reply to his opponents.

10m Join Most Paired Elements without an Intervening Comma [7i, p. 99].

- Last night's storm blew out *my electric blanket* and *my clock radio.*
- A graduating senior should know how to write *an effective business letter* and *a confident résumé.*

10n Use Commas and a Coordinating Conjunction to Separate Items in a Series [7j, p. 100].

- I used to sprinkle my writing with *commas, semicolons,* and *periods* as though they were salt and pepper.
- Now I use punctuation for *clarity, emphasis, logic,* and *variety.*

10o Learn the Uses of the Comma in Numbers, Dates, Addresses, Titles, and Degrees.

Number of More Than Four Digits

Commas should separate every three digits (counting from the right) of a number consisting of more than four digits: *109,368,452.* In four-digit numbers the comma is optional: *6083* and *6,083* are both correct.

No commas separate the digits of years *(2001),* telephone numbers, ZIP codes, serial numbers, and other figures meant to identify an item or place. Such figures are sometimes divided into segments by hyphens, as are Social Security numbers: *053-26-3537.*

Date

A comma should separate the day of the month and the year if the month is given first: *July 4, 1934.* If the sentence continues after the date, then the year, too, should be followed by a comma:

- July 4, 1934, was the date of her birth.

When the day is given first, no punctuation is necessary:

- She was born on 4 July 1934 in Peralta Hospital.

When only the month and the year are stated, commas before and after the year are optional. You can write either *July 1934 was the month of her birth* or *July, 1934, was the month of her birth.*

Address

- New York, New York
- 7713 Radnor Road, Bethesda, MD 20034

- Department of Economics, Simon Fraser University, Burnaby, B.C. V5A 156, Canada

Within a sentence, put commas both before and after the name of a state or province that identifies a specific town or geographic feature.

- Laramie, Wyoming, celebrates its Jubilee Days every July.
- Mount McKinley, Alaska, is the highest peak in North America.

10o

Title or Degree Following Name

As a rule, titles or degrees have been set off by commas on both sides:

- Herbert Moroni, Ph.D., was present.
- Adlai Stevenson, III, served on the committee.

     But the form without a comma—*Adlai Stevenson III*—is now more usual.

For the use of a comma to introduce a quotation, see 13j and 13k, page 155.

11 Semicolon and Colon

SEMICOLON

11a If Two Statements Are Closely Related in Meaning, Join Them with a Semicolon.

The punctuation mark that comes nearest in function to the semicolon is the period. But whereas a period keeps two statements apart as separate sentences, a semicolon shows that two statements within one sentence are intimately related. When one statement is a consequence of another or contrasts sharply with it, you can bring out that tight connection by joining them with a semicolon instead of with a comma and a coordinating conjunction (2a, p. 17):

- The University conducts art history classes in Europe; the accessibility of great museums and monuments gives students a firsthand sense of the subject.
- Some of those painters influenced Cézanne; others were influenced by him.

Note that when a semicolon is used, the second statement often contains a sentence adverb or transitional phrase (4k, p. 61) pointing out the logical relation between the two clauses:

- Misunderstanding is often the root of injustice; perfect under-
  SENT ADV
  standing, *however,* is impossible to attain.

● Some parents weigh every word they speak; others, *in contrast,* do not think twice about their harsh language.

TRANS PHRASE

11b Do Not Follow a Semicolon with a Sentence Fragment.

An unacceptable sentence fragment (1d, p. 11) is just as faulty when it follows a semicolon as when it stands alone.

DON'T:

x I used to be afraid to talk to people; *even to ask the time of day.*

FRAG

I always let my brother speak for me; *because he was everyone's buddy.*

FRAG

DO:

● I used to be afraid to talk to people; even asking the time of day was an ordeal. I always let my brother speak for me; he was everyone's buddy.

or:

● I used to be afraid to talk to people—even to ask the time of day. I always let my brother speak for me, because he was everyone's buddy.

11c In Appropriate Circumstances, Feel Free to Follow a Semicolon with a Conjunction.

There is nothing wrong with following a semicolon with a conjunction, so long as the second statement is an independent clause (11b). Do so if you want to make explicit the logical connection between the statements coming before and after the semicolon:

● All day long we loaded the van with our worldly goods; *but* when we were all ready to leave the next morning, full of eagerness for the trip, we saw that the van had a flat tire.

CONJ

A comma after *goods* would also be appropriate, but the semicolon recommends itself because the second statement already contains two commas. Thus the semicolon helps to show the main separation in the sentence.

11d If an Item in a Series Contains a Comma, Use Semicolons to Show Where the Items End [71, p. 102].

* The Director of Food Services said that during the renovation the students would have priority in the dining halls; that faculty members should plan to cook at home, eat elsewhere, or bring bag lunches to their offices; and that the college's neighbors, including several retired professors living nearby, would be barred from the student halls.
* Student dining halls include the Servery, which is located on the ground floor of the Student Union; the Cafeteria, temporarily relocated in Jim Thorpe Gymnasium; and the Rathskeller, now in the basement of Anne Bradstreet Hall.

COLON

11e Use a Colon to Show an Equivalence between Items on Either Side.

A colon introduces a restatement, a formal listing, or a quotation. Use a colon if you can plausibly insert *namely* after it:

* Dinner arrives: [*namely*] a tuna fish sandwich and a cup of tea.
* The bill is unbelievable: [*namely*] $8.50 for the sandwich and $1.95 for the tea.
* Samuel Johnson offered the following wise advice: [*namely*] "If you would have a faithful servant, and one that you like, serve yourself."

The *namely* test can help you avoid putting semicolons where colons belong and vice versa.

DON'T:

x The results of the poll were surprising; 7 percent in favor, 11 percent opposed, and 82 percent no opinion.

> *Namely* would be appropriate here; therefore the semicolon should be a colon.

x We slaved for years: we remained as poor as ever.

> *Namely* is inappropriate, since the second clause makes a new point. The colon should be a semicolon.

11f Make Sure You Have a Complete Statement before a Colon.

Like a semicolon, a colon must be preceded by a complete statement.

DON'T:
> FRAG

x *Occupations that interest me:* beekeeper, horse groomer, dog trainer, veterinarian.

DO:
> COMPLETE STATEMENT

• *Occupations involving animals interest me:* beekeeper, horse groomer, dog trainer, veterinarian.

But remember that unlike a semicolon, a colon need not be *followed* by a whole statement (11b, p. 135).

11g Do Not Allow a Colon to Separate Elements That Belong Together.

DON'T:
> V   D OBJ

x Before buying my Cavalier, I *tested: a Toyota Corolla, a Ford Tempo, and a Nissan Sentra.*

> The colon separates a verb from its three-part direct object. Note that this practice would still be wrong if the direct object had any number of parts and extended for many lines.

x Her favorite holidays *are:* $\overset{\text{V}}{}$ $\overset{\text{COMPL}}{\overbrace{\textit{Christmas, Halloween, and the Fourth}}}$ *of July.*

>   The colon separates a verb from its three-part complement (1a, p. 6).

x The exhibit contained work by many famous photographers,

$\underset{\text{PREP}}{\textit{such as:}}$ $\overset{\text{OBJ PREP}}{\overbrace{\textit{Avedon, Adams, Weston, and Lange.}}}$

>   The colon separates a preposition from its four-part object.

x The Renaissance naval adventurers set out *to:* $\overbrace{\textit{sack enemy cities,}}$
COMPLETION OF INF PHRASES
$\overbrace{\textit{find precious metals, and claim colonial territory.}}$

>   The colon separates the infinitive marker *to* from the completion of three infinitive phrases (p. 555). Even if you had a long series of such phrases, the colon would be wrong.

In each of the four examples above, you need only drop the colon to make the sentence acceptable.

11h Use No More Than One Colon in a Sentence.

Once you have supplied a colon, your reader expects the sentence to end with the item or items announced by the colon. A second colon makes a confusing effect.

> DON'T:
> x She needed three things: a new hat, warmer gloves, and boots that would be serviceable in all kinds of bad conditions: snow, slush, mud, and rain.

> DO:
> • She needed three things: a new hat, warmer gloves, and boots that would be serviceable in snow, slush, mud, and rain.

11i Use a Colon to Separate Hours and Minutes, to End the Salutation of a Business Letter, and to Introduce a Subtitle.

HOURS AND MINUTES:
- The train should arrive at 10:15 P.M.

SALUTATION:
- Dear Mr. Green:

SUBTITLE:
- *Virginia Woolf: A Biography*

12 Dash and Parentheses

Both dashes and parentheses, as well as commas, can be used to set off interrupting elements (4m, p. 63). The difference is that dashes call attention to the interrupting material, whereas parentheses suggest that it is truly subordinate in meaning.

Dash	—	most emphatic	The monsoon season—with incessant driving rain and flooding—causes much hardship.
Comma	,	"neutral"	The monsoon season, with incessant driving rain and flooding, causes much hardship.
Parentheses	( )	least emphatic	The monsoon season (with incessant driving rain and flooding) causes much hardship.

DASH

12a Use a Dash or Pair of Dashes to Offer an Emphatic Explanation, to Set Off a Striking Insertion, to Introduce a List Abruptly, or to Mark an Interruption of Dialogue.

EMPHATIC EXPLANATION:
- Narcissus was the most modern of mythological lovers—he fell in love with himself.

140

STRIKING INSERTION:

• Narcissus—the most modern of mythological lovers—fell in love with himself.

ABRUPT INTRODUCTION OF LIST:

• The new house has marvelous devices to let in light—skylights in the dining room, living room walls that slide open, and a breakfast porch constructed like a greenhouse.

12b

INTERRUPTION OF DIALOGUE:

• The man behind menaced us with his umbrella. "If you don't step aside, I'll—"

"This is a line for people with tickets," I said. "We're not—" But our dispute was cut short by the usher, who was urging the line forward.

If a character's speech "trails off" instead of being interrupted, an ellipsis (13m, p. 156) is more appropriate than a dash: *"We're not . . ."* Note that you should begin a new paragraph for each change of speaker.

12b If Your Main Sentence Resumes after an Interruption, Use a Second Dash.

When you begin an interruption with one dash, you must end it with another.

DON'T:

x Narcissus looked into a lake—so the story goes, and fell in love with his own reflection.

x Somehow my aunt sensed the danger—perhaps she realized that my uncle should have been home by then, and she phoned me to come over at once.

DO:

• Narcissus looked into a lake—so the story goes—and fell in love with his own reflection.

- Somehow my aunt sensed the danger—perhaps she realized that my uncle should have been home by then—and she phoned me to come over at once.

12c Use a Dash to Isolate an Introductory Element That Is Not the Grammatical Subject.

12e

In a sentence that makes a "false start" for rhetorical effect (26g, p. 307), you want to give a signal that the opening element is an appositive (4l, p. 62) rather than the subject of the verb. A dash serves the purpose:

- APP
- *Depression, compulsion, phobia, hallucination*—these disorders often require quick and emphatic treatment.

12d Make Sure Your Sentence Would Be Coherent If the Part within Dashes Were Omitted.

The elements of your sentence before and after the dashes must fit together grammatically.

DON'T:

x *Because* he paid no attention to her—he was riveted to his cable sports channel day and night—*so* she finally lost her temper.

Ask yourself if the sentence makes sense without the material between dashes: x *Because he paid no attention to her so she finally lost her temper.* Recognizing that this shortened sentence is grammatically askew, you can then correct the original.

DO:

- Because he paid no attention to her—he was riveted to his cable sports channel day and night—she finally lost her temper.

12e Do Not Use More Than One Dash or Pair of Dashes in a Sentence.

Dashes work best when used sparingly. Within a single sentence, one interruption marked by dashes should be the maximum.

DON'T:

x We cannot expect a tax reform bill—or indeed any major legislation—to be considered on its merits in an election year—a time
when the voters' feelings—not the country's interests—are up-
permost in the minds of lawmakers.

DO:

• We cannot expect a tax reform bill, or indeed any major legislation, to be considered on its merits in an election year—a time
when the voters' feelings, not the country's interests, are upper-
most in the minds of lawmakers.

( )
12f

PARENTHESES

12f Use Parentheses to Enclose and Subordinate an Incidental Element or to Provide Reference Information.

Parentheses are appropriate for sealing off and subordinating an in-
cidental illustration, explanation, comment, number, date, or citation:

ILLUSTRATION:
• Some tropical reptiles (the Galápagos tortoise, for example) sleep
in puddles of water to cool themselves.

EXPLANATION:
• A modem (a device for connecting a computer terminal to a central source of data) could easily be mistaken for an ordinary
telephone.

PASSING COMMENT:
• The Ouse (a rather pretty, harmless-looking river) is known to
literary people as the body of water in which Virginia Woolf
drowned herself.

NUMBER:
• The furniture will be repossessed in thirty (30) days.

DATE:
- The article on outcomes of psychotherapy appears in *The Behavioral and Brain Sciences* 6 (1983): 275–310.

CITATION:

- Guevara first began studying Marxism in Guatemala in 1954 (Liss 256–57).

12g Learn When to Supply End Punctuation for a Parenthetical Sentence within Another Sentence.

If your whole sentence-within-a-sentence is a statement, do not end it with a period:

- Shyness *(mine was extreme)* can be overcome with time.

But if you are asking a question or making an exclamation, do supply the end punctuation:

- Today I am outspoken *(who would have predicted it?)* and sometimes even eloquent.
- To be able to give a talk without panic *(what a relief at last!)* is a great advantage in the business world.

Notice that the parenthetical sentence-within-a-sentence does not begin with a capital letter.

12h When Placing a Parenthetical Sentence between Complete Sentences, Punctuate It as a Complete Sentence.

A whole sentence within parentheses, if it is not part of another sentence, must begin with a capital letter and contain end punctuation of its own, *within* the close-parenthesis mark:

- Shyness can be a crippling affliction. *(The clinical literature is full of tragic cases.)* Yet some victims suddenly reach a point where they decide they have been bullied long enough.

12i Do Not Allow Parentheses to Affect Other Punctuation.

Remember these two rules:

1. No mark of punctuation comes just before an open-parenthesis.

2. The rest of the sentence must keep to its own punctuation, as if the parenthetical portion were not there.

( )
12j

Thus, to decide whether a close-parenthesis mark should be followed by a comma, mentally disregard the interruption:

• Shyness *(mine was extreme)* can be overcome with time.

A comma after the close-parenthesis mark would make the following stripped-down sentence: *Shyness, can be overcome with time.* Since that sentence would wrongly separate a subject *(Shyness)* from its verb *(can be overcome)*, the comma must be omitted. (See 3r, p. 44.)

• My father was not as shy as I was *(otherwise he could not have succeeded in his work),* but he was soft-spoken and reserved.

The stripped-down sentence correctly links two independent clauses with a comma and a coordinating conjunction (2a, p. 17). Since the comma is appropriate without the parenthetical interruption, it is also appropriate with it.

12j Do Not Use Parentheses to Interrupt a Quotation.

Brackets (13p, p. 159), not parentheses, are required when you want to insert information or commentary into quoted material.

DON'T:

x "Joan (Benoit) has to be the favorite in this race," Nancy said.

DO:

• "Joan [Benoit] has to be the favorite in this race," Nancy said.

13 Quoting

Handling quoted material is more than a matter of following the procedures covered in this chapter. You want to quote only where the quoted language is important to your point; you want to avoid letting quotations crowd out your own reasoning; and you want to quote accurately and give proper acknowledgment of the source (37a, p. 472). Yet it is also good to know the small details of managing a quotation—introducing the words smoothly, showing just where they begin and end, and signaling where you have made an omission or inserted an explanatory word or phrase.

13a Recognize the Punctuation Marks Used with Quotations.

The marks used in handling quotations are double and single **quotation marks**, the **slash**, the **ellipsis**, and **brackets**.

NAME	FORM	FUNCTION
double quotation marks (13b)	" "	to mark the beginning and end of a quotation
single quotation marks (13c)	' '	to mark a quotation within a quotation
slash (13g)	/	to mark a line break in a brief quotation of poetry
ellipsis (13m)	. . .	to mark an omission from a quotation
brackets (13p)	[ ]	to mark an explanatory insertion within a quotation

Note that these marks have other functions as well.

MARK	OTHER FUNCTION	EXAMPLE
quotation marks	to show distance from a dubious or offensive expression	Hitler's "final solution" destroyed six million Jews.
slash	to indicate alternatives	Try writing an invoice and/or a purchase order.
	to mean "per" in measurements	ft./sec. (feet per second)
	to indicate overlapping times	the Winter/Spring issue of the journal
ellipsis	to show that a statement contains further implications	And thus he came to feel that he had triumphed over the government. How little he knew about the workings of bureaucracy. . . .
	to show that dialogue "trails off"	"What I am trying to tell you is . . . is . . ."
brackets	to insert material into a passage that is already within parentheses	(See, however, D. L. Rosenhan in *Science* 179 [1973]: 250–58.)

" "

13b

SETTING OFF A QUOTATION

13b Use Double Quotation Marks to Set Off Quoted Material That You Have Incorporated into Your Own Prose.

If you are representing someone's speech or quoting a fairly brief passage of written work—no more than five typed lines of prose or no more than two or three lines of poetry—you should **incorporate** the quotation. That is, you should make it continuous with your own text instead of **extracting** it by skipping lines and indenting it (13h, p. 152). Be sure to enclose an incorporated quotation in quotation marks. In North American (as opposed to British) English, those marks should be double (" "):

13c

- "Computers," as Bertini points out, "are unforgiving toward even the tiniest mistake in the instructions you give them."

13c Use Single Quotation Marks for a Quotation within a Quotation.

If the passage you are incorporating already contains quotation marks, change them to single marks (' '):

- E. F. Carpenter, writing in *Contemporary Dramatists,* says of Butterfield: "The playwright knows where his best work originated. 'Everything that touches an audience,' he told me, 'comes from memories of the period when I was down and out.'"

Double Quotation within a Quotation

Try to avoid quoting a passage that already contains single quotation marks; the effect will be confusing. But if you find no alternative, change those single marks to double ones. Then check carefully to see that your *three* sets of marks are kept straight (" ' " " ' "):

- Orwell's friend Richard Rees informs us that "when Socialists told him that under Socialism there would be no such feeling of being at the mercy of unpredictable and irresponsible powers, he remarked: 'I notice people always say "*under* Socialism." They look forward to being on top—with all the others underneath, being told what is good for them.'"

  Here the main quotation is from Rees. Since Rees quotes Orwell, Orwell's words appear within single marks. But when those words themselves contain a quotation, that phrase ("*under* Socialism") is set off with double marks.

13d When Quoting Dialogue, Indent for a New Paragraph with Each Change of Speaker.

After you have completed a quotation of speech, you can comment upon it without starting a new paragraph. You can also resume quoting the speaker's words after your own. But do indent for a new paragraph as soon as you get to someone else's speech.

" "

13e

> "I can't understand," I said, "how you can win world-class distance races without having been coached in high school or college."
> "Oh, but sir," he protested with a polite smile, "I have been running since I was a little child. In Kenya this is how we get from village to village."
> "Yes, yes, but where did you get your training?" This man seemed to defy everything I knew about the making of a great runner.
> "Oh, my *training!*" He threw his head back and laughed. "Mister reporter, *you* run every day, year after year, at 8,000 feet, carrying boxes and fuel and whatnot. Then please come back and tell me if you think you need some training!"

13e When Quoting Speech of More than One Paragraph, Put Quotation Marks at the Beginning of Each New Paragraph but at the End of Only the Final Paragraph.

In general, quotation marks come in pairs: for every mark that opens a quotation there must be another to close it. But there is one exception. To show that someone's quoted speech continues in a new paragraph, put quotation marks at the beginning of that paragraph, and keep doing so until the passage ends:

> "I have two things to bring up with you," she said. "In the first place, which of us is going to be keeping the stereo? I'd like to have it, but it's no big deal to me.
> "Second, what about the dog? I'm the one who brought her home as a puppy, and I intend to keep her!"

13f Learn How to Combine Quotation Marks with Other Marks of Punctuation.

1. Always place commas and periods inside the close-quotation marks. You do not have to consider whether the comma or period is part of the quotation or whether the quotation is short or long. Just routinely put the comma or period first:

- Francis Bacon said, "To spend too much time in study is sloth."
- "To spend too much time in study is sloth," said Francis Bacon.

2. Always place colons and semicolons outside the close-quotation marks:

- "Sloth": that was Bacon's term for too much study.
- Francis Bacon called excessive study "sloth"; I call it inefficiency.

3. Place question marks, exclamation points, and dashes either inside or outside the close-quotation marks, depending on their function. If they are punctuating the quoted material itself, place them inside:

- "Do you think it will snow?" she asked.
- "Of course it will!" he replied.

But put the same marks *outside* the close-quotation marks if they are not part of the question or exclamation:

- Was Stephanie a sophomore when she said, "I am going to have a job lined up long before I graduate"?

  I have told you for the last time to stop calling me your "little sweetie"!

4. When the quotation must end with a question mark or exclamation point and your own sentence calls for a closing period, drop the period:

- Grandpa listens to Dan Rather every evening and constantly screams, "Horsefeathers!"

5. Otherwise, the end punctuation of the quotation makes way for your own punctuation. For example, if the quoted passage ends with a period but your own sentence does not stop there, drop the period and substitute your own punctuation, if any:

- "I wonder why they don't impeach newscasters," said Grandpa.

  The quoted passage would normally end with a period, but the main sentence calls for a comma at that point.

" "

13f

6. When a quotation is accompanied by a footnote number, that number comes after all other punctuation except a dash that resumes your own part of the sentence:

- Bloomingdale's advertises women's skirts as "pencil-thin, get the point?"[6]
- Bloomingdale's advertises women's skirts as "pencil-thin, get the point?"[6]—but in fact the skirts come in all sizes.

7. When a quotation is incorporated into your text (without indention) and is followed by a parenthetical citation (37d, p. 488; 37e, p. 496), the parenthesis comes after the final quotation marks but before a comma or period—even if the comma or period occurs in the quoted passage:

- John Keegan begins his book about famous battles by confessing, "I have not been in a battle; nor near one, nor heard one from afar, nor seen the aftermath" (*The Face of Battle,* p. 15).

8. But if the incorporated quotation ends with a question mark or exclamation point, include it before the close-quotation marks and add your own punctuation after the parenthesis:

- He raises the question, "How would *I* behave in a battle?" (Keegan, p. 18).

9. If you extract a quotation (indent it and set it apart from your text), and if you then supply a parenthetical citation, place that citation after all punctuation on a separate line:

- Gladly will I sell
  For profit,
  Dear merchants of the town,
  My hat laden with snow.
  (Bashō, p. 60)

13g When Incorporating More Than One Line of Poetry, Use a Slash to Show Where a Line Ends.

You can incorporate as many as three lines of poetry instead of extracting them (13h). But if your passage runs beyond a line ending,
you should indicate that ending with a slash preceded and followed
by a space:

- In a snowstorm, says the noted Japanese poet Bashō, "Even a
  horse /Is a spectacle."

13h Extract a Longer Quotation from the Main Body of Your Text.

If your prose quotation extends beyond five typed lines, or if you are
quoting more than two or three lines of poetry, you should extract
the passage. In the examples below, the red numbers are keyed to
rules given on pages 153–154.

EXTRACTED PROSE:

Margot Slade points to the bond between siblings that

is like no other connection between human beings: ——— 1

5   ——— 2

    Welcome to the sibling bond, that twilight
    zone of relationships between brothers and
    sisters, and any combination thereof,
    where parents must walk but often fear to

3,4 | 7 —— tread. With good reason. As one well-
seasoned father put it: "Under most
circumstances, it can be suicide to ————→ 6
interfere."
—— Siblings generally constitute an
exclusive state—exclusive, that is, of
parents. They are the keepers of each
other's secrets and the supporters of
each other's goals. They can be friends
in the morning and enemies at night. ———— 5
(Slade 80)
———————— 2

" "

13h

Now let us see if this special relationship exists

between the famous pair of siblings under considera-

tion here.

The writer is quoting from Margot Slade's article, "Siblings: War and
Peace." For proper citation form see 37d, p. 488.

EXTRACTED POETRY:

In "Crossing Brooklyn Ferry" Whitman calls out to his

fellow citizens of the future as well as the present:—— 1

5
———————— 2
3,4 | 8— I am with you, you men and women of a generation,
or ever so many generations hence,
Just as you feel when you look on the river and
sky, so I felt,
Just as any of you is one of a living crowd,
I was one of a crowd, . . . ———————————— 5
———————— 2

By creating a bond with unborn Americans, Whitman pro-

phesies the coming greatness of his country.

1. In most cases, introduce the passage with a colon.

2. Separate the passage from your main text by skipping an extra
line above and below.

3. Indent the whole passage ten spaces from your left margin, or somewhat less if the quoted lines of poetry are very long.

4. If you are submitting a paper for a course, use single or double spacing according to your instructor's advice. But if you are writing for publication, double-space the passage, treating it just like your main text.

5. Omit the quotation marks you would have used to surround an incorporated quotation.

6. Copy exactly any quotation marks you find in the quoted passage itself.

7. In extracting prose, indent all lines equally if the passage consists of one paragraph or less. When you extract more than one paragraph of prose, indent by three spaces the first line of each full paragraph. If the first sentence in that quotation does not begin a paragraph in the original, do not indent it. Note that no indention of prose is called for unless the passage runs beyond a paragraph break in the source.

8. In extracting poetry, follow the spacing (beginnings and endings of lines) found in the original passage.

INTRODUCING A QUOTATION

13i If a Quotation Fits into One of Your Own Clauses or Phrases, Introduce It without Punctuation.

The way to decide which punctuation, if any, to use in introducing a quotation is to read the quoted matter as part of your own sentence. Use introductory punctuation only if it would have been called for anyway, with or without the quotation marks:

- Macbeth expresses the depth of his despair when he characterizes life as "a tale told by an idiot."

Since the quotation serves as an object of the writer's preposition *as*, a preceding comma would be wrong here (see 10c, p. 126). Note how smoothly the quoted passage completes the writer's sentence.

13j Follow an Introductory Tag with a Comma.

Even if you do not feel that a pause is called for, put a comma after an introductory clause such as *She said* or *He replied:*

- He said, "I'd like to comment on that."
- She replied, "Yes, you are always making comments, aren't you?"

If the tag follows or interrupts the quoted speech, it must still be set apart:

- "I'd like to comment on that," he said.
- "Yes," she replied, "you are always making comments, aren't you?"

13k Use either a Comma or a Colon to Introduce an Incorporated Quotation That Does Not Fit into Your Own Clause or Phrase.

You can choose between a comma and a colon to introduce a quotation that makes a new statement apart from your own language. The comma is more usual and less formal in effect.

- Gandhi, when asked what he thought of Western civilization, smiled and replied, "I think it would be a very good idea."

  A colon would be equally correct here, but it would mark a more formal pause.

- Surrounded by surging reporters and photographers, the accused chairman tried to hold them all at bay with one repeated sentence: "I will have no statement to make before tomorrow."

The colon is especially appropriate here because it matches *one repeated sentence* with the actual words of that sentence.

13l As a Rule, Use a Colon before an Extracted Passage.

Since an extracted quotation (13h, p. 152) appears on the page as an interruption of your prose, you should usually introduce it with a colon, implying a formal stop.

- Here is Macbeth's gloomiest pronouncement about life:

> it is a tale
> Told by an idiot, full of sound and fury,
> Signifying nothing.

Although you can introduce any extracted passage with a colon, you can make a smoother effect by dropping the punctuation if the passage begins with a fragment that completes your own sentence:

- Macbeth considers life to be

> a tale
> Told by an idiot, full of sound and fury,
> Signifying nothing.

A colon would be awkward here, since it would separate an infinitive (*to be*) from its complement (*a tale* . . .). Note that a comma would be unacceptable for the same reason.

OMITTING MATERIAL FROM A QUOTATION

13m Use an Ellipsis Mark to Show That Something Has Been Omitted from a Quotation.

If you want to omit unneeded words or sentences from a quoted passage, accuracy requires that you show where you are doing so.

WHOLE PASSAGE:

- As I have repeatedly stated, those claims, which irresponsible promoters of tax shelter schemes continue to represent as valid, have been disallowed every time they have come before the IRS.

PARTIAL QUOTATION:

- Gomez reports that "those claims . . . have been disallowed every time they have come before the IRS."

13n Distinguish between Three Kinds of Ellipsis.

Three Dots

If an omission is followed by material from the same sentence being quoted, type the ellipsis mark as three spaced periods preceded and followed by a space:

- She characterized her early years as "a bad joke . . . hardly a childhood at all."

Four Dots

Use four dots—a normal period followed by three spaced dots—if you are omitting (1) the last part of the quoted sentence, (2) the beginning of the next sentence, (3) a complete sentence or more, or (4) one or two complete paragraphs.

- She wrote, "I am always bored. . . . There is nothing here to keep me occupied."
- She described the apartment tower as "ridiculous, improbable. . . . I feel like a fairy princess who has been tucked away in the wrong castle by mistake."

If the sentence preceding your ellipsis ends with a question mark or exclamation point, keep that mark and add just three spaced dots:

- "Is Shaw," he asked, "really the equal of Shakespeare? . . . That seems extremely dubious."

• The champion shouted, "I am the greatest! . . . Nobody can mess up my pretty face."

A four-dot ellipsis is appropriate whenever your quotation skips material and then goes on to a new sentence, whether or not you are omitting material *within* a sentence. But note that you should always have grammatically complete statements on both sides of a four-dot ellipsis.

" "

13n

DON'T:

x She wrote, "I am always bored. . . . nothing here to keep me occupied."

Here the four-dot ellipsis is wrongly followed by a fragment.

Row of Dots

Mark the omission of a whole line or more of poetry, or of several paragraphs or more of prose, by a complete line of spaced periods.

POETRY:

Pope writes:

> First follow nature, and your judgment frame
> By her just standard, which is still the same;
>
> . . . .
>
> Life, force, and beauty must to all impart,
> At once the source, and end, and test of art.

Notice that the line of spaced periods is about the same length as the lines of poetry.

PROSE:

The authors continue:

> The panel based its conclusion on the belief that drugs should not be used for therapy unless absolutely necessary.
>
> . . . .
>
> If the nondrug regimen fails to bring blood pressure down to normal in three to six months, Dustan said, drug treatment

should be undertaken, starting with low doses. But if patients continue to exercise and watch their weight and salt intake, said the experts, they may be able to keep their drug taking to a minimum.

The writer is quoting from Matt Clark and Mary Hager's article, "A Nondrug Therapy for Hypertension."

For nearly all omissions of prose, however, four dots should serve.

" "

13p

13o Avoid Beginning a Quotation with an Ellipsis.

If you make a quoted clause or phrase fit in with your own sentence structure (13i, p. 154), you should not use an ellipsis mark to show that you have left something out.

DON'T:

ˣ The signers of the Declaration of Independence characterized George III as " . . . unfit to be the ruler of a free people."

DO:

• The signers of the Declaration of Independence characterized George III as "unfit to be the ruler of a free people."

INSERTING MATERIAL INTO A QUOTATION

13p Use Brackets to Insert Your Own Words into a Quotation.

To show that you are interrupting a quotation rather than quoting a parenthetical remark, be sure to enclose your interruption in brackets, not parentheses (12j, p. 145):

• "I hope to be buried in Kansas City [her birthplace]," she said.

> Parentheses here would indicate that the woman who wanted to be buried in Kansas City was referring to another woman's birthplace. The brackets show that it is the writer, not the woman, who is supplying the extra information.

[*sic*]

The bracketed and usually italicized Latin word *sic* (meaning "thus") signifies that a peculiarity—for example, a misspelling—occurs in the quoted material:

- He wrote, "I am teaching these kids how to live outdors [*sic*] without being afraid."

Do not abuse the legitimate function of [*sic*] by applying it sarcastically to claims that you find dubious.

DON'T:

x Are we supposed to believe the "humane" [*sic*] pretensions of the National Rifle Association?

The quotation marks are already sarcastic enough without [*sic*] to redouble the effect. But why not eliminate both devices and let the language of the sentence do its own work?

DO:

- Are we supposed to believe the humane pretensions of the National Rifle Association?

14 Forming and Spacing Punctuation Marks

To see how punctuation marks are normally handled by typewriter, examine the typescript essays beginning on pages 432, 500, and 510. For punctuation in manuscript, see page 509. In addition, note the following advice about forming marks and leaving or omitting spaces around them.

14a Learn the Three Ways of Forming a Dash.

Dashes come in three lengths, depending on their function.

1. A dash separating numbers is typed as a hyphen:

- pages 32-39
- October 8-14
- Social Security Number 203-64-7853

2. As a sign of a break in thought—its most usual function—a dash is typed as two hyphens with no space between:

- Try it--if you dare.

- They promise--but do not always come through with--
  overnight delivery.

3. Use four unspaced hyphens for a dash that stands in the place of an omitted word:

- He refused to disclose the name of Ms. ----.

> This is the only kind of dash that is preceded by a space;
> see 14g for the general rules.

14b Learn How to Form Brackets.

If your typewriter lacks keys for brackets, you can improvise them by either

1. typing slashes (/) and completing the sides with underlinings:
   /‾ ‾/

2. typing slashes and adding the horizontal lines later in ink:
   [ ]

3. leaving blank spaces and later writing the brackets entirely in ink: [ ]

14c Learn How to Form the Three Kinds of Ellipses.

1. An ellipsis (13n, p. 157) is formed with three spaced dots if it signifies the omission of material within a quoted sentence. Note that a space is left before and after the whole ellipsis as well as after each dot:

- "The government," she said, "appears to be
  abandoning its . . . efforts to prevent nuclear
  proliferation."

2. A four-dot ellipsis, signifying the omission of quoted material that covers at least one mark of end punctuation, begins with that *unspaced* mark:

- "The government," she said, "appears to be abandoning its formerly urgent efforts to prevent nuclear proliferation. . . . There may be a terrible price to pay for this negligence."

3. Leave spaces between all the dots of an ellipsis that covers a whole row, signifying the omission of one or more lines of poetry or several paragraphs or more of prose:

- The river glideth at its own sweet will:

  . . . .

  And all that mighty heart is lying still!

14d Learn the Two Ways of Spacing a Slash.

1. When a slash separates two quoted lines of poetry that you are incorporating into your text (13g, p. 152), leave a space before and after the slash:

- Shakespeare writes, "Shall I compare thee to a summer's day? / Thou art more lovely and more temperate."

2. But if your slash indicates alternatives or a span of time, leave no space before or after the slanted line:

- We are not dealing with an either/or situation here.
- The article will appear in the Winter/Spring issue of the journal.

14e Leave Two Spaces after a Period, a Question Mark, an Exclamation Point, or a Four-Dot Ellipsis.

p/form
14g

- The Chinese leaders appear to be ready for a new dialogue with the United States. Should we let this opportunity slip away? Certainly not! Remember the words of the Foreign Minister: "If we do not take steps to ensure peace, we may find ourselves drifting into war. . . . Our two nations can work together without agreeing about everything."

14f Leave One Space after a Comma, a Colon, a Semicolon, a Closing Quotation Mark, a Closing Parenthesis, or a Closing Bracket.

- Here is the real story, we believe, of last week's disturbance: it was not a riot but a legitimate demonstration. The city police chief thinks otherwise; but his description of the "riot" is grossly inaccurate. The chief (a foe of all progressive causes) erred in more than his spelling when he wrote of a "Comunist [sic] uprising."

14g Leave No Space before or after a Dash, a Hyphen, or an Apostrophe within a Word.

- Wilbur--a first-rate judge of toothpaste flavors--prefers Carter's Sparklefoam for its gum-tickling goodness.

14h When an Apostrophe Ends a Word, Leave No Space before Any Following Punctuation of That Word.

- This ranch, the Johnsons', has been in the family for generations.

14i When Two Marks Punctuate the Same Word, Put Them Together without a Space.

- Here is the true story of the "riot."
- When I heard the truth about the riot (as the police chief called it), I was outraged.
- The protest, which the police chief called the work of "Comunists" [sic], was actually organized by members of the business community.

14j Do Not Begin a Line with Any Mark That Punctuates the Last Word of a Preceding Line.

DON'T:

x Here is why Carol refuses to sign the petition
  : She objects to the dangerously vague language about waterfront development.

DO:

- Here is why Carol refuses to sign the petition: She objects to the dangerously vague language about waterfront development.

14k Do Not Carry an Ellipsis from One Line to the Next.

DON'T:

x Carol objected to the petition because of "the . .

. language about waterfront development."

DO:

• Carol objected to the petition because of "the . . .

language about waterfront development."

For combining quotation marks with other punctuation marks, see 13f, p. 150. For the spacing of periods within an abbreviation, see 20k, p. 237.

C CONVENTIONS

Conventions

In this section we consider rules affecting the form a word can take. These are small matters—if you get them right. If you do not, you will be handicapped in communicating your ideas. It is essential, then, to spell correctly and to be accurate in showing different forms of verbs, nouns and pronouns, and modifiers. And it is useful, if less urgent, to know where such conventions as italics, abbreviations, and written-out numbers are considered appropriate in a piece of writing. Once the conventions have become second nature, both you and your reader can put them out of mind and concentrate on larger issues.

15 Verb Forms

15a Note How Verbs Change Their Form to Show Person and Number in the Present Tense.

Within most **tenses** or time frames (15b), English verbs show no differences of form for person and number. That is, the verb remains the same whether its subject is the speaker, someone spoken to, or someone (or something) spoken about, and whether that subject is one person or thing or more than one. The past-tense forms of *move,* for example, look like this:

	SINGULAR	PLURAL
First Person	I moved	we moved
Second Person	you moved	you moved
Third Person	he, she, it moved	they moved

But in the most common tense, the present, the third-person singular verb is **inflected**—that is, it changes its form without becoming a different word.

	SINGULAR	PLURAL
First Person	I move	we move
Second Person	you move	you move
Third Person	he, she, it **moves**	they move

The third-person singular form of a present-tense verb ends in -*s*. If the base form of the verb ends in -*ch*, -*s*, -*sh*, -*x*, or -*z*, the addition is -*es*.

BASE FORM	THIRD-PERSON SINGULAR PRESENT
lurch	he lurches
pass	she passes
wash	Harry washes
fix	Betty fixes
buzz	it buzzes

**verb
15b**

In some spoken dialects of English, this third-person -*s* or -*es* does not occur. Standard written English, however, requires that you observe it. You may have to check your final drafts to be sure that your -*s* or -*es* endings are in place.

DON'T:

x When Meg *get* a new idea, she always *say* something worth hearing.

DO:

• When Meg *gets* a new idea, she always *says* something worth hearing.

15b Note How the Verb Tenses Are Formed in the Active Voice.

The various **tenses** or times are shown by changed forms of the base verb *(try—tried; go—went)* and through forms of *be* and *have* in combination with base *(try)* and participial *(trying)* forms *(will try, was trying, had tried, will have tried)*. Here, in the active voice only (see 15c for the passive), are the most commonly recognized tenses, shown in the third-person singular only.

TENSE	VERB FORM
present (action happening now)	laughs does
present progressive (action ongoing in the present)	is laughing is doing
present perfect (past action completed thus far)	has laughed has done
present perfect progressive (action begun in the past and continuing in the present)	has been laughing has been doing
past (completed action)	laughed did
past progressive (action that was ongoing in a previous time)	was laughing was doing
past perfect (action completed before another past time)	had laughed had done
past perfect progressive (ongoing action completed before another past time)	had been laughing had been doing
future (action to occur later)	will laugh will do
future progressive (ongoing action to occur later)	will be laughing will be doing
future perfect (action regarded as completed at a later time)	will have laughed will have done
future perfect progressive (ongoing action regarded as having begun before a later time)	will have been laughing will have been doing

verb 15b

Here are all the active-voice forms—first, second, and third person, singular and plural—for a verb, *walk,* in eight commonly used tenses.

ACTIVE VOICE		
Present:		
I	he, she, it	we, you (sing./pl.), they
walk	walks	walk

**verb
15b**

Present Progressive:		
I	he, she, it	we, you (sing./pl.), they
am walking	is walking	are walking
Present Perfect:		
I	he, she, it	we, you (sing./pl.), they
have walked	has walked	have walked
Past:		
I	he, she, it	we, you (sing./pl.), they
walked	walked	walked
Past Progressive:		
I	he, she, it	we, you (sing./pl.), they
was walking	was walking	were walking
Past Perfect:		
I	he, she, it	we, you (sing./pl.), they
had walked	had walked	had walked
Future:		
I	he, she, it	we, you (sing./pl.), they
will walk	will walk	will walk
Future Perfect:		
I	he, she, it	we, you (sing./pl.), they
will have walked	will have walked	will have walked

In the future tense, *I* and *we* can be accompanied by *shall* instead of *will. Shall* is normal in questions about plans:

● *Shall* we go to the movies?

In addition, some writers still keep to the once common use of *shall* for all first-person statements *(I shall go to the movies)* and for taking a commanding tone *(you shall go to the movies!).* But *will* is now usual in these functions. Keep to *will* unless you want to make an unusually formal effect.

Principal Parts of Irregular Verbs

All verbs have three **principal parts** used in tense formation: the infinitive or base form *(try)*, the past tense *(tried)*, and the past participle *(tried)*. You must be careful to get the right past participles of irregular verbs—that is, verbs that do not simply add *-d* or *-ed* to form both the past tense and the past participle *(tried)*. The past participle is used with forms of *have* and with auxiliaries *(could, would,* etc.) to form various other past tenses *(had tried, would have tried,* etc.).

Regular verbs form their principal parts simply by adding *-d* or *-ed* to the base, but **irregular verbs** change more radically.

verb
15b

	BASE	PAST TENSE	PAST PARTICIPLE
Regular	bake	baked	baked
	adopt	adopted	adopted
	compute	computed	computed
Irregular	choose	chose	chosen
	eat	ate	eaten
	write	wrote	written

To avoid errors in tense formation, study the principal parts of irregular verbs given below.

BASE	PAST TENSE	PAST PARTICIPLE
awake	awaked, awoke	awaked, awoke, awoken
be	was, were	been
beat	beat	beaten, beat
become	became	become
begin	began	begun
bend	bent	bent

**verb
15b**

BASE	PAST TENSE	PAST PARTICIPLE
bite	bit	bit, bitten
bleed	bled	bled
blow	blew	blown
break	broke	broken
bring	brought	brought
build	built	built
burst	burst	burst
buy	bought	bought
catch	caught	caught
choose	chose	chosen
come	came	come
cost	cost	cost
cut	cut	cut
deal	dealt	dealt
dig	dug	dug
dive	dived, dove	dived
do	did	done
draw	drew	drawn
dream	dreamed, dreamt	dreamed, dreamt
drink	drank	drunk
drive	drove	driven
eat	ate	eaten
fall	fell	fallen
feed	fed	fed
feel	felt	felt
fight	fought	fought
find	found	found
fit	fitted, fit	fitted, fit
fly	flew	flown

BASE	PAST TENSE	PAST PARTICIPLE
forget	forgot	forgotten, forgot
freeze	froze	frozen
get	got	gotten, got
give	gave	given
go	went	gone
grow	grew	grown
hang (an object)	hung	hung
hang (a person)	hanged	hanged
hear	heard	heard
hide	hid	hidden, hid
hit	hit	hit
hold	held	held
hurt	hurt	hurt
keep	kept	kept
kneel	knelt, kneeled	knelt, kneeled
knit	knit, knitted	knit, knitted
know	knew	known
lay (put)	laid	laid
lead	led	led
lean	leaned, leant	leaned, leant
leave	left	left
lend	lent	lent
let	let	let
lie (recline)	lay	lain
light	lighted, lit	lighted, lit
lose	lost	lost
make	made	made
mean	meant	meant
meet	met	met

verb
15b

BASE	PAST TENSE	PAST PARTICIPLE
pay	paid	paid
prove	proved	proved, proven
put	put	put
quit	quit, quitted	quit, quitted
read	read	read
rid	rid, ridded	rid, ridded
ride	rode	ridden
ring	rang	rung
run	ran	run
say	said	said
see	saw	seen
sell	sold	sold
send	sent	sent
set	set	set
shake	shook	shaken
shine	shone, shined	shone, shined (transitive)
shoot	shot	shot
show	showed	showed, shown
shrink	shrank	shrunk
shut	shut	shut
sing	sang, sung	sung
sink	sank	sunk
sit	sat	sat
sleep	slept	slept
slide	slid	slid, slidden
speak	spoke	spoken
speed	sped, speeded	sped, speeded
spend	spent	spent

verb
15b

BASE	PAST TENSE	PAST PARTICIPLE
spin	spun	spun
spring	sprang, sprung	sprung
stand	stood	stood
steal	stole	stolen
stick	stuck	stuck
sting	stung	stung
strike	struck	struck, stricken
swear	swore	sworn
swim	swam	swum
swing	swung	swung
take	took	taken
teach	taught	taught
tear	tore	torn
tell	told	told
think	thought	thought
throw	threw	thrown
wake	waked, woke	waked, woke, woken
wear	wore	worn
win	won	won
wring	wrung	wrung
write	wrote	written

verb
15b

For the tense forms of verbals—infinitives, participles, and gerunds—see 8h, p. 115.

Past Participle versus Past Tense

It is not enough to know the correct forms for the past participles of irregular verbs. You must also remember that past participles can form tenses only when they are combined with other words *(have gone, would have paid).* Do not use an irregular past participle where the past tense is called for.

DON'T:

x She *begun* her singing lessons last Tuesday.

x They *seen* him put on the wrong jacket.

x *We swum* across the pool.

DO:

verb
15c

• She *began* her singing lessons last Tuesday.

• They *saw* him put on the wrong jacket.

• We *swam* across the pool.

15c Learn the Tense Forms in the Passive Voice.

The **voice** of a verb shows whether its grammatical subject performs or receives the action it expresses. A verb is **active** when the subject performs the action *(Frankie shot Johnny)* but **passive** when the subject is acted upon by the verb *(Johnny was shot by Frankie.)*

ACTIVE VOICE:

• The paramedics *took* the old man to the hospital.

Note that the performers of the action (the paramedics) are also the grammatical subject.

PASSIVE VOICE:

• The old man *was taken* to the hospital by the paramedics.

Note that the performers of the action (the paramedics) are not the grammatical subject of the passive verb *was taken*.

One peculiarity of the passive voice is that you need not mention the performer of action at all: *Johnny was shot; The old man was taken to the hospital.*

Here are the passive-voice forms for the tenses whose functions are explained at 15b, page 171.

PASSIVE VOICE		
Present:		
I	he, she, it	we, you (sing./pl.), they
am shown	is shown	are shown
Present Progressive:		
I	he, she, it	we, you (sing./pl.), they
am being shown	is being shown	are being shown
Present Perfect:		
I	he, she, it	we, you (sing./pl.), they
have been shown	has been shown	have been shown
Past:		
I	he, she, it	we, you (sing./pl.), they
was shown	was shown	were shown
Past Progressive:		
I	he, she, it	we, you (sing./pl.), they
was being shown	was being shown	were being shown
Past Perfect:		
I	he, she, it	we, you (sing./pl.), they
had been shown	had been shown	had been shown
Future:		
I	he, she, it	we, you (sing./pl.), they
will be shown	will be shown	will be shown
Future Perfect:		
I	he, she, it	we, you (sing./pl.), they
will have been shown	will have been shown	will have been shown

verb
15c

For the use of *shall* as an alternative to *will,* see 15b, page 172.

For the stylistic uses and limitations of the passive voice, see 24g, p. 287.

15d Learn the Forms and Uses of the Indicative, Imperative, and Subjunctive Moods.

Verbs show certain other changes of form to convey the **mood** or manner of their action.

Indicative

Use the **indicative** mood if your clause is a statement or a question:

- The Secretary of State *advises* the President.
- *Does* the Secretary of State *advise* the President?

The forms of the indicative mood are those already given for normal tense formation (15b, p. 171; 15c, p. 179).

Imperative

Use the **imperative** mood for giving commands or directions, with or without an explicit subject:

- *Call* the police at once.
- You *stay* out of this!

The imperative mood uses the second-person form of the present tense.

Subjunctive

For a variety of less common purposes, use the **subjunctive** mood.

  1. Expressions of a wish in which *may* is understood:

- long *live* the Queen [not *lives*]
- *be* it known [not *is*]
- so *be* it [not *is*]
- *suffice* it to say [not *suffices*]

2. Conditions contrary to fact:

- He is, as it *were,* a termite gnawing at the foundations of our business.

    As it were is a fixed expression indicating that the writer is using a figure of speech (28g, p. 336) instead of making a literal statement.

- If I *were* on the moon now, I would tidy up the junk that has been left there. [not *was*]

- I wish I *were* in Haiti now. [not *was*]

verb

15d

3. *That* clauses expressing requirements or recommendations:

- The IRS requires that everyone *submit* a return by April 15. [not *submits*]

- It is important that all new students *be* tested immediately. [not *are*]

For nearly all verbs, the subjunctive differs from the indicative only in that the third-person singular verb loses its -s or -es: *come what may,* not *comes what may.* The verb *to be* uses *be* for "requirement" clauses *(I demand that she be here early)* and *were* for conditions contrary to fact *(if he were an emperor).*

See 8b, p. 108 for conditional sentences that express the imagined consequences of hypothetical conditions, as in *If he had taken that plane, he would be dead today.*

16 Plurals and Possessives

PLURALS

16a Form the Plural of Most Nouns by Adding -s or -es to the Singular.

class	classes
house	houses
shoe	shoes
summons	summonses
waltz	waltzes

16b Note the Differences in Plural Form among Nouns Ending in -o.

Most nouns ending in a vowel plus -o become plural by adding -s:

patio	patios
studio	studios

Nouns ending in a consonant plus -o become plural by adding -es:

potato	potatoes
veto	vetoes

But some plurals disobey the rule:

piano	pianos
solo	solos
soprano	sopranos

And some words have alternative, equally correct forms:

zero	zeros/zeroes
cargo	cargos/cargoes

plur
16d

Where your dictionary lists two forms, always adopt the first, which is more commonly used.

16c To Form the Plural of a Noun Ending in a Consonant plus -*y*, Change the -*y* to -*i* and Add -*es*.

army	armies
candy	candies
duty	duties
penny	pennies
warranty	warranties

16d To Make a Name Plural, Add -*s* or -*es* without an Apostrophe.

Add -*s* to most nouns:

Smith	the Smiths
Kennedy	the Kennedys
Helen	both Helens
Goodman	the Goodmans
Carolinas	two Carolinas

When a name ends in *-ch, -s, -sh, -x,* or *-z,* add *-es.* The extra syllable that results should be pronounced:

Burch	the Burches
Weiss	the Weisses
Fox	the Foxes
Perez	the Perezes

**plur
16f**

16e Form the Plural of a Noun Ending in *-ful* by Adding *-s* to the End.

cupful	cupfuls
shovelful	shovelfuls
spoonful	spoonfuls

Beware of the "genteel" but incorrect *cupsful, shovelsful,* etc.

16f Follow Common Practice in Forming the Plural of a Noun Derived from Another Language.

A number of words taken from foreign languages, especially Greek and Latin, keep their foreign plural forms. But some foreign-based words have also acquired English plural forms. The rule for deciding which plural to use is this: look it up!

Even so, the dictionary cannot settle your doubts in all cases. It may not tell you, for example, that the plural of *appendix* is *appendixes* if you are referring to the organ but either *appendixes* or *appendices* if you mean supplementary sections at the ends of books. Similarly, your dictionary may not reveal that while a bug has *antennae,* television sets have *antennas.* The way to get such information is to note the practice of other speakers and writers.

When in doubt, prefer the English plural.

SINGULAR	PREFER	NOT
cherub	cherubs	cherubim
crocus	crocuses	croci
curriculum	curriculums	curricula
sanatorium	sanatoriums	sanatoria
stadium	stadiums	stadia

But note that certain foreign plurals are still preferred.

plur
16f

SINGULAR	PLURAL
criterion	criteria
datum	data
phenomenon	phenomena
vertebra	vertebrae

Confusions between the singular and plural forms of these four terms are common. Indeed, *data* as a singular is often seen in scientific publications. Many careful writers, however, while avoiding the rare *datum,* use *data* only when its sense is clearly plural: *these data,* not *this data.*

Note that Greek and Latin derivatives ending in *-is* regularly change to *-es* in the plural.

SINGULAR	PLURAL
analysis	analyses
crisis	crises
parenthesis	parentheses
thesis	theses

16g To Form the Plural of a Word Presented *As* a Word, Add -*'s.*

Add an apostrophe and an -*s* to show the plural of a word you are discussing as a word, not as the thing it signifies:

- The editor changed all the *he*'s in Chapter 4 to *she*'s.

    Note how the writer's meaning is made clearer by the italicizing of each isolated word but not of the -*'s* that follows it.

plur
16h

16h Add -*s*, without an Apostrophe, to Form the Plural of Most Hyphenated Nouns, Capital Letters, Capitalized Abbreviations without Periods, Written-out Numbers, and Figures.

- two stand-ins
- the three Rs
- four RSVPs
- counting by fives and tens
- temperature in the nineties
- counting by 5s and 10s
- temperature in the 90s
- the 1980s

But some good writers prefer apostrophes with plural capitals and figures: *the three R's, the 1980's.* Even if you keep to the majority practice, use -*'s* wherever it is needed to avoid confusion.

DON'T:
x Charlene Armstrong Zeno uses her maiden name because she likes being called with the *A*s.

    Here the plural of *A* looks confusingly like the preposition *as.*

DO:
- Charlene Armstrong Zeno uses her maiden name because she likes being called with the *A*'s.

16i Add -'s to Form the Plural of an Uncapitalized Letter, an Abbreviation Ending with a Period, or a Lower-Case Abbreviation.

- *a*'s, *b*'s, and *c*'s
- the two *i*'s in *iris*
- too many *etc.*'s in your paper
- a shortage of M.D.'s
- thousands of rpm's

POSSESSIVES

A possessive form implies either actual ownership *(my neighbor's willow, Alice's typewriter)* or some other close relation (a *stone's throw, the Governor's enemies)*. Nouns and some pronouns form the possessive either by adding an apostrophe with or without an -s or by preceding the "possessed" element with *of: my husband's first wife, her parents' car, the wings of the canary.*

16j Add -'s to Form the Possessive of a Singular Noun.

- farm's
- Bill's
- Hayakawa's

Follow the rule even if the singular noun ends with an -s sound:

- horse's
- bus's
- quiz's
- Les's
- Jones's
- Keats's

Exception for Certain Names

In names of more than one syllable, the *-s* after the apostrophe is optional when it might not be pronounced.

PRONOUNCED *-S*	UNPRONOUNCED *-S*
Dickens's	Dickens'
Berlioz's	Berlioz'
Demosthenes's	Demosthenes'

poss
16l

Whichever of these practices you follow, make sure you keep to it throughout a given piece of writing.

16k Watch for Certain Unusual Singular Possessives.

Where an added *-s* would make for three closely bunched *-s* sounds, use the apostrophe alone:

- Moses'
- Ulysses'
- Jesus'

Note also that in certain fixed expressions *(for ——— sake)* the possessive *-s* is missing: *for goodness' sake, for conscience' sake, for righteousness' sake.* Some writers even drop the apostrophe from such phrases.

16l Make Most Plural Nouns Possessive by Adding an Apostrophe Alone.

- several *days'* work
- the *Americans'* views
- the *dictionaries'* definitions
- the *Stuarts'* reigns
- the *Beatles'* influence

16m If a Plural Noun Does Not End in *-s,* Make It Possessive in the Same Way You Would a Singular Noun.

- the *children's* room
- those *deer's* habitat
- the *mice's* tracks
- the *alumni's* representative

16n Keep the Apostrophe in a Plural Possessive of Time.

poss
16o

In expressions like *two years' parole,* many writers now drop the apostrophe: *two years parole.* But since that practice is widely regarded as wrong, you would do well to keep to the rule:

- in two days' time
- a three months' increase in prices
- five years' worth of wasted effort

16o In Compound Possessives Showing "Joint Ownership," Give the Possessive Form Only to the Final Name.

When two or more words are "joint possessors," make only the last one possessive:

- Laurel and *Hardy's* comedies
- John, Paul, George, and *Ringo's* movie
- Sally and *Vic's* restaurant

But give the possessive form to each party if different things are "owned":

- *John's, Paul's, George's,* and *Ringo's* personal attorneys met to see if the Beatles could be kept from splitting up.

16p To Make a Hyphenated Term Possessive, Add -'s to the Last Element.

- the mayor-*elect's* assistant
- my daughter-in-*law's* career

16q Do Not Add an Apostrophe to a Pronoun That Is Already Possessive in Meaning.

**poss
16q**

DON'T	DO
his'	his
her's, hers'	hers
our's, ours'	ours
your's, yours'	yours
their's, theirs'	theirs
who'se	whose

Note also that the possessive pronoun *its* (like *his*) has no apostrophe. *It's* is the correct form for the contraction of *it is* but a blunder for the possessive *its*. Similarly, *who's* is the correct contraction for *who is* but a blunder for the possessive *whose*.

DON'T:
x This album is *her's*.
x Why don't you drive *our's* and we drive *your's*?
x The dog seems to have lost *it's* collar.
x This is the man *who's* computer broke down.

DO:
- This album is *hers*.
- Why don't you drive *ours* and we drive *yours*?
- The dog seems to have lost *its* collar.
- This is the man *whose* computer broke down.

DON'T:

x The college canceled *it's* Saturday night film series.

x *Its* a baby girl!

x *Its'* a baby girl!

x *Whose* going to make the announcement?

DO:

• The college canceled *its* Saturday night film series.

• *It's* a baby girl!

• *Who's* going to make the announcement?

poss
16r

16r Do Not Confuse Plural and Possessive Forms.

In going over your drafts, watch for any confusion between plural and possessive forms. Note these differences.

SINGULAR	PLURAL	SINGULAR POSSESSIVE	PLURAL POSSESSIVE
temple	temples	temple's	temples'
pass	passes	pass's	passes'
squash	squashes	squash's	squashes'
annex	annexes	annex's	annexes'
Ford	Fords	Ford's	Fords'

DON'T:

x The two *priest's* made many *contribution's* to the parish.

x The *Kennedy's* have been stalked by tragedy.

x In many *place's* the *oceans* depth is unknown.

x The *clocks* hands stopped all across the city.

DO:

• The two *priests* made many *contributions* to the parish.

• The *Kennedys* have been stalked by tragedy.

• In many *places* the *ocean's* depth is unknown.

• The *clocks'* hands stopped all across the city.

16s To Avoid an Awkward Possessive, Make Use of the *of* Construction.

Wherever an -'s possessive sounds awkward, consider shifting to the *of* form. Suppose, for example, your "possessing" term or your "possessed" one is preceded by several modifiers. You can get rid of the bunched effect by resorting to *of*.

poss
16s

DON'T:
x the revised and expanded edition's index

DO:
• the index of the revised and expanded edition

A possessive form following a word in quotation marks may sound all right but look awkward on the page. Again, prefer the *of* construction.

DON'T:
x "Eleanor *Rigby*"'s melody

DO:
• the melody of "Eleanor Rigby"

Watch, too, for an unnatural separation of the -'s from the word it belongs with.

DON'T:
x the house on the corner's roof

DO:
• the roof of the house on the corner

Finally, nouns for inanimate (nonliving) things often make awkward possessives.

DON'T:
x the *page's* bottom
x social *chaos's* outcome

DO:

- the bottom of the page
- the outcome of social chaos

16t Notice Which Indefinite Pronouns Cannot Form the Possessive with -'s.

Some indefinite pronouns (3m, p. 39) form the possessive in the same manner as nouns: *another's, nobody's, one's.* But others can be made possessive only with *of:*

poss
16u

of	all	few	several
	any	many	some
	both	most	such
	each	much	

DON'T:

x I have two friends in Seattle, and I can give you *each's* address.

DO:

- I have two friends in Seattle, and I can give you the address of each.

16u Master the Other Uses of the Apostrophe.

Contractions

Use an apostrophe to join two words in a contraction:

did not	didn't
have not	haven't
can not, cannot	can't
she will	she'll
we will	we'll
they are	they're
he is	he's
he has	he's
you have	you've

Beware of placing the apostrophe at the end of the first word instead of at the point where the omission occurs.

DON'T:

x He *did'nt* have a chance.

x They *have'nt* done a thing to deserve such punishment.

DO:

- He *didn't* have a chance.
- They *haven't* done a thing to deserve such punishment.

poss
16u

Omission of Digits

Use an apostrophe to mark the omission of one or more digits of a number, particularly of a year: *the summer of '85*. In dates expressing a span of time, however, drop the apostrophe: *1847–63*. And omit the apostrophe when you are shortening page numbers: *pp. 267–91*.

Certain Past Participles

Use an apostrophe to form the past participle of a verb derived from an abbreviation or a name:

- Benitez was *K.O.'d* in the twelfth round.
- They *Disney'd* the old amusement park beyond recognition.

17 Comparing Adjectives and Adverbs

17a Recognize the Forms Showing Degrees of Adjectives.

Most adjectives can be **compared,** or changed to show three **degrees** of coverage.

POSITIVE DEGREE	COMPARATIVE DEGREE	SUPERLATIVE DEGREE
wide	wider	widest
dry	drier	driest
lazy	lazier	laziest
relaxed	more relaxed	most relaxed
agreeable	more agreeable	most agreeable
wide	less wide	least wide
dry	less dry	least dry
lazy	less lazy	least lazy
relaxed	less relaxed	least relaxed
agreeable	less agreeable	least agreeable

The base form of an adjective is in the **positive degree:** *thin*. The **comparative degree** puts the modified word beyond one or more items: *thinner* (than he is; than everybody). And the **superlative degree** unmistakably puts the modified word beyond all rivals within its group: *thinnest* (of all).

The comparative and superlative degrees of adjectives are formed in several ways.

1. For one-syllable adjectives: *wide, wider, widest* (but *less wide, least wide*).

2. For one- or two-syllable adjectives ending in *-y*, change the *-y* to *-i* and add *-er* and *-est: dry, drier, driest; lazy, lazier, laziest* (but *less lazy, least lazy*).

3. For all other adjectives of two or more syllables, put *more* or *most* (or *less* or *least*) before the positive form: *relaxed, more relaxed, most relaxed (less relaxed, least relaxed)*.

4. For certain "irregular" adjectives, supply the forms shown in your dictionary. Here are some common examples.

POSITIVE DEGREE	COMPARATIVE DEGREE	SUPERLATIVE DEGREE
bad	worse	worst
good	better	best
far	farther, further	farthest, furthest
little	littler, less, lesser	littlest, least
many, some, much	more	most

17b   Recognize the Forms Showing Degrees of Adverbs.

Like adjectives, adverbs can be compared: *quickly, more quickly, most quickly; less quickly, least quickly.* Note that *-ly* adverbs—that is, nearly all adverbs—can be compared only by being preceded by words like *more* and *least.* But some one-syllable adverbs do change their form: *hard/harder/hardest, fast/faster/fastest,* etc.

17c Avoid Redundancy in Comparing Adjectives and Adverbs.

Be careful not to "double" the comparison of an adjective or adverb.

DON'T:

x more funnier

x most warmest

x less darker

x least brightest

DO:

• funnier

• warmest

• less dark

• least bright

DON'T:

x more quicklier

x more closelier

x more sooner

DO:

• more quickly

• more closely

• sooner

ad
17c

18 **Spelling**

If spelling causes you trouble, do not label yourself a poor speller and leave it at that; work to eliminate the wrong choices. You can attack the problem on two fronts, memorizing the right spellings of single words and learning rules that apply to whole classes of words. We will cover both of these strategies below.

If there is one key to better spelling, it is the habit of consulting your college dictionary whenever you are in doubt (27a, p. 313). You need not pick up the dictionary until you have completed a draft, but you should check your final copy carefully for both habitual misspellings and typing errors.

TROUBLESOME WORDS

18a Keep a Spelling List.

Keep an ongoing spelling list, including not only the words you have already misspelled in your essays but also words whose spelling looks odd to you when you see them in published sources.

The most serious misspellings are not those that would eliminate you from the finals of a spelling contest but slips with ordinary words. If you regularly make such slips, you may not be able to cure them simply by noting the correct versions. You will need to jog your memory with a special reminder. Try a three-column spelling list, using the middle column to show how the real word differs from the misspelling.

MISSPELLING	REMEMBER	CORRECT SPELLING
(seperate)	not like *desperate*	sep*a*rate
(alot)	one word is not *a lot*	a lot
(hypocracy)	not like *democracy*	hypocri*s*y
(heighth)	get the *h* out of here!	height
(concieve)	*i* before *e* except after *c*	conce*i*ve
(mispell)	don't *miss* this one!	mis*s*pell
(fiting)	doesn't sound like *fighting*	fi*tt*ing
(beautyful)	*y* misspell it?	beaut*i*ful
(wierd)	a *weird* exception to *i* before *e*	we*i*rd
(goverment)	*govern* + *ment*	govern*m*ent
(complection)	*x* marks the spots	comple*x*ion

sp
18b

18b Note How Spelling Differs among English-Speaking Countries.

Many words that are correctly spelled in British English are considered wrong in American English. Canadian English resembles British in most but not all features. Study the following differences, which are typical.

AMERICAN	CANADIAN	BRITISH
cent*er*	cent*re*	cent*re*
flav*or*	flav*our*	flav*our*
preten*se*	preten*ce*	preten*ce*
real*ize*	real*ize*	real*ise*
trave*l*er	trave*ll*er	trave*ll*er

18c Beware of Words That Sound or Look Alike.

Note these differences:

accept *(receive)*, except *(exclude, excluding)*
adapt *(change for a purpose)*, adopt *(take possession)*
advice (noun), advise (verb)
affect (verb: *influence;* noun: *feeling*), effect (verb: *bring about*; noun: *result*)
all ready *(all prepared)*, already *(so early)*
all together *(everyone assembled)*, altogether *(entirely)*
allusion *(passing reference)*, illusion *(deceiving appearance)*
altar (of a church), alter *(change)*
ante- *(before)*, anti- *(against)*
bare (adjective: *naked;* verb: *expose*), bear *(carry, endure)*
beside *(at the side of)*, besides *(in addition to)*
bias *(prejudice)*, biased *(prejudiced)*
born *(brought into the world)*, borne *(carried)*
breadth *(width)*, breath (noun: *respiration*), breathe (verb: *take breath*)
business *(job)*, busyness *(being busy)*
by (preposition), buy *(purchase)*
capital *(governmental city, funds)*, capitol *(statehouse)*
chord *(tones)*, cord *(rope)*
cite *(mention)*, sight *(view)*, site *(locale)*
climactic *(of a climax)*, climatic *(of a climate)*
coarse *(rough)*, course *(direction, subject)*
complement (noun: *accompaniment*; verb: *complete*), compliment *(praise)*
comptroller *(financial officer)*, controller *(regulator)*
council *(committee)*, counsel *(advice, attorney)*
descent *(lowering)*, dissent *(disagreement)*
desert *(barren area, abandon)*, dessert *(last course in meal)*

device (noun: *instrument*), devise (verb: *fashion*)

die *(expire)*, dying *(expiring)*; dye *(color)*, dyeing *(coloring)*

discreet *(prudent)*, discrete *(separate)*

dual *(double)*, duel *(fight)*

elicit *(draw forth)*, illicit *(unlawful)*

eminent *(prominent)*, imminent *(about to happen)*

envelop *(surround)*, envelope (for mailing)

every day *(each day)*, everyday *(normal)*

every one *(each one* of specified items), everyone *(everybody)*

fair *(just)*, fare *(charge)*

sp
18c

faze *(daunt)*, phase *(period)*

forbear *(refrain)*, forebear *(ancestor)*

foreword *(preface)*, forward *(ahead)*

hangar (for airplanes), hanger (for coats)

it's *(it is)*, its *(of it)*

lead (noun: *metal;* verb: *direct;* adjective: *head*), led (past tense of
  verb *lead*)

lessen *(reduce)*, lesson *(teaching)*

lightening *(getting lighter)*, lightning *(flash)*

loath *(reluctant)*, loathe *(despise)*, loathsome *(disgusting)*

loose *(slack)*, lose *(mislay)*, losing *(mislaying)*

material *(pertaining to matter)*, materiel *(military supplies)*

miner *(digger)*, minor *(lesser, under legal age)*

moral *(ethical)*, morale *(confidence)*

naval *(nautical)*, navel *(bellybutton)*

passed *(went by)*, past *(previous)*

peace *(tranquillity)*, piece *(part)*

persecute *(single out for mistreatment)*, prosecute *(bring to trial)*

personal *(individual)*, personnel *(employees)*

pray *(implore)*, prey *(victim)*

precede *(go ahead of)*, proceed *(go forward)*

predominant (adjective), predominate (verb)

prejudice (noun), prejudiced (past participle, adjective)

principal (adjective, noun: *chief*), principle (noun: *rule*)

prophecy *(prediction)*, prophecies *(predictions)*, prophesy *(predict)*, prophesies *(predicts)*

prostate *(gland)*, prostrate *(prone)*

rack *(framework)*, wrack *(ruin)*

rain *(precipitation)*, rein *(restrain)*, reign *(rule)*

some time *(span of time)*, sometime *(at an unspecified time)*, sometimes *(now and then)*

stationary *(still)*, stationery *(paper)*

suppose (verb), supposed (past participle)

tack *(course)*, tact *(discretion)*

than (for comparison), then *(at that time)*

their *(belonging to them)*, there *(that place)*, they're *(they are)*

to *(toward*, infinitive marker), too *(also, excessively)*, two *(one plus one)*

track *(path)*, tract *(area, treatise)*

waive *(relinquish)*, wave (verb: *move to and fro*; noun: *spreading movement*)

weather *(state of the atmosphere)*, whether *(if)*

who's *(who is)*, whose *(of whom)*

wreak *(inflict)*, wreck *(ruin)*

your *(of you)*, you're *(you are)*

sp
18d

18d Check the Spelling of Words with Unusual Pronunciations.

Words Having Silent Letters

column	Wednesday
mortgage	withdrawal
sword	

Words Having Letters Unpronounced by Some Speakers

environment	recognize
government	strength
pumpkin	

Words Frequently Mispronounced

1. Added or erroneous sound:

sp
18d

athlete	(not athalete)
escape	(not excape)
height	(not heighth)
memento	(not momento)
pejorative	(not perjorative)
wintry	(not wintery)

2. Sound sometimes left unpronounced:

arctic	surprise
candidate	temperament
probably	temperature
quantity	veteran
sophomore	

3. Sounds sometimes wrongly reversed:

jewelry	(not jewlery)
modern	(not modren)
nuclear	(not nucular)
perform	(not preform)
professor	(not perfessor)
realtor	(not realator)
perspiration	(not prespiration)

18e Review Other Commonly Misspelled Words.

A good way to begin your private spelling list (18a, p. 198) is to look through the following commonly misspelled words, along with those already mentioned above, and pick out the ones that trouble you. (The letters *C/B* indicate Canadian and British forms wherever they differ from American.)

sp
18e

absence
accidentally
accommodate
acknowledgment
across
actually
address
adolescence, adolescent
aggravate, aggravated,
    aggravating
aggress, aggressive, aggression
aging
allege
all right
altogether
always
analysis, analyses (plural)
analyze
anesthesia
annihilate
apparent
appearance
appreciate, appreciation
aquatic
argument
assassin, assassination

assistant, assistance
attendance
bachelor
balloon
beggar
benefit, benefited, *C/B:*
    benefitted
besiege
bigoted
bureau
bureaucracy, bureaucratic
burglar
bus
cafeteria
calendar
camouflage
category
ceiling
cemetery
changeable
commit, commitment
committee
competent
concomitant
conscience
conscious

consensus

consistent, consistency

consummate

control, controlled, controlling

controversy

convenience, convenient

coolly

corollary

correlate

correspondence

corroborate

counterfeit

criticism, criticize

deceive

defendant

defense, *C/B:* defence

definite, definitely

deity

dependent

desirable

despair

desperate, desperation

destroy

develop, development

dilapidated

dilemma

disastrous

discipline

dispensable

divide

divine

drunkenness

duly

ecstasy

eighth

emanate

embarrass, embarrassed, embarrassing

equip, equipped, equipment

evenness

exaggerate

exceed

excellent, excellence

exercise

exhilarate

existence

exorbitant

expel

extraordinary

fallacy

familiar

fascinate

fascist

February

fiend

fiery

finally

forehead

foresee, foreseeable

forfeit

forgo

forty

fourth

friend

fulfill

fulsome

sp
18e

futilely
gases
gauge
glamour, glamorous
grammar, grammatically
greenness
grievance, grievous
gruesome
guarantee
guard
handkerchief
harangue
harass
heroes
hindrance
hoping
idiosyncrasy
imagery
immediate
impel
inadvertent
incidentally
incredible
independent, independence
indestructible
indispensable
infinitely
innuendo
inoculate
interrupt
irrelevant
irreparable, irreparably

irreplaceable, irreplaceably
irresistible, irresistibly
jeopardy
judgment, *C/B:* judgement
knowledge, knowledgeably
laboratory
legitimate
leisure
length
library
license, *C/B:* licence
loneliness
lying
maintenance
maneuver
manual
marriage
marshal (verb and noun),
    marshaled, marshaling
mathematics
medicine
millennium, millennial
mimic, mimicked
mischief, mischievous
missile
naïve, naïveté
necessary
nickel
niece
noncommittal
noticeable, noticing
occasion

occur, occurred, occurring,
  occurrence
omit, omitted, omitting,
  omission
opportunity
optimist, optimistic
paid
pajamas
parallel, paralleled
paralysis, paralyze
parliament
pastime
perceive
perennial
perfectible, perfectibility
permanent
permissible
phony
physical
physician
picnicked, picnicking
playwright
pleasant
pleasurable
possess, possession
practically
practice, *C/B:* practice, noun;
  practise, verb
prairie
privilege
probably
pronunciation

propaganda
propagate
psychiatry
psychology
pursue, pursuit
putrefy
quizzes
rarefied
realize
receipt
receive
recipe
recognizable
recommend
refer, referred, referring
regretted, regretting
relevant, relevance
relieve
remembrance
reminisce, reminiscence
repellent
repentance
repetition
resistance
restaurant
rhythm
ridiculous
roommate
sacrilegious
said
schedule
secretary

sp
18e

seize
sergeant
sheriff
shining
shriek
siege
significance
similar
smooth (adjective and verb)
software
solely
soliloquy
sovereign, sovereignty
specimen
sponsor
stupefy
subtlety, subtly
succeed, success
succumb
suffrage
superintendent
supersede
suppress
surprise
symmetry
sympathize
tariff
tendency
terrific
than
therefore
thinness

thorough
threshold
through
traffic, trafficked, trafficking
tranquil, tranquillity
transcendent, transcendental
transfer, transferred,
    transferring
tries, tried
truly
unconscious
unmistakable, unmistakably
unnecessary
unshakable
unwieldy
vacillate
vacuum
vegetable
venomous
vengeance
vice
vilify, vilification
villain
wield
withhold
woeful
worldly
worshiped, worshiping, *C/B:*
    worshipped, worshipping
writing
yield

SPELLING RULES

18f Notice How Words Change When They Add Suffixes.

A **suffix** is one or more letters that can be added at the end of a word to make a new word (*-ship, -ness,* etc.) or a new form of the same word (*-ed, -ing,* etc.). Since many spelling mistakes are caused by uncertainty over whether and how the root word changes when the suffix is tacked on, you should go over the following rules. (If a rule is hard to follow, you can get the point by studying the sample words that follow it.)

sp
18f

1. Change a final *-y* preceded by a consonant to *-i* when making formations other than the plural.

beauty	beautiful
easy	easily
happy	happier, happiest
hurry	hurries
imply	implies
ordinary	ordinarily
salty	saltier
tyranny	tyrannical
ugly	ugliness

2. Do not drop the final *-y* of a word adding *-ing.*

embody	embodying
gratify	gratifying
hurry	hurrying
study	studying

3. When adding a suffix that begins with a vowel, usually drop a final -e.

desire	desir<u>a</u>ble
drive	dri<u>v</u>ing
future	futu<u>r</u>istic
hope	hop<u>i</u>ng
impulse	impul<u>s</u>ive
mate	mat<u>i</u>ng
sincere	since<u>r</u>ity
suicide	suici<u>da</u>l

sp
18f

Exceptions: In words ending in -ce or -ge, retain the "s" or "j" pronunciation by keeping the -e before a suffix that begins with a or o.

notice	notic<u>e</u>able
peace	peac<u>e</u>able
courage	courag<u>e</u>ous
manage	manag<u>e</u>able

And note two further exceptions:

acre	acr<u>e</u>age
mile	mil<u>e</u>age

4. Usually keep the final -e of a word when adding a suffix that begins with a consonant.

advance	advanc<u>e</u>ment
precise	precis<u>e</u>ly
safe	saf<u>e</u>ly
tame	tam<u>e</u>ness

Exceptions: Look out for a few words that drop the -e before adding a suffix beginning with a consonant.

argue	argument
judge	judgment (in American English)
nine	ninth
true	truly

5. In a one-syllable word having a final consonant that is preceded by a single vowel, double the consonant before adding a suffix beginning with a vowel.

beg	begging
chop	chopper
clip	clipped
fun	funny
thin	thinnest

sp
18f

6. In a word of more than one syllable having a final consonant that is preceded by a single vowel, follow these suffix rules.

   a. If the word is accented on its last syllable, double the consonant before adding a suffix that begins with a vowel.

begín	beginning
detér	deterrent
contról	controlled
occúr	occurrence
prefér	preferring
regrét	regrettable

   b. If the accent does not fall on the last syllable, do not double the final consonant.

bárgain	bargained
díffer	difference
ópen	opener
stámmer	stammering
trável	traveler (in American English)

c. If, in adding the suffix, the accent shifts to an earlier syllable, do not double the final consonant.

infér	ínference
prefér	préference
refér	réference

18g Remember the Old Jingle for *ie/ei*.

i before *e*	(achieve, believe, friend, grieve)
except after *c*	(deceive, ceiling, receive)
or when sounded like *a*	
as in *neighbor* and *weigh*	(freight, neighbor, vein, weigh)

Exceptions:

ancient	efficient	leisure	seize
conscience	foreign	science	weird

18h Overcome the Confusion between *-sede*, *-ceed*, and *-cede*.

supersede	This is the only English word that ends in *-sede*.

exceed proceed succeed	Only three words end in *-ceed*.

accede concede intercede precede recede secede	Several words end in *-cede*.

HYPHENATION RULES

Another source of uncertainty in spelling is doubt as to whether a word contains a hyphen. Short of looking up every questionable word, you can observe certain rules. For the sake of keeping together the whole discussion of hyphens, we begin with conventions for dividing words at the end of a line.

18i Observe the Conventions for Dividing Words at Line Endings.

sp
18i

In a manuscript or typescript, where right-hand margins are normally uneven, avoid breaking words at line endings. Just finish each line with the last word you can complete. When you must hyphenate, observe the following conventions:

1. Divide words at syllable breaks as marked in your dictionary. Spaces or heavy dots between parts of a word indicate such breaks: *en•cy•clo•pe•di•a.*

2. Never divide a one-syllable word, even if you might manage to pronounce it as two syllables *(rhythm, schism).*

3. Do not leave one letter stranded at the end of a line *(o-ver, i-dea)*, and do not leave a solitary letter for the beginning of the next line *(Ontari-o, seed-y).*

4. If possible, avoid hyphenating the last word on a page.

5. If a word is already hyphenated, divide it only at the fixed hyphen. Avoid x *self-con-scious, ex-Pre-mier.*

6. You can anticipate what your dictionary will say about word division by remembering that:

   a. Double consonants are usually separated: *ar-rogant, sup-ply.*

   b. When a word has acquired a double consonant through the adding of a suffix, the second consonant belongs to the suffix: *bet-ting, fad-dish.*

   c. When the root of a word with a suffix has a double consonant, the break follows both consonants: *stall-ing, kiss-able.*

18j   Use a Hyphen to Separate Certain Prefixes from the Root Words to Which They Are Attached.

A **prefix** is a letter or group of letters that can be placed *before* a root word to make a new word. (Compare **suffix,** 18f, p. 209.) Dictionaries do not always agree with each other about hyphenation after a prefix, but the following guidelines will enable you to be consistent in your practice.

All-, ex-, self-

Words beginning with *all-, ex-,* and *self-,* when these are prefixes, are hyphenated after the prefix:

- all-powerful
- ex-minister
- self-motivated

Note that in words like *selfhood, selfish, selfless,* and *selfsame,* the accented syllable *self* is not a true prefix; no hyphen is called for.

Prefixes with Names

Prefixes before a name are always hyphenated:

- pre-Whitman
- un-American
- anti-Soviet

Words Like Anti-intellectual and Cooperate

Prefixes ending with a vowel sometimes take a hyphen if they are followed by a vowel, especially if the two vowels are the same:

- anti-intellectual
- co-op
- semi-invalid

The hyphen prevents ambiguity and mispronunciation, as in *coop.*

But prefixed terms that are very common are less likely to be misconstrued, and many double vowels remain unhyphenated:

- cooperate
- coordinate
- preempt
- reentry

Some dictionaries recommend a dieresis mark over the second vowel to show that it is separately pronounced: *reëntry.* In contemporary prose, however, you will not come across many instances of the dieresis.

sp
18k

Constructions Like <u>Pre- and Postwar</u>

When a modifier contains compound prefixes, the first prefix usually stands alone with a hyphen, whether or not it would take a hyphen when joined directly to the root word:

- There was quite a difference between *pre-* and postwar prices.
- *Pro-* and antifascist students battled openly in the streets of Rome.

18k Follow Your Dictionary in Hyphenating a Compound Noun or Verb.

Many compound words (formed from more than one word) are hyphenated in most dictionaries: *bull's-eye, secretary-treasurer, spring-cleaning, water-ski* (verb only), etc. Many others, however, are usually written as separate words (*fire fighter, head start, ice cream, oil spill,* etc.) or as single unhyphenated words (*earring, scofflaw, scoutmaster, skydive,* etc.). To make matters more confusing, practice is always in flux; as compound terms become more familiar they tend to lose their hyphens. All you can do, then, is be alert to the compound words you see in print and consult an up-to-date dictionary whenever you are in doubt.

181 Study the Guidelines for Hyphenating Compound Modifiers.

Before Modified Term

A **compound modifier** (containing more than one word) is usually hyphenated if it meets two conditions:

1. it comes before the term it modifies, and
2. its first element is a modifier.

These two conditions are met in the following examples:

- a MOD
  well-trained philosopher
- a MOD
  short-tempered umpire
- some MOD
  deep-ocean drilling
- MOD
  nineteenth-century art
- an MOD
  out-of-work barber

In such phrases the hyphens sometimes prevent confusion. Consider what would happen, for example, if you wrote:

- a short tempered umpire
- some deep ocean drilling

Is the umpire short in stature but tempered in judgment? Is it the drilling rather than the ocean that is deep? When hyphens are added, a reader can see at once that *short* is part of the compound modifier *short-tempered* and that *deep* is part of the compound modifier *deep-ocean*. In such a case the hyphen tells us not to take the next word to be the modified term.

If the first word in a compound modifier is a noun, as in *school program administrator,* do not put a hyphen after it. A noun generally runs a low risk of being mistaken for a modifier of the next word. The following phrases are correct:

- the MOD
  the *ocean salinity* level
- a MOD
  a *barbecue sauce* cookbook
- a MOD
  a *mercury vapor* lamp

But do use a hyphen if the initial noun is followed by a modifier:

- a MOD
  a *picture-perfect* landing
- that MOD
  that *time-honored* principle

> Here the hyphens are needed to show that the initial noun does not stand alone; it is part of a compound modifier.

Even when the first part of a compound modifier is itself a modifier, leave it unhyphenated if it forms a familiar pair with the following word and if there is no danger of confusion:

- MOD
  the *Modern Language* Association

- MOD
  an *electric typewriter* store

- MOD
  the *happy birthday* card

As you can see, compound modifiers pose especially sensitive problems of hyphenation. Call on your good judgment: use a hyphen where it is needed to prevent ambiguity, but leave it out if you think your reader can get along without it.

After Modified Term: *Well Trained*

When a compound modifier *follows* the modified term, the hyphen usually disappears:

- The philosopher was *well trained.*
- A barber *out of work* resents people who cut their own hair.

sp
18l

Modifiers Like <u>Barely Suppressed</u>

When a compound modifier contains an adverb in the *-ly* form, it does not have to be hyphenated in any position. There is no danger of ambiguity, since the adverb, clearly identifiable *as* an adverb, can only modify the next word:

- a *barely suppressed* gasp
- an *openly polygamous* chieftain
- a *hypocritically worded* note of protest

Modifiers Like <u>Fast-Developing</u>

Adverbs lacking the *-ly* form do run the risk of ambiguity. Whether they come before or after the modified term, you should always hyphenate them:

- a *fast-developing* crisis
- a *close-cropped* head of hair
- The traffic was *slow-moving.*

Modifiers with Fixed Hyphens

If you find that a modifier is hyphenated in the dictionary, keep it hyphenated wherever it occurs:

- She was an *even-tempered* instructor.
- She was *even-tempered.*

18m Study the Guidelines for Hyphenating Numbers.

Numbers <u>Twenty-one</u> to <u>Ninety-nine</u>

Always hyphenate these numbers, even when they form part of a larger number:

- Two hundred *seventy-five* years ago, religious toleration was almost unknown.

Number as Part of a Modifier

If the number and the term it modifies work together as a modifier, place a hyphen after the number:

* A *twelve-yard* pool is hardly long enough for swimming.

Noun Formed from Hyphenated Number

Hyphenate a noun formed from an already hyphenated number:

* The seats were reserved for *sixty-five-year-olds*.

sp
18n

Fractions with and without Hyphens

Hyphenate a fraction only if you are using it as a modifier.

AS MODIFIER:

* The luggage compartment was *five-eighths* full.

NOT AS MODIFIER:

* *Five eighths* of the space had already been taken.

In the first sentence, *five-eighths* modifies the adjective *full*. In the second, *five eighths* is the subject of the verb.

Some good writers, however, overlook this distinction. In your reading you will find that the more common fractions such as *one quarter* and *two thirds* are sometimes left unhyphenated even when they serve as modifiers. When in doubt, you would still do well to follow the rule.

18n Use a Hyphen to Connect Numbers Expressing a Range.

* pages 37–49 (the pages 37 through and including 49)
* September 11–October 4 (from September 11 through October 4)
* 1978–1985 (from 1978 through 1985)

19 Capitals

19a Capitalize the First Letter of Every Sentence or Intentional Sentence Fragment.

- *She* will need help when she moves.
- *Count* on me.
- *Will* you be able to come over on Sunday?
- *With* pleasure!

Whole Sentence within a Sentence

If a sentence within a sentence is a quotation or a representation of someone's thoughts, begin it with a capital letter:

- Leslie asked Mark, "*Will* you dismantle the stereo for me?"
- Mark thought, *Let's* hope she saved the original packing boxes.

19b If You Are Not Quoting Speech or Representing Someone's Thoughts, Do Not Capitalize the First Letter after a Colon.

- Home was never like this: *twenty-four* roommates and a day starting at 5:00 A.M.
- I finally understood how the Air Force makes a pilot of you: *after* the crowded barracks, every cadet yearns for the solitude of flight.

19c Capitalize the First Word of a Sentence in Parentheses Only If the Parenthetic Sentence Stands between Complete Sentences.

CAPITALIZED:

- In the Air Force we learned to fly. (*We* also learned a good deal about life on the ground.) I would not have traded the experience for any other.

UNCAPITALIZED:

- Life in the Air Force (*the* Army and Navy never attracted me) was just what the doctor ordered for a lazy, smart-aleck eighteen-year-old.

cap
19d

19d Learn When to Capitalize within a Quotation.

Capitalize the first letter of a quotation only if (1) it is capitalized in the original, (2) it represents the beginning of a speaker's sentence, or (3) it begins your own sentence.

CAPITALIZED IN THE ORIGINAL:

- Ben Jonson believed that "*Talking* and eloquence are not the same: to speak, and to speak well, are two things."

BEGINNING OF A SPEAKER'S SENTENCE:

- Leslie told Mark, "*After* you dismantle the stereo, bring the truck around to the back."

BEGINNING OF THE WRITER'S OWN SENTENCE:

- "*When* to stop" is the crucial lesson a dieter must learn.

When a quotation does not meet any of these three tests for capitalization, leave its first letter in lower case:

- The lawyer told the squabbling couple he would help them "*only* if you can learn to take turns speaking."

    The quotation is a subordinate clause (1c, p. 9), not a full statement.

19e Capitalize the First, the Last, and All Other Important Words in a Title or Subtitle.

If an article, a coordinating conjunction, or a preposition does not occur in the first or last position, leave it in lower case:

- *The House of the Seven Gables*
- *The Mismeasure of Man*
- *For Whom the Bell Tolls*

cap
19g

Do capitalize the first letter of a subtitle:

- *Peasants into Frenchmen: The Modernization of Rural France, 1870–1914*
- "Male Gymnasts: The Olympic Heights"

19f Capitalize Both Parts of Most Hyphenated Terms in a Title.

The Modern Language Association recommends that you capitalize both parts of a hyphenated term in a title:

- *Fail-Safe*
- *Through the Looking-Glass*
- *Self-Consuming Artifacts*

When an obviously minor element is included in a hyphenated term, however, leave it uncapitalized:

- "A Guide to Over-*the*-Counter Medications"

19g Capitalize the Name of a Person, Place, Business, or Organization.

- Joyce Carol Oates
- Western Hemisphere

- New Canaan, Connecticut
- Lifeboat Associates
- Canadian Broadcasting Corporation
- Xerox Corporation

19h Capitalize an Adjective Derived from a Name.

- Shakespearean
- Malthusian
- the French language
- Roman numerals

But note the lower-case *roman type, italic type.*

19i Capitalize a Family Relation If It Is a Name or Part of a Name but Not If It Merely Identifies the Relationship.

NAME OR PART OF NAME (CAPITALIZED):
- Everyone has seen posters of *Uncle* Sam.
- Oh, *Mother*, I miss you!

NOT PART OF NAME (UNCAPITALIZED):
- My *uncle* Sam bought me my first baseball mitt.
- I cabled my *mother* when I reached Athens.

19j Capitalize a Rank or Title Only When It Is Joined to a Name or When It Stands for a Specific Person.

CAPITALIZED:
- General Dwight D. Eisenhower
- The Colonel was promoted in 1983.

UNCAPITALIZED:
- Two *generals* and a *colonel* attended the parade.

19k Capitalize Certain High Offices Even When No Particular Occupant Is Being Discussed.

- the Queen of England
- the President of the United States
- the Secretary of Defense
- the Chief Justice of the United States

    There is no such office as *Chief Justice of the Supreme Court.*

**cap
19l**

19l Capitalize the Name of a Specific Institution or Its Formal Subdivision, but Not of an Unspecified Institution.

When you are designating a particular school, museum, etc., or one of its departments, use capitals:

- Museum of Modern Art
- University of Chicago
- the Department of Business Administration
- Franklin High School

Subsequent, shortened references to the institution or department are sometimes left uncapitalized:

- She retired from the *university* last year.

    But *University* would also be correct here.

Do not capitalize a name that identifies only the *type* of institution you have in mind:

- a strife-torn *museum*
- Every *university* must rely on contributions.
- She attends *high school* in the daytime and *ballet school* after dinner.

19m Capitalize a Specific Course of Study but Not a General Branch of Learning.

CAPITALIZED:
- Physics 1A
- Computer Science 142B

UNCAPITALIZED:
- He never learned the rudiments of *physics*.
- Her training in *computer science* gained her a job as a programmer.

If a branch of learning is a language, however, capitalize it: *German, English, Japanese.*

cap
19n

19n Capitalize a Sacred Name but Not a Word Derived from It.

Whether or not you are a believer, use capitals for the names of deities, revered figures, and holy books:

- the Bible
- the Gospels
- God
- the Lord
- He, Him, His [referring to the Judeo-Christian deity]
- the Virgin Mary
- the Koran

But in general, do not capitalize a word derived from a sacred name:

- biblical
- godlike
- scriptural
- the gospel of getting ahead

19o Capitalize the Name of a Specific Historical Event, Movement, or Period.

- the Sixties
- the Bronze Age
- the Civil War
- the Romantic poets
- the Depression

19p Capitalize a Day, a Month, or a Holiday but Not a Season or the Numerical Part of a Date.

CAPITALIZED:
- next Tuesday
- May 1985
- Christmas
- Passover
- Columbus Day

UNCAPITALIZED:
- next fall
- a winter storm
- July twenty-first
- the third of August

19q Capitalize the Name of a Group or Nationality but Not of a Looser Grouping.

CAPITALIZED:
- Moslem
- Hungarian
- Friends of the Earth

UNCAPITALIZED:
- the upper class
- the underprivileged
- environmentalists

19r Capitalize a Geographic Direction Only If It Is Part of a Place Name or a Widely Recognized Section of the Country.

CAPITALIZED:
- Northwest Passage
- Southeast Asia
- The South and the Midwest will be crucial in the election.

UNCAPITALIZED:
- northwest of here
- Go west for two miles and then turn south.

19s Reproduce a Foreign Word or Title As You Find It in the Original Language.

- *Weltanschauung* (Ger.: world view)
- *una cubana* (Sp.: a Cuban woman)
- *La terre* (title of a French novel: *The Earth*)

19t Notice That a Word May Have Different Meanings in Its Capitalized and Uncapitalized Forms.

- The Pope is a *Catholic*. [He belongs to the Church.]
- George has *catholic* tastes. [His tastes are wide-ranging.]
- He became a *Democrat* after he married Rosa. [He joined the party.]
- Tocqueville saw every American farmer as a *democrat*. [He believed that they all supported the idea of equality.]

20 Italics, Abbreviations, Numbers

ITALICS

Ordinary typeface is known as **roman**, and the thin, slightly slanted typeface that contrasts with it is **italic**—as in *these three words*. In manuscript or typescript, "italics" are actually indicated by underlining.

MANUSCRIPT:

- *The Great Gatsby*

TYPESCRIPT:

- The Great Gatsby

PRINT:

- *The Great Gatsby*

20a Italicize the Title of a Book, Play, Film, or Long Musical Work, Taped or Recorded Album, or Radio or Television Series, but Use Quotation Marks for Other Titles.

ITALICS:

One Hundred Years of Solitude	[a novel]
Paradise Lost	[a long poem published as a whole volume]
Waiting for Godot	[a play]
Casablanca	[a film]
New York Times	[a newspaper]
Popular Mechanics	[a magazine]
The Firebird	[a long musical work]
The Smithsonian Collection of Classic Jazz	[a record album]
A Prairie Home Companion	[a radio series]
The Odd Couple	[a television series]

**ital
20a**

QUOTATION MARKS:

"Araby"	[a short story]
"To Autumn"	[a poem]
"The Political Economy of Milk"	[a magazine article]
"Magic and Paraphysics"	[a chapter of a book]
"Eleanor Rigby"	[a song]

Note the following special conditions.

1. In the name of a newspaper, include the place of publication in the italicized title:

• She read it in the *Philadelphia Inquirer.*

The article preceding the place name is usually not italicized (or capitalized).

2. The title of a poem, story, or chapter may also be the title of the whole volume in which that smaller unit is found. Use italics only when you mean to designate the whole volume:

- "The Magic Barrel" [Bernard Malamud's short story]
- *The Magic Barrel* [the book in which Malamud's story was eventually republished]

ital
20b

3. Some publications, especially newspapers, use italics sparingly or not at all. If you are writing for a specific publication, follow its style. If not, observe the rules given here.

4. Do not italicize or use quotation marks around the Bible and its divisions.

DO:
- the Bible
- the New Testament
- Leviticus

5. When one title contains another title that would normally be italicized, make the embedded title roman. That is, you should not underline it.

- She was reading *The Senses of* Walden to get ideas for her paper.

20b Italicize a Foreign Word That Has Not Yet Been Adopted as a Common English Expression.

STILL "FOREIGN" (ITALICIZE):
- *la dolce vita*
- *sine qua non*
- *La Belle Époque*
- *Schadenfreude*

FAMILIAR IN ENGLISH (DO NOT ITALICIZE):
- ad hoc
- blitzkrieg
- cliché
- de facto
- guru
- junta
- sushi

Latin Abbreviations

Latin abbreviations are often italicized, but the tendency is now to leave them in roman. For example, according to the general practice these may be left in roman:

cf.	et al.	i.e.	viz.
e.g.	f., ff.	q.v.	vs.

See 20g, p. 233, for the meanings of these and other abbreviations used in documentation.

Translating a Foreign Term

When translating into English, put the foreign term in italics and the English one in quotation marks:

- The Italian word for "the book" is *il libro;* the French is *le livre.*

The Modern Language Association also allows a translation to be placed within single quotation marks without intervening punctuation:

- *ein wenig* 'a little'
- They called the Fiat 500 *Topolino* 'little mouse.'

20c Italicize the Name of a Ship.

- *Queen Elizabeth II*
- *Cristoforo Colombo*

But do not italicize abbreviations such as *SS* or *HMS* preceding a ship's name:

- SS *Enterprise*

20d Use Italics or Quotation Marks to Show That You Are Treating a Word *as* a Word.

- When Frank and Edith visited the rebuilt neighborhoods of their childhood, they understood the meaning of the word *gentrified.*

  It would be equally correct to keep *gentrified* in roman type and enclose it in quotation marks: "gentrified."

20e To Add Emphasis to a Quoted Expression, Italicize the Key Element.

If you want to emphasize one part of a quotation, put that expression in italics. And to show that the italics are your own rather than the author's, follow the quotation with a parenthetical acknowledgment such as *emphasis added*:

- The author writes mysteriously of a "*rival* system of waste management" (emphasis added).

20f Use Italics Sparingly to Emphasize a Key Expression in Your Own Prose.

To distinguish one term from another or to lend a point rhetorical emphasis, you can italicize (underline) some of your own language:

- No doubt she can explain where she was in the month of June. *But what about July?* This is the unresolved question.

Beware, however, of relying on emphatic italics to do the work that should be done by effective sentence structure and diction. Prose that is riddled with italics makes a frenzied effect.

DON'T:

x The hazard from *immediate radiation* is one issue—and a *very important* one. But the *long-term* effects from *improper waste storage* are *even more crucial*, and *practically nobody* within the industry seems to take it seriously.

This passage would inspire more confidence if it lacked italics altogether.

ABBREVIATIONS

20g Use Abbreviations in Parenthetical Citations, Notes, Reference Lists, and Bibliographies.

For purposes of documentation (Chapter 37), you can use the following abbreviations.

ABBREVIATION	MEANING
anon.	anonymous
b.	born
bibliog.	bibliography
©	Copyright
c. or ca.	about (with dates only)
cf.	compare (not *see*)
ch., chs.	chapter(s)
d.	died
diss.	dissertation
ed., eds.	editor(s), edition(s), edited by
e.g.	for example (not *that is*)
esp.	especially
et al.	and others (people only)
etc.	and so forth (not interchangeable with *et al.*)
f., ff.	and the following (page or pages)
ibid.	the same (title as the one mentioned in the previous note)
i.e.	that is (not *for example*)
introd.	introduction
l., ll.	line(s)

ms., mss.	manuscript(s)
n., nn.	note(s)
N.B.	mark well, take notice
n.d.	no date (in a book's imprint)
no., nos.	number(s)
p., pp.	page(s)
pl., pls.	plate(s)
pref.	preface
pt., pts.	part(s)
q.v.	see elsewhere in this text (literally *which see*)
rpt.	reprint
rev.	revised, revision; review, reviewed by (beware of ambiguity between meanings; if necessary, write out instead of abbreviating)
sc.	scene
sec., secs., sect., sects.	section(s)
ser.	series
st., sts.	stanza(s)
tr., trans.	translator, translation, translated by
v.	versus (legal citations)
viz.	namely
vol., vols.	volume(s)
vs.	verse, versus

abbr
20h

Note that *passim*, meaning "throughout," and *sic*, meaning "thus," are not to be followed by a period; they are complete Latin words. For the function of *sic*, see 13p, p. 160.

20h Learn Which Abbreviations Are Allowable in Your Main Text.

Allowed in Main Text

Some abbreviations are considered standard in any piece of writing, including the main body of an essay:

1. *Mr., Ms., Mrs., Dr., Messrs., Mme., Mlle., St.,* etc., when used before names. Some publications now refer to all women as *Ms.,* and this title has rapidly gained favor as a means of avoiding designation of marital status.

2. *Jr., Sr., Esq., M.D., D.D., D.D.S., M.A., Ph.D., LL.D.*, etc., when used after names.

3. abbreviations of, and acronyms (words formed from the initial letters in a multiword name) for, organizations that are widely known by the shorter name: *CIA, FBI, ROTC, NOW, NATO, UNESCO*, etc. Note that very familiar designations such as these are usually written without periods between the letters.

4. *B.C., A.D., A.M., P.M., mph* These abbreviations should never be used apart from numbers (x *in the P.M.*). *B.C.* always follows the year, but *A.D.* usually precedes it: *252 B.C.*, but *A.D. 147.*

5. places commonly known by their abbreviations: *U.S., D.C., USSR,* etc.

**abbr
20h**

Inappropriate in Main Text

	DON'T	**DO**
1. titles	the Rev., the Hon., Sen., Pres., Gen.	the Reverend, the Honorable, Senator, President, General
2. given names	Geo., Eliz., Robt.	George, Elizabeth, Robert
3. months, days of the week, and holidays	Oct., Mon., Vets. Day	October, Monday, Veterans Day
4. localities, cities, counties, states, provinces, and countries	Pt. Reyes Natl. Seashore, Phila., Sta. Clara, N.M., Ont., N.Z.	Point Reyes National Seashore, Philadelphia, Santa Clara, New Mexico, Ontario, New Zealand
5. roadways	St., La., Ave., Blvd.	Street, Lane, Avenue, Boulevard
6. courses of instruction	Bot., PE	Botany, Physical Education
7. units of measurement	ft., kg, lbs., qt., hrs., mos., yrs.	feet, kilogram, pounds, quart, hours, months, years

Technical versus Nontechnical Prose

In general, you can do more abbreviating in technical than in nontechnical writing. See the following examples.

TECHNICAL WRITING	OTHER PROSE
km	kilometer(s)
mg	milligram(s)
sq.	square

abbr 20i

Even in general-interest prose, however, abbreviation of a much-used term can be a convenience. Give one full reference before relying on the abbreviation:

- Among its many services, the Harvard Student Agency (HSA) sponsors the *Let's Go* series of travel books for students. HSA also functions as a custodial agency, rents photographic equipment and linens, acts as an employment clearinghouse, and caters parties.

20i Be Consistent in Capitalizing or Not Capitalizing Abbreviations Following Times.

Authorities disagree over A.M. and P.M. versus *a.m.* and *p.m.* Either form will do, but do not mix them.

DON'T:

x She was scheduled to arrive at 11 a.m., but we had to wait for her until 2 P.M.

DO:

- She was scheduled to arrive at 11 a.m., but we had to wait for her until 2 p.m.

or

- She was scheduled to arrive at 11 A.M., but we had to wait for her until 2 P.M.

20j Learn Which Kinds of Abbreviations Can Be Written without Periods.

Good writers differ in their preference for periods or no periods within an abbreviation. Practice is shifting toward omission of periods. In general, you can feel safe in omitting periods from abbreviations written in capital letters:

- JFK
- USSR
- IOU
- NJ

abbr
20k

Note that *N.J.*, with periods, is an option for abbreviating *New Jersey* but not for supplying a mail code before a ZIP number: *NJ 08540.*
But most abbreviations that end in a lower-case letter still require periods:

- Brit.
- Chi.
- Inc.
- i.e.

Note that there are commonly recognized exceptions: *mph, rpm,* etc. Also, abbreviations for metric measures are usually written without periods: *ml, kg,* etc.

20k Leave Spaces between the Initials of a Name, but Close Up Other Abbreviations and Acronyms.

SPACED:
- T. S. Eliot
- E. F. Hutton
- A. J. P. Taylor

UNSPACED:

- e.g.
- A.M. (or a.m.)
- Ph.D.
- CIA

NUMBERS AND FIGURES

num
201

201 Know Which Circumstances Call for Written-out Numbers.

Technical versus Nontechnical Prose

In scientific and technical writing, figures *(67)* are preferred to written-out numbers (*sixty-seven*), though very large multiples such as *million, billion,* and *trillion* are written out. Newspapers customarily spell out only numbers *one* through *nine* and such round numbers as *two hundred* and *five million.* In your nontechnical prose, prefer written-out numbers for the whole numbers *one* through *ninety-nine* and for any of those numbers followed by *hundred, billion,* etc.:

TECHNICAL PROSE	NONTECHNICAL PROSE
3/4	three-quarters
4	four
93	ninety-three
202	202
1500 (or 1,500)	fifteen hundred
10,000	ten thousand
38 million	thirty-eight million
101 million	101 million
54 billion	fifty-four billion
205 billion	205 billion

Special Uses for Written-out Numbers

1. In nontechnical prose, write out a concise number between one thousand and ten thousand that you can express in hundreds: not *1600* but *sixteen hundred.* This rule does not apply to dates, however.

2. Write out round (approximate) numbers that are even hundred thousands:

- Over six hundred thousand refugees arrived here last year.

3. Always write out a number that begins a sentence.

- *Eighty-four* students scored above grade level.

  But if the number would not ordinarily be written out, it is usually better to recast the sentence.

- The results were less encouraging for *213* other takers of the test.

  It would have been awkward to begin the sentence with *Two hundred thirteen.*

4. Write out a whole hour, unmodified by minutes, if it appears before *o'clock, noon,* or *midnight: one o'clock, twelve noon, twelve midnight.* Do not write *twelve thirty o'clock* or *12:30 o'clock.*

Special Uses for Figures

1. Use figures with abbreviated units of measure:

- 7 lbs.
- 11 g
- 88 mm

2. If you have several numbers bunched together, use figures regardless of the amounts:

- Harvey skipped his birthday celebrations at ages 21, 35, and 40.

3. When two or more related amounts call for different styles of representation, use figures for all of them:

• The injured people included 101 women and 9 children.

4. Use figures for all of the following:

   a. apartment numbers, street numbers, and ZIP codes:

• Apt. 17C, 544 Lowell Ave., Palo Alto, CA 94301.

   b. tables of statistics.

   c. numbers containing decimals: *7.456, $5.58, 52.1 percent.*

   d. dates (except in extremely formal communications such as wedding announcements): *October 5, 1985; 5 October 1985; October 5th.*

   e. times, when they precede *A.M.* or *P.M.* (*a.m.* or *p.m.*): *8 A.M., 6 P.M., 2:47 P.M.*

   f. page numbers: *p. 47, pp. 341–53.*

   g. volumes *(vol. 2)*, books of the Bible *(2 Corinthians)*, and acts, scenes, and lines of plays *(Macbeth I.iii.89–104).*

20m Use Roman Numerals Only Where Convention Requires Them.

In general, **Roman numerals** *(XI, LVIII)* have been falling into disuse as **Arabic numerals** *(11, 58)* have taken over their function. But note the following exceptions.

1. In some citation styles, upper- and lower-case Roman numerals are still used in combination with Arabic numerals to show sets of numbers in combination. Thus *Hamlet III.ii.47* refers to line 47 in the second scene of the play's third act.

2. Use Roman numerals for the main divisions of an outline (32b, p. 399).

3. Use lower-case Roman numerals to cite pages at the beginning of a book that are so numbered:

- (Preface v)
- (Introduction xvi–xvii)

4. Use Roman numerals as you find them in the names of monarchs, popes, same-named sons in the third generation, racing boats, etc.:

- Elizabeth II
- Leo IV
- Orville F. Schell III
- *Australia II*

num
20n

The following list will remind you how Roman numerals are formed.

1	I	10	X	50	L	200	CC
2	II	11	XI	60	LX	400	CD
3	III	15	XV	70	LXX	499	CDXCIX
4	IV	19	XIX	80	LXXX	500	D
5	V	20	XX	90	XC	900	CM
6	VI	21	XXI	99	XCIX	999	CMXCIX
7	VII	29	XXIX	100	C	1000	M
8	VIII	30	XXX	110	CX	1500	MD
9	IX	40	XL	199	CXCIX	3000	MMM

20n Distinguish between the Uses of Cardinal and Ordinal Numbers.

Numbers like *one, two,* and *three (1, 2, 3)* are called **cardinal numbers;** those like *first, second,* and *third (1st, 2d, 3d;* note the shortened spelling) are called **ordinal numbers.** The choice between cardinal and ordinal numbers is usually automatic, but there are several differences between spoken and written convention:

SPEECH	WRITING
Louis the Fourteenth	Louis XIV
July seventh, 1984	July 7, 1984 *or* 7 July 1984
But:	
July seventh [no year]	July 7th *or* July seventh

num

20n

Note that the rules of choice between written-out numbers and figures are the same for cardinal as for ordinal numbers (20l, p. 238).

Adverbial Ordinal Numbers

The word *firstly* is now rarely seen; *first* can serve as an adverb as well as an adjective.

ADJECTIVE:
- The *first* item on the agenda is the budget.

ADVERB:
- There are several items on the agenda. *First,* . . .

When you begin a list with *first,* you have the option of continuing either with *second, third,* or with *secondly, thirdly.* For consistency of effect, drop all the *-ly* forms:

- Let me say, *first,* that the crisis has passed. *Second,* I want to thank all of our employees for their extraordinary sacrifices. And *third,* . . .

But as soon as you write *secondly,* you have committed yourself to *thirdly, fourthly,* etc.

Finally, beware of mixing cardinal and ordinal forms.

DON'T:
x *One,* a career as a writer presents financial hardship. *Second,* I am not sure I have enough emotional stamina to face rejection. *Third,* . . .

For consistency, change *One* to *First.*

II EFFECTIVE EXPRESSION

D PARAGRAPHS

Paragraphs

Once you have mastered paragraph form, you have an invaluable means of keeping your reader's interest and approval. Although each sentence conveys meaning, an essay or paper or report is not a sequence of sentences but a development of one leading point through certain steps of presentation. Those steps are, or ought to be, paragraphs.

The sentences within an effective paragraph support and extend one another in the service of a single unfolding idea, just as the paragraphs themselves work together to make the thesis persuasive. In key respects, then, you can think of the paragraph as a mini-essay. Like the full essay, a typical paragraph

1. *presents one main idea;*

2. *conveys thoughts that are connected both by logical association and by word signals;*

3. *often reveals its main idea in a prominent statement, usually but not always toward the start;*

4. *usually supports or illustrates that idea;*

5. *may also deal with objections or limitations to that idea, but without allowing the objections to assume greater importance than the idea itself; and*

6. *may begin or end more generally, taking an expanded view of the addressed topic.*

In one sense nothing could be easier than to form paragraphs; you simply indent the first word of a sentence by five spaces. But those indentions must match real divisions in your developing thought if you are to keep your reader's respectful attention. All readers sense that a new paragraph signals a shift: a new subject, a new idea, a change in emphasis, a new speaker, a different time or place, or a change in the level of generality. By observing such natural breaks and by signaling in one paragraph how it logically follows from the preceding one, you can turn the paragraph into a powerful means of communication.

21 Paragraph Unity and Continuity

UNITY

21a Highlight Your Leading Idea.

As a rule, every effective paragraph has a leading idea to which all other ideas in the paragraph are logically related. A reader of your essays or papers should be able to tell, in any paragraph, which is the **main sentence** (often called *topic sentence*)—the sentence containing that one central point to be supported or otherwise developed in the rest of the paragraph.

It is true that in some prose—descriptions, narratives, and the parts of a report that present data or run through the steps of an experimental procedure—many paragraphs contain no single sentence that stands out as the main, controlling one. Such a paragraph can be said to have an implied main sentence: "This is the way it was," or "These are the procedures that were followed." But in college essays and term papers, which call chiefly for explanation and argument (30a, p. 371), you should try to see that each paragraph contains not only a leading idea but an easily identified main sentence as well.

We will see (Chapter 22) that a main sentence can occur anywhere in a paragraph if the other sentences are properly subordinate to it. More often than not, however, a main sentence comes at or near the beginning:

main
sentence

{ Societies, of course, play down their problems, put their best foot forward and try to make a good impression on visitors, but Soviet society, with the special vanity of its utopian ideology, takes this tendency to extremes. No more dramatic example of staging a show to impress foreigners took place during my stay in Russia than the facelifting given Moscow just before President Nixon's visit in the summer of 1972. Entire blocks of old buildings were burned down and carted away. Hundreds of people were moved out. Streets were widened and repaved, buildings repainted, trees and lawns planted, fringed with fresh flowerbeds put in practically on the eve of his arrival. Even our building, far from the Kremlin, was spruced up a bit on the odd chance that Nixon might show up. Under the czars this was called "Potemkinizing," after the prince who erected fake villages along the highway used by Catherine the Great to impress her with the wealth of his region. Nowadays, Russians call it *pokazukha,* for show.

¶ unity
21b

—HEDRICK SMITH, *The Russians*

Here the main sentence, after offering a general observation about the care any society takes to impress visitors, makes the key assertion that Soviet society "takes this tendency to extremes." The paragraph then illustrates this leading idea with details of "the facelifting given Moscow" just before President Nixon's 1972 visit, and it concludes by showing that the tradition of "Potemkinizing" goes back to pre-Soviet times. Even though the paragraph moves between general statements and an extended example, the strongly controlling effect of the main sentence never lapses.

21b Do Not Contradict Yourself.

A paragraph can include negative as well as positive considerations, but it should never "change its mind," canceling one point with a flatly contrary one.

DO:

- A.   The seepage of dioxin into a community's water supply always terrifies everyone once it has been discovered. Citizens naturally expect the Environmental Protection Agency and the guilty industry to remove the source of risk as soon as possible. Unfortunately, however, this chemical is so incredibly toxic in small doses that decades may pass before the threat to public health is truly over.

DON'T:

x B. The seepage of dioxin into a community's water supply always terrifies everyone once it has been discovered. Citizens naturally expect the Environmental Protection Agency and the guilty industry to remove the source of risk as soon as possible. Yet many people react to the crisis quite calmly, refusing to worry about cancer, birth defects, and other proven results of contact with dioxin.

Each of these paragraphs ends with a sentence that "goes against" the preceding two sentences. In paragraph A, however, there is no contradiction; the writer simply turns from one aspect of the dioxin problem (citizens' demand for a speedy solution) to a more serious aspect (long-term toxicity). But in paragraph B the writer says two *incompatible* things: that everyone is alarmed and that some people are not alarmed. The writer of paragraph B could eliminate the contradiction by rewriting the opening sentence.

¶ unity
21c

DO:

• The seepage of dioxin into a community's water supply provokes mixed reactions once it has been discovered. Citizens naturally expect the Environmental Protection Agency and the guilty industry to remove the source of risk as soon as possible. Yet many people react to the crisis quite calmly, refusing to worry about cancer, birth defects, and other proven results of contact with dioxin.

21c Keep to the Point.

A paragraph that shows strong internal continuity (21e, p. 251), hooking each new sentence into the one before it, can cover a good deal of ground without appearing disunified. Every sentence, however, should bear some relation to the leading idea—either introducing it, stating it, elaborating it, asking a question about it, supporting it, raising a doubt about it, or otherwise reflecting on it. A sentence that does none of those things is a **digression**—an irrelevancy. Just one digression within a paragraph may be enough to sabotage its effectiveness.

Suppose, for example, paragraph A on dioxin (21b) contained this sentence: *The Environmental Protection Agency, like the Federal Communications Commission, is an independent body.* Even though that statement deals with the EPA, which does figure in the paragraph, it has no bearing on the paragraph's leading idea: that dioxin can remain hazardous for decades. Thus the statement amounts to a digression. Unless the writer decided to switch leading ideas, the digression would have to be eliminated in a later draft.

21d Give Your Leading Idea the Last Word.

¶ unity
21d

If it is sometimes useful to include statements that limit the scope of a paragraph's leading idea or that raise objections to it (22b, p. 263), you should try never to *end* a paragraph with such a statement. Final positions are naturally emphatic. If your last sentence takes away from the main idea, you will sound indecisive or uncomfortable, and the paragraph will lack emphasis.

INDECISIVE:

x A. One reason for the recent popularity of Hollywood autobiographies must surely be the decline of serious fiction about important, glamorous people. We know that readers crave intimacy with the great, and we also know that modern novelists have ignored that craving. What people no longer get from fiction, they now seek in true confessions from Tinseltown. Of course, other factors must be at work as well; literary fads are never produced by single causes.

FIRM:

• B. One reason for the recent popularity of Hollywood autobiographies must surely be the decline of serious fiction about important, glamorous people. Of course, other factors must be at work as well; literary fads are never produced by single causes. But we do know that readers crave intimacy with the great, and we also know that modern novelists have ignored that craving. What people no longer get from fiction, they now seek in true confessions from Tinseltown.

Notice that these paragraphs say the same thing but leave the reader with different impressions. Paragraph A trails off, as if the writer were having second thoughts about the leading idea. Paragraph B gets its "negative" sentence about *other factors* into a safely unemphatic position and then ends strongly, reinforcing the idea that was stated in the opening sentence. The confident treatment of an objection makes the paragraph supple rather than self-defeating.

CONTINUITY

21e Respond to the Previous Sentence.

To maintain **continuity,** or linkage between sentences or whole paragraphs, you need to write each new sentence with the previous one in mind. You want your reader to feel that one statement has grown naturally out of its predecessor—an effect that comes from picking up some element in that earlier sentence and taking it further.

If, for example, the most recent sentence in your draft reads *The economic heart of America has been shifting toward the Sunbelt,* you could maintain continuity in any of the following ways, depending on the point you wish to make:

¶ con
21e

- The economic heart of America has been shifting toward the Sunbelt. But how much longer will this trend continue? [Ask a question.]

- The economic heart of America has been shifting toward the Sunbelt. The recent history of Buffalo, New York, is a case in point. [Illustrate your point.]

- The economic heart of America has been shifting toward the Sunbelt. It may be, however, that the country also has a quite different kind of heart—one that is not so easily moved. [Limit your point.]

- The economic heart of America has been shifting toward the Sunbelt. Without forgetting that trend, let us turn now to less obvious but possibly more important developments. [Provide a transition to the next idea.]

- The economic heart of America has been shifting toward the Sunbelt. If so, it can only be a matter of time before the moral or spiritual heart of the country is similarly displaced. [Reflect on your point; speculate.]

In short, reread the sentence you have just written and ask yourself, "All right, what follows from this?" What follows may be

1. a question (or further question);

2. an answer (if the sentence above is a question);

3. support or illustration of the point just made;

4. a limitation or objection to the point just made;

5. further support or illustration of an earlier point, or further limitation or objection to an earlier point;

6. a transition; or

7. a conclusion or reflection appropriate either to the sentence above or to the whole idea of the paragraph.

¶ con
21f

21f Include Signal Words and Phrases.

Though you may sometimes want to delay stating your paragraph's leading idea (22b, p. 263), you should never put your reader to the trouble of puzzling out hidden connections. By using unmistakable **signals of transition** from sentence to sentence, you can let the reader see at a glance that a certain train of thought is being begun, developed, challenged, or completed.

Those signals are chiefly words or phrases indicating exactly how a statement in one sentence relates to the statement it follows. The possible types of relation, along with examples of each type, are these:

CONSEQUENCE:
- therefore, then, thus, hence, accordingly, as a result

LIKENESS:
- likewise, similarly

CONTRAST:
- but, however, nevertheless, on the contrary, on the other hand, yet

AMPLIFICATION:
- and, again, in addition, further, furthermore, moreover, also, too

EXAMPLE:
- for instance, for example

CONCESSION:
- to be sure, granted, of course, it is true

INSISTENCE:
- indeed, in fact, yes, no

SEQUENCE:
- first, second, finally

RESTATEMENT:
- that is, in other words, in simpler terms, to put it differently

¶ con
21f

RECAPITULATION:
- in conclusion, all in all, to summarize, altogether

TIME OR PLACE:
- afterward, later, earlier, formerly, elsewhere, here, there, hitherto, subsequently, at the same time, simultaneously, above, below, farther on, this time, so far, until now

Notice how a careful use of transitional signals brings out the logical connectedness of sentences in the following paragraph:

In the winter of 1973–74 drivers lined up all over America to fill their gas tanks. *But* it was not merely a question of a fifteen-minute wait and back on the road again. *On the contrary,* cars often began to congregate at dawn. *Similarly,* walkers appeared early on frigid mornings with an empty five-gallon can in one hand and a pint of steaming coffee in the other, determined to wait out the chill and avoid disappointment. Everybody had to wait. *As a result,* high-school kids took Saturday morning jobs as gas line sitters; spouses drove their mates to work and spent the rest of the day in line; and libraries had a surge of activity as people decided to catch up on their reading while waiting. *All in all,* Americans were at their best during that bizarre season, abiding by the new rules as if a place in the gas line had been guaranteed to everyone by the Bill of Rights.

In addition to signal words that show logical connections, you can gain continuity through words indicating that something already treated is still under discussion. Such signal words make sense only in relation to the sentence before.

PRONOUNS:
- Ordinary people know little about the causes of inflation. What *they* do know is that *they* must earn more every year to buy the same goods and services.

DEMONSTRATIVE ADJECTIVES:
- Mark Twain died in 1910. Since *that* date American literature has never been so dominated by one writer's voice.

¶ con
21f

REPEATED WORDS AND PHRASES:
- We should conserve fossil fuels on behalf of our descendants as well as ourselves. Those *descendants* will curse us if we leave them without abundant sources of light and heat.

IMPLIED REPETITIONS:
- Some fifty Americans were trapped in the embassy when the revolution broke out. *Six more* managed to scramble onto the last helicopter that was permitted to land on the roof.

One key word, repeated several times, can do much to knit a paragraph together. Thus in the following paragraph the name *Ottawa* (italicized here for emphasis) is artfully plucked out from other names:

Perhaps a visitor cannot truly understand the country until he has traveled from the genteel poverty of the Atlantic coast with its picturesque fishing villages and stiff towns through the Frenchness of sophisticated Quebec cities and rural landscapes, past the vigorous bustling Ontario municipalities and industrial vistas, over mile after mile of wheat fields between prairie settlements into the lush and spacious beauty of British Columbia; but he must also visit *Ottawa* and the House of Commons. *Ottawa* the stuffy, with its dull-looking houses, its blistering summer heat, its gray rainy afternoons; *Ottawa* the beautiful, on a snowy day when the government buildings stand tall and protective, warmly solid above the white landscape; on a sunny spring afternoon with the cool river winding below, and people moving easily through the clean streets, purposeful but not pushed. Even during the morning and evening traffic rushes, *Ottawa* seems to remain sane.

—EDITH IGLAUER, "The Strangers Next Door"

In the first sentence *Ottawa* belatedly emerges as the key name among several; it gains importance by being weighted singly against all the "travelogue" references before the semicolon. In the second sentence (or intentional sentence fragment) the name is used insistently and fondly. And the author exploits this effect in her final sentence, using the name yet again to reinforce her idea that Ottawa stands apart from the rest of Canada.

¶ con
21g

21g Keep Related Sentences Together.

You can serve continuity by keeping together sentences that all bear the same general relation to the paragraph's leading idea. To simplify, let us reduce all such relations to *support* and *limitation* (p. 261). Sentences that support the leading idea by restating it, illustrating it, offering evidence for its truth, or expanding upon it belong in an uninterrupted sequence. So do all sentences that limit the leading idea by showing what it does *not* cover or by casting doubt on it.

Continuity is especially threatened when a paragraph contains two isolated sets of limiting sentences. To see why, examine the following draft paragraph:

limitation	x Not many people would want to endure the lonely hours, the aches and pains, and the probable injuries awaiting anyone who trains seriously for a marathon.
main sentence	The pride, however, that comes from finishing one's first marathon makes all the struggle seem worthwhile.
limitation	But is it really worthwhile? What does running twenty-six miles in glorified underwear have to do with real life? But for veteran marathoners, long-
support	distance racing *is* real life, while all other claims on their time are distractions or nuisances.

Here the direction established by the main sentence is promarathon. But that direction is opposed twice in the course of the paragraph; the main sentence is hemmed in by qualifications, and the reader is bounced back and forth between "pro" and "con" points. Compare:

limitation	Not many people would want to endure the lonely hours, the aches and pains, and the probable injuries awaiting anyone who trains seriously for a marathon. Is all the effort worthwhile? More than once, no doubt, exhausted beginners must ask themselves what running twenty-six miles in glorified underwear has to do with real life.
main sentence	Yet the pride that comes from finishing one's first marathon makes all the struggle seem worthwhile. And for
support	veteran marathoners, long-distance running *is* real life, while all other claims on their time are distractions or nuisances.

¶ con
21h

Now the paragraph's shuffling between pros and cons has been replaced by *one* definitive pivot on the signal word *Yet*. One such turn per paragraph is the maximum you should allow yourself. To observe that principle, make sure that your limiting and supporting sentences remain within their own portion of the paragraph—with the limiting sentences first to keep them from "having the last word."

For further discussion of the kind of paragraph that pivots to its leading idea, see 22b, p. 263.

21h Link Sentences through Varied and Repeated Structure.

A further means of making the sentences of a paragraph flow together is to give them some variety of structure. In particular, avoid an unbroken string of choppy sentences, each consisting of one statement unmarked by pauses (see 26e, p. 304).

Within certain limits, however, you can show continuity by *repeating* a sentence pattern. Those limits are that (a) only parts of paragraphs, not whole paragraphs, lend themselves comfortably to such effects, and (b) the sentences so linked must be parallel in meaning. When you want to make their association emphatic, you can give them the same form.

The following paragraph relates American history textbooks to a transformed society. Notice how the writer makes use of identical structures in two sentences to underscore the changes in America that have made history books less predictable than they used to be:

> But now the texts have changed, and with them the country that American children are growing up into. *The society that was once uniform is now* a patchwork of rich and poor, old and young, men and women, blacks, whites, Hispanics, and Indians. *The system that ran so smoothly* by means of the Constitution under the guidance of benevolent conductor Presidents *is now* a rattletrap affair. The past is no highway to the present; it is a collection of issues and events that do not fit together and that lead in no single direction.
>
> —FRANCES FITZGERALD, *America Revised: History Schoolbooks in the Twentieth Century*

¶ con
21h

Note how another author provides continuity through a series of similarly constructed questions about human fate:

> Why did my child, or any one of millions of children, die before he had the chance to grow out of infancy? Why was my child, or any child, born crippled in mind or body? Why has my friend or relative, or anyone's friend or relative, disintegrated in his mind, and then lost both his freedom and his destiny? Why has my son or daughter, gifted as they were with many talents, wasted them and been deprived of them? Why do such things happen to any parent at all? And why have the creative powers of this boy or that girl been broken by a tyrannical father or a possessive mother?
>
> —PAUL TILLICH, "The Riddle of Inequality"

Finally, in the next paragraph a critic of urban planning gains emphatic continuity through two sets of identical structures:

> But look what we have built with the first several billions: Low-income projects that become worse centers of delinquency, vandalism and general social hopelessness than the slums they were supposed to replace.

Middle-income housing projects which are truly marvels of dullness and regimentation, sealed against any buoyancy or vitality of city life. Luxury housing projects that mitigate their inanity, or try to, with a vapid vulgarity. Cultural centers that are unable to support a good bookstore. Civic centers that are avoided by everyone but bums, who have fewer choices of loitering place than others. Commercial centers that are lackluster imitations of standardized suburban chain-store shopping. Promenades that go from no place to nowhere and have no promenaders. Expressways that eviscerate great cities. This is not the rebuilding of cities. This is the sacking of cities.

—JANE JACOBS, *The Death and Life of Great American Cities*

¶ con
21i

The body of this paragraph consists of intentional sentence fragments (1e, p. 15), each of which takes its sense from the writer's opening words: *But look what we have built. . . .* An entirely different parallelism of structure brings the paragraph to its emphatic end: *This is not the rebuilding of cities. This is the sacking of cities.* The writer has risked annoying us with relentless hammer blows, but her shifting to a second variety of patterning prevents monotony.

21i Link One Paragraph to the Previous One.

Just as linked sentences help to establish the internal continuity of a paragraph, so linked paragraphs help to establish the continuity of a whole essay or paper. Of course your paragraphs must actually *be* logically connected, not just appear so. But once again you can bring out the connections through conjunctions like *but* or *yet* and through sentence adverbs and transitional phrases like *thus, however, in fact,* and *on the contrary.* And the linkage is surest of all in a paragraph whose first sentence refers directly to a point made in the previous sentence: *These problems, however, . . . ; Nevertheless, that argument can be answered;* etc.

Note, for instance, how the sample essay on pages 432–437 frequently "answers" the end of one paragraph with the beginning of the next one:

We pass by, disappointed and vaguely bothered.
  And perhaps vaguely envious as well. . . .

Why, then, is there something unsettling about watching her electronic trance?

I can only answer for myself. . . .

In particular, I am worried about three implications of the headset vogue: a growing dependency on artificial means of staying calm, decreased contact with reality, and a corresponding shrinkage of concern for other people.

First, the matter of dependency. . . .

For Sally, in contrast, the music *is* the action; reality will get through to her only when it is compatible with her mental Muzak.

But what worries me most about the headphone wearers is their social—and therefore political—indifference. . . .

One can always raise the volume if the world's troubles approach too near.

Of course I am overdramatizing here; we are not yet a nation of callous zombies. . . .

¶ con
21j

Enumeration

One rather formal but occasionally helpful way of linking paragraphs is to enumerate points that have been forecast at the end of the earlier paragraph. If you assert, for example, that there are three reasons for favoring a certain proposal or four factors that must be borne in mind, you can begin the paragraphs that follow with *First, . . . , Second, . . . ,* and so on.

21j Link Several Related Paragraphs in a Block.

A relatively long essay typically develops in groups of paragraphs that address major points. Within each of these **paragraph blocks,** one paragraph will usually state the dominant idea and the others will develop it. A writer working, for example, from the "rent control" outline on page 401 might decide to introduce Part III, the heart of the argument, with a "thesis" paragraph marking a major shift in emphasis:

Such is the promise that advocates of rent control offer to students who are weary of expensive housing and long trips to campus. If the promise could be even partially realized, it might be worth giving rent control another try. Unfortunately, there is no reason to think that another experiment would work better than all previous ones. However bad the present housing crisis is, you can be sure that rent control would make it worse.

Then four paragraphs, covering points A through D in the outline, would follow, making a single paragraph block about the disappointing results of rent control.

22 PARAGRAPH DEVELOP- MENT

Most of the advice you may have seen about constructing paragraphs deals with just one kind of development, which we will call *direct* (22a). Direct paragraphs are indeed the most common type. Capable writers, however, also feel at home with other ways of putting a paragraph together. For simplicity's sake we will recognize three patterns—the *direct,* the *pivoting,* and the *suspended* paragraph. They illustrate classic ways of combining the types of sentences most frequently found in paragraphs:

1. a **main sentence,** which carries the paragraph's leading idea;

2. a **supporting sentence,** which backs or illustrates the leading idea; and

3. a **limiting sentence,** which "goes against" the leading idea by raising a negative consideration either before or after that idea has been stated.

261

22a Master the Direct Pattern.

In a **direct paragraph,** the most usual pattern, you place the main sentence at or near the beginning, before you have mentioned any limiting (negative) considerations. The "Moscow" paragraph (p. 248), the second "Hollywood" paragraph (p. 250), the "gas shortage" paragraph (p. 253), the "Ottawa" paragraph (p. 254), the "urban planning" paragraph (p. 257), and this present paragraph all exhibit the direct pattern. The following student example is typical:

¶ dev 22a

main sentence { Horseback riding is, of course, the main feature of the ranch, and the stable of horses is impressive. Housed across the road from the ranch complex, the horses roam several acres of pasture that stretch right up to the road. Situated near the road is a large pond, which affords a spectacular view each evening as the horses make their way across the field to drink from the pond. Four rides are scheduled each day, and each evening before dinner the wranglers carefully assign horse to rider according to riding ability and the person's physical stature. Riders follow a trail that takes them on a ninety-minute expedition through the forest. For those who prefer not to gallop through the woods, a horse-drawn cart provides an equally scenic ride.

Here the opening sentence provides a leading idea which is then "made good" in the five sentences of development that follow it.

Note that a direct paragraph, just like an essay whose thesis is stated near the outset, can comfortably include *limiting* considerations—those that "go against" the leading idea. In the following student paragraph, for example, the writer can afford to offer a "con" remark, which is placed strategically between the main sentence and two final sentences of support for that statement:

main sentence { The "greenhouse effect," whereby the temperature of the atmosphere rises with the increased burning of hydrocarbons, may have devastating consequences for our planet within a generation or two. Similar scares, it is

limiting sentence { true, have come and gone without leaving any lasting mark. Yet there is an important difference this time.

supporting sentences { We know a good deal more about the greenhouse effect and its likely results than we knew, say, about invasions from outer space or mutations from atomic bomb tests. The greenhouse effect is already under way, and there are very slender grounds for thinking it will be reversed or even slowed without a more sudden cataclysm such as all-out nuclear war.

Direct paragraphs, then, can follow two models, one including and one omitting limiting sentences:

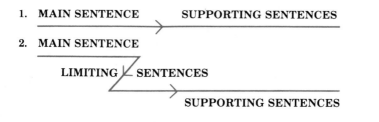

1. **MAIN SENTENCE   SUPPORTING SENTENCES**

2. **MAIN SENTENCE**

   LIMITING   SENTENCES

                    SUPPORTING SENTENCES

¶ dev
22b

22b Master the Pivoting Pattern.

A **pivoting paragraph** not only delays the main sentence but begins by "going against it" with one or more limiting sentences. Characteristically, the pivoting paragraph then turns sharply ("pivots") toward the main sentence, usually announcing that shift of emphasis with a conspicuous signal word such as *but* or *however*. The leading idea, once announced, then dominates the rest of the paragraph. The opening paragraph of this chapter (p. 261) typifies the pattern. Its third sentence, containing the pivoting word *however,* reverses the paragraph's direction while stating the leading idea, which is then illustrated in the remaining sentences.

Notice how the following student paragraph pivots neatly on the word *But* and then develops its leading idea:

limiting sentence { When we think of Gandhi fasting, plastering mud poultices on his belly, and testing his vow of continence by sharing a bed with his grand-niece, we can easily regard him as an eccentric who happened to be politically

pivot to the main sentence { lucky. *But* the links between his private fads and his political methods turn out to be quite logical. Gandhi's

supporting sentences { pursuit of personal rigors helped him to achieve a rare degree of discipline, and that discipline allowed him to approach political crises with extraordinary courage. The example of his self-control, furthermore, was contagious; it is doubtful that a more worldly man could have led millions of his countrymen to adopt the tactic of nonviolent resistance.

Similarly, the classic pivoting signal *however* shows us that the third sentence of this next paragraph is making a reversal of emphasis:

¶ dev 22b

Health experts always seem to be telling Americans what *not* to eat. Cholesterol, salt and sugar are but a few of the dietary no-no's that threaten to make dinnertime about as pleasurable as an hour of push-ups. In a report last week on the role of nutrition in cancer, *however,* a blue-ribbon committee of the National Academy of Sciences offered a carrot—as well as oranges, tomatoes and cantaloupes—along with the usual admonitory stick. While some foods appear to promote cancer and should be avoided, said the panel, other comestibles may actually help ward off the disease.

—MATT CLARK and MARY HAGER,
"A Green Pepper a Day"

The further you venture from the direct pattern, the more important it is to guide your reader with signal words such as *but* or *however.* You can also make your pivot, if you prefer, by means of a whole sentence such as *That is no longer the case.* The next sentence can then state your leading idea. And once in a while you can pivot on something as small as a single italicized word. In the following student paragraph, for instance, the word *needs*—italicized in the original— reverses the writer's emphasis:

limiting sentences { I don't usually like valet parking; in most cases, it is just a pretentious attempt at fancifying a restaurant that needs fancifying. In usual circumstances, people

pivot to the main sentence { can park on their own. Tesoro's Restaurant *needs* valet parking. Cars are squeezed into its far from adequate parking lot, leaving no space for opening a door wide enough. Other cars make their own stalls and line the residential streets. Neighborhood complaints about blocked driveways are not uncommon, and it is not odd at all to see ticketed cars cramped illegally close to hydrants.

supporting sentences {

A scheme of the pivoting paragraph would look like this:

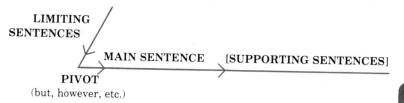

LIMITING SENTENCES

MAIN SENTENCE   [SUPPORTING SENTENCES]

PIVOT
(but, however, etc.)

¶ dev
22c

The brackets around "Supporting Sentences" indicate that a pivoting paragraph can end with its main sentence. More commonly, though, the main sentence is supported by one or more following sentences. In pivoting paragraphs already used as sample passages, for instance, the main sentence of the first "dioxin" paragraph (p. 248) comes at the end, whereas the main sentence of the "marathon training" paragraph (p. 255) is followed by support. So are the main sentences of the "Gandhi" and "nutrition" paragraphs just examined.

22c Master the Suspended Pattern.

The final pattern to master is the **suspended paragraph**—that is, a paragraph building to a climax or conclusion by some means other than a sharp reversal of direction. In a suspended paragraph the main sentence always comes at or near the end. Instead of taking a sharp turn, like the pivoting paragraph, it moves from discussion or exemplification to leading idea, maintaining the reader's sentence-by-sentence interest until it arrives at a statement that brings things together at last:

DISCUSSION   **MAIN SENTENCE**

Thus:

discussion

> A man who once developed printed circuits for computers begs on street corners for enough coins to buy another bottle of cheap port. A woman whose husband walked out when she couldn't stop drinking at home sits stupefied on a park bench, nodding senselessly at passers-by. An anxious teenager raids her parents' liquor closet at every opportunity. These people, though they have never met, suffer from the same misfortune. If they were placed together in a room, each of them might recognize the others as alcoholics. Yet what they have most in common is their inability to see *themselves* as alcoholics—and this is the very worst symptom of

main sentence

> their disease. For until the alcoholic's self-deception can be broken down, not even the most drastic cure has a chance of success.

Or again:

discussion

> In the early fourteenth century, northern Europe was subjected to a terrible famine. Meanwhile, economic instability caused whole kingdoms to go bankrupt. Then in 1348–50 the worst plague in history ravaged the Continent, killing perhaps half the population. It is little

main sentence

> wonder, therefore, that this was a period of profound social and political unrest; the supposedly stable order of feudalism had proved helpless to cope with various forms of disaster.

Looking back on the "discussion" sentences in these paragraphs, we could regard them as providing support for the leading idea. But we cannot perceive a sentence as "supporting" if we have not yet been told what it supports. By withholding that information until the end, the suspended paragraph establishes itself as the most dramatic pattern as well as the hardest to manage.

Once you feel at ease with the suspended paragraph, you will find it especially useful as a means of introducing or concluding an essay (Chapter 23). An opening paragraph that ends with its main sentence—a sentence revealing either your topic or your thesis—can gradually awaken the reader's interest and eagerness to move ahead. And a suspended final paragraph allows you to finish your essay with a "punch line"—an excellent tactic if you have saved a strong point for the end.

22d   Keep to a Manageable Paragraph Length.

There is no single "right" size for all paragraphs. In newspaper reporting, where the purpose is to communicate information with a minimum of analysis, paragraphs consist of one, two, or three sentences at the most. Paragraphs of dialogue also tend to be short; most writers indent for every change of speaker. So, too, scientific and technical journals favor relatively brief paragraphs that present facts and figures with little rhetorical development. And essayists vary considerably among themselves, both in their preference for short or long typical paragraphs and in the paragraph sizes they use within a given essay.

¶ dev
22d

Even so, it is possible to tell at a glance whether your essay paragraphs fall within an acceptable range. If you hardly ever write paragraphs of more than three brief sentences, you are erring on the side of choppiness. Readers will suspect that you have no great interest in exploring your ideas. And if your typical paragraph occupies nearly all of a typewritten, double-spaced page, you are being long-winded, making your reader work too hard to retain the connection between one leading idea and the next. The goal is to show careful sentence-by-sentence thought within a paragraph without allowing the main idea to lose its prominence.

Avoiding the Choppy Paragraph

If you have a tendency to write brief, stark paragraphs in which the main sentence is accompanied by just one or two other short sentences, reread one of your main sentences and ask yourself what else a reader might want to know about its implications. Do any of its terms need explaining? Where does it lead? What questions or objections does it call to mind? The new statements thus generated can become supporting or limiting sentences (22a, p. 262) that will flesh out the skeleton of your draft paragraph.

Suppose, for example, your draft paragraph looks like this.

CHOPPY DRAFT PARAGRAPH:

Acid rain has been destroying the forests of Canada. Although it blows northward from the United States, no one is sure that American factories are the only guilty ones. The damage is extensive, and it may take a court case to find out who is liable.

To gather material for a more developed paragraph, ask yourself what else your reader might profit from knowing:

> —*What questions might be asked about acid rain?* What is it? Is the damage irreversible? Can it be prevented?

> —*What objections might be raised to the charge that American factories are responsible for destroying the forests of Canada?* Are there other possible causes? Are American factory emissions mixed with those from Canada itself?

> —*Where does the issue of acid rain lead?* For example, to questions of legal liability for "pollution at a distance."

¶ dev
22d

Your revised, adequately developed paragraph might look like this:

ADEQUATELY DEVELOPED PARAGRAPH:

American factories, we are told, have been discharging atmospheric wastes that drift northward and fall on Canada as acid rain, destroying valuable forests. At present it remains uncertain how extensive the damage is, whether it is irreversible, and whether the pollution could be effectively stopped at its source. Indeed, we cannot be sure that American factories are the only guilty ones. Yet there is little reason to doubt that those factories are the primary source of acid rain and that the damage being caused is very considerable. If so, a landmark case of liability for "pollution at a distance" would seem to be in the offing.

Avoiding the Bloated Paragraph

If you see that your draft essay or paper contains a bloated paragraph—one that goes on and on without a strong sense of purpose—

seek out its main sentence. If you cannot find it, decide what you want your leading idea to be. As soon as you are sure you have a leading idea, check to see that every sentence has some bearing on it. In some cases your long paragraph will split neatly into two new ones, but you should never indent for a fresh paragraph without verifying that both units are internally complete.

Many draft paragraphs begin purposefully but bloat as the writer gets absorbed in details.

BLOATED DRAFT PARAGRAPH:

limiting sentence
{ x 1. If a person feels guilty about something, the obvious thing to do is to get that guilt out in the open.

main sentence
{ 2. But many people take a different approach, one that only makes matters worse: they try to stifle their bad feelings by means of depressants or stimulants such as alcohol, methedrine, or marijuana.

¶ dev 22d

supporting sentences
{ 3. A friend of mine felt guilty about getting low grades. 4. Her solution was to stay high nearly all the time. 5. But of course that made her get even lower grades and it thus redoubled her guilt, so she had even more bad feelings to hide in smoke. 6. I tried to talk to her about her problems, but she was already too depressed to allow anyone to get through to her. 7. Finally, she left school. 8. I lost touch with her, and I never did learn whether she straightened herself out. 9. I think that people like her deserve a lot of pity, because if she hadn't been so sensitive in the first place, she wouldn't have had the guilt feelings that sent her into a tailspin. 10. People who just don't care are sometimes better off.

This begins as a competent pivoting paragraph, contrasting two approaches to the problem of handling guilty feelings and providing an example of the second, self-defeating, approach. The momentum, however, begins to drag as the writer shifts attention to herself in sentence 6, and the paragraph falls apart completely at sentence 9, which escapes the control of the main sentence, number 2. Revising for economy and relevance, the writer decided to do without the sentences about herself and her compassionate attitude.

ADEQUATELY FOCUSED PARAGRAPH:

limiting sentence { If a person feels guilty about something, the obvious thing to do is to get that guilt out in the open. But many

main sentence { people take a different approach—one that only makes matters worse. They try to stifle their bad feelings with

supporting sentences { stimulants or depressants such as alcohol, methedrine, or marijuana. A friend of mine, for example, feeling guilty about her low grades, tried to stay high nearly all the time. The result was that she got even worse grades, felt guiltier still, smoked even more dope, and eventually dropped out of school. Her supposed remedy had become a major part of her problem.

¶ dev
22d

After establishing a middle-sized paragraph as your norm, you can depart from the norm with good effect. A reader who comes across a somewhat longer paragraph will know that a particularly complex point is being developed. Occasionally you can insert a very short paragraph—a sentence or two, or even a purposeful sentence fragment—to make a major transition, a challenge, an emphatic statement, or a summary. The emphasis comes precisely from the contrast between the short paragraph and the more developed ones surrounding it.

23 Special Paragraphs

OPENING PARAGRAPHS

A good introductory paragraph customarily accomplishes three things. It catches your reader's interest; it establishes the voice and stance of your essay or paper (32d–32f, pp. 405–411); and—usually but not always—it reveals the one central matter you are going to address. Only rarely does a shrewd writer begin by blurting out the thesis and immediately defending it. The standard function of an introduction is to *move toward* disclosure of the thesis in a way that makes your reader want to come along.

But if your mind goes blank when you try to write the opening paragraph, delay the opener until you have drafted subsequent paragraphs. Some writers routinely compose in that order, and nearly all writers return to adjust and polish their opening to suit the rest of the essay.

23a Avoid the Deadly Opener.

An experienced reader can usually tell after two or three sentences whether the writer commands the topic and will be able to make it attractive. Whatever else you do, never slip your reader one of the following classic sleeping pills:

1. *The solemn platitude:*

   x Conservation is a very important topic now that everyone is so interested in ecology.

   Ask yourself if *you* would continue reading an essay that began with such a colorless sentence.

2. *The unneeded dictionary definition:*

   x The poem I have been asked to analyze is about lying. What is lying? According to *Webster's Eighth New College Dictionary,* to lie is "1: to make an untrue statement with intent to deceive; 2: to create a false or misleading impression."

   Ask yourself if your reader is actually in the dark about the meaning of the word you are tempted to define. *Lie* obviously fails that test.

3. *Restatement of the assignment, usually with an unenthusiastic declaration of enthusiasm:*

   x It is interesting to study editorials in order to see whether they contain "loaded" language.

   If you are actually interested, you would do well to *show* interest by beginning with a thoughtful observation.

4. *The bald statement of the thesis:*

   x In this essay I will prove that fast food restaurants are taking the pleasure out of eating.

   But you are also taking the pleasure out of reading. You want to *approach* your thesis, not to drop it on the reader's foot like a bowling ball that has slipped out of your grasp.

5. *The "little me" apology:*

   x After just eighteen years on this earth, I doubt that I have

spec ¶ 23a

acquired enough experience to say very much about the purpose of a college education.

Is this going to whet your reader's appetite for the points that follow?

23b Master the Funnel Opener.

Perhaps the most common device for introducing a topic or thesis (30c, p. 375) is the so-called **funnel opener**. This paragraph begins with an assertion that covers a broader area than your topic will; it is an "umbrella sentence," giving your reader a wide perspective and a context for understanding the actual topic when it is stated. Then in subsequent sentences the funnel opener narrows to the topic or thesis, which is usually revealed at or near the end of the paragraph.

The following example shows the pattern:

> Only a few politicians have taken a craftsman's pride in self-expression, and fewer still—Caesar, Lord Clarendon, Winston Churchill, De Gaulle—have been equally successful in politics and authorship. Of these, Churchill may be the most interesting, for he was not only among the most voluminous of writers, but also commented freely on the art of writing. He was, in fact, a writer before becoming a politician.
>
> —MANFRED WEIDHORN, "Blood, Toil, Tears, and 8,000,000 Words: Churchill Writing"

By the end of this paragraph we know that the topic will be Churchill's writing, but we arrive at that knowledge by sliding down the funnel:

those politicians who took pride in self-expression

those who were equally successful in politics and authorship

the most interesting of these: Churchill

Churchill as writer

spec ¶
23b

23c Master the Baited Opener.

A **baited opener** is an introductory paragraph that not only saves its main idea for last (22c, p. 265) but also teases the reader by withholding a clear sense of the essay's topic. We are drawn ahead in the hope of getting our bearings:

> First off, I want to say that as far as I am concerned, in instances where I have not personally and deliberately sought it out, the only difference between music and Muzak is the spelling. Pablo Casals practicing across the hall with the door open—being trapped in an elevator, the ceiling of which is broadcasting "Parsley, Sage, Rosemary, and Thyme"—it's all the same to me. Harsh words? Perhaps. But then again these are not gentle times we live in. And they are being made no more gentle by this incessant melody that was once real life.
>
> —FRAN LEBOWITZ, "The Sound of Music: Enough Already"

spec ¶
23c

This paragraph arouses interest without revealing whether the essay will be about having a "tin ear," missing a music education, or some other music-related topic. Only the final sentence tells us that the subject is the incessant music that accompanies us as we try to live our daily lives.

Or again, note this surprising two-paragraph opening of a brief essay:

> Natasha Crowe, a close acquaintance of mine, recently received an unsolicited invitation from Joanne Black, senior vice president of the American Express Co.'s Card Division. "Quite frankly," the letter began, "the American Express Card is not for everyone. And not everyone who applies for Card membership is approved." Tasha (as she is affectionately called) ignored the letter. A few weeks later she received a follow-up offer from a different vice president, Scott P. Marks Jr. "Quite frankly," Mr. Marks reminded her, "not everyone is invited to apply for the American Express Card. And rarer still are those who receive a personal invitation the second time."
>
> Despite the honor, Tasha has continued to disregard this and similar invitations she has lately been receiving. For one thing, she has no job. Her savings are minimal. Her credit history is essentially a vacuum and therefore her credit rating, I'd imagine, is lousy. She doesn't even speak English. She's my cat, and I love her.
>
> —STEVEN J. MARCUS, "How to Court a Cat"

23d Sharpen Your Opening Sentence.

If your first paragraph is the most important one, its first sentence is your most important sentence as well. When that sentence betrays boredom or confusion, you reduce your chances of gaining the reader's sympathy. If it is crisp and tight and energetic, its momentum can carry you through the next few sentences at least. This is why some people take pains to make that first sentence *epigrammatic*—pointed and memorable. Thus one writer begins a review of a book about Jewish immigrants by declaring:

> The first generation tries to retain as much as possible, the second to forget, the third to remember.
>
> —THEODORE SOLOTAROFF, review of
> *World of Our Fathers,* by Irving Howe

spec ¶
23e

Another wittily begins an essay on divorce:

> There was a time when a woman customarily had a baby after one year of marriage; now she has a book after one year of divorce.
>
> —SONYA O'SULLIVAN, "Single Life in a Double Bed"

And a student writer advocating gun control begins:

> Thousands of people in this country could make an overwhelming case for the banning of handguns, except for one inconvenient fact: they aren't so much *in* the country as *under* it, abruptly sent to their graves with no chance to protest or dissuade. Arguing with a gun nut may be futile, but have you ever tried arguing with a gun?

TRANSITIONAL PARAGRAPHS

23e Keep a Transitional Paragraph Concise.

Try not to devote a substantial paragraph to the task of maneuvering from one part of your essay to the next:

DON'T:

x We have now seen that the question of human rights posed at the beginning of this essay cannot be easily answered, and that, specifically, two serious considerations stand in our way. The first of those considerations has now been dealt with, though not perhaps as fully as some readers might prefer. It is time now to go on to the second point, after which we can return to our original question with a better sense of our true options.

Such a paragraph merely tells your reader that you are having trouble making things fit together smoothly.

From time to time, however, you may want to devote a *brief* paragraph to announcing a major shift of direction. Do so concisely, with a minimum of distraction from the sequence of ideas.

spec ¶
23f

DO:

● But how can such violations of human rights be swept under the rug? Unfortunately, as we will see, the method is simple and practically foolproof.

CLOSING PARAGRAPHS

23f Avoid the Deadly Conclusion.

Readers want to feel, at the end of a piece of writing, that it has truly finished and not just stopped like some toy soldier that needs rewinding. Further, they like to anticipate the end through a revealing change in tone or intensity or generality of reference.

Though you may not always come up with a punchy conclusion, you can avoid certain lame devices that would threaten your good relations with your reader. Check your draft endings against the following cautions:

1. Do not merely repeat your thesis.

2. Though you can look beyond your thesis (23g), do not embark on a completely new topic.

3. Do not pretend to have proven more than you have.

4. Do not apologize or bring your thesis into doubt. If there is anything that requires an apology, fix it!

Remember that readers come away from an essay with the last paragraph ringing in their ears. If you end by sounding bored or distracted or untrustworthy or hesitant, you are encouraging your readers to discount everything you have worked so hard to establish.

23g Look Beyond Your Thesis in a Closing Paragraph.

Just as you can lead to your thesis by beginning on a more general plane (23b, p. 273), so you can end by looking beyond that thesis, which has now been firmly established. Thus, in a paper defending the thesis that unilateral disarmament is a dangerous and unwise policy, a student writer concluded as follows:

spec ¶
23h

> There is no reason to expect, then, that the world would be safer if we laid down our arms. On the contrary, we could do nothing more fool-hardy. *We must look to other means of ensuring our security and that of the nations we have agreed to protect.*

The sentence we have emphasized "escapes" the thesis, posing a relevant goal for some future investigation. But note that it does so without embarking on a new topic; it provokes thought by looking further in the direction already taken.

23h Save a Clinching Statement for Your Closing Paragraph.

Remember that the final position within any structure—sentence, paragraph, or whole essay—is naturally emphatic. To take advantage of that fact, delay writing your conclusion until you have found material that bears reemphasizing or expanding. Look especially for a striking quotation or story that might drive your point home. You can either end with that passage or, as in these two examples, add a final comment of your own:

Robert M. Hutchins has described the editors of *Britannica 3* as pioneers. After they had established their design "the question became one of execution . . . there were no models to imitate and no horrible examples to shun." One of those deficiencies has been made good by *Britannica 3* itself: they have their horrible example now.

—SAMUEL McCRACKEN, "The Scandal of *Britannica* 3"

23i Try Recalling Your Opening Paragraph in Your Closing One.

Look for ways of making your concluding paragraph show some evident, preferably dramatic, relation to your introductory one. If you already have a sound first paragraph and are groping for a last one, reread that opener and see if it contains some hint that you can now develop more amply. Here, for instance, is the concluding paragraph of the essay (quoted on p. 263) that began by asking whether Mahatma Gandhi was nothing more than a religious fanatic:

spec ¶
23j

Gandhi's arguments reveal an underlying shrewdness. Far from betraying the dogmas of a fanatic, they are at once moral and cunningly practical. His genius, it seems, consisted in an unparalleled knack for doing right—and, what isn't quite the same, for doing the right thing. It is hard to come up with another figure in history who so brilliantly combined an instinct for politics with the marks of what we call, for lack of a better name, holiness.

Note how the writer has put his opening question into storage until it can be answered decisively, with a pleasing finality, in his closing lines.

23j If Your Essay Is Brief, Feel Free to Omit a Concluding Paragraph.

A short essay may make its point thoroughly within five hundred words; your readers will be insulted or bored by a heavy-handed reminder of the points they have just finished reading. Sometimes a brief concluding paragraph—consisting of no more than one or two sentences—can effectively end a short essay. But you can also save one of your strong supporting points for the last paragraph, counting on an emphatic final sentence to give a feeling of completion.

E SENTENCES

Sentences

Strong sentences have much in common with strong paragraphs and whole essays, including a clear idea, emphatic placement of that idea, and subordination of other elements. You can think of the fully developed sentence as a skeletal paragraph containing major and minor components that ought to be easy for a reader to spot:

	ESSAY		PARAGRAPH		SENTENCE
MAJOR	Thesis	=	Leading Idea	=	Assertion, Question, or Exclamation
MINOR	Supporting Paragraphs		Supporting Sentences		Modifying Clauses and Phrases

On each level—essay, paragraph, sentence—your chief purpose in redrafting should be to highlight the major element and to see that it is adequately backed by minor elements that are clearly subordinate to it.

The chapters in Part E assume that you can already write complete sentences that make a grammatically coherent statement (Chapters 1 and 2). You may want to review several chapters in Part A if you feel uncertain about fundamentals of usage. But since you have already succeeded in getting countless sentences onto paper, we start our discussion not with the blank page but with draft sentences that a student writer might want to improve. Our keynote will be revising to make your meaning easier to grasp and your sentences more pleasant and varied.

24 Distinct Expression

24a Recognize Your Main Idea.

Since your chief concern in writing any sentence is to communicate an idea, the logical starting point for revision is to locate that idea and see if you have conveyed it as clearly as possible. Some sentences—those with two or more independent clauses (1c, p. 9) joined by words like *and* or *but*—will prove to have more than one main idea, but every full sentence that makes a statement or asks a question will contain at least one. The act of isolating it can often show you where a problem of unclear expression lies.

The following sentences illustrate main ideas with and without relation to other elements. The main ideas are italicized:

1. *The professional basketball season now runs from September through the middle of June.*

    The whole sentence is a main idea.

2. *The players are always tired,* and *they find it hard to take every game seriously.*

    The sentence makes two statements that receive equal emphasis. Both are main ideas.

3. *So many teams make the playoffs,* furthermore, *that first-place finishes within a division are scarcely important.*

> One word, *furthermore,* stands apart from the interrupted main idea, relating it to a previous statement. Note that the first italicized group of words requires the second one to complete its meaning; together they make one main idea.

4. *Would the players,* one wonders, *have longer careers if they were given more rest?*

> Note that a main idea can be a question (or an exclamation) as well as a statement.

5. Although basketball may have replaced baseball as the national pastime, *we might do better to pass a little more time between seasons.*

> The main idea—the one that could stand by itself—does not begin until after the word *pastime.* Note that it makes full sense without the *Although* clause.

**vague
24b**

Note that in a grammatically complete sentence a main idea (a) is always an independent clause, and (b) may contain a subordinate clause, as in sentence 3 above *(that first-place finishes . . . are scarcely important).* You find a main idea by asking yourself which parts of the sentence *cannot be omitted* if the statement, question, or exclamation is to make sense.

24b Align Your Meaning with Grammatically Important Words.

Your reader wants above all to get the point of your sentence—to take in your main idea without difficulty. When you go back to revise a draft sentence, mentally isolate that set of words and study it with fresh, doubting eyes, as if you did not know what the writer had in mind. Does the idea make immediate sense? If not, the reason is probably that you have not yet put the essential parts of your idea into the grammatically strongest elements.

The strongest elements in a sentence are generally a *subject* and a *verb*, possibly linked to either a *direct object* or a *complement* (1a, p. 6):

     SUBJ   V
- The *committee exists.*

     SUBJ   V
- The *committee meets* on Tuesdays.

     SUBJ   V   D OBJ
- The *committee is drafting* a *report.*

     SUBJ   V   COMPL
- The *committee is* an official *body.*

     SUBJ   V   COMPL
- The *committee seems prepared.*

Consider this "correct" but unimpressive sentence:

     SUBJ   V
x The *departure* of the fleet *is thought* to be necessarily conditional on the weather.

vague

24b

Here the essential grammatical elements are a subject and verb, *The departure . . . is thought.* This is scanty information; we must root around elsewhere in the sentence to learn what is being said *about* the departure. The idea is that bad weather—here tucked into a prepositional phrase, *on the weather*—may delay the fleet's departure. Once we recognize that point, we can get *weather* into the subject position and replace the wishy-washy construction *is thought to be conditional on* with a verb that transmits action to an object.

DO:

     SUBJ   V   D OBJ
- *Bad weather may keep* the *fleet* at anchor.

Notice that we now have three grammatically strong elements—a subject, a verb, and a direct object—that do carry significant meaning.

DON'T:

     SUBJ   V
x The *thing* the novelist seems to say *is* that the human race is lacking what is needed to keep from being deceived.

This whole sentence is a main idea whose subject and verb convey no information: *the thing is.* To find the writer's meaning we must disentangle various embedded infinitives, subordinate clauses, and prepositional phrases, each of which adds a little more strain to our memory.

DO:

      SUBJ   V

• *Human beings,* the novelist seems to say, necessarily *deceive*

    D OBJ
themselves.

Now the subject and verb do convey information. The key grammatical elements, subject–verb–direct object, bear the chief burden of meaning: *Human beings deceive themselves.* And as a result of this realignment, the main idea now takes up just five words instead of twenty-three. Notice how the commas make it easy for a reader to tell where that main idea is being interrupted.

**vague
24c**

24c Watch for Impossible Predication.

Predication—saying something about a grammatical subject—is the essence of all statement. In first-draft prose, however, writers sometimes yoke subjects and predicates that fail to make sense together. The most extreme such breakdown is *mixed construction* (3a, p. 28), whereby a reader cannot even locate the subject: x *What they promised on the phone it was very different.* But predication can also go awry if the writer asks a subject to perform something it could not possibly do.

DON'T:

             SUBJ   V

x The *capabilities* of freshmen in high school *function* on an adult

                                                  PRED
level.

Can capabilities function? No; they are abstractions, (28f, p. 334), not agents. People or things function, and they do so because they possess certain capabilities. Thus the revised sentence must reflect that fact.

DO:

SUBJ   V
- *Freshmen* in high school <u>*are* capable of functioning like adults.</u>
                                     PRED

or

SUBJ   V
- *Freshmen* in high school <u>*have* the capabilities of adults.</u>
                              PRED

or

          SUBJ   V
- The *capabilities* of freshmen in high school <u>*match* those of adults.</u>
                                        PRED

You can see that the problem in impossible predication often lies in treating an abstraction as if it were a performer of action. Once you have hit upon a subject like *capabilities* (or *inventiveness, symmetry, rationality, reluctance,* etc.), your predicate must reflect the fact that you are not writing about an agent.

> **vague**
> **24 d**

24d Avoid an Overstuffed Statement.

Check your drafts for formless sentences that do not distinguish primary from subordinate elements.

DON'T:

S V
x *It is* what she recalled from childhood about the begonia gardens that were cultivated in Capitola that drew her to return to that part of the coastline one summer after another.

Since such a sentence demands that all of its elements be kept in mind until the point eventually becomes clear, the sentence often will require two readings. The solution, as we will see more fully in the next chapter, lies in shortening the main idea and clearly setting the minor elements apart.

DO:

- Summer after summer, drawn by her childhood recollections of

SUBJ   V

the Capitola begonia gardens, *she returned* to that portion of the coastline.

Note how, through a separating out of significant elements, the sentence becomes more dramatic and easier to grasp. Its main idea, instead of being thirty-one words jostling together in a mass, is a readily understood eight-word statement: *she returned to that portion of the coastline.*

24e Do Not Overuse the Verb *to Be.*

vague

24f

You can make your drafts more expressive by cutting down on uses of the colorless, actionless verb *to be (is, are, were, had been,* etc.).

"CORRECT" BUT ACTIONLESS:

x It *was* clear that the soprano *was* no longer in control of the high notes that *had been* a source of worry to her for years.

STRONGER:

- Clearly, the soprano *had lost* control of the high notes that *had been worrying* her for years.

The action-bearing verbs in the revised version trim away needless words—notably the plodding prepositional phrases *in control, of worry,* and *to her*—and convey the key activities of losing and worrying.

24f Convey Action through a Verb, Not a Noun.

As the example in 24e illustrates, a sentence whose main idea is indistinct typically uses nouns instead of verbs to express the action.

That is, the action becomes an abstract state such as *control of the high notes* and *a source of worry*. By moving the action into verbs *(had lost, had been worrying),* you allow your reader to feel the energy of your statement. Notice the relative vitality of the following *DO* examples.

DON'T:

x Many young single people are in a financial arrangement that enables them to have joint ownership of a house.

DO:

• Many young single people arrange their finances so that they can own a house jointly.

DON'T:

x A single parent stands in need of occasional relief from the endless responsibilities of workplace and household.

DO:

• Sometimes a single parent must get away from the endless responsibilities of workplace and household.

vague
24 g

The *DON'T* examples above are not "wrong"; they just place a little more strain on the reader's patience than is necessary.

24g In Most Contexts, Prefer the Active Voice.

In addition to choosing verbs that show action (24f), you can keep your sentences distinct by generally preferring the active to the passive voice in your verbs: not *was done* but *did,* not *is carried* but *carries.* The trouble with passive verbs is twofold: they can never take direct objects, and they oblige the performer to go unnamed or to be named only in a postponed and minor sentence element.

DON'T:

x *It is believed* by the candidate that a ceiling *must be placed* on the budget by Congress.

x Their motives *were applauded* by us, but their wisdom *was doubted.*

Note how you can save words and impart vividness by substituting active forms.

DO:

- The candidate *believes* that Congress *must place* a ceiling on the budget.
- We *applauded* their motives but *doubted* their wisdom.

In scientific writing, which often stresses impersonal, repeatable procedures rather than the individuals who carried them out, passive verbs are common. You can also use them in essay prose whenever you want your emphasis to remain on the person or thing acted upon. Suppose, for example, you are narrating the aftermath of an accident. Both of the following sentences would be correct, but you might have good reason to prefer the second, passive one:

vague
24h

ACTIVE VERB:

- Then three hospital attendants and the ambulance driver *rushed* Leonard into the operating room.

PASSIVE VERB:

- Then Leonard *was rushed* into the operating room.

Although the second sentence is less vivid, it keeps the focus where you may want it to be, on the injured man.

Passive verbs, then, are not automatically "wrong." As you revise your prose, look at each passive form and ask yourself whether you have a good justification for keeping it.

24h Use Delaying Formulas Sparingly and Only for Special Emphasis.

If one of your sentences begins with a subject-deferring expression such as *it is* or *there were,* take a close look at the subject (it is the *weather;* there was a *princess).* That "announced" word stands out emphatically in its unusual position. If you have a special reason for highlighting it, your delaying formula may be justified:

- It is the weather that causes her arthritis to act up.
- There was a princess whose hair reached the ground.

    In the first of these sentences, *weather* is isolated as the cause of the arthritis; in the second, the writer succeeds in getting an intended "fairy tale" effect.

More often than not, however, delaying formulas show up in first-draft prose simply because the writer is postponing commitment to a clearly stated main idea. The price of delay is that, without any gain in emphasis, essential information is pushed further back into subordinate parts of the sentence (see 24b, p. 282). Frequently the result is an awkward and indistinct statement.

DON'T:

x *There is* no reason to suspect that *there is* much difference between what she wrote in her last years and what she felt when *it was* not so easy for her to be candid in her thirties.

vague
24 i

DO:

- Her statements in her last years probably express ideas she already held, but was censoring, in her thirties.

    Note how much more easily you can take in the revised sentence; you do not have to hold your breath until you can discover what the statement is about. The complete grammatical subject, *Her statements in her last years,* immediately gives us our bearings.

24i Avoid an Unnecessary *That* or *What* Clause.

Look at the last *DON'T* example above in 24h *(There is no reason to suspect that . . .).* Part of the indistinctness of that sentence comes from its *that* and *what* clauses, which further tax the reader's patience. Such clauses can, it is true, serve a good purpose—for example, arousing a curiosity that can then be emphatically answered:

- *What he needed* above all, after eight hours of steady questioning, was simply a chance to close his eyes.

In much first-draft prose, however, *that* and *what* clauses serve only to nudge the intended statement along in little jerks.

DON'T:

x At the present time, the realities of nuclear terror are such *that* countries *that* possess equal power find, when they oppose each other, *that* the weapons *that* carry the most force are precisely the weapons *that* they cannot use.

DO:

- In this age of nuclear terror, equal adversaries are equally powerless to use their strongest weapons.

vague
24 i

Here thirty-nine words have been compressed into sixteen, and a slack, cud-chewing sentence has become tight and balanced *(equal adversaries are equally powerless)*. And notice how the grammatical core of the sentence (24b, p. 282) has been given something definite to convey: not *realities are such* but *adversaries are powerless*. Strong, message-bearing elements of thought have been moved into subject-verb-complement positions, where they normally belong.

25 Subordination

The first thing to do with any draft sentence is to see if you can make its main idea more distinct (Chapter 24). In doing so, you will usually find yourself **subordinating** certain parts of the sentence—placing them in secondary positions. As you make these elements clearly minor you indicate to your reader that another element is primary.

25a Subordinate to Highlight Your Main Idea.

When one of your thoughts in a sentence is less important than another, you should put it into a subordinate structure. Thus, if your draft sentence says *The government collects billions of dollars in taxes, and it must meet many obligations,* you should recognize that by using *and* you have given equal weight to two independent remarks. Are they of equal importance in your own mind? If you decided that you really meant to stress the collecting of money, you would want to turn the statement about meeting obligations into a subordinate element:

- The government collects billions of dollars in taxes *because it*
  SUBORD EL
  has many obligations to meet.

But if you wanted to stress the meeting of obligations, you would subordinate the remark about collecting money:

                                                          SUBORD EL
- The government meets its obligations *by collecting billions of dollars in taxes.*

When you make an element subordinate, it will usually fit into one of the following (left-column) categories. Note how subordinating words like *because, where,* and *although* (1c, p. 9) not only spare us the trouble of locating the main idea but specify the relation between that idea and the subordinate element.

	WITHOUT SUBORDINATION	**WITH SUBORDINATION**
Time	The earthquake struck, and then everyone panicked.	Everyone panicked *when* the earthquake struck.
Place	William Penn founded a city of brotherly love. He chose the juncture of the Delaware and Schuylkill rivers.	*Where* the Schuylkill River joins the Delaware, William Penn founded a city of brotherly love.
Cause	She was terrified of large groups, and debating was not for her.	*Because* she was terrified of large groups, she decided against being a debater.
Concession	He claimed to despise Vermont. He went there every summer.	*Although* he claimed to despise Vermont, he went there every summer.
Condition	She probably won't be able to afford a waterbed. The marked retail prices are just too high.	*Unless* she can get a discount, she probably won't be able to afford a waterbed.
Exception	The grass is dangerously dry this year. Of course I am not referring to watered lawns.	*Except for* watered lawns, the grass is dangerously dry this year.
Purpose	The Raiders moved to Los Angeles. They hoped to find bigger profits there.	The Raiders moved to Los Angeles *in search of* bigger profits.
Description	The late Edward Steichen showed his reverence for life in arranging the famous exhibit "The Family of Man," and he was a pioneer photographer himself.	The late Edward Steichen, *himself a pioneer photographer,* showed his reverence for life in arranging the famous exhibit "The Family of Man."

sub
25a

25b Gain Clarity through Free Subordination.

In the right-hand column of the chart above, note that all but two of the italicized elements are set apart from the main ideas by commas. They are **free** in the sense of standing alone. By contrast, the sentences *Everyone panicked when the earthquake struck* and *The Raiders moved to Los Angeles in search of bigger profits* contain **bound** subordinate elements—that is, they are tied together with the main ideas. Here are some further contrasts:

BOUND:	**FREE:**
The Germany *that he remembered with horror* had greatly changed.	Germany, *which he remembered with horror,* had greatly changed.
Germany was now inclined toward neutralism *instead of being fiercely militaristic.*	*Instead of being fiercely militaristic,* Germany was now inclined toward neutralism.
Hitler had vanished from the scene *along with everything he stood for.*	*Along with everything he stood for,* Hitler had vanished from the scene.

sub
25b

In general, bound elements are **restrictive** or defining, and thus they should not be set off by commas (see 4j, p. 58). Free elements, being **nonrestrictive** or nondefining, should be set apart. But since any phrase or subordinate clause at the beginning of a sentence can be followed by a comma (4h, 4i, pp. 56–57), a restrictive element that comes first can be free—that is, followed by a comma:

RESTR AND FREE
• *In September or October,* heating bills begin to rise.

The distinction between free and bound elements is a valuable one for mastering an efficient style. When one of your draft sentences is clumsily phrased, you can often attack the problem by looking for bound elements and then setting them free.

WITH BOUND SUBORDINATION:

x The censorship *that is not directly exercised by a sponsor when a program is being produced* may be exercised in many instances by the producers themselves.

WITH FREE SUBORDINATION:

• *Even when a sponsor does not directly censor a program*, the producers often censor it themselves.

   Note the importance of the comma after *program,* leaving the reader in no doubt about where the main idea begins. Observe, too, that the revised sentence shifts from passive to active verbs (24g, p. 287). Use of the passive voice almost always results in the addition of bound prepositional phrases *(by a sponsor, by the producers)*.

WITH BOUND SUBORDINATION:

x Nuclear power is an energy source *whose enormous risks to health and safety are out of scale in importance with the fact that it accounts for less than five percent of energy production in the United States.*

   Here a main idea has been glued tight to eight subordinate elements: two subordinate clauses *(whose enormous risks . . . , that it accounts for . . .)* and six prepositional phrases *(to health and safety, of scale, in importance, with the fact, of energy production, in the United States).* The result is an unnecessarily heavy demand on the reader's patience; the sentence offers no resting place and no clear sign of its logical structure.

WITH FREE SUBORDINATION:

• Although nuclear power accounts for less than five percent of our energy production, it poses enormous risks to health and safety.

   Subordination does lead to clarity in this revision, for the comma sets the subordinate element apart from the main idea. We thus get two crucial advantages: the main idea now takes up only eight words, and the *Although* construction immedi-

sub
25b

ately tells us what the sentence's logic will be *(although x, nevertheless y).*

When you find a lengthy, labored main idea in a draft, then, look for ways of shortening it by turning bound subordinate elements into free ones.

25c Place a Free Subordinate Element Emphatically.

One important feature of free subordinate elements is that they can be moved without a radical loss of meaning. How can you tell where a free element would make the best effect? If you do not trust your ear, you can apply one of the following three principles:

1. *Explaining or placing conditions on an assertion.* If your free element explains your main idea or puts a condition on it, you should consider placing the free element *first.* In that position it will allow your reader to follow your logic from the start:

sub
25c

- *Unless scientists come up with a better explanation,* we will have to lend our belief to this one.
- *Although he finished the test in time,* he missed many of the answers.
- *Because he becomes nervous whenever he isn't listening to music,* he wears earphones while he works.

In first-draft prose, main ideas tend to come first, with limiting or explanatory elements dragging behind. Get those elements into early positions; they will show that you have the entire logic of the sentence under control. And since last positions tend to be naturally emphatic, you can generally make a stronger effect by putting your main idea after your free subordinate element.

2. *Adding to an assertion.* If your free element, instead of explaining the main idea or placing a condition on it, merely adds a further thought about it, you should place that free element *after* the main idea:

- Her smile disguised her fierce competitiveness, *a trait revealed to very few of her early teammates.*
- His life revolved around his older brother, *who never ceased making unreasonable demands.*

3. *Modifying one part of an assertion.* If your free element modifies a particular word or phrase, consider placing it *right after* that element:

- Cézanne's colors, *earthy as his native Provence,* are not adequately conveyed by reproductions.
- They gave me, *a complete newcomer,* more attention than I deserved.

A less usual but sometimes effective position is *right before* the modified element:

- *Earthy as his native Provence,* Cézanne's colors are not adequately conveyed by reproductions.

sub
25d

25d Avoid Vague Subordination.

We have already noted that subordination in itself is not automatically a good thing. Sometimes you can make a sentence more distinct not by adding subordination but by sharpening a vague subordinate element or eliminating it altogether.

In rereading your drafts, watch especially for tags like *in terms of, with regard to,* and *being as.* Such routine expressions fail to specify how the subordinated element relates to the main idea.

DON'T:

x *In terms of swimming,* she was unbeatable.

Here a rather pompous subordinate element hints at a cloudy connection between swimming and being unbeatable. The connection can be stated more straightforwardly.

DO:

- *As a swimmer* she was unbeatable.

or

- She was an unbeatable swimmer.

DON'T:

x He felt sympathetic *with regard to their position.*

DO:

- He sympathized with their position.

DON'T:

x *Being as it was noon,* everyone took a lunch break.

DO:

- Everyone took a lunch break at noon.

Other potentially vague subordinators include *with, as, as to, in the area of, in connection with, in the framework of, along the lines of, pertaining to,* and *as far as.*

**sub
25 d**

DON'T:

x *With all that he says about the English,* I believe he has misrepresented them.

DO:

- I believe he has altogether misrepresented the English.

DON'T:

x *As far as finals,* I hope to take all of them in the first two days of exam week.

> To be correct in usage the writer would have to say *As far as finals are concerned,* . . . But unless there is some special reason for singling out finals, a more concise statement would be preferable.

DO:

- I hope to take all of my finals in the first two days of exam week.

26 Emphasis and Variety

EMPHASIS

26a Match Two Elements That Belong Together.

You can write more forceful sentences by making your main ideas distinct (Chapter 24) and by highlighting them through the subordination of secondary elements (Chapter 25). In addition, you can revise to give the same grammatical structure to elements that are closely related in meaning. Such **matching,** or bringing into *parallelism* (Chapter 7), is emphatic because it makes logical relations immediately apparent to your reader. The idea is to have your grammar reinforce your meaning, not only through the choice of a main subject and verb but also through the structural aligning of key words, phrases, and clauses.

To appreciate this advantage, compare two passages that convey the same information:

  A. Animals think *of* things. They also think *at* things. Men think primarily *about* things. Words are symbols that may be combined in a thousand ways. They can also be varied in the same number of ways. This can be said of pictures as well. The same holds true for memory images.

B. Animals think, but they think *of* and *at* things; men think primarily *about* things. Words, pictures, and memory images are symbols that may be combined and varied in a thousand ways.

—SUSANNE K. LANGER, "The Lord of Creation"

Passage A, a classically choppy paragraph, takes seven sentences and fifty-one words to say what passage B says in two sentences and thirty-one words. In passage B, seven main ideas are condensed to four, with a corresponding gain in understanding. And the key to this concentration is matching—of paired clauses *(Animals think, but they think . . .),* of conspicuously equal halves of a sentence marked by a semicolon, of nouns in a series *(Words, pictures, and memory images),* and of verb forms *(combined and varied).* Passage B inspires confidence in the writer's control; we feel that she could not have packed her sentences with so much matching structure if she had not known exactly what she wanted to say.

Most instances of matching involve two items that are conspicuously equivalent in emphasis. The following table shows how such items can be matched, with or without conjunctions (joining words such as *and* and *or*).

**emph
26a**

PATTERN	EXAMPLE
x and *y*	She was tired of *waiting* and *worrying*. *(x = waiting, y = worrying)*
x or *y*	If he had continued that life, he would have faced death *in the electric chair* or *at the hands of the mob.*
x,y	He strode away, *the money in his hand, a grin on his face.*
x:y	He had *what he wanted: enough cash to buy a new life.*
x;y	*He wanted security; she wanted good times.*

As you can see from these few examples, matching can involve units as small as single words *(waiting* and *worrying)* or as large as whole statements *(he wanted security* and *she wanted good times).*

For problems of usage and punctuation arising with parallelism, see Chapter 7, pages 89–102.

26b Use Anticipatory Patterns.

In the boxed sentences above, each *y* element comes as a mild surprise; we discover that a matching structure is in process only when we reach the second item. Other matching formulas, however, anticipate the pairing of items by beginning with a "tip-off" word.

emph
26b

PATTERN	EXAMPLE
both *x* and *y*	$\overset{x}{}$ $\overset{y}{}$ *Both* guerrillas *and* loyalists pose a threat to the safety of reporters covering foreign revolutions.
either *x* or *y*	$\overset{x}{}$ *Either* reporters should be recognized as neutrals *or* they $\overset{y}{}$ should not be sent into combat zones.
neither *x* nor *y*	$\overset{x}{}$ $\overset{y}{}$ *Neither* the competition of networks *nor* the ambition of reporters justifies this recklessness.
whether *x* or *y*	Reporters must wonder, when they wake up each morning in a foreign city, *whether* they will be gunned $\overset{x}{}$ $\overset{y}{}$ down by the loyalists *or* kidnapped by the guerrillas.
more (less) *x* than *y*	$\overset{x}{}$ It is *more* important, after all, to spare the lives of $\overset{y}{}$ journalists *than* to get one more interview with the typi- cal freedom fighter.

not *x* but *y*	It is *not* the greed of the networks, however, *but* the changed nature of warfare that most endangers the lives of reporters.
not only *x* but also *y*	Now reporters covering a guerrilla war find it hard *not only* to distinguish "friendly" from "unfriendly" elements *but also* to convince each side that they are not working for the other one.
so *x* that *y*	Such reporting has become *so* risky *that* few knowledgeable journalists volunteer to undertake it.

emph
26b

Note how the first word of the anticipatory formula prepares us for the rest. As soon as we read *both* or *either* or *so*, we know what kind of logical pattern has begun; we are ready to grasp complex paired elements without losing our way. Anticipatory matching always means improved readability—provided, of course, that the grammar and punctuation of your sentence make the intended structure clear.

To see how anticipatory patterns can aid a reader, compare an imagined first-draft passage with the actual finished version:

A. He swore a lot. He would swear at absolutely anybody. For him it was just the natural thing to do. The people who worked for him probably thought he was angry at them all the time, but it wasn't necessarily true. A man like that could have been just making conversation without being angry at all, for all they knew.

B. He swore so often and so indiscriminately that his employees were sometimes not sure whether he was angry at them or merely making conversation.

—NORA EPHRON, "Seagram's with Moxie"

Passage A uses more words to make more assertions, yet it never lets us see where it is headed. Nora Ephron's more economical passage B uses two anticipatory structures—*so x and so y that z* and *whether he was x or y*—to pull elements of thought into alignment without squandering whole sentences on them.

26c Use Balance for Special Emphasis.

When a sentence uses emphatic repetition to achieve matching (26a), it shows **balance**. A balanced sentence usually does two things: (1) it *repeats a grammatical pattern,* and (2) it *repeats certain words so as to highlight key differences.* Thus the two halves of *He wanted security; she wanted good times* use the same subject-verb-object pattern and the same verb, *wanted,* in order to contrast *he* with *she* and *security* with *good times.*

You can see the ingredients of balance in the following *aphorisms,* or memorable sentences expressing very general assertions:

emph
26c

- What is *written without effort* is in general *read without pleasure.* (Samuel Johnson)
- We must indeed *all hang together,* or, most assuredly, we will *all hang separately.* (Benjamin Franklin)
- Democracy substitutes *election by the incompetent many* for *appointment by the corrupt few.* (George Bernard Shaw)

Notice in each instance how the writer has used identical sentence functions to make us confront essential differences: *written/read, effort/pleasure, together/separately, election/appointment, incompetent/ corrupt, many/few.*

The art of creating balance consists in noticing elements of sameness and contrast in a draft sentence and then rearranging your grammar so that those elements play identical grammatical roles.

DRAFT SENTENCE:
- Love of country is a virtue, but I think that it is more important today to love the human species as a whole.

BALANCED VERSION:

- Love of country is a virtue, but love of the human species is a necessity.

    The first sentence is adequately formed, but it still reads like an idea-in-the-making, the transcript of a thought process. The second, radically concise, sentence uses balance to convey authority and finality.

26d Make Your Series Consistent and Climactic.

One indispensable form of matching (26a) is the **series** of coordinated items, three or more elements in parallel sequence. A series tells your reader that the items it contains each bear the same logical relation to some other part of the sentence.

- *Declining enrollments,* $\overset{x}{}$ *obsolete audio equipment,* and $\overset{y}{}$ *hostility from the administration* $\overset{z}{}$ have hurt the language departments.

emph
26d

This says that *x, y,* and *z* are comparable factors, each making its contribution to the effect named. Such a condensed, immediately clear statement could replace as many as three rambling sentences in a draft paragraph.

Although the parts of a series must be alike in form, they may have different degrees of importance or impact. Since the final position is by far the most emphatic one, that is where the climactic item should go:

- He was prepared to risk everything—*his comfort, his livelihood, even his life.*

    If you try to put *his life* into either of the other positions in the series, you will see how vital a climactic order is.

As the example above shows, you do not always have to put *and* or *or* before the last member of a series. Omitting the conjunction can give the series an air of urgency or importance:

- A moment's *distraction, hesitation, impatience* can spell doom for an aerialist.

Again, if you want to make a crowded or overwhelmed effect, you can omit the commas and put coordinating conjunctions between all members of the series:

- No sooner does one international crisis fade from the headlines than a new one arrives, *an Angola or Nicaragua or Lebanon or El Salvador.*

For problems of usage and punctuation arising with series, see 7k and 7l, pages 101–102.

VARIETY

26e Include Significant Pauses to Combat Choppiness.

Bear in mind that your prose will be read not in isolated sentences but in whole paragraphs. You, too, should read your drafts that way, checking to see that the sentences within each paragraph sound comfortable in one another's company. If they seem abrupt and awkward, the problem may be a discontinuity of thought. Yet your sentences can be related in thought and still feel unrelated because they are too alike in structure. Watch especially for **choppy sentences**—a monotonous string of brief, plain statements containing few if any internal pauses. What you want instead is movement between relatively plain sentences and sentences that do contain pauses.

Not all pauses, however, are equally useful in providing variety for a reader. The commas between items in a series (7j, p. 101) have little effect, for those items are all "heading the same way." But even the smallest free element (25b, p. 293), properly set off by punctuation, makes for a **significant pause,** for it calls attention to the relation of one part of the sentence to another. Notice the stylistic value of effective sentence combining.

CHOPPY:

x The bill passed the Senate. It was defeated in the House.

IMPROVED:

> FREE EL
- *Although the bill passed the Senate,* it was defeated in the House.

CHOPPY:

x Our coach talked about next week's game. He said it will be crucial.

IMPROVED:

> FREE EL
- *According to our coach,* next week's game will be crucial.

CHOPPY:

x The chairman of the board decided to resign. He was mindful of the plunge in earnings.

IMPROVED:

> FREE EL
- *In view of the plunge in earnings,* the chairman of the board decided to resign.

var
26e

CHOPPY:

x Such a woman can be helpful to us. She can be our advocate.

IMPROVED:

> FREE EL
- Such a woman, *furthermore,* can help us by becoming our advocate.

In addition, a pause marked by the comma separating two independent clauses works against choppiness:

- The bill passed the Senate, but it was defeated in the House.
- Earnings plunged, and the chairman of the board decided to resign.

See Chapter 4 for the relevant comma rules.

26f Use an Occasional Question or Exclamation.

Usually an idea-in-progress appears as a succession of statements, or **declarative sentences.** But to show strong feeling, to pinpoint an issue, to challenge your reader, or simply to enliven a string of sentences, you can make use of a strategically placed question or exclamation:

- *What are we to make of such a fuss over the tiny, frigid, wind-blasted Falkland Islands?* Let us begin with the subject of off-shore oil.
- And this is all the information released so far. *Does anyone doubt that the Congressman has something to hide?*
- *A million tons of TNT!* The power of this bomb was beyond anyone's imagination.
- Once the grizzlies were deprived of garbage, their population declined steeply. *So much for the "back to nature" school of bear management!*

var
26g

Note, in the second of these examples, that the writer asks the question without expecting an answer, for the question "answers itself." Such a **rhetorical question** can work well for you in driving home an emphatic point. Since rhetorical questions have a coercive air, however, you should use them sparingly.

26g Practice the Emphatic Interruption.

To give special emphasis to one statement or piece of information, try turning it into an interruption of your sentence:

- The street Jerry lived on—*it was more like an alley than a street*—was so neighborly that he scarcely ever felt alone.
- The hot, moist summer air of Florida—*people call it an instant steambath*—makes an air conditioner a necessity in every home and office.
- A woman of strong opinions—*her last movie grossed $50 million, and she calls it a turkey*—she is not exactly a press agent's dream come true.

As you can gather, dashes are the normal means of punctuating an emphatic interruption.

In a variation on the interruptive pattern, you can begin your sentence with a lengthy element—for example, a series (26d, p. 303)—and follow it with a dash announcing that the grammatical core of the sentence is about to begin:

- *Going to hairdresser school, marrying the steady boyfriend, having the baby, getting the divorce*—everything in her life seemed to follow some dreary script.

Such a sentence takes the reader off guard by making a **false start.** We assume at first that the opening element will be the grammatical subject, but we readjust our focus when we see that the true subject will come after the dash. (The first element is actually in apposition to the subject; see 4l, p. 62.)

26h Practice Inverted Syntax.

Readers normally expect subjects to come before verbs, but for that very reason you can gain emphasis by occasionally reversing, or **inverting,** that order. The subject becomes more prominent when it is held back:

- In the beginning was the *Word.*
- Most important of all, for the would-be tourist, is a *passport* that has not expired.

Similarly, any sentence element that has been wrenched out of its normal position and placed first gets extra attention:

- *Not until then* had he understood how miserable he was.
- *Never again* will she overlook the threat of an avalanche.

Again:

- *About such a glaring scandal* nothing need be said.

The subject and verb, *nothing* and *need*, are in the usual sequence, but the writer begins with a prepositional phrase that would normally come last.

26i Practice the Cumulative Sentence.

A **cumulative sentence** is one whose main idea is followed by one or more free subordinate elements (25b, p. 293). It is called *cumulative* because it "accumulates" or collects modifying words, phrases, or clauses after the heart of the statement is complete. The following sentences, encountered earlier, are typical:

- Her smile disguised her fierce competitiveness, *a trait revealed to very few of her early teammates.*
- He was prepared to risk everything—*his comfort, his livelihood, even his life.*

- No sooner does one international crisis fade from the headlines than a new one arrives, *an Angola or Nicaragua or Lebanon or El Salvador.*

The beauty of the cumulative pattern is that it offers refinement without much risk of confusing the reader. Since the basic structure of the sentence is complete before the end-modifiers (italicized above) begin, your reader has a secure grasp of your idea, which you can then elaborate, illustrate, explain, or reflect on. And since much of our speech follows the cumulative model of statement-plus-adjustment, a cumulative sentence on the page can make a pleasantly conversational effect, as if one afterthought had brought the next one into mind.

26j Practice the Suspended Sentence.

If you substantially delay completing your main idea, forcing your reader to wait for the other shoe to drop, you have written a **suspended sentence** (often called a *periodic sentence.*) Through its use of delaying elements (italicized in the following examples), a suspended sentence can be an effective means of leading to a climax:

- It appears that their success was due more to the influence of their father, *so dominant in the worlds of business and politics that every door would open at his bidding,* than to any merits of their own.

- The states argued that they had indeed complied, *if compliance can mean making a good-faith effort and collecting all the required data,* with the federal guidelines.

- If you are still unused to the idea of gasohol, you will certainly not be ready to hear that some diesel engines will soon be running on *that most humble and ordinary of products, taken for granted by homemakers and never noticed by auto buffs,* vegetable oil.

26k Listen for Sentence Rhythm.

When rereading your draft sentences, check them for **rhythm,** or a pleasing alternation

ŏf stréssed ănd únstrĕssed sýllăbĭes.

The five words we have marked for voice stress are so rhythmical as to be *metrical*—that is, they show a regular alternation between syllables that are accented and those that are not. Meter is common in traditional verse but rare in prose, where the ideal is simply to avoid jarring effects and, insofar as possible, to make the occasional stresses emphasize your meaning rather than clash with it.

To see how the words in a completely unrhythmical sentence pull against one another, listen to this made-up example:

x The subject of rhythm in speech or writing is one of those subjects that deal with complex sets of interrelationships between multiple but not altogether specifiable variables such as rise-fall patterns and the like, which makes it a sea-to-wave and wave-to-wave kind of thing.

Significant pauses (26e, p. 304) are almost absent here; we have to plod ahead two or three words at a time, trying not to lose the idea. All the nouns, furthermore, have about the same degree of stress on their accented syllables, and there are no noticeably emphatic brief phrases among the longer ones. Read the sentence aloud and you will hear its monotony.

Now compare this with the actual words of H. W. Fowler:

> Rhythmic speech or writing is like waves of the sea, moving onward with alternating rise and fall, connected yet separate, like but different, suggestive of some law, too complex for analysis or statement, controlling the relations between wave and wave, waves and sea, phrase and phrase, phrases and speech.
>
> —H. W. FOWLER, *A Dictionary of Modern English Usage*

Although this sentence is elaborate in structure, we grasp it without much difficulty as it proceeds. Fowler's commas are like architectural supports that spare us the necessity of trying to bear the weight of the whole sentence at once. We see that one main clause is going to govern a sequence of phrases that will carry us along *like waves of the sea,* and our voice pauses naturally on accented syllables: *like wáves of the séa, móving ónward.* These long, heavily stressed vowels make a pleasing contrast with harsher, more staccato phrases like *Rhýthmic spéech or wríting.* Fowler has illustrated his principle of complex relationship in the act of naming it—as, for example, in his "like but different" sets of three-word phrases:

**var
26k**

- connected yet separate, like but different
- waves and sea, phrase and phrase, phrases and speech

To return from Fowler's example to the first one is like going from navigation to seasickness.

The lesson here is that in reading and writing you should use your ear as well as your brain. Although the principles that go to make up a pleasing rhythm are too obscure to be stated as advice, by reading good stylists you can pick up a feeling for graceful and emphatic cadences.

F WORDS

Words

To convey your ideas successfully, you need to know words well and to respect their often subtle differences from one another. Specifically, when revising your drafts you should make sure that your words

1. *mean what you think they mean;*

2. *are appropriate to the occasion;*

3. *are concise;*

4. *are neither stale, roundabout, nor needlessly abstract;*

5. *show control over figurative, or nonliteral, implications; and*

6. *use "sound effects" to the advantage of your meaning.*

Chapters 27 and 28 discuss these requirements of **diction,** *or word choice, concentrating first on appropriateness of meaning and then on ways of imparting vividness and energy to your language. In Chapter 29 you will find an alphabetical list of expressions that cause diction problems for many student writers.*

27 Appropriate Meaning

27a Use Your College Dictionary.

To make progress in your control of **denotation,** or the dictionary meaning of words, it is essential that you own a college dictionary such as *The Random House College Dictionary, Funk and Wagnalls Standard College Dictionary, Webster's New World Dictionary of the American Language, Webster's New Collegiate Dictionary,* or *The American Heritage Dictionary of the English Language.* These volumes are large enough to meet your daily needs without being too cumbersome to carry around. Once you learn from the prefatory guide to your dictionary how to interpret its abbreviations, symbols, and order of placing entries, you can find in it most—perhaps all—of the following kinds of information:

spelling	usage levels
parts of speech	syllable division
definitions	principles of usage
synonyms	abbreviations
antonyms	symbols
alternate forms	biographical and given names
pronunciation	places and population figures
capitalization	weights and measures
derivations	names and locations of colleges

To see what a college dictionary can and cannot do, look at *Random House*'s entry under *fabulous:*

a. spelling and syllable divisions

d. part of speech

c. pronunciation

f. derivation

b. main accent

e. definitions

> **fab•u•lous** (fab′yə ləs), *adj.* **1.** almost unbelievable; incredible. **2.** exceptionally good or unusual; marvelous; superb. **3.** told or known through fables, myths, or legends. [<L *fābulōs(us)*] — **fab′u•lous•ly,** *adv.* — **fab′u•lous•ness,** *n.* — **Syn. 1.** amazing, astonishing, astounding. **3.** fabled. — **Ant. 1.** usual. **3.** actual, historical.

g. other parts of speech

i. antonyms

h. synonyms

The entry shows, in the following order:

mean
27a

a. how the word is spelled and the points where syllable divisions occur *(fab-u-lous);*

Comment: The lower-case *f* shows that *fabulous* is not normally capitalized.

If this word could be spelled correctly in different ways, the less common form would appear in a separate entry with a cross reference to the more common form; thus the entry for *reenforce* merely sends you to *reinforce*. In your writing, use the spelling under which a full definition has been given.

Syllable division is not completely uniform from one dictionary to another, but you cannot go wrong by following your dictionary's practice in every case. (You can also spare yourself trouble by not breaking up words at all; a little unevenness in right-hand margins is normal.)

b. where the main accent falls *(fab′);*

Comment: If the word has another strongly stressed syllable, like *hand* in *beforehand,* you would find it marked with a secondary accent: *bi • for′* hand′.

c. how the word is pronounced;

Comment: The pronunciation key at the bottom of every pair of pages reveals, among other things, that ə = *a* as in *alone.* (One dictionary's key will differ from another's.) College dictionaries make no attempt to capture regional or nonstandard pronunciations, like *x* n$\overline{oo}$′ *kul • ər* for n$\overline{oo}$′kl$\overline{e}$ *ər (nuclear).*

d. the part of speech *(adj.* for *adjective);*

Comment: Some words, like *can* and *wait,* occupy more than one part of speech, depending on the context. Definitions are grouped according to those parts of speech. Transitive verbs (those that take an object—1a, p. 5) are usually listed separately from intransitive verbs (those that take no object). Thus *Random House* gives all the intransitive senses of *wait (v.i.),* as in *Wait for me,* before the transitive senses *(v.t.),* as in *Wait your turn!*

e. three definitions of *fabulous;*

Comment: No dictionary lists definitions in the order of their acceptability. The dictionary illustrated here begins with the most common part of speech occupied by a given word and, within each part of speech, offers the most frequently encountered meaning first. Some other dictionaries begin with the earliest meaning and proceed toward the present. The system used in your dictionary is clearly set forth in the prefatory material, which you should read through at least once.

mean 27a

f. the word's derivation from the first three syllables of the Latin word *fabulosus;*

Comment: The derivation or *etymology* of a word is given only if its component parts are not obviously familiar—as they are, for example, in *freeze-dry* and *nearsighted.* Many symbols are used in stating etymologies; look for their explanation in the prefatory material of your dictionary.

g. an adverb and a noun stemming from the main word;

> *Comment: Fabulously* and *fabulousness* are "run-on entries," words formed by adding a suffix (18f, p. 209) to the main entry.

h. synonyms of definitions 1 and 3;

> *Comment:* In most dictionaries a word with many apparent synonyms—words having the same or nearly the same meaning—is accompanied by a "synonym study" explaining fine differences. Thus, this dictionary's entry for *strength* concludes:

> **—Syn. 4.** STRENGTH, POWER, FORCE, MIGHT suggest capacity to do something. STRENGTH is inherent capacity to manifest energy, to endure, and to resist. POWER is capacity to do work and to act. FORCE is the exercise of power: *One has the power to do something. He exerts force when he does it. He has sufficient strength to complete it.* MIGHT is power or strength in a great degree: *the might of an army.*

nean
27a

This would be useful information if you were wondering which of the four similar words to use in a sentence. If you looked up *power, force,* or *might,* you would find a cross reference to the synonym study under *strength.*

i. antonyms (words with the opposite meaning) of definitions 1 and 3.

> *Comment:* If you are searching for a word to convey the opposite of a certain term, check its listed antonyms. But if you still are not satisfied, look up the entries for the most promising antonyms and check their synonyms. This will greatly expand your range of choice.

So much for *fabulous.* But other sample entries would reveal still further kinds of information:

1. *inflected forms.* Some entries show unusual inflected forms—
that is, changes in spelling expressing different syntactic functions. You will find unusual plurals *(louse, lice)*; unusual principal parts of verbs *(run, ran, run*—see 15b, p. 173); pronoun
forms *(I, my, mine,* etc.); comparative and superlative degrees
of adjectives *(good, better, best*—see 17a, p. 195).

2. *restrictive labels.* The entry will show how a word's use may be
limited to a particular region *(Southern U.S., Austral., Chiefly
Brit.);* to an earlier time or a particular occasion *(Archaic, Obs.,
Poetic)*; to a particular subject *(Bot., Anat., Law);* and, most
important for the writer, to a level of usage for words not clearly
within standard American English *(Nonstandard, Informal,
Slang).*

3. *usage study.* Beyond its usage labels, your dictionary may offer
especially valuable discussions of usage problems surrounding
certain controversial words or meanings, such as *ain't, different
from/than,* or *hardly* with negative forms:

> —**Usage.** HARDLY, BARELY, and SCARCELY all
> have a negative connotation, and the use of any
> of them with a supplementary negative is con-
> sidered nonstandard, as in *I can't hardly wait* for
> *I can hardly wait.*

**mean
27b**

27b Keep a Vocabulary List.

The only way to be certain that you have broadened your written
vocabulary is to try out new words in your papers, risking an occasional inaccuracy while gradually building your store of useful words.
But how are you to acquire those words in the first place?

Many student writers rely heavily on a *thesaurus,* or dictionary of
synonyms and antonyms. Synonyms, however, are rarely exact, and
the thesaurus will not indicate fine differences of meaning. If you
consult a thesaurus, do so to jog your memory of words already known,

not to get fancy new language into your prose. The best way to build vocabulary is to notice how unfamiliar words are used by published authors and to keep a record of your discoveries.

By taking the following steps, you can systematically increase the number of words whose meanings you have mastered:

1. Whenever someone criticizes your use of a word or you come across an unfamiliar word in your reading, look it up or make a note of it until you can get back to your dictionary.

2. After you have looked it up, write the word and its definition in a section of your notebook set aside for useful words.

3. Every time you add an entry, quickly scan the previous entries to see if you have mastered them yet. Cross out entries that you now consider to be part of your normal working vocabulary.

To supplement your vocabulary list, go over the Index of Diction in Chapter 29 (pp. 341–366). Make an entry for each word whose indicated meaning is new to you. Note especially those terms that get easily confused (*affect* versus *effect, imply* versus *infer,* etc.). If you tend to use either term in the pair incorrectly, add both of them to your list.

27c Use Words in Established Senses.

English is probably the fastest-changing of all languages, and yesterday's error often becomes today's standard usage. As a writer, however, you should be concerned not with anticipating shifts in taste but with communicating your ideas effectively. Many readers are upset by diction that is being used in some capricious or momentarily popular way. By being conservative in your choice of words, you can avoid arousing automatically negative responses to the content of your work.

Many fad words have a common feature: they usually belong to one part of speech but are being used as another. Sometimes a suffix (18f, p. 209) such as -*wise* or -*type* has been added to turn a noun into an adjective or adverb.

DON'T:

x *Gaswise,* the car is economical.

x *Preferencewise,* she is looking for a *commuter-type* car.

DO:

• The car gets good mileage.

• She wants a car suitable for commuting.

More often, one part of speech simply takes over another.

DON'T:

x It was a *fun* party.

x She *authored* the book in 1983.

x We *gifted* the newlyweds with a toaster.

x Mark is a *together* person.

x I would give anything for an *invite* to the party.

DO:

• The party was *fun.*

• She *wrote* the book in 1983.

• We *gave* the newlyweds a toaster.

• Mark is a *confident, competent* person.

• I would give anything for an *invitation* to the party.

mean
27c

The use of nouns as adjectives deserves special mention in an age of spreading bureaucracy. Standard English allows many such *attributive nouns,* as they are called, as in *mountain time, night vision, cheese omelet,* and *recreation director.* But officials have a way of jamming them together in a confusing heap. A frugal governor, for example, once proposed what he called a *community work experience program demonstration project.* This row of nouns was meant to describe, or perhaps to conceal, a policy of getting welfare mothers to pick up highway litter without receiving any wages. As a student writer, you would be wise to avoid changing the customary part of speech of a word or piling up attributive nouns.

27d Control Connotations.

The prime requirement for controlling meaning is to know the *denotations,* or dictionary definitions, of the words you use. (See 27a and 27b.) But words also have important **connotations**—further suggestions or associations derived from the contexts in which the words have been habitually used. By and large, you will not find connotations in your dictionary; you have to pick them up from meeting the same words repeatedly in reading and conversation. Of course you cannot expect to learn all the overtones of every English word. But as a writer you can ask yourself whether the words you have allowed into your first drafts are appropriate to the occasion. When you are unsure, think of related words until you find one that conveys appropriate associations.

Take, for example, the words *store, shop,* and *boutique.* Because of the contexts in which the words most often appear, they *connote* different things. When we think of a *store,* we think of an establishment where merchandise is sold. A *shop* suggests a smaller establishment selling a specific type of goods, or a department in a larger store, such as the *card shop* at Field's. A *boutique* is a small shop that specializes in fashionable items, often clothing or accessories for women. If you were writing about the corner grocery that keeps your neighborhood in bread, milk, and other staples seven days a week, you would want to call it a *store.* To call it a *shop* or a *boutique* would undercut your purpose in pointing out the establishment's diverse and ordinary stock.

Consider two further examples, *complex* versus *complicated* and *workers* versus *employees.* Although the members of each pair are close in denotation, their connotations differ. Suppose you wanted to characterize an overelaborate instruction manual. Would you call it *complex* or *complicated?* We hope you would choose *complicated,* which can imply not just intricacy but more intricacy than is called for. And if you were criticizing harsh factory conditions, you would want to write about mistreated *workers,* not mistreated *employees.* These words denote the same people, yet *employees* characterizes them from a corporate point of view, whereas *workers* calls to mind laborers whose interests and loyalties may be quite different from those of the company.

Note that there is such a thing as getting connotations too lopsidedly in favor of your own position on an issue. Suppose, for example, you were writing an essay about discourtesy among adolescents. If you chose the term *young thugs* to characterize teenagers, you would certainly be making your feelings clear, but you would also be *prejudging* your thesis (31d, p. 390), forcing your reader to respond emotionally with you or against you. In revising your essays, tone down any inflammatory language that seems to convey ready-made conclusions.

27e Avoid Racist and Sexist Language.

Since you are writing to convince, not to insult, nothing can be gained from using offensive terms. Racial slurs like *nigger, honky,* and *wop,* demeaning stereotypes like *pushy Jew* and *dumb Swede,* and sexually biased phrases such as *lady driver, female logic,* and *typical male brutality* make any fair-minded reader turn against the writer.

The problem of sexism in language deserves special discussion because it goes beyond any conscious wish to show prejudice. In recent decades people have been increasingly realizing that long-accepted conventions of word choice imply that women are inferior or are destined for restricted roles. To keep sexist language out of your prose, then, it is not enough to avoid grossly insulting terms like *tomato* and *broad;* you must be watchful for subtler signs of condescension as well.

If, for example, you call William Shakespeare *Shakespeare,* why should you call Emily Dickinson *Miss Dickinson* or, worse, *Emily?* Such names imply that a woman who writes poems is not really a poet but a "poetess," a "lady poet," or even a "spinster poet." Write about *Dickinson's poetry,* thus giving it the same standing you would the work of any other author. Similarly, use *sculptor* and *lawyer* for both sexes, avoiding such designations as *sculptress* and *lady lawyer.* And do without *coed,* which suggests that the higher education of women is an afterthought to the real (male) thing. Make your language reflect the fact that, in North America at any rate, men and women are now considered equally eligible for nearly every role except those of mother and father.

mean
27e

Tact is necessary, however, in deciding how far to go in changing traditional expressions. The ideal is to avoid sexism without sacrificing clarity and ease of expression. If you wrote *actor* for *actress* and *waiter* for *waitress,* for example, your readers would be confused; rightly or wrongly, common usage still recognizes separate terms for male and female performers of those functions. But when in doubt, choose a sex-neutral term: not *mankind* but *humanity,* not *man-made* but *artificial.*

-Person

Try to find nonsexist alternatives to awkward *-person* suffixes, which sound ugly to many readers of both sexes.

SEXIST	NONSEXIST BUT AWKWARD	PREFERABLE
chairman	chairperson	chair, head
Congressman	Congressperson	Representative
mailman	mailperson	letter carrier
policeman	policeperson	officer
weatherman	weatherperson	meteorologist

**mean
27e**

The Pronoun Dilemma

Perhaps the sorest of all issues in contemporary usage is that of the so-called **common gender.** Which pronouns should you use when discussing an indefinite person, a "one"? Traditionally, that indefinite person has been "male": *he, his, him,* as in *A taxpayer must check his return carefully.* For the centuries in which this practice went unchallenged, the masculine pronouns in such sentences were understood to designate not actual men but people of either sex. Today, however, many readers find those words an offensive reminder of second-class citizenship for women. Remedies that have been proposed include using the phrase *he or she* (or *she or he*) for the common gender, treating singular common words as plural *(A taxpayer must check* *their return),* combining masculine and feminine pronouns in forms like *s/he,* and using *she* in one sentence and *he* in the next.

Unfortunately, all of these solutions carry serious drawbacks. Continual repetition of *he or she* is cumbersome and monotonous; many readers would regard *A taxpayer must check their return* as a blunder, not a blow for liberation; pronunciation of *s/he* is uncertain; and the use of *she* and *he* in alternation, though increasingly common, risks confusing the reader by implying that two indefinite persons, a female and a male, are involved.

To avoid such awkwardness, follow these five guidelines:

1. Use *she* whenever you are sure the indefinite person would be female (a student in a women's college, for example):

    • Someone who enters a nunnery must sacrifice everything from *her* former life.

2. Do not use *she* for roles that have been "traditionally female" but are actually mixed: secretary, school teacher, laundry worker, etc. Female pronouns in such contexts imply an offensive prejudgment about "women's place." Use plural forms to show a sex-neutral attitude.

DON'T:
x A kindergarten teacher has *her* hands full every day.

DO:
• Kindergarten teachers have *their* hands full every day.

mean
27e

3. Use an occasional *he or she* or *she or he* to indicate an indefinite person:

    • When a driver is stopped for a traffic violation, *he or she* would do well to remain polite.

    But be sparing with this formula; it can quickly become annoying.

4. Avoid the singular whenever your meaning is not affected.

DON'T:

x A taxpayer must check *his* return.

DO:

• Taxpayers must check *their* returns.

5. Omit the pronoun altogether whenever you can do so without awkwardness.

ACCEPTABLE:

• Everyone needs *his or her* vacation.

BETTER:

• Everyone needs *a* vacation.

27f Avoid Jargon.

Jargon is specialized language that appears in a nonspecialized context, thus giving a technical flavor to statements that would be better expressed in everyday words. When you are writing a paper in, say, economics, anthropology, or psychology, you can and should use terms that are meaningful within the field: *liquidity, kinship structure, paranoid,* and so forth. But those same terms become jargon when used out of context.

mean
27f

DON'T:

x My liquidity profile has been weak lately.

DO:

• I have been short of cash lately.

DON'T:

x Her kinship structure extends from coast to coast.

DO:

• Her family is scattered from coast to coast.

DON'T:

x Roland was really paranoid about the boss's intentions.

DO:

• Roland was suspicious of the boss's intentions.

Most jargon today comes from popular academic disciplines such as sociology and psychology, from government bureaucracy, and from the world of computers. Here is some of the more commonly seen jargon, accompanied by everyday equivalents that would usually be preferable.

JARGON	ORDINARY TERM
access (v.)	enter, make use of
behaviors	acts, deeds, conduct
correlation	resemblance, association
cost-effective	economical
counterproductive	harmful, obstructive
ego	vanity, pride
facilitate	help, make possible
feedback	response
finalize	complete
input	response, contribution
interface (v.)	meet, share information with
maximize	make the most of
obsession	strong interest
parameters	borders
prioritize	prefer, rank
reinforcement schedule	inducements
sociological	social
syndrome	pattern
trauma	shock
user-friendly	uncomplicated

mean
27f

You can put jargon to good comic or ironic use, but when you find it appearing uninvited in your drafts, revise.

27g Avoid Euphemisms.

A **euphemism** is a squeamishly "nice" expression standing in the place of a more direct one. Some words that began as euphemisms, such as *senior citizen* and *funeral director,* have passed into common usage, but you should try to avoid terms that still sound like ways of covering up a meaning instead of conveying it. Euphemisms often conceal a devious political or commercial motive. If you want to be regarded as candid and trustworthy, do not write *discomfort* for *pain, memory garden* for *cemetery, pass away* for *die, relocation center* for *concentration camp,* and so forth.

DON'T:

x The Governor is concerned about *human resources development.*

DO:

• The Governor is concerned about *unemployment.*

DON'T:

x The candidate issued a press release *declaring* that her earlier remarks about her opponent were now to be considered *inoperative.*

DO:

• The candidate issued a press release *admitting* that her earlier remarks about her opponent had been *untrue.*

DON'T:

x We are recalling all late models because the bearings *at variance with production code specifications* may *adversely affect vehicle control.*

DO:

• We are recalling all late models because the *defective* bearings may cause drivers to *lose control of the steering.*

**mean
27g**

28 Liveliness

28a Prefer Middle Diction in Most Contexts.

Different situations call for different levels of diction (word choice), from the slang that may be appropriate in a letter to a friend, to the formal language expected in a legal document, to the technical terms demanded by a scientific report. But whenever you are writing outside such special contexts, you should aim for **middle diction**—language that is neither too casual to convey serious concern nor too stiff to express feeling.

The best way to recognize levels of diction is to be an observant reader of different kinds of prose and a close listener to conversations. But if you have studied Latin or a "Latinate" modern language such as Spanish, French, or Italian, you have a head start toward spotting formal English diction. All the words in the right column below are both formal and Latinate:

SLANG	MIDDLE DICTION	FORMAL DICTION
mug	**face**	visage
kicks	**pleasure**	gratification
threads	**clothes**	attire
specs	**glasses**	spectacles
rip off	**steal**	expropriate
big-mouthed	**talkative**	voluble

28b Be Concise.

Your reader's attention will depend in large part on the ratio between information and language in your prose. **Wordiness,** or the use of more words than are necessary to convey a point, is one of the most common and easily corrected flaws of style. The fewer words you can use without harm to your meaning, the better.

WORDY	CONCISE
among all the problems that exist today	among all current problems
an investment in the form of stocks and bonds	an investment in stocks and bonds
at the present time	now
due to the fact that	because
during the course of	during
for the purpose of getting rich	to get rich
for the simple reason that	because
in a very real sense	truly
in spite of the fact that	although
in the not too distant future	soon
in view of the fact that	since
it serves no particular purpose	it serves no purpose
majoring in the field of astronomy	majoring in astronomy
my personal perference	my preference
on the part of	by
owing to the fact that	because
proceeded to walk	walked
rarely ever	rarely
seldom ever	seldom
the present incumbent	the incumbent
to the effect that	that

livel 28b

Avoiding Redundancy

A **redundancy** is an expression that conveys the same meaning more than once—for example, *circle around,* which says "go around around." The difference between writing *She circled the globe* and x *She circled around the globe* is that in the second version the word *around* delivers no new information and thus strains the reader's patience.

Examine your drafts to see if they contain redundancies, and be uncompromising in pruning them. The following examples are typical.

REDUNDANT	CONCISE
adequate enough	adequate
advance planning	planning
both together	both
but yet	but
contributing factor	factor
deliberate lie	lie
equally as far	as far
exact same symptoms	same symptoms
few in number	few
final outcome	outcome
free gift	gift
join together	join
large in size	large
past experience	experience
past history	history
refer back	refer
set of twins	twins
share in common	share
shuttle back and forth	shuttle
two different reasons	two reasons

livel 28b

Avoiding Circumlocution

All redundancies fall into the broader category of **circumlocutions**—that is, roundabout forms of expression. But some circumlocutions, instead of saying the same thing twice, take several words to say almost nothing. Formulas like *in a manner of speaking* or *to make a long story short,* for example, are simply ways of making a short story long. Watch especially for cumbersome verb phrases like *give rise to, make contact with,* and *render inoperative;* prefer *arouse, meet, destroy.* And if you mean *because,* do not reach for *due to the fact that.* When five words do the work of one, all five are anemic.

CIRCUMLOCUTION	CONCISE EXPRESSION
He was of a kindly nature.	He was kind.
It was of an unusual character.	It was unusual.
My father and I have differences about dating.	My father and I differ about dating.
At this point in time . . .	Now . . .
I finally made contact with my supervisor.	I finally met my supervisor.
The copy that is pink in color is for yourself.	Keep the pink copy.
She suspected she would be in an unemployment-type kind of situation when the overflow of customers due to the Christmas shopping circumstances was no longer in effect.	She suspected she would be laid off after the Christmas rush.

livel
28c

28c Prune Intensifiers.

In conversation most of us use **intensifiers**—"fortifying" words like *absolutely, basically, certainly, definitely, incredibly, intensely, just, of course, perfectly, positively, quite, really, simply,* and *very*—without pausing to worry about their meaning. And in telling stories or expressing opinions we veer toward the extremes of *fantastic, terrific, sensational, fabulous,* and *awful, horrible, terrible, dreadful.* Our listeners know how to allow for such exaggeration. Most written prose, however, aims at a more measured tone. Look through your drafts for intensifiers, and see how many of them you can eliminate without subtracting from your meaning. Your revised work will not only be more concise and therefore less taxing to read, it will also sound more assured. Readers sense that intensifiers are morale-building words meaning *maybe* or *I hope;* doing without such terms is a sign of your confidence that you are making a sound case for your ideas.

WITH INTENSIFIERS:

x It was another *very* routine start to a two-week vacation. I *definitely* had no fixed plans other than *simply* flying to Denver. I knew Colorado was a *fantastic* state, and *basically* that is all I thought about as I settled into my assigned seat. As the aircraft door was about to be closed, a man walked in and occupied the vacant seat next to me. He mumbled something to me in an *absolutely* foreign accent. The departure was *very* uneventful. All we *really* did was try to kill time, but the book he was reading *just* attracted my interest: *Cave Exploring in the USA.* I *certainly* was curious and asked him if cave exploring interested him. That was when he explained—*incredibly*—that in France he was a professional cave explorer. After the dinner service ended we talked, and his stories of days underground were *positively* fascinating. Finally, he invited me to join him, and I *quite* happily accepted.

**level
28c**

WITHOUT INTENSIFIERS:

• It was another routine start to a two-week vacation. I had no fixed plans other than flying to Denver. I knew Colorado was an exceptional state, and that is all I thought about as I settled into my assigned seat. As the aircraft door was about to be closed, a man walked in and occupied the vacant seat next to me. He mumbled something in a foreign accent. The departure was uneventful. All we did was try to kill time, but the book he was reading attracted my interest: *Cave Exploring in the USA.* I was curious and asked him if cave exploring interested him. That was when he explained that in France he was a professional cave explorer. After the dinner service ended we talked; his stories of days underground were fascinating. Finally, he invited me to join him, and I happily accepted.

28d Put Your Statements in Positive Form.

Negative ideas are just as legitimate as positive ones; you may have to point out that something did not happen or that an argument leaves you unconvinced. But the negative modifiers *no* and *not* sometimes make for wordiness and a slight loss of readability. If you write *We are not in agreement,* you are asking your reader to go through two steps, first to conceive of agreement and then to negate it. But if you simply write *We disagree,* you have saved three words and simplified the mental operation. The gain is small, but good writing results from a sum of small gains.

Of course you need not develop a phobia against every use of *no* or *not.* Observe, however, that negatively worded sentences tend to be slightly less emphatic than positive ones. Compare:

NEGATIVE	POSITIVE
She did not do well on the test.	She did poorly on the test.
He was not convicted.	He was acquitted.
They have no respect for rationing.	They despise rationing.
It was not an insignificant amount.	It was a significant amount.

livel 28e

28e Avoid Clichés.

A **cliché** is a trite, stereotyped, overused expression such as *throw money around* or *bring the house down.* Clichés are *dead metaphors* —that is, they are figures of speech that no longer sound figurative. When someone writes *off the wall* or *the bottom line,* no reader sees a wall or a line. On the other hand, a writer could blunder into causing people to see real bricks by saying *On the first day that June worked in the construction crew, Steve fell for her like a ton of bricks.* (For such accidentally revived clichés, see 28g, p. 338.) But the usual effect of clichés is not unintended comedy but simple boredom. The reader feels that the writer is settling for prepackaged language instead of finding the exact words to convey a particular thought. And matters are not improved by the apologetic addition of *so to speak* or *as the saying goes*. When you need to apologize for any expression, change it.

The worst thing about cliché-ridden prose is its predictability. As soon as we register one element of the cliché, the rest of it leaps to mind like an advertising jingle:

pleasingly . . . plump

lines of . . . communication

the foreseeable . . . future

the pieces . . . of the puzzle . . . fall into place

The resultant prose—*to be brutally frank*—is a *far cry* from being a *sure winner* in the *hearts and minds* of readers *from every walk of life*.

Three lists of clichés follow. List A includes examples of gross clichés, which you can spot fairly easily and eradicate as you revise. List B includes less obvious clichés, pairs of seemingly inseparable adjectives and nouns, clusters that choke out your originality as a writer. List C consists of pat expressions that say too little in a wordy and predictable manner.

livel
28e

LIST A: GROSS CLICHÉS

a needle in a haystack	quiet as a mouse
blind as a bat	rule with an iron fist
carve a niche for oneself	sly as a fox
drive one to distraction	smart as a whip
happy as a lark	sow one's wild oats
live like a king	the top of the heap
make a beeline for	tough as nails
old as the hills	

LIST B: "INSEPARABLE" PAIRS

bounce back	supreme moment
flawless complexion	tempestuous affair
grave danger	unforeseen obstacles
high spirits	vicious circle
integral part	vital role
nuclear holocaust	

LIST C: PAT EXPRESSIONS

after all is said and done	in this day and age
at this point in time	it goes without saying
far be it from me	it stands to reason
in a very real sense	once and for all
in the final [last] analysis	

28f   Revise toward Concreteness.

livel
28f

Concrete words name observable things or properties like *classroom* and *smoky*; **abstract** words convey ideas like *education* and *pollution*—nonphysical things that we can grasp only with our minds, not with our senses. Of course there are gradations between the extremes: a *university* is more concrete than *education* but less so than a *classroom,* a distinct physical place. The more concrete the term, the more vivid it will be to a reader.

Whenever you are describing something or telling a story, you can hardly go wrong by making your successive drafts more concrete. Suppose you are trying to characterize your new typewriter, which you have praised in your first draft as *extremely modern.* That is an abstract judgment that could mean anything to anyone. What precisely is modern about the machine? In revising, think about *the daisy wheel printing unit, the automatic return, the automatic correction, the sixteen-character memory, the programmable margin settings,* and so forth. Get the concrete details into your essay, convincing your reader that your general statements rest on observations.

Even in papers of explanation and argument (30a, p. 372), where the thesis is necessarily an abstract idea, concrete language will help you provide supporting details and retain your reader's interest. Here, for example, are two versions of a student paragraph. In drafting the first, the writer was evidently thinking of himself as a social-science major. When asked to revise for an essay audience, he looked for ways of turning abstract statements into concrete ones:

A. Lasting trauma from early stress is probably causally related to two factors: heritability of susceptibility and the age at which the stress occurs. In infant rhesus monkeys, certain members of the experimental population prove more susceptible to permanent disturbance than others; heritability is thus an indicated factor. Furthermore, the entire population yields a finding of greater vulnerability when administration of stress occurs between the precise ages of two and seven months. Such a finding suggests that among humans, too, a period of maximum vulnerability may obtain.

B. A recent study of rhesus monkeys may offer us some clues to the way people react—and sometimes don't react—to early stress. Baby monkeys who have been put into solitary cages tend to become feisty and to stay that way. We might have expected as much. But some monkeys, oddly, act normal again almost as soon as they have rejoined their fellows; it seems that they have inherited a resistance to trauma. Furthermore, the most aggressive monkeys turn out to be those who were isolated within a precise period, between the ages of two and seven months. If these findings carry over to humans, we can see why it is risky to generalize about the effects of *all* early stress. What matters may not be whether you suffered in infancy, but who your parents were and exactly when your ordeal occurred.

livel
28f

Neither of these paragraphs abounds in concrete language, but the relative concreteness of passage B helps to explain why it is easier to grasp and more pleasurable to read. Note that weighty, awkward abstractions like *heritability of susceptibility* have disappeared and that we now see *Baby monkeys . . . in solitary cages,* not a *population* that has undergone *administration of stress.*

28g Sharpen Your Figurative Language.

If you think about an essay topic imaginatively as well as rational-
ly, you will find yourself likening the material before you to other
things. Such resemblances can lead you to choose a comparison-and-
contrast framework for the whole essay or, on a smaller scale, to use
an occasional *analogy* (30i, p. 385) to make a point more vivid. But
even on the level of single words and phrases you can heighten interest
and clarity by stating one thing in terms of another. The nonliteral
diction that expresses imaginative comparison is called **figurative
language.**

Simile and Metaphor

Two closely related figures of speech allow you to draw imaginative
likenesses. A **simile,** by including the word *like* or *as,* explicitly acknowledges that a comparison is being made.

SIMILE:

- *Like* a patio rotisserie, George's mind always keeps turning at
  the same slow rate, no matter what is impaled on it.

  George's mind is explicitly compared to a rotisserie.

livel
28g

A **metaphor** omits *like* or *as.*

METAPHOR:

- George's hedgeclipper mind gives a suburban sameness to everything it touches.

  George's mind is compared to hedgeclippers, but without either
  of the explicit terms of comparison, *like* or *as.*

In theory a metaphor is a more radical figure of speech than a
simile, for it asserts an identity, not just a likeness, between two
things (George's mind "is" a gardening tool). But in practice one kind
of figure can be as striking as the other. What counts is not the choice
between simile and metaphor but the suitability of the *image,* or word
picture, to your intended meaning. The two images about George, for
example, call to mind not only his conformism but also his specifically
suburban background (the carefully tended hedge, the patio rotisserie).

The Extended Figure of Speech

If you do have a suitable image, you may find that it is not altogether self-explanatory. Without running the image into the ground, you can sometimes add a sentence or two that clarifies its implications. Thus a student writer *extended* her simile:

- For me, the idea of going on for an advanced degree is like that of rowing across the ocean. Perhaps I could do it and perhaps I couldn't. But what, I wonder, is waiting for me on the other side, and isn't there some faster and safer way of getting there? Until I know the answers to these questions, I intend to keep my feet planted on familiar soil.

So, too, a professional author added a clarifying sentence of elaboration to a striking simile:

- This generation thinks—and this is its thought of thoughts—that nothing faithful, vulnerable, fragile can be durable or have any true power. Death waits for these things as a cement floor waits for a dropping light bulb. The brittle shell of glass loses its tiny vacuum with a burst, and that is that.

—SAUL BELLOW, *Herzog*

level
28g

In either of these passages one further sentence might have produced tedium. Both images are pursued just long enough to give us the full thought lying behind them.

Avoiding Mixed Metaphor

If you remain aware of the fact that you are using figurative language and if you check to see that each image is carried through in a consistent way, you will avoid the embarrassment of **mixed metaphor**— the clashing of one image with another.

MIXED METAPHOR:

x Although some analysts feel that the Presidential primary system is the wrong game plan for choosing the best nominee, they forget that primaries are an important mirror and proving ground of our democracy. To be sure, candidates can get burned out on the hustings. ·

> But by diving into the very heart of state and county politics, the survivors of this pressure cooker can acquire a hands-on feeling for the people they hope to govern.

This passage begins with a sports metaphor, *game plan,* but before the first sentence is over we have been taken through two more incompatible images, a *mirror* and a *proving ground.* The next sentence tells us that candidates can get *burned out on the hustings* (literally, speaking platforms)—a mixed metaphor that unintentionally suggests a public execution. And finally, those candidates who survive the *pressure cooker* are said to be *diving into* a *heart* where they can get a *hands-on feeling.* Emergency surgery in the kitchen? Clearly, this writer likes to reach for the handiest figurative language without taking responsibility for its implications.

EFFECTIVE METAPHOR:

- A tiger in the jungle of politics, he was a pussycat around the house.

  —CLIFTON DANIEL, "Presidents I Have Known"

  The images of *tiger* and *pussycat* are closely related, and the writer (characterizing his father-in-law, Harry Truman) fully controls the different implications of the two terms.

livel 28g

- Technology has given Goliath a club so heavy he cannot lift it. And it has given every David a sling: mass communications.

  —LEWIS M. BRANSCOMB, "Taming Technology"

  The figures of David and Goliath are drawn from the same biblical story. The extended metaphor neatly captures the writer's thesis: that technology is of more value to the "little people" of the world than to governments and corporations.

Perhaps you feel that you can avoid mixed metaphors by shunning figurative language altogether. But insofar as you do, your prose will be flat and colorless. Besides, it is not really possible to be completely unfigurative. Many ordinary terms and nearly all clichés (28e, p. 332) are *"dead metaphors"*—that is, they contain the faint implication of an image which we are not supposed to notice as such (the *leg* of a table, a *blade* of grass). When clichés are used in close succession, they mischievously come back to life as mixed metaphors:

x *Climbing to the heights* of oratory, the candidate *tackled* the issue.

x Either we *get a handle* on these problems or we are all *going down the drain.*

x You can't *sit on your hands* if a recession is developing, because *you don't know where the bottom is.*

x This was a report on *the population of the United States broken down by age and sex.*

Figurative language, then, can be tricky. When you intend an abstract meaning, you have to make sure that your dead metaphors stay good and dead. But when you do wish to be figurative, see whether your image is vivid, fresh, and consistent. Literal statement may be safe, but a striking figure carried through consistently can unify and intensify your sentences.

28h Watch for Sound Patterns.

Knowing that repeated sounds draw attention, you can sometimes use them deliberately, as Mark Twain did in referring to

* the *calm confidence* of a *Christian* with four aces,

livel
28h

or as Thomas Paine did in writing

* These are the *times* that *try* men's souls,

or as Theodore Roosevelt did in advising his countrymen to

* *Speak softly* and carry a big *stick.*

In these examples the "poetic" quality goes along with the effort to make a concisely emphatic statement.

Unless you are after some such effect, however, beware of making your reader conscious of rhymes *(the side of the hide)* or alliteration *(pursuing particular purposes)* or repeated syllables *(apart from the apartment).* These snatches of "poetry" usually result from an unconscious attraction that words already chosen exert on subsequent choices. Having written *the degradation,* you write *of the nation* because the *-ation* sound is in your head. You may have to read your first draft aloud, attending to its sound and not its sense, in order to find where you have lapsed into jingling.

Abstract Latinate words—the ones that usually end in *-al, -ity, -ation,* or *-otion*—are especially apt to make a repetitive sound pattern. It is worth the pains to rewrite, for example, if you find bunched words like *functional, essential, occupational,* and *institutional* or *equality, opportunity, parity,* and *mobility.*

Finally, watch for clusters of prepositions that stand out annoyingly:

x A lot *of* journalists *of* different points *of* view were there.

x They learned a lesson *from* her conclusions *from* the incident.

Compare:

• Many journalists holding different points of view were there.

• Her conclusions from the incident taught them a lesson.

livel
28h

29 An Index of Diction

To supplement your vocabulary list (27b, p. 317), go over the list of "words that look or sound alike" (18c, p. 200). Make an entry for every distinction that you do not already have under control. Then repeat the procedure for the following Index of Diction, which probably contains many unfamiliar points. As your vocabulary list grows, review it from time to time, deleting entries that you are sure you no longer need. The ideal is to start with as large a list as necessary and gradually trim it as you gain more mastery of word choice.

The Index of Diction does not dwell on differences between dialect expressions, slang, and informal usage. It simply labels *colloq.* ("colloquial") any terms that are inadvisable for use in college essays and papers.

The following abbreviations appear in the Index of Diction.

adj.	adjective, adjectival
adv.	adverb, adverbial
ambig.	ambiguous, having more than one possible meaning
awk.	awkward
colloq.	colloquial, to be avoided in standard written English
compl.	complement
conj.	conjunction
coord.	coordinating
e.g.	for example
i.e.	that is
inf.	infinitive
intrans.	intransitive: the verb takes no object
jarg.	jargon
n.	noun
neg.	negative
obj.	direct object
part.	present participle
plu.	plural
p.p.	past participle
prep.	preposition, prepositional
pro.	pronoun
redt.	redundant, conveying the same meaning twice
S.E.	standard written English
sing.	singular
subj.	subject of a verb
subord.	subordinating
syn.	synonym, a word having the same meaning as another
trans.	transitive: the verb takes an object
v.	verb
x	marks an illustration of a typical mistake or awkward construction

d
29

above (n., adj.)   Stuffy in phrases like x *in view of the above* and x *for the above reasons.* Wherever possible substitute *therefore, for these reasons,* etc.

A.D.   Should precede the date: *A.D. 1185.* Note that it is redt. to write x *in the year A.D. 1185,* since *A.D.* already says "in the year of our Lord" (Latin *anno Domini*).

affect, effect   As a v., *affect* means to *influence: Rain affected the final score. Affect* may also be used as a n. meaning *feeling* or *emotion.* The v. *effect* means to *bring about* or *cause: She effected a stunning reversal.* When *effect* is a n., it means *result: The effect of the treatment was slight.*

afraid   See *frightened.*

again, back   Redt. after *re*-prefixed words that already contain the sense of *again* or *back: rebound, reconsider, refer, regain, reply, resume, revert,* etc. Do not write x *refer back.*

ain't   Colloq. for *is not, are not.*

all, all of   Use either *all* or *all of* when separable items are involved: *All of the skillets were sold.* When there are no items to be counted, use *all* without *of: All her enthusiasm vanished; He was a hermit all his life.*

all that   Colloq. in sentences like x *I didn't like her all that much.*

also   Do not use as a coord. conj.: x *She owned two cars, also a stereo.* Try *Along with her two cars, she also owned a stereo.* Here *also* serves its proper function as an adv.

A.M., P.M.   These abbreviations, which most writers now capitalize, should not be used as nouns: x *at six in the A.M.* And do not accompany *A.M.* or *P.M.* with *o'clock,* which is already implied. Write *six A.M.* or *six o'clock* but not x *6 A.M. o'clock.*

d
29

among, between *Among* is appropriate when there are at least three separable items: *among his friends; among all who were there.*

Between can be used for any plu. number of items, though some writers reserve it for two items (also see *between*). The more widely recognized difference is that *among* is vaguer and more collective than *between,* which draws attention to each of the items:

- They hoped to find one good person *among* the fifty applicants.
- The mediator saw a basis for agreement *between* management and the union.

amount, number For undivided quantities, use *amount of: a small amount of food.* For countable items, use *number of: a small number of meals.* The common error is to use *amount* for *number,* as in x *The amount of people in the hall was extraordinary.*

analyzation A mistake for *analysis.*

angry See *mad.*

any more, anymore Only the first is S.E. Do not write x *They don't make disposable diapers the way they used to anymore.*

anybody, any body; nobody, no body; somebody, some body The first member of each pair is an indefinite pro.: *Anybody can see.* . . . The others are adj.-n. pairs: *Any body can be dissected.*

anyway, any way, anyways *Anyway* is an adv.: *There is no hope, anyway. Any way* is an adj.-n. pair: *I have not found any way to do it. Anyways* is colloq.

anywheres Colloq. for *anywhere.*

apt, liable, likely Close in meaning. But some writers reserve *liable* to mean *exposed* or *responsible* in an undesirable sense: *liable to be misunderstood; liable for damages. Likely* means *probably destined: She is likely to succeed. Apt* is best used to indicate habitual disposition: *They are apt to complain when you tell them to work faster.*

argue, quarrel These can be syns., but *argue* also has a special meaning of *make a case*, without overtones of quarrelsomeness.

around If you mean *about*, it is better to write *about: about five months*, not x *around five months*.

as (conj., prep.) The subord. conj. *as* in the sense of *because* is often ambig.: x *As she said it, I obeyed*. Does *as* here mean *because* or *while?* Use *because* if you mean *because*.
Do not use *as* to mean *whether* or *that:* x *I cannot say as I do*.

as, like *As* is usually a conj. introducing an adv. clause, and *like* is usually a prep. introducing a prep. phrase.

CONJUNCTION:
• *As* the forecaster predicted, it rained all day.

PREPOSITION:
• *Like* anyone else, she has made her share of mistakes.

In speech, many people use *like* as a conj.: x *Like he said, . . .* This is inadvisable written usage.
Note that when *as* is a prep., it differs in meaning from *like:*

• He runs *like* a deer.
• He is running *as* the vegetarian candidate.

as, such as Not syns. Do not write x *The burglar's bag contained many items, as masks, screwdrivers, and skeleton keys. Such as* would be appropriate.

as far as . . . Be sure to complete this formula with *is/are concerned*. Do not write x *As far as money, I have no complaints*. Try *As far as money is concerned, I have no complaints*, or *As for money, I have no complaints*, or, better, *I have no complaints about money*.

as good as, as much as Colloq. when used for *practically:* x *He as good as promised me the job*.

aspect   A much overworked term. Literally, an *aspect* is a *view from a particular vantage*. Moving around an object, you see various *aspects* of it. Instead of using *aspect* as a syn. for *consideration* (x *The problem has five aspects*), try to use the term with at least a hint of concreteness: *When the issue is regarded from this perspective it shows a wholly new aspect.*

author (v.)   Widely used, but also widely condemned as substandard: x *He has authored four novels.* Use *has written,* and keep *author* as a n.

back of   Colloq. for *behind:* x *You can find it back of the stove. Behind* is also preferable to *in back of.*

bad   Do not use as an adv. meaning *badly* or *severely:* x *It hurt him bad.*

being (part.)   Often redt.: x *The city is divided into three districts, with the poorest being isolated from the others by the highway.* Either *with* or *being* should be dropped.

bemused   Means *bewildered,* not *amused.*

**d
29**

better than   Colloq. as a syn. of *more than:* x *Better than half an hour remained.*

between   Can be used for more than two items (see *among, between*), but it does require at least two. Do not write either x *Hamlet's conflict is between his own mind* or x *The poems were written between 1983–84.* In the second sentence *1983–84* is one item, a period of time. Try *The poems were written between 1983 and 1984.*

   Between always requires a following *and,* not *or.* Avoid x *The choice is between anarchy or civilization.*

between each, between every   Because *between* implies at least two items, it should not be joined to sing. adjs. like *each* and *every:* x *He took a rest between each inning.* Try *He rested after every inning* or *He rested between innings.*

between you and I A "genteel" mistake for *between you and me.* As twin objs. of the prep. *between*, both pros. must be objective in case.

bi- A treacherously ambig. prefix. It always means *twice;* but what is being doubled, e.g., in *biweekly?* If the weeks are doubled, *biweekly* means *every two weeks*; if the times are doubled, it means *twice a week* or *semiweekly.* Find a clearer phrase: *every other week, twice a week.*

bored Should be followed by *by* or *with,* not *of.* Avoid x *He was bored of skiing.*

broke (adj.) Colloq. both in the sense of *having no money* and as the p.p. of *break:* x *The faucet was broke.* Prefer *broken* for this meaning.

bunch, crowd (n.) A *bunch* is a dense collection of *things;* a *crowd,* of *people* or *animals.* Avoid x *a bunch of my friends.*

but that, but what These are awk. equivalents of *that* in clauses following an expression of doubt: x *I do not doubt but that you intend to remain loyal.*

calculate See *figure.*

calculated See *designed.*

can, may Both are now acceptable to indicate permission. *May* has a more polite and formal air: *May I leave?*

can not, cannot Unless you want to underline *not,* always prefer *cannot,* which makes the negative meaning immediately clear.

cause, reason Not syns. A *cause* is what produces an effect: *The earthquake was the cause of the tidal wave.* A *reason* is someone's *professed motive or justification*: *He cited a conflict of interest as his reason for not accepting the post.* Note that the actual *cause* of his refusal could have been something quite different.

cause is due to Redt. Write *The cause was poverty,* not x *The cause was due to poverty.*

d
29

censor, censure (n.) A *censor* is an official who judges whether a publication or performance will be allowed. *Censure* is vehement criticism. *The censor heaped censure on the play.*

center around Since a center is a point, *center around* is imprecise. *Center on* or *center upon* would be better: *The investigation centered on tax evasion.*

character Often redt. x *He was of a studious character* means, and should be; *He was studious.*

class (**v.**) *Classify* is preferable. Avoid x *He classed the documents under three headings.*

commence Usually pompous for *begin, start.*

compare, contrast *Compare* means either *make a comparison* or *liken.* To compare something *with* something else is to make a comparison between them; the comparison may show either a resemblance or a difference. To compare something *to* something else is to assert a likeness between them.

To *contrast* is to emphasize *differences*: *She contrasted the gentle Athenians with the warlike Spartans.* As a v., *contrast* should be followed by *with.*

d
29

comprise, compose, constitute *Comprise* means *embrace, include*: *The curriculum comprises every field of knowledge. Compose* and *constitute* mean *make up*: *All those fields together compose* [or *constitute*] *the curriculum.* The most common mistake is to use *comprise* as if it meant *compose:* x *The parts comprise the whole. Is comprised of* is not an adequate solution: x *The whole is comprised of the parts.* Try *The whole comprises the parts* or *The parts compose the whole.*

concept, conception, idea The broadest of these terms is *idea,* and you should prefer it unless you are sure you mean one of the others. A *concept* is an abstract notion characterizing a class of particulars: *the concept of civil rights.* A *conception* is a particular idea, often erroneous: *She had an odd conception of my motives.* Note that *idea* would have been suitable even in these examples.

concur in, concur with You *concur in* an action or decision: *He concurred in her seeking a new career.* But you *concur with* a person or group: *He concurred with her in her decision.*

conscious, aware Almost syns., but you can observe a difference. People are *conscious* of their own perceptions but *aware* of events or circumstances.

consensus Avoid this n. unless you mean something very close to unanimity. And beware of the redt. x *consensus of opinion* and x *general consensus. Opinion* and *general* are already contained in the meaning of *consensus.*

considerable Colloq. in the sense of *many* (items): x *Considerable dignitaries were there.* Use the word to mean *weighty, important*: *The costs were considerable*; *The Secretary-General is a considerable figure.*

consist of, consist in Something *consists of* its components: *The decathlon consists of ten events. Consist in* means *exist in* or *inhere in*: *Discretion consists in knowing when to remain silent.*

contemptible, contemptuous Very different. *Contemptible* means *deserving contempt. Contemptuous* means *feeling or showing contempt. They felt contemptuous of such a contemptible performance.*

continual, continuous *Continual* means *recurring at intervals. Continuous* means *uninterrupted.* A river flows *continuously* but may overflow its banks *continually* through the years.

**d
29**

contrary to Since *contrary* is an adj., avoid constructions in which *contrary to* serves as an adv. modifier: x *Contrary to Baldwin, Orwell is not directly concerned with race.* This sentence makes it appear that Orwell is "contrary to Baldwin," whereas the writer means to compare the two authors' *concerns.* Try *Orwell, unlike Baldwin, is not directly concerned with race.* Save *contrary to* for sentences like *The order to surrender was contrary to everything they had been taught.*

convey Do not follow with a *that* clause: x *They conveyed that they were happy.* Choose a n. as obj.: *They conveyed the impression that they were happy.*

convince, persuade Often treated as syns., but you can preserve a valuable distinction by keeping *convince* for *win agreement* and *persuade* for *move to action.* If I *convince* you that I am right, I may *persuade* you to join my cause. Avoid x *He convinced his father to lend him the car.*

could of Always a mistake for *could have.*

couple, pair *Couple* refers to two items that are united. It is colloq. when the items are only casually linked: x *I have a couple of points I want to raise with you.* When you do use *couple of,* be sure not to drop the *of*: x *a couple reasons.*

   Pair refers to two things that are inseparably joined in function or feeling: *The Joneses are a couple, but they are not much of a pair.*

   Prefer *pairs* to *pair* for the plu.: *four pairs of shoes,* not x *four pair of shoes.*

   Verbs governed by *couple* or *pair* are generally plu., although a sing. v. could be appropriate in a rare case: *A couple becomes a trio when the first child is born.*

criteria Always plu.: *these criteria.* The sing. is *criterion.*

data Opinion is divided over the number of *data,* which is technically the plu. form of *datum.* The safe course is to continue treating *data* as plu.: *These data have recently become available.*

deduce, deduct Both form the same n., *deduction,* but *deduce* means *derive* or *infer* and *deduct* means *take away* or *detract. He deduced that the IRS would not allow him to deduct the cost of his hair dryer.*

depend Do not omit *on* or *upon,* as in x *It depends whether the rain stops in time.* And avoid *it depends* without a following reason: x *It all depends* is incomplete.

designed, calculated Misused in passive constructions where no designing agent is envisioned: x *The long summer days are designed* *to expose your skin to too much ultraviolet light.* Try *The long summer days are likely to expose your skin to too much ultraviolet light.* Again, do not write x *This medicine is perfectly calculated to turn you into an addict.* Try *This medicine is apt to turn you into an addict.*

differ from, differ with   To *differ from* people is to *be different from* them; to *differ with* them is to *express disagreement with* them: *The Sioux differed from their neighbors in their religious practices; they differed with their neighbors over hunting rights.*

different from, different than   Some readers regard *different than* as an error wherever it occurs. But most readers would not object to *different than* when it helps to save words. *The outcome was different than I expected* is more concise than *The outcome was different from what I expected.*

disinterested, uninterested   Many writers use both to mean *not interested,* but in doing so they lose the unique meaning of *disinterested* as *impartial*: *What we need here is a disinterested observer.* Reserve *disinterested* for such uses. Avoid x *She was completely disinterested in dancing.*

doubtless(ly)   Since *doubtless* is already an adv., the *-ly* is excessive: *She will doubtless be ready at eight.*

d
29

drastic   Once meant *violent,* and still retains a sense of harshness and grim urgency. Avoid x *a drastic improvement.*

dubious, doubtful   An outcome or a statement may be *dubious,* but the person who calls it into question is *doubtful* about it. Though some writers overlook the distinction, you would do well to keep *doubtful* for the mental state of harboring doubts.

due to   Do not use adverbially, as in x *Due to her absence, the team lost the game.* In such a sentence use *because of* or *owing to,* and save *due to* for sentences like *The loss was due to her absence.*

effect   See *affect.*

e.g., i.e. Often confused. The abbreviation *e.g.* means *for example*; it can be used only when you are *not* citing all the relevant items. The abbreviation *i.e.* means *that is*; it can be used only when you are giving the *equivalent* of the preceding term. In the main text of an essay or paper, it is best to write out *for example* and *that is*.

Once you have written *e.g.*, do not add *etc.*, as in x *See, e.g., Chapters 4, 7, 11, etc.* The idea of unlisted further examples is already present in *e.g.*

enhance Does not mean *increase,* as in x *I want to enhance my bank account.* It means *increase the value or attractiveness of,* as in *He enhanced his good reputation by performing further generous acts.* In order to be enhanced, something must be already valued.

Note that the quality, not the person, gets enhanced. Avoid x *She was enhanced by receiving favorable reviews.*

enormity, enormousness Not syns. *Enormity* means *atrocious wickedness.* Do not write x *the enormity of his feet.*

enthuse Looks like a plausible substitute for *show enthusiasm,* but it has not won full acceptance. Be safe and prefer the longer expression.

d 29

escape (v.) When used with an obj., it should mean *elude,* as in *They escaped punishment.* Avoid x *They escaped the jail.* Make *escaped* intrans. here: *They escaped from the jail.*

especially, specially, special *Especially* means *outstandingly*: *an especially interesting idea. Specially* means *for a particular purpose, specifically*: *This racket was specially chosen by the champion.*

Watch for meaningless uses of *special*: x *There are two special reasons why I came here.* This would make sense only if there had been many reasons, only two of which were special ones. Just delete *special.*

et al. Means *and other people,* not *and other things.* It belongs in citations, not in your main text.

etc. Means *and other things,* not *and other people. Et al.* serves that rival meaning. In formal prose, use a substitute expression such as *and so forth.*

Do not use *etc.* after *for example* or *such as*: x *America is composed of many ethnic groups, such as Germans, Poles, Italians, etc.*

eventhough A mistake for *even though.*

everywheres A mistake for *everywhere.*

exceeding(ly), excessive(ly) *Exceeding* means *very much; excessive* means *too much.* It is not shameful to be *exceedingly rich,* but to be *excessively rich* is a demerit.

except Do not use as a conj., as in x *She told him to leave, except he preferred to stay.* Keep *except* as a prep. meaning *excluding*: *He remembered everything except his toothbrush.*

expect Mildly colloq. in the sense of *suppose, believe*: x *I expect it will snow tomorrow.*

facet A *facet* is one of the surfaces of a gem; thus it comes into view as the gem is turned. When you use *facet,* try to keep some sense of this shift in perspective: *An unexpected facet of the problem appears when we adopt the migrant workers' point of view.* Simply as a syn. of part, *facet* is stale: x *Let us address three facets of the issue.*

d

29

factor A *factor* is an *element helping to produce a given result,* as in *They overlooked several factors in seeking the causes of the riot.* Do not use *factor* simply as a syn. of *item* or *point.* Note that *contributing factor* is always redt.

feel, feeling Many careful writers prefer to keep *feel* a v. and *feeling* a n. Thus they would avoid x *She has a sensitive feel for the piano.*

few, little *Few* refers to things or persons that can be counted; *little* refers to things that can be measured or estimated but not itemized. *Few people were on hand, and there was little enthusiasm for the speaker.*

fewer, less, lesser, least *Fewer* refers to numbers, *less* to amounts: *fewer members, less revenue.* Beware of advertising jarg.: x *This drink contains less calories.* Since the calories are countable, only *fewer* would be correct here.

Lesser is an adj. meaning *minor* or *inferior: The lesser emissaries were excluded from the summit meeting. Least* is the superlative of *little.* As an adj. it should be used only when more than two items are involved: *That was the least of her many worries.*

Note that *fewer in number* is redt.

figure, calculate Colloq. as syns. of *think, suppose,* or *believe*: x *They figured she would be too frightened to complain.*

flaunt, flout Widely confused. To *flaunt* is to *display arrogantly: They flaunted their superior wisdom.* To *flout* is to *defy contemptuously: They flouted every rule of proper behavior.* The common error is to use flout for *flaunt*: x *The pitcher flouted his unbeaten record.*

flunk Colloq. for *fail,* as in x *He flunked Biology 23.*

for example See *etc.*

fortuitous Means *by chance,* whether or not an advantage is implied. Do not allow *fortuitous* to mean simply *favorable, auspicious,* or *lucky*: x *How fortuitous it was that fate drew us together!*

free, freely *Free* can serve as both an adj. and an adv., meaning, among other things, *without cost.* If you write *I give it to you freely,* you are conveying something else: *I give it to you without mental reservation.* Do not be afraid to write *I give it to you free* if you mean *without charging you.*

frightened, scared, afraid You are *frightened* or, more informally, *scared* by an immediate cause of alarm; you are *afraid* of a more persistent danger or worry: *He was frightened [scared] by noises in the middle of the night; he was afraid he would have to buy a watchdog.*

fulsome Does not mean *abundant*; it means *offensively insincere.* Thus it would be wrong to write x *I love the fulsome scents of early spring.*

d
29

fun Colloq. as an adj., as in x *a fun party.*

gender Reserve for grammar, not sex. Avoid x *He went to Sweden to have his gender changed.* Note also that a gender can be *masculine* or *feminine,* but not *male* or *female.*

good, well *You look good tonight* means that you are attractive. *You look well tonight* means that you do not look sick.

guess Colloq. as a syn. of *suppose:* x *I guess I should give up trying.*

had better Do not shorten to *better,* as in x *You better pay attention.*

half a Do not precede with a redt. *a,* as in x *He was there for a half a day.*

hanged, hung The regular p.p. of *hang* is *hung,* but you should use *hanged* when referring to capital punishment: *He was hanged for his crimes; his lifeless body hung from the noose.*

hang-up Colloq. for *problem, reservation, inhibition, perversion.* All these terms can be used precisely, but *hang-up* cannot.

hard, hardly Both can be advs. Fear of using *hard* as an adv. can lead to ambiguity: x *She was hardly pressed for time.* This could mean either *She was rushed* or, more probably, *She was scarcely rushed.* There is nothing wrong with writing *She was hard-pressed for time.* Note the hyphen, however.

d
29

high, highly *High* can be an adv. as well as an adj. Prefer it to *highly* in expressions like *he jumped high, a high-flying pilot.* An antique vase may be *highly prized* and therefore *high-priced* at an auction.

hopefully Many readers accept this word in the sense of *it is hoped,* but others feel strongly that *hopefully* can mean only *in a hopeful manner.* Keep to this latter meaning if you want to give no offense. Write *He prayed hopefully* but not x *Hopefully, his pains will subside.*

how Avoid in the sense of *that,* as in x *I told her how I wouldn't stand for her sarcasm any more.*

how ever, however   Distinct terms. *How ever are you going to untie that knot? You, however, know more about it than I do.*

However is correct in the sense of *in whatever manner*: *However you consider it, the situation looks desperate.*

i.e.   Means *that is*; see *e.g.*

if not   Potentially ambig., as in x *There were good reasons, if not excellent ones, for taking that step.* Does this mean that the reasons decidedly were not excellent or that they may indeed have been excellent? Try *but not excellent ones* or *indeed, excellent ones,* depending on the intended sense.

ignorant, stupid   Often confused. To be *ignorant* of something is simply not to know it: *Newton was ignorant of relativity.* An *ignorant* person is one who has been taught very little. A *stupid* person is mentally unable to learn: *The main cause of his ignorance was his stupidity.*

implicit, explicit, tacit   *Implicit* can be ambig., for it means both *implied* (left unstated) and *not giving cause for investigation.* Consider, e.g., x *My trust in her was implicit.* Was the trust left unstated, beyond question, or both? Try *My trust in her was left implicit* or *My trust in her was absolute.*

Explicit is the opposite of *implicit* in the sense of *implied*: *In his will he spelled out the explicit provisions that had previously been left implicit. Tacit* is close to this sense of *implicit,* but it means *silent, unspoken*; its reference is to speech, not to expression in general.

imply, infer   Widely confused. To *imply* is to *leave an implication*; to *infer* is to *take an implication. She implied that she was ready to leave the company, but the boss inferred that she was bluffing.* The common error is to use *infer* for *imply*.

in back of   See *back of.*

in case   Can usually be improved to *if*: *If* [not *in case*] *you do not like this model, we will refund your money.* Save *in case* for *in the event*: *This sprinkler is provided in case of fire.*

d

29

in connection with   See *in terms of.*

in terms of, along the lines of, in connection with   Vague and wordy. Instead of writing x *In terms of prowess, Tarzan was unconquerable,* just write *Tarzan was unconquerable.* Similarly, x *He was pursuing his studies along the lines of sociology* should be simply *He was studying sociology.*

include   Do not use loosely to mean *are,* as in x *The Marx Brothers included Groucho, Harpo, Chico, and Zeppo.* Only when at least one member is unnamed should you use *include*: *The Marx Brothers included Harpo and Zeppo.*

Note also that *include* is inappropriate after you have already indicated a limitation: x *Two of my reasons include my drive for success and my wish to please my mother.*

individual (n.)   Often pompous for *person*: x *He was a kind-hearted individual.* Use *individual* where you want to draw attention to the single person as contrasted with the collectivity, as in *Our laws respect the individual.*

inside of   Widely regarded as colloq., and can always be shortened to *inside.*

inspite of   A mistake for *in spite of.*

is because   See *reason is because.*

is when, is where   Often involved in faulty predication: x *A war is when opposing countries take up arms*; x *Massage is where you lie on a table and . . .* Match *when* only with times, *where* only with places: *When she was ready, she went where she pleased.* Most predication problems can be solved by changing the v.: *A war occurs when . . .*

kind of, sort of, type of   When used at all, these expressions should be followed by the sing.: *this kind of woman.* But *such a woman* is preferable.

Sort of and *kind of* are awk. in the sense of *somewhat,* and they are sometimes followed by an unnecessary *a*: x *He was an odd sort of*

d
29

a king. Do not use *sort of* or *kind of* unless your sentence needs them to make sense: *This kind of bike has been on the market for only three months.*

leave, let   Have different senses in clauses like *leave him alone* and *let him alone.* The first means *get out of his presence*; the second means *don't bother him* (even if you remain in his presence).

level (n.)   Overworked in the vague, colorless sense illustrated by x *at the public level*; x *on the wholesale level.* Use only when the idea of degree or ranking is present: *He was a competent amateur, but when he turned professional he found himself beyond his level.*

lie, lay   If you mean *repose,* use the intrans. *lie: lie down.* The trans. *lay* means, among other things, *set* or *put: lay it here.*
   All forms of these verbs are troublesome. The following sentences use three common tenses correctly:

PRESENT	PAST	PRESENT PERFECT
I lie in bed.	I lay in bed.	I have lain in bed.
I lay down my cards.	I laid down my cards.	I have laid down my cards.

like   See *as, like.*

likely   Weak as an unmodified adv.: x *He likely had no idea what he was saying.* Some readers would also object to x *Very likely, he had no idea what he was saying.* Try *probably,* and reserve *likely* for adj. uses: a *likely story.*

likewise   An adv., not a conj. You can write *Likewise, Myrtle failed the quiz,* but not x *Jan failed the quiz, likewise Myrtle.*

literally   Means *precisely as stated, without a figurative sense.* If you write x *I literally died laughing,* you must be writing from beyond the grave. Do not use *literally* to mean *definitely* or *almost.* It is properly used in a sentence like *The poet writes literally about flowers, but her real subject is forgiveness.*

lot, lots Somewhat colloq. in the sense of *many*: x *I could give you lots of reasons. A lot* and *lots* make distinctly colloq. advs., too: x *She pleases me lots.* Try *very much.*

mad, angry *Mad* means *insane.* It is colloq. in the sense of *angry*: x *They were mad at me.*

majority Do not use unless you mean to contrast it with *minority*: *The majority of the members voted to disband the club.* In x*the majority of the time,* the term is out of place because *time* does not contain members that could be counted as a majority and a minority.

many, much *Many* refers to countable items, *much* to a total amount that cannot be divided into items (see *amount, number*): *Many problems make for much difficulty.* Do not write x *There were too much people in the line.*

media Increasingly used as a sing. term, but since it is the plu. of *medium,* you would still do well to keep it plu. Write *The media are to blame.*

militate, mitigate Often confused. To *militate* is to *have an adverse effect.* It is followed by *against,* as in *His poor eyesight militated against his becoming a pilot. Mitigate* means *reduce* (an unpleasant effect). It always takes an obj., as in *The doctor's cheerful manner mitigated the pain.*
   The common error is to use *mitigate* for *militate,* as in x *Their stubborn attitude mitigated against their chances of success.*

mix, mixture Many careful writers prefer to keep *mix* a v. and *mixture* a n. Thus they would avoid x *There was a fascinating mix of interests around the table.*

most Colloq. as an adv. meaning *almost*: x *We were most dead by the time we got there.*

much less Avoid x *Skiing is difficult, much less surfing.* The *much less* construction requires an initial negation, as in *He has not even appeared, much less begun his work.*

d
29

muchly   A mistake for *much.*

myself   Do not use this intensive pro. merely as a substitute for *I* or *me*: x *My friends and myself are all old-timers now;* x *She gave the book to Steve and myself.* Save *myself* for emphatic or reflexive uses: *I myself intend to do it; I have forgiven myself.*

not too, not that   Colloq. when used to mean *not very*: x *She was not too sure about that*; x *They are not that interested in sailing.*

nothing like, nowhere near   Do not use in place of *not nearly,* as in x *I am nothing like* [or *nowhere near*] *as spry as I used to be.*

nowheres   A mistake for *nowhere.*

numerous   Properly an adj. You can write *He still had numerous debts,* but avoid x *Numerous of his debts remained unpaid.*

occur, take place   The narrower term is *take place,* which should be used only with scheduled events. Avoid x *The storm took place last Tuesday.*

off of   Should be either *off* or *from*: *She jumped off the bridge* or *She jumped from the bridge.* Avoid x *She jumped off of the bridge.*

oftentimes   Colloq. for *often.*

old-fashion   Colloq. for *old-fashioned.*

on, upon, up on   *On* and *upon* mean the same thing, but you should save *upon* for formal effects: *She swore upon her word of honor.* Note that *up on* is not the same as *upon*: *He climbed up on the ladder.*

on account of   Never preferable to *because of.*

only   Do not use as a conj.: x *He tries to be good, only his friends lead him astray.* Keep *only* as an adj. or adv.: *That is his only problem; he only needs some better advice.*

d
29

oral, verbal *Oral* means *by mouth*; *verbal* means *in words,* whether or not the words are spoken. Write *a verbal presentation* only if you have in mind a contrast with some form of communication that bypasses words.

other than that Considered awk.: x *Other than that, I can follow your reasoning.* Try a more definite expression: *except for one point, apart from this objection,* etc.

other times Do not use as an adv., as in x *Other times she felt depressed.* Use the complete prep. phrase *at other times.*

otherwise Allowable as an adv. meaning *in other respects* or *differently: Otherwise, I feel healthy; She decided otherwise.* But do not use *otherwise* to replace the adj. *other:* x *He loved old buildings, Victorian and otherwise.*

ourself Should be *ourselves.*

outside of Should be *outside.* And in figurative uses you should prefer *except for:* not x *outside of these reasons* but *except for these reasons.*

part, portion A *part* is a *fraction of a whole*; a *portion* is a *part allotted to some person or use.* Thus you should avoid x *A large portion of the ocean is polluted.*

phenomena Not a sing. word, but the plu. of *phenomenon.*

place Some readers regard terms like *any place, no place,* and *some place* as colloq. It is safer to write *anywhere, nowhere, somewhere.* If you do use a *place* term, note the two-word spelling.

plan The v. is best followed by *to,* not *on: He plans to run,* not x *He plans on running.* Note that since *plan* implies a future action, expressions like x *plan ahead* and x *future plans* are redt.

plus Not a coord. conj.: x *He was sleepy, plus he had not studied.* Nor is it a sentence adv.: x *She enjoyed her work; plus, the hours were*

d
29

good. Keep *plus* as a prep. with numbers: *Two plus two is four.* Look for a syn. when you are not dealing in numbers: x *Her challenging work plus her long vacations made her happy.* Try *and* or *along with.*

poorly   Colloq. in the sense of *ill* or *sick*: *I feel poorly today.* Keep as an adv.: *I performed poorly on the exam.*

popular   Implies favor with large numbers of people. Avoid when you have something smaller in mind: x *The hermit was popular with his three visitors*; x *That idea is not very popular with me.*

possible   Do not use as an adv.: x *a possible missing airliner.* Try *possibly.*

pressure   Has not gained full acceptance as a v.: x *He pressured us to agree.* Try *pressed.*

quote (n.)   Widely considered colloq. when used to mean *quotation,* as in x *this quote,* or written in the plu. to mean quotation marks, as in x *She put quotes around it.* In formal writing, take the trouble to use the full terms *quotation* and *quotation marks.*

d
29

raise, rise   As a v. *raise* is trans.: *raise your arm. Rise* is intrans.: *rise and shine.* Do not confuse these words.
  As a n. *raise* is by now fully accepted: *a raise in pay.*

real   Colloq. as an adv., as in x *I am real committed.* Prefer *really.*

reason is because   A classic predication error. You can write either *She stayed home because of her health* or *The reason was her health,* but it is redt. to write x *The reason she stayed home was because of her health.*

rebut, refute   To *rebut* an argument is to *speak or write against* it; to *refute* an argument is to *disprove* it. The common error is to use *refute* for *rebut:* x *You may be right, but I will refute what you said.*

reckon   Colloq. for *suppose, think*: x *I reckon I can handle that.* Use in the sense of *count* or *consider*: *She is reckoned an indispensable member of the board.*

relation, relationship   These overlap in meaning, and some writers use *relationship* in all contexts. But *relation* is preferable when you mean an abstract connection: *the relation of wages to prices.* Save *relationship* for mutuality: *the President's relationship with the press.*

relevant   Requires a following prep. phrase: x *The course was extremely relevant.* To what?

replace   See *substitute.*

reticent   Does not mean *reluctant,* as in x *They were reticent to comply.* It means *disposed to be silent,* as in *Reticent people sometimes become talkative late at night.*

scared   See *frightened, scared, afraid.*

similar   Means *resembling,* not *same.* Avoid x *Ted died in 1979, and Alice suffered a similar fate two years later.* Try *the same fate.*
   Do not use *similar* as an adv. meaning *like*: x *This steak smells similar to the one I ate yesterday.* Try *like the one.*

since   An indispensable word, but watch for ambiguity: x *Since she left, he has been doing all the housework.* Here *since* could mean either *because* or *from then until now.* Try *because* or *ever since.*

d
29

sit, set   With few exceptions, *sit* is intrans.: *She sat down.* Set is usually trans.: *They set the banquet table.* You can of course write *She sat her baby in the high chair* and *The sun set,* but avoid x *I set there sleeping* or x *I want to sit these weary bones to rest.*

some   Do not use as an adv. meaning *somewhat,* as in x *He worried some about his health.* Try *He was somewhat worried about his health.*

something   Avoid as an adv. meaning *somewhat,* as in x *He is something over six feet tall.* Note also that x *He smells something awful* is both ambig. and colloq. in the intended sense of *He smells bad.*

somewheres   A mistake for *somewhere.*

sort of   See *kind of.*

special, specially   See *especially.*

structure (v.)   Overused as a syn. of *order, arrange,* or *construct.* Some readers insist that it can only be a n. Avoid x *Give me a moment to structure my thoughts.*

substitute, replace   *Substitute* takes as its obj. the new item that is supplanting the old one: *He substituted margarine for butter. Replace* takes as its obj. the item being abandoned: *She replaced the butter with margarine.* Note that these sentencs are recounting the same act.

such as   See *etc.*

suppose to   A mistake for *supposed to,* as in x *We are suppose to watch our manners.*

sure   Colloq. as an adv.: x *She sure likes muffins.* Since *surely* would sound awk., try *certainly.*

d 29

sympathy for, sympathy with, sympathize with   To feel *sympathy for* someone is to experience compassion: *She has sympathy for the people of Bangladesh. Sympathy with* is a feeling of kinship or identity: *Her sympathy with Gloria Steinem made her a feminist.* To *sympathize with,* however, is once again to experience compassion: *She sympathized with the poor.*

that   Beware of using *that* as an unexplained demonstrative adj.: x *He didn't have that much to say.* How much is *that* much?
   In restrictive clauses (4j, p. 58), prefer *that* to *which*: *Texas is the state that fascinates me.*

theirself, theirselves   Mistakes for *themselves.*

those kind, type, etc.   Should be *that kind, type,* etc. But prefer *such,* which is more concise: not x *that kind of person* but *such people.*

thusly   A mistake for *thus.*

till, until, til, 'til, 'till   *Till* and *until* are interchangeable. The other three forms are inappropriate.

too   Avoid as a syn. of *very*: x *It was too good of you to help.*

try and   Should be *try to*: not x *Try and do better* but *Try to do better.*

type   Colloq. in place of *type of*: x *You are a headstrong type person.* But *type of* is itself objectionably wordy; try *You are headstrong.*

usage, use   Widely confused. Save *usage* for contexts implying convention or custom: *English usage; the usages of our sect.* Avoid x *They discouraged the usage of cocaine* or x *Excessive usage of the car results in high repair bills.* Substitute *use* in both sentences.

    Even *use of* often proves wordy: x *By his use of symbolism Ibsen establishes himself as a modern playwright.* Why not just *By his symbolism Ibsen establishes himself as a modern playwright*?

use (v.), utilize; use (n.), utilization   *Utilize* and *utilization* are almost always jarg. for *use.* To *utilize* is properly to *put to use* or to *turn a profit on,* and it makes sense when coupled with an abstraction: *to utilize resources.* But the word has a dehumanizing air; prefer *use* in ordinary contexts. Note that *utilization* is almost four times as long as *use,* which can always stand in its place.

use to   In an affirmative past construction, be sure to write *used to,* not *use to*: x *They use to think so*; x *They are not use to the cold.* In addition, certain past neg. constructions with *use* always sound awk.: x *Didn't she use to take the bus?* Try *She used to take the bus, didn't she?*

verbal, oral   See *oral.*

d
29

violently   Not a syn. of *strongly*, as in x *I violently oppose your program*. Only thugs and terrorists oppose programs *violently*, causing actual physical damage.

ways   Avoid in the sense of *distance*: x *It was only a short ways*. The right form is *way*.

what ever, whatever   Distinct terms. *What ever will we do about the heating bills? Whatever we do, it will not solve the problem.*

where   Do not use in place of *whereby*, as in x *T'ai-chi is an exercise regimen where one slowly activates every muscle group*. *Whereby,* the right word here, means *by means of which*. Save *where* for actual places: *That storefront studio is where we study T'ai-chi.*

where . . . at   Redt. and colloq., as in x *She had no idea where he was at*. Always delete the *at*.

-wise   Acceptable when it means *in the manner of*, as in *clockwise* and *lengthwise*, and when it means *having wisdom: penny-wise and pound-foolish; a ring-wise boxer*. Note the hyphens in this second set of examples.

   Avoid *-wise* in the sense of *with respect to*: x *taxwise, agriculturewise, conflict resolutionwise*. Such terms do save space, but many readers find them ugly. Look for concise alternatives: not x *the situation taxwise* but *the tax situation*; not x *America's superiority agriculturewise* but *America's superiority in agriculture*.

with   See *being*.

would like for   Colloq. in sentences like x *They would like for me to quit*. Try *They would like me to quit*.

III APPLICATIONS

III APPLICATIONS

G THE COLLEGE ESSAY

The College Essay

An **essay** *is a relatively brief piece of nonfictional prose that tries to make a point in an interesting way. To explain:*

1. It is fairly brief. *Some classic essays occupy only a few paragraphs, and in a composition course you may be asked to keep your first essays to 500 words. But an essay generally falls between two and twenty-five typed, double-spaced pages. Under that minimum, the development of thought that typifies an essay would be hard to manage. Above that maximum, people might be tempted to read the piece in installments like a book. A good essay makes an unbroken reading experience.*

2. It is nonfiction. *An essayist tries to tell the truth or to speculate about possible changes in the world we all recognize. If the essay contains a story or a description, we presume that the details have not been made up for effect.*

3. It makes a point. *An essay characteristically tells or explains something, or expresses an attitude toward something, or supports or criticizes something—an opinion, a person or place, a work of art, an institution, a movement. A poem or a novel may also do these things, but it does them incidentally; it appeals above all to the reader's imagination. An essay directly addresses a* topic *or specific subject, and its usual aim is to win sympathy or agreement to the point or* **thesis** *it is maintaining.*

4. It is meant to be engaging. *An essay should arouse curiosity, convince the reader that the main idea is worth bothering about, and move toward a satisfyingly conclusive finish.*

To be an effective essayist you must be willing to strike some balances. You will want to tell the truth, but first make people interested in hearing it; write with conviction, but consider whether your ideas and attitudes will stand up under criticism; supply evidence, but not become a bore about it; be purposeful, but not follow such a predictable pattern that your reader's attention slackens.

30 Arriving at a Topic

30a Recognize the Essay Modes.

Whole essays and parts of essays have traditionally been divided into four basic types or rhetorical **modes**, according to their varying tasks and aims.

MODE	TASK	AIM
1. Description	Picture	Make vivid to the reader
2. Narration	Recount	Tell the reader what happened
3. Explanation	Define Divide Illustrate Analyze a process Compare and contrast Analogize Show causes and effects	Make the reader understand
4. Argument	Defend a position	Win the reader's agreement

Note that the first two modes, **description** and **narration**, are presentational; they ask the writer to call scenes or episodes to the reader's mind. The third mode, **explanation**—often called *exposition*—characterizes most college writing assignments; the pursuit of knowledge is by and large the pursuit of explanations. And **argument**, the final but not necessarily the most important or difficult mode, appeals to facts, descriptions, narrations, and/or explanations in order to support a position on an issue. An argument typically *rebuts* (gives reasons for rejecting) an opposing position in the hope of *refuting* it (proving it wrong).

To see the logical relations among the four modes, we can locate them on a scale with immediate experience at one end and abstraction from experience at the other:

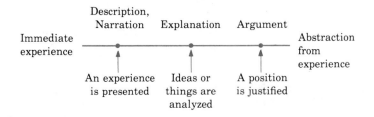

Does a given passage aim chiefly to represent something that can be remembered in its physical actuality? Then it must be either *description* or *narration.*

topic
30a

Does the passage aim chiefly to help us understand the nature or function of something or to see its relation to other things? Then this is a passage of *explanation.*

Does the passage try to convince us that a certain view or policy is preferable to another? Then we are dealing with *argument*—the rhetorical mode that stands at the greatest distance from immediate experience.

Suppose, for example, you were thinking about discussing the subject of *bubonic plague,* a disease that flourished in the Middle Ages and that remains dangerous today on a smaller scale.

In a *description* you might give your reader a detailed, physically vivid account of the symptoms: fever, boils, discoloration, chills, etc.

In a *narration* you might tell how the plague swept through Europe in 1348–49—or, in a personal vein, how you recently had to change your camping plans when health authorities found that rodents were dying from the disease.

In an *explanation* you might show how the plague bacillus is transmitted by rats and their fleas.

And in an *argument* you might support as essential, or oppose as no longer necessary, public health regulations designed to prevent outbreaks of the plague.

Most of your college essays will probably incorporate two or more of the modes—moving, say, from explanation to narration and back again as you seek to influence your reader in different ways. But since explanation and, to a lesser extent, argument are the modes that dominate college writing, we will concentrate below on the devising of essays that call for a strong central idea backed by evidence.

30b Recognize the Flexibility of the Composing Process.

Some students make things hard for themselves by conceiving of "good writing" as a one-time challenge—a brass ring to be seized or, more probably, missed on their first and only try. In their view the world is already divided into the lucky few who "can write" and all the others who cannot. What they fail to realize is that, by and large, *writing is rewriting.* Even the most accomplished authors start with drafts that would be woefully inadequate except *as* drafts—that is, as means of getting going in an exploratory process that will usually include a good many setbacks and shifts of direction. To feel dissatisfied with a sample of your prose, then, is not a sign of anything about your talent. The "good writer" is the one who can turn such dissatisfaction to a positive end by pressing ahead with the labor of revision, knowing that niceties of style will come more easily once an adequate structure of ideas has been developed.

And how will you arrive at such ideas? Many students believe that sheer inspiration or luck must be the answer; they furrow their brows and hope that a light bulb will flash over their heads. When it does not, they lose heart. But experienced writers know that good ideas, instead of dropping (or not dropping) from the sky, must be generated

**topic
30b**

by activities that place one thought into relation with another. And one of those activities is writing itself. In the labor of writing you will be forced to zero in on connections, comparisons, contrasts, illustrations, contradictions, and objections, any of which may point you toward a central idea or alter the one you began with.

Thus the finding of that idea, or *thesis,* is not a fixed early stage of the composing process, but a concern that is urgent at first and will probably become urgent again when you run into trouble or realize that a better idea has come into view. The sooner you arrive at a thesis—by any means, including random writing—the better; but your choice is being continually tested until you are ready to type up the final copy of your essay. At any moment you may find yourself having to take more notes, argue against a point you favored in an early draft, or throw away whole pages that have been made irrelevant by your improved thesis. Do not imagine that such annoyances set you apart from other writers; they put you in the company of the masters.

So, too, the other "stages of composing" normally leak into one another. Although you cannot complete your organizing, for example, until you have arrived at a thesis, unexpected problems of organization may point the way to a better thesis. Even a simplified diagram of your options at such a moment would look complex:

topic 30b

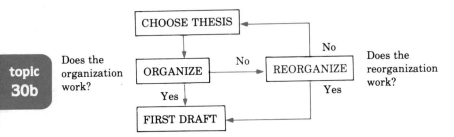

And even the revising of paragraphs for internal unity may prompt a more fundamental change of direction. Writing is almost never a linear process; it typically doubles back on one phase because a later one has opened new perspectives.

Thus, though we will discuss composing as a logical sequence of steps, its actual order in any one instance defies summary. At nearly every point you are free either to move ahead or to reconsider a previous decision. A reasonably ample flow chart for composing, then, would look like this:

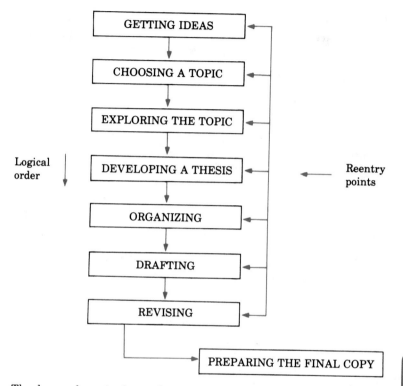

The lesson here is that, wherever your composing hits a snag, it is normal and useful to double back. Such rethinking is nothing to be alarmed about; it is the usual means by which weak ideas and structures give way to stronger ones.

30c Recognize the Differences between a Subject Area, a Topic, and a Thesis.

The key to writing a successful college essay is a strong and clear *thesis*—that is, a central idea to which everything else in your essay will contribute. You cannot get by with only a *topic* or, worse, a *subject area*.

Subject Area

A **subject area** is a large category within which you hope to find your actual topic—the specific question you will address. Thus, if you are asked to "recount a personal experience" or "discuss open admission to college" or "write an essay about *Catch-22*," you have been given not topics but subject areas: a personal experience, open admission to college, *Catch-22*.

Topic

The **topic** of an essay is the particular, focused issue or phenomenon being addressed. Thus, within the subject area "Open Admission to College," some workable topics might be:

The effect of open admission on "high potential" students

My debt to the policy of open admission

Why did open admission become popular in the late 1960s?

The success (or failure) of open admission

Is open admission a means to social equality?

Notice that these topics take up considerably more words than "Open Admission to College." Potential "topics" expressed in few words may be subject areas in disguise.

**topic
30c**

Thesis

Your **thesis** is the one ruling idea you are going to propose *about* your topic. Thus a thesis is never material to be investigated. It is always an *assertion*—an idea you will support in the body of your essay. And because it always makes a claim, a thesis lends itself to expression in one clear sentence.

Here is a chart that illustrates the contrast between a subject area, a topic, and a thesis. Notice that two possible theses are given for each topic.

SUBJECT AREA	TOPIC	THESIS
Open admission to college	The success of open admission	1. The success of open admission in my large urban college can be measured by the effectiveness of our basic instruction in reading and writing. 2. Unconventional students admitted under a policy of open admission have had a positive influence on the education of traditional students.
A personal experience	My night in jail	1. After my night in jail I will have more respect for prisoners' rights. 2. My night in jail helped to make me a safer driver.
Agricultural production	The effect of mechanization on farm employment	1. The typical farm employee has changed from a migrant laborer to a sophisticated regular with the skills to operate large machines. 2. Many migrant farm laborers have become the unskilled unemployables of the cities.
Civil liberties	Phone tapping as an issue of civil liberties	1. When government officials place innocent citizens under observation and routinely tap one another's phones, everyone's civil liberties are threatened. 2. Despite its infringement of civil liberties, phone tapping is the most effective device the government has for procuring evidence in criminal cases.

topic
30c

30d Narrow Your Subject Area.

Once you recognize that you have been given a subject area rather than a topic, you can work toward possible topics by dividing and subdividing the subject area. That maneuver will not in itself present you with a topic. "Chicago," for instance, is narrower than "Illinois," and "Lakeshore Drive" is narrower still, but all three lack a suitable focus; they remain subject areas because no question has yet been asked about them. Yet the process of breaking a large subject area into several smaller ones may bring such questions into mind.

If all you have to go on is the vast subject area "Education," for example, you can start by noting as many *categories* of education as you can. It may help to think of the categories as sets of opposites:

Education:
  private/public
  religious/secular
  vocational/academic
  lower/higher

Which of these categories do you feel most comfortable with? Write it down and run through the categorizing operation again:

Higher education:
  undergraduate/graduate
  science/humanities/engineering
  privately supported/state-supported/federally supported

topic 30d

Now study each item in your second list and ask what *issues or questions* it raises in your mind. One of them should prove to be an acceptable topic. Thus, if you are looking at *federally supported education,* you might ask these questions:

1. How much influence does the government exercise on admissions policies?

2. Do professors in a federally supported institution enjoy greater academic freedom than those in a privately supported institution?

3. Has the program of federal loans to students been cut back too far?

4. To what extent can the government insist that men's and women's athletic programs be equally funded?

5. What is the effect of tying federal aid to student responsibilities, such as registering for the draft?

30e Get Ideas from Your Experience.

Instructors sometimes assign essays of a certain structural type (for example, comparison and contrast) without specifying a subject area or a topic. When you find yourself thus free to choose a topic, think at once about your own interests and areas of special knowledge—activities, skills, attitudes, problems, and unique or typical experiences. The reason is simple: what doesn't interest you is not likely to engage a reader, whereas it is easy to be convincing when you can draw on firsthand information.

Reviewing Course Work and Recent Reading

One source of interest may be your course work in composition or any other discipline. Have you come across a significant problem in the assigned reading? If you have been taking notes during class, do the notes contain questions or observations that could lead to a thesis? Wherever you have recorded doubts or strong agreement or connections with ideas of your own, you may have in hand the beginnings of an essay.

So, too, you can search for topics in the books and magazines that happen to be within easy reach. The goal, of course, is not to copy someone else's words or ideas (see 37a, p. 472), but to find an issue that meets up with experience or knowledge or an opinion of your own.

topic
30e

Keeping a Journal

Your search for ideas will be easier if you keep a **journal**. Unlike a diary, which has no restriction of focus, a journal is a daily record of your experience and thoughts within a certain area. A typical journal, for example, might trace your progress in understanding musical theory or mastering computer skills; alternatively, it could store your reflections about life in general, your plans and ambitions, your ideas for short stories you hope to write, and so forth. You may even be asked to keep a journal about your efforts and problems in this very course. Whatever material it deals with, a journal can point you toward a topic by reminding you of already developed interests and opinions.

30f Try Freewriting.

If you have ever told yourself or others, *I don't know what I want to say until I've written it out,* consider yourself normal. Writing *is* a primary way of arriving at ideas, and teachers have increasingly been recognizing that fact. By forcing yourself to hook up nouns and verbs, subjects and predicates, you can draw forth insights that you didn't know you possessed.

You can even begin writing before having any idea of what your topic will be. When you feel stymied, assign yourself a ten- or fifteen-minute stint of **freewriting**. The trick is to put pen to paper at "Go" and to keep writing until "Stop" without pausing between your sentences or fragments of sentences. If you get stuck, just repeat a key word in the last sentence you have written and build a further statement around it. And even if one freewriting session appears to take you nowhere, a second one, started a few minutes later, may pick up on thoughts that were not quite ready for expression in a first effort.

Here, for example, are two passages of freewriting that a student produced in quick succession:

topic 30f

FIRST FREEWRITING:

Well, what do I have to say? Not much it appears! Sitting here "free" writing, so they tell me. How free is freewriting on demand, with the stopwatch ticking? Freedom in general—it always confuses me. I never know whether it's supposed to be freedom to go out and do something you'd like to, or freedom to keep somebody else from doing something mean to you. Anyway, would sure like to be free from freewriting! What is so sacred about exactly ten minutes worth of this stuff? How about nine or eleven? Stuck for ideas—ugh! Well, just keep pushing this pencil until time's up. . . .

SECOND FREEWRITING:

OK, maybe something here after all. Idea of freedom. *Total* freedom is empty, unattractive, boring—we always have something in mind to be free *for*—i.e. something that won't leave us so free any more. E.g., religious freedom usually means spending that freedom on some belief and/or practice—some "service." Or does it? What about unbelievers? I guess they have a right to a freedom that stays negative: no, thanks. . . . But historically, the fighters for freedom have always been people with strong beliefs of their own. Luther, Jefferson, Lincoln, King . . . Maybe an essay here? "Freedom For or Freedom From"?

Although neither of these passages has the grammatical completeness and the logical continuity of finished essay prose, and although the writer is clearly uncomfortable with an imposed task, his struggle to keep writing finally yields a likely-looking idea.

30g Try Brainstorming.

Freewriting (30f) teases forth ideas by means of our natural tendency to link one sentence with the previous one. **Brainstorming,** in contrast, works by the opposite principle, discontinuity. To brainstorm is to toss out suggestions without regard for their connections with one another. Since no development is called for, nothing stands in the way of your leaping from one notion to a completely unrelated one.

You can brainstorm by yourself, listing random words and phrases as they occur to you, scribbling across a notepad, or talking into a tape recorder. Or you can work in a group, either among friends or in the classroom, where the "notepad" is a shared chalkboard. In discussion or reflection, certain ideas will begin to look more fruitful than others—and you are on your way toward a topic.

**topic
30g**

When brainstorming works, it sometimes evolves naturally into freewriting as one hastily mentioned idea starts to look more interesting than the others:

Freedom / freedom fighters / free-for-alls / freed slaves / "free gifts" / I.e., come-ons for renting (or buying) a car, going to grand opening, etc. What's really free—nothing! Who pays? The customers, of course; extra costs added back into prices. Notice that "free gifts" come only when the customers aren't buying. . . .

By this point the writer already has a clear topic in view: the hidden costs and motives behind "free" merchandise.

30h Use Notes to Develop Your Thoughts.

You should take notes throughout the composing process, raising previously unforeseen questions, commenting on earlier notes, jotting down changes of plan, and reminding yourself of the next two or three points you ought to cover. Even if you are working from an outline 32b, p. 399, your notes can overrule any segment of it.

When your essay is supposed to deal with an assigned text, your note taking should begin during your reading of the text. Do you own the book? If so, mark it up. Underline passages that look significant and write comments and questions in the margins. Wherever one part of the text helps you to understand another part, make a marginal cross reference such as "see p. 134." And as soon as you have finished reading or, preferably, rereading, get your miscellaneous impressions onto paper so that you can begin dealing with *them* instead of with the whole text. Of course you will need to keep returning to the text, but now you can do so with specific, pointed questions in mind.

Some writers use uniform-sized index cards for all their notes, restricting themselves to one idea per card, but you may prefer full pages of scratch paper. In either case, you can use your notes to quote passages from your reading, record or summarize facts, make comparisons, launch a trial thesis as it occurs to you, express doubts or warnings, or comment on your comments—developing a dialogue of pros and cons.

topic
30i

30i Test Your Trial Topic.

Once you are sure you have arrived at a topic rather than a subject area, you may feel so relieved that you yearn to start the actual writing of your essay. But that would be a mistake. In the first place, your writing will quickly bog down if you still lack a thesis—a main point that answers the question implied or stated in your topic. And second, how do you know that the first topic to come to mind is the best one for your purpose? Your **trial topic** should stay on probation until you are sure it can pass six tests:

1. Is this trial topic still too broad?

2. Is it likely to sustain my interest?

3. Is it appropriate to my intended audience?

4. Can it lead to a reasonable thesis?

5. Does it involve enough complexity—enough "parts"—for development at essay length?

6. Do I have enough supporting material to work with?

If, without further thought, you can answer all of these questions positively, consider yourself lucky. More probably, you will need to explore your trial topic by one or more of the following means.

Focused Freewriting or Brainstorming

If freewriting and brainstorming can lead to preliminary ideas for an essay, they can also help you to explore a trial topic. The same rules apply (see pp. 380–382). The only difference is that now you begin with a definite focus and try to keep it—developing, not miscellaneous thoughts about anything, but specific features of the trial topic. As before, the idea is to set aside worries about correctness of organization and expression and to see what happens.

Asking Reporters' Questions

Another simple yet surprisingly helpful way to expand your view of the trial topic is to run through the standard list of questions reporters are supposed to answer in covering a story: *who? what? when? where? how? why?* Unlike a reporter, of course, you are not trying to make sense of a single event, yet the procedure can work because it keeps returning you to the same material from fresh perspectives.

Suppose your trial topic were the merits of a proposed law that encouraged recycling of glass by requiring a five-cent returnable deposit on all bottles. Asking the six standard reporters' questions, you might come up with answers like these:

Who? The elected officials of your community or state.

What? Pass a law requiring a five-cent deposit on every returnable bottle.

topic
30i

When? At the next session of the city council or legislature; law to take effect at start of next calendar year.

Where? Only within the boundaries of this community or state.

How? Fix penalties for noncompliance by sellers of bottles, give the law wide publicity, warn first offenders, then begin applying penalties.

Why? Reduce waste and pollution; raise public consciousness about conservation; cut prices through use of recycled glass.

Any of these brief notes could carry you beyond your first thoughts and lead to an adequately focused thesis. Given inflation, for example, will a five-cent deposit be large enough to ensure returns? Will there be special problems associated with putting the law into effect so soon? If the law applies only within a small geographic area, will consumers take their business elsewhere? Are the penalties for noncompliance too strict? Not strict enough?

Applying Explanatory Strategies

Whether or not you intend to write a whole essay of explanation, you can explore your trial topic by considering it in the light of the classic explanatory strategies: *definition, division, illustration, process analysis, comparison and contrast, cause and effect,* and *analogy.* These maneuvers are so basic to thinking in general that you can hardly fail to stimulate new trains of thought by reviewing them in turn.

**topic
30i**

Definition: How does a law differ from a regulation? A misdemeanor from a felony? What kinds of containers would be included or excluded?

Division: What are the separate provisions of the bill? What types of stores would be affected?

Illustration: Which communities and states have already established deposit laws? What reports of success or failure are available? Do we have case histories of bottling companies and grocery chains that have accommodated themselves to the law, of individuals who were prosecuted, of others who have made a subsistence living by collecting other people's empty bottles for refund?

Process analysis: How will violations of the law come to public notice, arrive at a prosecutor's desk, and be subsequently handled? Does the law allow unknowing violations to be treated differently from outright defiance? If so, at what point would such a difference be recognized? And what flow of payments and reimbursements is expected between the consumer, the grocer, and the distributor?

Comparison and contrast: In what ways does this law resemble others that have been enacted elsewhere? How does it differ from them? Are the conditions (commercial, political, environmental) in this community or state like those elsewhere, or must special factors be taken into account? Do young and older people hold different views of the law?

Cause and effect: What events and trends have made passage of the law likely or unlikely? What differences in consumers' behavior would the law bring about? Would littering be significantly curtailed? In the long run, would prices of bottled products go up or down?

Analogy: How can the positive or negative aspects of this law be dramatized by statement in terms of some quite different measure?

Any number of good possibilities could grow out of such questions. Thus, *definition* of a misdemeanor might help you to decide whether the law carries adequate or excessive penalties for noncompliance. After *division,* the breaking of the topic into smaller units, you could ask whether "mom and pop" stores would be more inconvenienced by the law than supermarket chains. Examples *illustrating* existing laws elsewhere could be powerful evidence of workability or unworkability. *Process analysis* might show how flexible or inflexible the proposed law would be in implementation. *Comparisons and contrasts* could have obvious relevance to judgments about the wisdom of the law. *Cause and effect* reasoning could extend your thoughts in two directions, back to origins and forward to consequences; the latter would be crucial for an essay of argument. And once you decided which side you were on, you could draw an *analogy* to emphasize your position:

topic
30i

Pro: Asking people to recycle bottles is like asking them to subsidize medical care for the aged. Some will want to, many won't, and the program will get nowhere. In one case as in the other, the goal of *general* compliance requires that a tax be imposed.

Con: A swimmer who ties her feet together may feel especially noble and self-sacrificing, but she isn't going to win a race. If we pass this deposit law, we too will think ourselves morally superior to neighboring communities (states)—and we too will find that we are handicapping ourselves right out of business.

31 Developing a Reasonable Thesis

31a Write Out a One-Sentence Trial Thesis.

Let us assume that, using one or more of the strategies described in the previous chapter, you have arrived at a *trial thesis*, or preliminary idea for your essay. Do not simply mull that thesis over in your head. Write it out in one clear sentence that you can then consider from several angles. That sentence may or may not eventually find its way into the body of your essay. Its function for now is to let you make sure that you have *one* central idea—not zero, not two—and that it looks sufficiently challenging and defensible. To these ends it is important that you keep to the one-statement limitation. Though your trial thesis can contain several considerations, one point should control all the others.

Typical trial theses for an essay about instituting a bottle law (30i, p. 383) might be these:

EXPLANATORY TRIAL THESES:

Increased fear that the environment is becoming polluted and that raw materials are growing scarce has provided broad-based support for laws requiring deposits on returnable bottles.

The passage or failure of bottle-deposit legislation in any given state or community can be directly correlated with the proportion of voters under age thirty.

ARGUMENTATIVE TRIAL THESES:

The minor inconvenience of paying a deposit and having to return empty bottles to a store is far outweighed by the benefits that all citizens would receive from a well-drafted law requiring the deposits.

A deposit law would not only hurt small business people by adding to their expenses and reducing their sales but also result in more, not less, pollution because of the increased trucking it would require.

None of these four examples is good or bad in itself; everything would depend on whether the writer had appropriate material on hand to make a convincing case. But all four trial theses meet the requirement of presenting just one main idea.

31b Limit the Scope of Your Thesis.

A thesis that quickly proves unworkable may suffer from too broad a scope. Remember that you have only a short essay in which to develop your idea successfully. Instead of discarding a thesis that seems to lead nowhere, try recasting it in narrower terms, replacing vague general concepts with more definite ones.

TOPIC	THESIS TOO BROAD	THESIS IMPROVED
The popularity of garage sales	Garage sales reflect the times we live in.	Garage sales circulate goods during periods of high inflation and high unemployment. ["The times" are carefully defined.]
A "star wars" missile defense system	We need to invest in a "star wars" missile defense system.	Although extremely costly, a "star wars" missile defense system may be our only safeguard against nuclear war. [Considerations of cost and safeguarding our future are both expressed in the thesis.]

**thesis
31b**

Late marriages as a phenomenon of the eighties	Late marriages are creating a different kind of American family life.	Because marriage is often postponed to accommodate careers, North Americans are creating a new kind of family in which parents are old enough to be their children's grandparents. [Reason for late marriage and a detailed explanation of "different" belong in the thesis.]

Faulty Generalization

When you write out a trial thesis, examine it for telltale danger words like *all, none, no, any, always, never, only,* and *everyone.* Such all-inclusive terms usually signal the presence of **faulty generalization,** the illegitimate extension of *some* instances to cover *all* instances of something. Suppose, for example, you want to argue that *There is no reason to delay immediate adoption of a national health insurance program.* Ask yourself: no reason at all? Will I be anticipating *all* possible reasons in my essay? Perhaps I can avoid unnecessary trouble by making my thesis more modest: *Adoption of a national health insurance program would answer needs urgently felt by the poor, minorities, and the chronically ill.*

You should be especially wary of faulty generalization if you find that you have written a thesis that covers centuries of history or makes sweeping judgments of right and wrong.

thesis
31b

DON'T:

x The decay of our culture has been accelerating every year.

x The West is guided by Christian morals.

x The purpose of evolution is to create a higher form of human being.

Encyclopedias of support could not establish the plausibility of such theses. Consider: (1) What universally recognized indicators of "cultural decay" do we have, and how could anyone show that cultural decay has been "accelerating every year"? (2) Can something as vague and various as "the West" be said to be "guided" by certain "morals"? How will the writer explain away all the brutalities of the past twenty centuries? (3) How has the writer been able to discover a purpose hidden from all professional students of evolution?

Keeping Personal Experience in Perspective

We have said that personal experience can be an important source of ideas for a college essay (30e, p. 379). Yet you should also recognize the risks of generalizing from such experience. If the question, for instance, is whether the human species has an innate aggressive instinct, you may feel inclined to look in your heart and say either yes or no. To do this, however, would be to rely on guesswork and an inadequate sample of just one case. The same lapse occurs when a foreign-born writer asserts, x *The idea that immigrants want to become "Americanized" is contradicted by all experience,* meaning *I, for one, do not want to be "Americanized."* Someone else writes, x *Professors actually enjoy making students suffer,* meaning *I had an ugly experience in History 10.* Personal experience can usefully illustrate a thesis, but the thesis itself should rest on more public grounds.

31c Avoid a Weaseling or Circular Thesis.

A **weaseling thesis** asserts so little that it expresses nothing more than the writer's wish to stay out of trouble.

thesis
31c

DON'T:

x A deposit law is very controversial.

x Although some people approve of a deposit law, others do not.

To secure interest in your topic you must propose an idea that will require support and illustration to be made convincing. Turn back to 31a, page 386, for "deposit law" theses that do take the necessary degree of risk.

A **circular thesis** doubles back on itself, saying only what is already implied by some of its language.

DON'T:

x The growing popularity of sports shows that people are more interested in athletics than ever before.

x Contact sports should be banned because they involve the violent impact of one body on another.

If the popularity shows the popularity, or if contact is bad because it involves contact, the trial thesis is biting its own tail.

DO:

• The growing popularity of sports expresses nostalgia for a more physically challenging existence.

• Contact sports should be banned because they whet an unhealthy appetite for violence and harm.

Whether or not you agree with these revised trial theses, at least they escape circularity.

31d Do Not Beg the Question.

Beware of settling an issue in advance by posing it in "loaded" language. Such **begging the question** (prejudging the issue) is apparent in each of the following argumentative theses.

DON'T:

x A. It is inadvisable to let hardened criminals out of prison prematurely so that they can renew their war on society.

x B. Society has no right to lock up the victims of poverty and inequality for indefinite periods, brutalizing them in the name of "rehabilitation."

Writers A and B are addressing the same issue, but each of them has settled it in advance. The word *prematurely* already contains the idea that many convicts are released too soon, and other terms—*hardened criminals, renew their war*—reinforce the point. For writer B there is no such thing as a criminal in the first place. Prisoners have already been defined as *victims,* and imprisonment is equated with *brutalizing*. Similarly, the quotation marks around *rehabilitation* dismiss the possibility that a criminal might be taught to reform. The trouble here is that both writers A and B, in their eagerness to sweep away objections, are portraying themselves as close-minded. No one will want to read an essay whose very thesis forbids all disagreement.

Of course your thesis should convey an attitude, but it should do so in fair language.

DO:

- A. The policy of releasing prisoners on probation has not justified the social risks it involves.
- B. If the goal of prisons is to rehabilitate, the prison system must be considered on balance to be a failure.

Note that these two versions are just as hard-hitting as the ones they replace; the difference is that their language does not beg the question.

31e Avoid Either-Or Reasoning.

Make sure your thesis does not pull the alarmist trick of **either-or reasoning**—that is, pretending that the only alternative is something awful. Thus a writer favoring legal abortion might claim, x *We must legalize abortion or the world will become disastrously overpopulated,* and a writer on the opposite side might reply, x *We must prevent legal abortion or the family will cease to exist.* Both writers would be delivering an ultimatum. *Which do you choose, overpopulation or legal abortion? What will it be, legal abortion or the survival of the family?* The choice is supposed to be automatic. All a reader must do, however, to escape the bind is to think of one other possibility. Is there no means to control population except through abortion? Might legal abortion have some lesser consequence than the destruction of family life? Your wisest course would be to admit that people favoring an opposite stand from yours have good reasons for their view—reasons that you do not find decisive. If the issue *were* one of total right versus total wrong, you would probably be wasting your time writing about it.

thesis
31e

31f Avoid *Post Hoc* Explanation.

Bear in mind that two events or conditions can be associated in time without being related as cause and effect. Perhaps this seems obvious, but most of us become superstitious when partisan feelings or pet beliefs are involved. Democrats claim that Republican administrations "cause" economic recessions; Republicans call their rival "the war party" because most wars have erupted when Democrats were in power; and some people support their beliefs by arguing that their dreams were fulfilled or that a certain result followed their witnessing an unusual phenomenon: "I saw a black cat and then lost control of the car"; "I landed my job after I saw a rainbow." This fallacy goes by its Latin name, ***post hoc ergo propter hoc:*** "after this, therefore because of it."

> **POST HOC THESIS:**
> x Aspirin cures colds, as can be seen from the fact that a cold will disappear just a few days after you begin taking regular doses of aspirin.

> **REVISED THESIS:**
> • Though aspirin relieves some cold symptoms, the idea that any currently available medicine "cures" a cold is not supported by evidence.

31g Be Fair to an Opposing Point of View.

thesis
31g

Misstating the Opposing Case: The Straw Man

In formulating your thesis, be careful not to distort a position contrary to your own. Such distortion creates a so-called **straw man**—that is, an imaginary opponent that can be all too easily knocked over. Thus, if the question is whether students should be allowed to serve on faculty committees, a writer would be creating a straw man with this thesis: *Faculty efforts to keep the student body in a state of perpetual childhood must be resisted.* Here the specific issue—the pros and cons of student participation—has conveniently disappeared behind the straw man of wicked faculty intentions. A fairer thesis would be *If* *faculty members really want to make informed judgments about conditions on campus, they ought to welcome student voices on their committees.*

Attacking Personalities: Ad Hominem *Argument*

Still another fallacious shortcut is to attack the people who favor a certain position rather than the position itself. This is known as *ad hominem* (Latin, "to the man") argument. Sometimes such an argument tells us real or invented things about somebody's character or behavior. The implication is that if we disapprove of certain people, we had better reject the idea that has become linked with them. More often the writer simply mentions that a despised faction such as "Communism" or "big business" supports the other side.

DON'T:

x By now we should all recognize the dangers of national health insurance, a scheme for which subversives have long been agitating.

x The benefits of home videotaping are obvious to everyone except the money-crazed Hollywood moguls who stand to lose by it.

DO:

• To judge from the British example, national health insurance might impose an intolerable burden on our economy.

• Although movie executives are understandably worried about competition from home videotaping, they would do better to adapt to the new technology instead of trying to have it banned.

thesis

31g

As politicians realize, *ad hominem* attacks do often have their desired effect. Because none of us has time to think through the pros and cons of every public issue, we sometimes rely on surface clues; if certain "bad guys" are revealed to be on one side, we automatically favor the other. As citizens, though, we ought to recognize that the *ad hominem* appeal is a form of bullying. And as writers, we ought to get along without the cheap advantage it affords. If you *can* win an argument on its merits, do so; if you cannot, you should change your position or even your whole topic.

31h Develop a Full Thesis Statement That Mentions the Most Important Elements of Your Case.

Let us suppose that your thesis is no longer on trial: it has passed the tests of definiteness and reasonable scope, and you are ready to go with it. At this point you would do well to take an extra step that may look unnecessary at first. Cast your thesis into a **full thesis statement**—a sentence that not only names your main point but also includes its most important parts, supplies reasons why that point deserves to be believed, and/or meets objections to it. This statement will probably be long and cumbersome. Never mind: it will *not* appear anywhere in the body of your essay. It is simply a private guide which will help you (a) be completely sure that you are in control of your material and (b) choose a sound organization for your essay's parts (32a, p. 397).

Sometimes your unexpanded thesis will already possess the complexity that can carry you into the work of organizing. We have already met one such thesis/thesis statement: *A deposit law would not only hurt small business people by adding to their expenses and reducing their sales but also result in more, not less, pollution because of the increased trucking it would require.* Here we see three crucial factors begging to be made structurally prominent: added expense, reduced sales, increased pollution. The writer is ready to decide on an effective order for these main supporting points.

More often than not, though, a thesis will be too simple in form to serve as a thesis statement. The remedy is to spell out some of the large considerations that made you adopt the thesis in the first place. You can add *main details, reasons,* and/or *objections,* all of which will become prominent units of your organization.

Including Main Details

Suppose your tested and approved thesis is a sentence as plain as this: *Chinese farming methods differ strikingly from American ones.* Fine—but are you sure you know exactly which differences you will be emphasizing in your essay? Now is the time to clear up any lingering doubt by working those differences into a full thesis statement.

Since you will eventually have to choose an order of presentation for your main details, why not decide right now, as you are drawing

thesis
31h

up your thesis statement? The final position is generally the most emphatic one, whether the unit be a sentence, a paragraph, or a whole essay. Think, then, about the relative importance of your points and arrange them accordingly within your thesis statement:

DO:

- Chinese farming differs strikingly from American farming in its greater concern for using all available space, its handling of crop rotation, its higher proportion of natural to manufactured fertilizers, and, above all, its emphasis on mass labor as opposed to advanced machinery.

Here you already have a complete blueprint for a brief essay, which you could begin writing without delay.

Supplying Reasons

In some theses the main statement does not lend itself to the kind of expansion we have just considered. Yet you can always find more "parts" for your essay—and thus for your full thesis statement—by listing the reasons why you think the thesis deserves to be believed. Suppose, for example, you intend to maintain that *The first year of college often proves to be a depressing one.* That is a fair beginning, but it tells you only that *x proves to be y.* How is a whole paper going to result from such a simple declaration? Ask yourself, then, why or in what ways you find that year typically depressing.

If you tell why in one or more *because* clauses, your thesis statement becomes an organizational blueprint:

thesis
31h

- The first year of college often proves to be a depressing one, because many students have moved away from their parents' homes for the first time, because it is painful to be separated from established friends, and because homework and grading are usually more demanding than they were in high school.

Now you have laid out the nature of your explanation: you are reasoning from an effect (depression) to its causes, which you will discuss one by one in your essay.

Meeting Objections

If your thesis is controversial—and all argumentative theses and many explanatory theses are—you should expect to deal with at least one major objection to it. Typically, you will want to handle that point either through *refutation* or through *concession*—that is, either by showing that the objection is wrong or by granting its truth while showing that it does not overrule your thesis.

Since the objection will be discussed in your essay, it should also appear in your full thesis statement. Include that objection in an *although* clause:

- *Although some students find their freshman year exciting and rewarding,* many others find it depressing, because they have moved away. . . .

Again, suppose you intend to maintain that the government should not insist on equal expenditures for men's and women's athletic programs in college. You know that to be convincing you will have to blunt the force of at least one strong point on the opposing side. Get that point into your full thesis statement, add your positive reasons, and you are ready to go:

- *Although men and women in college should certainly have equal opportunities to participate in sports,* the government should not insist on equal expenditures for men's and women's athletic programs, because in colleges where a football program exists it requires disproportionately high expenditures, and because such a program can produce income to support the entire spectrum of men's and women's athletics.

**thesis
31h**

A mouthful! But, again, a thesis statement is only a roadmap, not an excerpt from your essay. You need not try to make it concise. It will succeed in its purpose if it allows you to move confidently to the next phase of planning.

32 Organizing and Drafting

32a Find the Most Effective Organization for Your Ideas.

The key to arriving at a sound essay structure is to put yourself in your reader's place. Beginning in ignorance, your reader wants to know certain things that fall into a natural order:

1. what is being discussed;
2. what the writer's point is;
3. why objections, if any, to that point are not decisive;
4. on what positive grounds the point should be believed.

As a diagram, then, the most reliable essay structure would look like this:

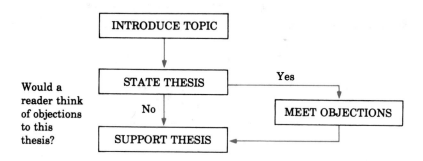

If you try to rearrange this common order, you will find it difficult. How, for example, could a reader want to know the writer's thesis before knowing the issue at stake? Why ask for supporting evidence before knowing what it is evidence *for*? Even the optional part of the sequence, the handling of objections, falls into a logical place. When (as in any argument) it does become important to address objections, the handiest place to do so is right after the thesis has been revealed— for that is where the objections are most likely to occur to the reader and hence to threaten the writer's credibility.

Using the Full Thesis Statement as a Guide

org
32a

By following the simplified model just discussed you can derive the structure of a brief essay directly from your full thesis statement.

1. The *topic,* the first element of the model, is known from the thesis statement because it is the question answered by the thesis.

2. The *thesis* is directly named in the thesis statement.

3. If the thesis contains an *although* clause, at least one important *objection* has been isolated.

4. *Because* clauses in the thesis statement specify the final element of structure, the main points of support for the thesis.

Moving beyond a Fixed Pattern

The principles of organization mentioned above will serve you best if you take them as a starting point rather than an inflexible guide. There are things the model cannot do—choices you must settle either through a detailed outline (32b) or through problem solving as you work your way through a draft. Specifically, the model

—does not tell you how to catch a reader's interest;

—does not say how many objections, if any, you should deal with, or whether they should be met by concession or by refutation (p. 396);

—does not say how much space you should devote to any single point; and

—does not indicate whether you will need a formal concluding paragraph.

Thus your developing sense of problems, opportunities, and paragraph-by-paragraph tactics should be your final guide.

Suppose, for instance, you notice that the best positive evidence for your thesis consists of points that also answer main objections. In that case it would be wasteful to treat objections and supporting evidence separately. Or, again, the decision to include or skip a summary paragraph at the end is a matter of weighing available alternatives. If your essay is long and complex, a conclusion is probably called for. But if you saved a decisive point of evidence, a revealing incident, or a striking sentence, you may be well advised to end dramatically with that clincher and omit a concluding paragraph.

org
32b

32b Suit an Outline to Your Purpose.

An outline can be an important aid to your composing, but to make good use of it you must first appreciate what it *cannot* do. Briefly, it cannot replace a sound thesis.

Some writers, equating an outline with "good organization," are tempted to go directly from a subject area or topic (30c, p. 376) to an outline:

DONT:

x Topic: Commercial Airlines
  I. Relation to Military
  II. The Jet Age
  III. Fare Wars in the 1980s
  IV. Future of the Industry

An explanatory or argumentative essay, you recall, must pursue a point from beginning to end. In contrast, the outline above merely identifies assorted subtopics that the writer hopes to cover. It is actually doing the writer a disservice by giving off a false appearance of order and purpose. Be sure, then, that any outline of your own is preceded by and derived from a thesis statement. Even if some parts of your outline look like subtopics, you will know that they represent necessary steps in the case you will be making for your thesis.

Competent writers differ greatly in their fondness for an outline. If, like some of them, you find that you simply cannot work from an outline in writing your first draft, you should nevertheless make an outline of that draft when you have finished it. There is no better way of spotting redundancies and inconsistencies that need fixing.

Scratch Outline

If your essay is going to be brief and you simply need to decide on an order for several paragraphs, you will be adequately served by a **scratch outline**—that is, one showing no subordination of some points to others.

Suppose, for instance, you had hit upon the following thesis statement for an explanatory 600-word essay: *Although television and radio both cover news developments and sports events, their styles are necessarily different, TV leaning toward "editorial" and radio toward "reportorial" coverage.* A serviceable scratch outline of your paragraphs might look like this:

¶1 { **1.** TV and radio cover many of the same happenings, e.g., news developments and sports events.

org
32b

2. Thesis: But the two styles differ. Because TV can show what radio has to describe, TV has more air time to comment on events.

3. News developments (films clips of speeches, interviews, battles, election returns, etc.): only on TV are the events partly allowed to speak for themselves, with occasional or follow-up commentary by news analysts.

4. Sports events: TV, relatively free from reporting what is happening, includes more commentary than radio does.

5. In summary: TV coverage doesn't abolish the spoken word, but because we can *see,* the balance tips toward "editorial" as opposed to radio's "reportorial" coverage.

Subordinated Outline

For longer and more complex essays you may want to use a **subordinated outline**—one that shows, through indention and more than one set of numbers, that some points are more important than others.

Suppose, for instance, you had decided to write a thousand-word argument opposing rent control of off-campus housing, and you were satisfied with the following thesis statement: *Although off-campus rent control is aimed at securing reasonable rents for students, it would actually produce four undesirable effects: establishment of an expensive, permanent rent-control bureaucracy; landlord neglect of rental property; a shortage of available units; and a freezing of currently excessive rents.* Knowing that your argument would be fairly complex, you might want to draw up a full outline:

**org
32b**

   I. The Problem Is That Students Now Face Hardships in Securing Adequate Housing.
     A. Students are currently subject to rent gouging.
     B. High rents force many students to live far from campus.

  II. The Promise Is That Rent Control Will Guarantee Reasonable Rents near Campus.

 III. The Reality Is That the Actual Effects of Rent Control Would Be Undesirable.

A. An expensive, permanent rent-control bureaucracy would be established.
B. Landlords would neglect rent-controlled property.
C. The shortage of units would *worsen,* because:
   1. Owners would have no incentive to increase the number of rental units.
   2. Competition for rent-frozen units would be more intense.
D. Currently excessive rents would be frozen, thus ruling out any possible reduction.

Notice that this outline establishes three degrees of importance among your ideas. The Roman numerals running down the left margin point to the underlying structure of the essay, a movement from problem to promise to reality. These main categories come straight from the thesis statement. The *problem* is the topic itself; the *promise* is the "although" consideration, which is taken care of early; and the *reality,* the thesis itself, consists of the "four undesirable effects" of off-campus rent control.

At the next level of subordination, the indented capital letters introduce ideas that contribute to these larger units. The problem, says Part I of the outline, has two aspects: rent gouging and the forcing of students to seek lower rents far from campus. By listing those aspects as *A* and *B,* you assign them parallel or roughly equivalent status in your argument.

Points A through D in Part III are also parallel, but one of them, C, is supported in turn by two narrower points. By assigning those two points Arabic numerals and by a further indention from the left margin, you indicate to yourself that these considerations go to prove the larger idea just above them. Thus the three sets of numbering/lettering and the three degrees of indention display the whole logic of your essay.

org
32b

Sentence versus Topic Outline

The example just given is a **sentence outline**, using complete sentences to state every planned idea. A sentence outline is the safest kind, because its complete statements ensure that you will be making assertions, not just touching on subjects, in every part of your essay.

But if you are confident of keeping your full points in mind, you can use the simpler **topic outline**, replacing sentences with concise phrases:

I. The Problem
   A. Rent Gouging
   B. Students Forced to Live Far from Campus (etc.)

The form you choose for an outline is hardly an earthshaking matter; just be sure the outline gives you enough direction, and do not waste time elaborating an outline until it is more intricate and hairsplitting than your essay itself.

Keeping Outline Categories in Logical Relation

If you do use subordination in an outline, observe that one heading or subheading should always have at least one mate—no *I* without *II,* no *A* without *B.* The reason is that headings and subheadings represent divisions of a larger unit, either a more general point or the thesis of the whole essay. It is of course impossible to divide something into just one part. If you have a lonesome *A* in a draft outline, work it into the larger category:

ILLOGICAL:
x I. Problems
   A. Excessive Noise
 II. Cost Factors
   A. Overruns

BETTER:
• I. Problems of Excessive Noise
 II. Cost Overruns

org
32b

In addition, you should always check a draft outline to make sure that all the subheadings under a given heading logically contribute to it. Do not try to tuck in irrelevant items just because you find no other place for them; that would defeat the whole purpose of outlining, which is to keep your essay coherent and logical in moving from one idea to the next.

32c Consider Your Audience and Purpose.

Even with a full thesis statement and an outline in hand, you will not want to begin writing mechanically—just churning out the material you have decided to present. Rather, it is time to focus on your goal: to make a certain kind of impression on a certain reader. Your **rhetoric**, in other words, must be geared to the specific audience and purpose you have in mind.

This advice may leave you uneasy if you think of rhetoric in its casual meaning of insincere, windy language, as in *Oh, that's just a lot of rhetoric.* But in its primary meaning rhetoric is simply *the strategic placement of ideas and choice of language*—the means of making an intended effect on a reader or listener. Rhetoric need never call for deceptive prose; it calls, rather, for making a strong case by satisfying your audience's legitimate expectations.

Instructor as Audience

Even in a composition course, where practice with various forms of writing is the goal, you at least know who the main audience for every assignment will be. It is your instructor—not, however, as a unique individual, but as someone who will try to represent generally accepted standards of careful, sympathetic reading.

Classmates as Audience

You can also get the desired sense of contact if, while you compose, you think of your classmates as your audience. This is not to say that you should write in chummy slang. Rather, if you think of trying to convince people like yourself, you will get a reliable sense of what needs proving, what you can take for granted, and what tone to adopt (32d, p. 406). It is true that classmates sometimes apply "the rules" with a strictness that may make your instructor look easygoing by comparison. But your classmates share your world in important ways, and you can usually trust their good sense. If the student sitting next to you would choke on some contrived generalization, leave it out. If you suspect that the class as a whole would say *Make that clearer* or *Get to the point,* do so. Your instructor will be delighted by any essay that would impress most of your classmates.

32d Choose between a Personal and an Impersonal Voice.

Voice refers to the "self" projected by a given piece of writing. The relevant question to ask is not "what am I really like?" but "what is the nature of this occasion?" For certain occasions you will want to maintain a formal, impersonal air, while in others you will want readers to feel much closer to you as an individual.

Consider the following deliberat ly impersonal paragraph.

IMPERSONAL VOICE:

Asked to compare the benefits of academic jobs with jobs in government or business, over 90% of humanities graduate students cited greater flexibility in the use of time. Two-thirds or more mentioned freedom to do as one wished, opportunities to experiment with differing life-styles, and ability to flout social conventions. On the down side, one-quarter to two-fifths expressed suspicion that a teaching job would carry less social prestige and less job security. They were divided almost evenly on whether teaching would involve less leisure or more. The chief drawback to the academic career identified by the majority was relatively lower earning power.

—ERNEST R. MAY and DOROTHY G. BLANEY, *Careers for Humanists*

The authors of this passage want to show a serious, well-informed audience that they are reliable transmitters of information. They do not refer even distantly to their own experiences, opinions, or feelings; nor do they ask their readers for anything beyond attention to the reported results. In this deliberately neutral prose, "the facts speak for themselves." The absence of intimacy is a deliberate stylistic effect, well suited to the businesslike work of conveying information. Whenever that is your chief purpose—as, for example, in a report of facts you have uncovered or of laboratory results you have obtained—you will want to adopt such an **impersonal voice**.

The following student paragraph illustrates an opposite effect.

PERSONAL VOICE:

Eating the catered meals they serve on airplanes is always a memorable experience. In the first place, you have to admit it is exciting to open that little carton of salad oil and find a stream of Thousand Islands dressing rocketing onto your blouse. Then, too, where else would you be able to dig into a *perfectly* rectangular chicken? And let's not forget the soggy, lukewarm mushrooms which are accused by the menu of having "smothered" the geometrical bird. They look and taste exactly like the ear jacks that are forever falling off your rented headset. Come to think of it, what *do* they do with those jacks when the flight is over?

This writer, using a **personal voice**, everywhere implies that she is drawing on her private experience, and she insists on an involved response by addressing her reader as an individual: *you have to admit; your blouse; where else would you be able; your rented headset.* Since the "facts" in this passage are not facts at all but witty exaggerations of widely shared inconveniences, the writer wants us to gather that she is saying at least as much about her own wry, mildly cynical attitude toward life as she is about airline food.

By choosing an appropriate voice, you also help to establish the **tone,** or quality of feeling, of your essay, paper, or report. An impersonal voice necessarily carries a dry, factual tone, but a personal voice can be intense, respectful, supportive, fanciful, mocking, worldly, authoritative, etc., depending on your purpose. Compare the wry tone of the "airline food" passage, for example, with that of the following lines by Martin Luther King, Jr., addressing a "letter" to eight Alabama clergymen who had urged him to proceed cautiously in seeking racial justice. Both voices are personal, but King's tone is noble and angry:

org
32d

We know through painful experience that freedom is never voluntarily given by the oppressor; it must be demanded by the oppressed. Frankly, I have yet to engage in a direct-action campaign that was "well timed" in the view of those who have not suffered unduly from the disease of segregation. For years now I have heard the word "Wait!" It rings in the ear of every Negro with piercing familiarity. This "Wait" has almost always meant "Never." We must come to see, with one of our distinguished jurists, that "justice too long delayed is justice denied."

—Martin Luther King, jr.,
Why We Can't Wait

Here is the rhetoric of a writer who knows that he cannot bank on much agreement from his immediate readers; after all, they had just written *him* a highly critical letter. Instead of swallowing his feelings, King defiantly stands on his own authority: *I have yet to engage in a direct-action campaign that was "well timed" . . . ; for years now I have heard the word "Wait!"* He and other black activists *know through painful experience* what the eight timid clergymen will never know about how freedom is won; and he and *every Negro* have a personal basis for asserting that *"Wait" has almost always meant "Never."*

Choice of Governing Pronoun

Notice that the **governing pronoun** you choose for your essay helps to establish a consistent voice. If you call yourself *I,* you are guaranteeing at least a degree of personal emphasis. Even greater intimacy is implied if, like the "airline food" writer, you presume to call your reader *you.* That pronoun can quickly wear out its welcome, however; a reader resents being told exactly what to think and feel. If, like King, you occasionally shift from the personal *I* to the community *we,* you can imply a sense of shared values between yourself and all fair-minded readers. And if you want a strictly formal, impersonal effect, you should refer to yourself rarely, if at all—and then only as a member of the indefinite "editorial" *we,* as in *We shall see below. . . .*

32e Generally Prefer a Forthright Stance.

Most essays and nearly all college papers, like the prose of this present book, are meant to be taken "straight." Readers sense that the writer is taking a **forthright stance**—a straightforward, trustworthy rhetorical posture. Thus they assume that the writer is being sincere in making assertions and in endorsing certain attitudes while disapproving of others.

The following paragraph from a freshman essay shows the usual features of the forthright stance:

When this University switched from quarters to semesters, my first reaction was dismay over my shortened summer. The last spring quarter ended in mid-June; the first fall semester began in August. Was this what the new order would be like—a general speedup? It took me a while to realize that my lost vacation was not a permanent feature of the semester system but a one-time inconvenience. Now that I have survived nearly two whole semesters, I am ready to admit that there is much to be said for the changed calendar. As for vacations, those five weeks of freedom around Christmas have turned my vanished summer into a trivial, faded memory.

Note how this writer, using middle diction (28a, p. 327) and maintaining an earnest manner, carefully lays out the reasons why she had first one reaction and then another to the semester system. Whether or not she is being strictly accurate in recalling her feelings, she gives us no cause to doubt any of her statements.

32f Note the Special Effects of an Ironic Stance.

Once in a while, instead of taking the usual forthright stance (32e), a writer may strike an **ironic stance**, saying one thing in such a way as to express a different or even opposite meaning. Irony is delicious when it works and disastrous when it does not. Before practicing it, you should understand what kinds of opportunities and difficulties it typically presents.

Irony can be either subtle or broad and either local or sustained. Local and subtle irony, lasting only for a sentence or two and scarcely striking the reader's attention, can enter into any essay possessing a personal voice (32d). Take, for example, the sentence *Recovery from an all-out nuclear attack would not be quite the routine project that some officials want us to believe.* The irony here, barely noticeable at first, is concentrated on the word *quite.* Taken at face value, the sentence claims that recovery from an all-out nuclear attack would be *almost* routine. But of course the writer means just the reverse—that there would be nothing routine about it. The word *quite* serves two ironic functions, twitting the business-as-usual mentality of the bureaucrats and hinting, through *understatement,* at the unspeakable horror of an actual nuclear attack. After such a sentence, the writer would want to shift to a straightforward stance and paint the gruesome details.

Broad irony, in contrast to the subtle kind, is deliberately outrageous in turning the world upside down to make fun of some disapproved policy or position. The idea is to *pretend to take seriously* a

org
32f

ridiculous extension of that policy or position and to run through its consequences with seeming enthusiasm. Thus, in the most famous example of broad irony, Jonathan Swift's "A Modest Proposal" suggested that the Irish children who were being starved by English absentee landlords could be profitably butchered and sold as meat for their persecutors' tables. Swift was not of course putting forward any such plan; he was ironically exposing the landlords' inhumanity.

For a modern sample of broad irony, consider the following excerpts from an essay mocking the bewildering options faced by consumers after the breakup of the national telephone monopoly in 1984. The writer pretends that gas and electricity, too, are about to be deregulated:

With the proposed breakup of PG&E, many subscribers have been thrown into confusion over exactly *how* it will work once gas and electricity are distributed according to age, sex and zip code. . . .

Using guidelines established in the recent AT&T breakup, the new PG&E will become Gasco and ElectroCorp, with customers billed for each, either by the month or triannually, depending. Those over sixty-five will be billed weekly. . . .

Subscribers to Gasco will have their choice of gas and, in some cases, meter readers. Those with gas ranges and gas heaters can choose between gas piped in from Alaska (more expensive but hotter) and gas that comes directly from local gas lines (more toxic but cheaper). People who use a lot of gas and not much electricity—or vice versa—will be able to decide which of several smaller gas and electric companies they prefer.

Major gas users may find it more economical to forgo Gasco and subscribe to either Big Boy Gas or FumeCo, "no-frills" companies able to supply low-cost gas on a prorated, per-annum, prix-fixe basis. Those with a greater demand for electricity may decide to go with Specific Gas & Electric, which has a twenty-four-hour service that provides energy to customers "by the appliance." Here is how it works. Say you have a washing machine, a gas stove, a TV set, two radios and a canary. When your bill arrives, there will be a separate page for each appliance under 540 milliwicks. . . .

It is, of course, still possible to rent a utility pole or gas main by the month, but it's probably cheaper to buy your own, if you're a regular user of either gas or electricity. The average utility pole costs anywhere from $175 to $250, and comes in various sizes and decorator colors; the most popular is the Evergreen, which clamps onto any standard back-fence jack.

org
32f

"But I never *bought* a gas main before," you may say. You are not alone. Many people have not, so it's going to mean a period of adjustment for many. Tough.

Most neighborhoods have utility pole and gas main boutiques, where one may drop in and ask to look at the various models available. Or you might want to attend a natural gas show at the Civic Auditorium. No one but you can be the ultimate judge of the *kind* of gas main that will best fit your daily needs. . . .

—Gerald Nachman,
"Your Home Guide to Energy Divestiture"

If you have a fruitful premise to work with—one like "Let's pretend that Irish children can be sold as table meat" or "Let's pretend that energy is going to be deregulated as the phone business was"—you can build a whole essay upon broad irony, working out the various implications of the absurd situation you have created. But if you are just poking fun at others or yourself, you would do well to keep your irony relatively low-keyed. A whole essay taking the stance of the "airplane food" passage (p. 406), for example, would become tiresome.

By adopting a less blatant ironic stance, one that only gradually becomes apparent to us, another student writer is able to sustain a whimsical effect:

**org
32f**

Powerful people never walk aimlessly. You'll never see James Bond stop in the middle of a room and look around, scratching his head. I went directly for the blackjack table because I was aimed for it. I stood behind a woman, maybe my age, waiting for her cards. She got ten more dollars out of the wide-open purse in her lap. In it was her room key chain with 312 embossed in gold. Her nervousness proved her a novice at the game and the casino—she was too well-dressed to be a regular. I smiled at her hand. Too much sophistication won't allow a man to smile at a stranger. "I'll hold." She laid her cards down and lost. "Why didn't you tell me? Didn't you see my hand?" I got the waitress. "Bambi [I saw her name tag], would you be so kind as to send a bottle of champagne to room 312?" I gave her the $25 covering the room service charge. I looked down at the woman still seated at the blackjack table (down is the direction of the most powerful eyes) and explained, "You see, I make it a point not to get involved in the games played. Had I misled you, you might not come back." This stunned her and the dealer. The waitress shuffled off to do as I said. I walked back to the hallway to prove that it wasn't a pick-up. In the elevator up to my room, I finally exhaled, having sucked in my stomach throughout the whole adventure, and cursed myself for having blown $25 on someone I didn't even know. . . .

We are never quite sure, in reading this passage, whether the writer's main target is the artificiality of "James Bond" conventions or his own fantasy of being a "powerful person." But precisely because we are not being bludgeoned by obvious sarcasms, we are eager to keep reading.

If you plan to submit an essay of broad irony, check with your instructor first. Many writing assignments have important purposes that cannot be met once you have adopted the broad-ironical stance. Beware of reaching for irony simply because you would rather not fulfill the terms of the assignment.

32g Mix Improvising with Planning in Writing Your First Draft.

Even after much preparation, you may feel some resistance to committing your first draft to paper. If the opening paragraph (23a–23d, pp. 271–275) looms as an especially big obstacle, try skipping it and starting with a later one. If you seem to be losing momentum in the middle of a sentence, shift into a private shorthand that will keep you from worrying about the fine points of expression; you can return to them later. And instead of writing, you may find it easier to talk into a tape recorder and then transcribe the better parts. Whether you write or dictate, do not be afraid to include too much, to leave blank spaces, or to commit errors of usage and punctuation. What matters is that you move ahead, understanding that you will have a substantial job of revision to do (Chapter 33).

org
32g

Do not be alarmed if you find new possibilities coming into view as you finish one sentence and struggle to begin the next one. Some of your best ideas—perhaps even a radically improved thesis—can be generated by that friction between the written sentence and the not-yet-written one. So long as you anticipate the need to reconsider and reorganize after your first draft is complete, the tug of war between plans and inspirations should result in a subtler, more engaging paper than you originally expected to submit.

33 Revising

33a Anticipate the Need to Revise.

Many students are willing enough to revise their work but are held back by two misconceptions. First, they suppose that revision begins only when an essay is nearly ready to be turned in; and second, they think that revision involves only a tidying up of word choice, spelling, punctuation, and usage. But experienced writers revise their prose even while they are first producing it—adding, deleting, replacing, and rearranging material at every opportunity (see 30b, p. 373). They never assume that any given draft will be the last one. And they stand ready to make *conceptual* and *organizational* changes as well as *editorial* ones.

If you have access to a word processor, you will find revising a text much simplified. The word processor allows you to move, delete, or insert a passage without having to do substantial retyping.

Seeking Responses to a Draft

If you could put a draft aside for a week or two, you would see flaws in it that a quick reading cannot uncover. Unfortunately, student writers rarely have that luxury. But perhaps a classmate, a roommate, a writing lab tutor, or your instructor may be willing to advise you about needed revisions. You, of course, must be the final judge of which advice to take and which to disregard as unreliable. Yet by posing key questions, you can actually oblige people to give you their best judgment. Ask them:

1. Can you accurately state my thesis?

2. What is the main impression (positive or negative) my essay has made on you?

3. Have I left you with any unanswered questions? If so, what are they?

4. What points need further—or less—development?

5. Are my opening and closing paragraphs effective?

6. Which words strike you as "off" in meaning, tone, correctness of usage, or spelling?

These questions form only a fraction of the checklist you should apply to your own work (33e, p. 420), but anyone who addresses all of them will be doing you a considerable favor.

33b Attend to Conceptual and Organizational Revision.

Because sentence-by-sentence composing (32g, p. 411) often leads to new ideas, you must read through your completed draft to be sure it makes a consistent impression. Do not hesitate to alter your thesis or even reverse it if you become more swayed by objections than by supporting points. Such a shift can be painful and time-consuming, but in the long run it will spare you many hours of trying to show interest in ideas that you now consider fatally weak.

rev
33b

You should be prepared to make less sweeping conceptual changes as well. Have you exaggerated your claims? Are your explanations clear? Do you need to supply more evidence? Give your conceptual revisions top priority; there is no reason to tinker with phraseology if the whole direction of your essay has to be changed.

After you have made necessary changes in your ideas, check your draft to see if your points appear in a logical and persuasive order. Have you placed your thesis prominently? Have you waited to unveil it until you have attracted the reader's interest and clearly identified the topic? Have you avoided digressions, or passages that stray from the issue at hand? Have you avoided redundancy, or needless repetition of assertions? Are all of your quotations succinct and necessary? And have you included all necessary information—for example, the setting for your discussion of an event, the rules of a little-known game, or the plot of an unassigned novel? Here as elsewhere the key to successful revision is to "play reader" and probe for sources of puzzlement or dissatisfaction.

33c Attend to Editorial Revision.

Though editorial revision is rarely the most important kind, it does cover the greatest number of problems. They range from such finicky matters as citation form (Chapter 37) to such broad ones as the striking of an appropriate voice and stance. In every case, effective revision flows from putting the reader's convenience ahead of your own.

FEATURE	REVISE FOR	HELPS READER TO
voice, stance	appropriateness to audience and purpose	appreciate tone and point of view
paragraphs	unity, continuity, development	see relations between major and minor points
sentences	distinctness, subordination, emphasis, variety	follow ideas, avoid tedium
words	appropriateness, liveliness	get clear information, avoid jarring effects
grammar, usage, punctuation, spelling, other conventions	conformity with standard written practice	concentrate on substance of essay
citation form	fullness, exactness, consistency	have access to secondary information

rev
33c

For an idea of how instructors typically draw attention to editorial problems and how students then revise, consider the following made-up paragraph and the **symbols for comment and revision** (see the inside back cover) that have been added to it:

Once people [have gone to the trouble of acquiring the capacity to treat everyone] as equals, they can *wdy* work with others for the common good. A great ex- *exagg* ample is how the Los Angeles area handled it's pol- *sp* lution problem. Everyone was aware of the stifling smog. But the majority of these people were will- *ref* ing only to complain. One group of citizens, how- ever came up with a creative plan for carpooling. *p* Providing an incentive, one lane of freeway was set *dm* aside for cars carrying three or more people. [But after a short period of time,] the committment was *sp* abandoned. [Because of the godawful traffic jams in *colloq* the other lanes.] It was a promising idea, but most *ref* people are made [less upset by smog so that] they *comp* actually prefer it to traffic jams in freeway *red* lanes.

pred chop frag pass • *¶ unity*

rev
33c

The most important of these markings is *¶unity*, since it calls for a substantial rewriting that would automatically eliminate some of the smaller problems. But if the student were to address those problems as they stand, the diagnoses and the most likely remedies would be these.

SYMBOL	PROBLEM AND SOLUTION	UNREVISED VERSION	REVISION
wdy	the expression is wordy; make it more concise	Once people have gone to the trouble of acquiring the capacity to treat everyone as equals	Once people can recognize others as equals
		after a short period of time	soon
exagg	the expression is overstated; tone it down	A great example	One example
pred	faulty predication; do away with the mismatch between subject and predicate	One example is how . . .	One example is the handling . . . ; *or* Consider, for example, how Los Angeles handled . . .
sp	spelling error; look the word up and spell it correctly	it's	its
		committment	commitment
chop	choppy sentences: several plain, brief sentences in a row; introduce variety of structure	A great example is how Los Angeles . . . willing to complain.	Consider, for example, how Los Angeles handled its pollution problem. Even though everyone was aware of the stifling smog, few people were willing at first to do anything more than complain.
ref	pronouns or demonstratives lack clear, explicitly stated antecedents; make the reference clear	these people	residents
		It was a promising idea	The carpooling plan was a promising idea

rev
33c

p	punctuation error; correct it	One group of citizens, however came up with	One group of citizens, however, came up with
dm	dangling modifier; supply an agent to perform the action	Providing an incentive, one lane of freeway was set aside	Providing an incentive, county officials set aside
colloq	the expression falls beneath the level of diction appropriate to this paper; find a midddle-level substitute	godawful	serious
frag	sentence fragment; rewrite or combine to form a grammatically complete sentence	Because of serious traffic jams in the other lanes.	But because of serious traffic jams in the other lanes, the commitment was soon abandoned.
pass	unnecessary use of passive voice; shift to active voice	most people are made less upset	most people would rather
comp	faulty comparison; match the compared terms or completely recast the expression	most people are made less upset by smog so that	most people prefer smog to traffic jams; *or* most people find smog less offensive than traffic jams
red	this expression repeats an earlier one; rephrase it	traffic jams in the other lanes . . . traffic jams in freeway lanes	. . . most people prefer lung congestion to traffic congestion

rev
33c

As for ꓩ *uni'ty*, notice that the writer began by asserting that *people can work for the common good* but then went on to illustrate a nearly opposite point, that *most people cannot put the public interest before their immediate convenience.* Until that contradiction is resolved, no amount of tinkering can make the paragraph effective.

To weigh the writer's options, ask yourself which idea shows more regard for real experience, the initial one or the one that surfaced in the drafting process. It is really no contest. *Working with others for the common good* is a limp "motherhood" concept, wishful and unprovocative. The conflict between selfish private habits and the common good is a more balanced, less simplistic notion—one that indicates the writer's ability to face facts. Thus the writer would do well to skip the moralizing and rethink the whole thesis. An eventual, radically improved version of the paragraph might look like this:

When selfish private habits and the common good come into conflict, the outcome is likely to be all too predictable. Take a recent example from Los Angeles, where everyone's health would be safe-guarded by a significant reduction in automobile exhausts. Acting on the suggestion of a citizens' group, county officials tried to promote carpooling by setting aside one lane of each freeway for cars carrying three or more people. If it had worked, this plan would have enabled everyone to breathe more easily. The plan had to be dropped, however, when so few people cooperated that motorists refus-ing to share rides were hopelessly clogging the re-maining lanes. Forced to choose between lung congestion and traffic congestion, Los Angelenos will take lung congestion every time.

33d Make Your Title Definite.

Do not bother thinking of a title until you have finished at least one draft, and be ready to change titles as your later drafts change emphasis. If you begin with a title, it will probably indicate little more than the subject matter treated in your essay. Replace it later with a title expressing your *view of* that subject matter, or at least posing the question answered by your thesis. Thus, asked to write about revision, do not remain satisfied with "Revision" or "Revising College Essays"; such toneless titles suggest that you have no thesis at all. Instead, try something like "The Agony of Revision," "Revision as Discovery," or "Is an Essay Ever Really Finished?" Each of those versions tells the reader that you have found something definite to say.

That impression will be especially strong if you can make your title surprising and vivid. Look for a striking figure of speech (28g, p. 336) that could suggest your thesis with pointed wit. One common device is to combine such a phrase with a more straightforwardly informative subtitle:

- Downhill All the Way: My Melting Career as a Ski Racer
- Going High for the Rebound: Drugs and Professional Basketball

If your essay contains especially significant phrases (original or quoted), see if any of them could be borrowed for your title. One freshman student, for example, began a prizewinning essay about *Hamlet* with the following paragraph:

rev
33d

```
While showing Guildenstern how to play the re-
corder, Hamlet remarks that it is "as easy as
lying" (III.ii.343).  In a sense, much of the
play's meaning is expressed in this line.  Almost
every character in Hamlet is to some extent living
a lie: hiding thoughts, playing a role, trying to
deceive another character.  Claudius conceals his
```

```
crime; Hamlet feigns madness; private schemes pre-
vail.  In the end, Hamlet may even be deceiving
himself, forcing himself into a role of avenger
when he may not actually fit.
```

For a title, the writer chose "As Easy As Lying"—a phrase that stirred curiosity and gave promise of a well-considered, original thesis.

33e Test Your Draft against a Checklist for Revision.

Since you cannot always count on having a friendly critic available, you will need to test your drafts yourself against standards that readers commonly hold. The following questions form a checklist that you can consult as soon as you have finished a draft or two. Running through the questions, you may be able to pinpoint any remaining problems and locate the relevant discussions of them in this book.

A CHECKLIST FOR REVISION

1. Does my title indicate that I have a point to make (33d)?
2. Do I have a clear, properly limited, and interesting thesis (31a–31g, pp. 386–393)?
3. Have I adequately supported my thesis (32a–32b, pp. 397–404)?
4. Have I dealt with probable objections to my thesis (31g–31h, pp. 392–396)?
5. Is my thesis conspicuously stated (33b, p. 413)?
6. Are my voice and stance appropriate to my audience and purpose (32d–32f, pp. 405–411)?
7. Are my paragraphs unified and fully developed (21, 22, pp. 247–270)?
8. Does my first paragraph attract the reader's interest (23a–23d, pp. 271–275)?
9. Have I made clear and helpful transitions between paragraphs (21i–21j, pp. 258–260)?

rev
33e

10. Does my last paragraph give enough sense of completion (23f–23i, pp. 276–278)?

11. Are my sentences clear and efficient (24, 25, pp. 281–297)?

12. Do my sentences show enough emphasis and variety of structure (26, pp. 298–310)?

13. Do my words mean what I think they mean (27a–27b, pp. 313–318)?

14. Are my words appropriate to the occasion (27c–27g, pp. 318–326)?

15. Is my language as lively as the occasion allows (28, pp. 327–340)?

16. Have I looked up the spelling of doubtful words (18, pp. 198–219)?

17. Have I kept to standard written usage (1–8, pp. 5–116)?

18. Does my punctuation bring out my meaning (9–12, pp. 119–145)?

19. Have I followed correct form for capitals, italics, abbreviations, and numbers (19–20, pp. 220–242)?

20. Have I followed correct form for quoting other people's words (13, pp. 146–160)?

21. Have I supplied all necessary documentation and followed a standard form for doing so (37, pp. 472–498)?

33f Observe Standard Typescript Form in Your Final Copy.

rev
33f

No matter how many changes you make between drafts, the essay you eventually submit should look unscarred, or nearly so. It should also meet certain technical requirements of form. The following advice reflects general practice and should be followed whenever your instructor does not specify something different.

---

1. Type your essay if possible, using standard-sized (8½″ × 11″) unlined white paper of ordinary weight, not onionskin. If you must write longhand, choose paper with widely spaced lines or write on every other line. Type with an unfaded black ribbon or write in dark ink. Use only one side of the paper.

2. Put your name, the course number, your instructor's name and the date of submission on four double-spaced lines at the upper right corner of your first page, above your title. Skip four lines between your title and the beginning of your text.

3. If you are asked to supply a thesis statement and/or an outline, put them on a separate page along with your name, the course number, your instructor's name, the date of submission, and the title of your essay. Repeat the title on your first page of text. (See p. 512 for an example.)

4. Allow at least one-inch margins on all four sides of each page of your main text. Your right margins need not be even. In a hand-written essay, be sure to leave as much space as in a typewritten one.

5. Leave the first page of text (and notes and bibliography, if any) unnumbered, but put unpunctuated Arabic numerals (2, 3, 4) in the upper right corners of subsequent pages.

6. Double-space your whole paper, including any reference list (37c, p. 479), endnotes (37e, p. 490), or bibliography (37e, p. 477). Single-space any footnotes (37e, p. 490). Follow your instructor's specifications for the spacing of extracted quotations (13h, p. 152).

7. Indent the first line of each paragraph by five type-spaces, or, in a handwritten essay, about an inch. Do not skip extra lines between paragraphs. Indent extracted quotations (13h, p. 152) by ten spaces.

8. Retype any pages on which you had to make more than a few last-minute changes. Otherwise, type those changes or write them clearly in ink, using the following conventions:

   a) Remove unwanted letters with a diagonal slash:
      indigestio/n

   b) Remove unwanted words by running a line through them:
      ~~nasty~~

   c) Replace a letter by putting the new letter above your slash:
      compo/ition
         s
      compo/ition

   d) Replace words by putting the new word above your canceled one:
                    writer
      please every ~~reader~~

e) Add words or letters by putting a caret (∧) at the point of insertion and placing the extra words or letters above it:

```
                notable
      Another∧feature of this device
```

f) Separate words or letters by placing a vertical line between them:

```
      steel and|iron
```

g) Close up separated letters with a curved line connecting them from above:

```
      hic⌒cup
```

h) Transpose (reverse) letters or words with a curved enclosing line:

```
      Al⸨ic⸩e, ⸨Carroll Lewis⸩
```

i) Indicate a paragraph break by inserting the paragraph symbol before the first word of the new paragraph:

```
      depends on development. ¶ Transitions, too, have a
      certain importance.
```

j) Run two paragraphs together by connecting them with an arrow and writing **no ¶** in the margin:

```
      She has found a way of turning "nothing" time into
      pleasure or learning⌐
          ↳ Isn't that better than having some trivial
no¶   chitchat on the sidewalk?
```

9. Carefully proofread your final copy, looking especially for typing errors. Check all quotations against your notes or, better, against the printed passages.

10. Make sure you have assembled your pages in order. Fasten them with a paper clip or, second best, with a staple.

11. Make a carbon copy of your essay or photocopy it, and retain the copy until you get the original back. Keep the graded original at least until the course is over. These steps will protect you if your instructor should mislay an essay or misrecord a grade.

rev
33f

For the forming and spacing of punctuation marks, see Chapter 14, pages 161–166. For citation form, see 37c–37f, pages 479–498.

34 One Essay from Start to Finish

A freshman student, asked to save her notes and drafts, found herself with a week and a half in which to write a thousand-word essay on any topic within the subject area "Technology and the Quality of Life." She knew that her topic would have to be narrower than that. In her earliest notes she mulled over several possibilities:

Computers . . . too broad. Subject doesn't seem to fascinate me anyway.

Cordless phones: nothing here? So you can take the phone into the kitchen without tripping over the cord. That's nice, but so what?

VCR's: Betamax etc. OK in theory—no real ideas yet.

Portable headsets—maybe something here? The world is getting divided into people who do and don't live inside those things.

Robots in factories?

Janet liked the idea of writing about radios and tape players that can be carried in a pocket and played through earphones, but she didn't yet know *why* she liked it or what she wanted to say about it. To explore her trial topic, she began with reporter's questions (30i, p. 383), seeing if any of the answers would lead her further:

Who? Joggers, bicyclists, misc. pedestrians, students crossing campus. . . . Mostly middle-class.

What? Walkman, etc.

When? Any waking hours. . . . Addiction?

Where? Buses, streets, workplaces, running trails, elevators, lavatories—where *not*? Urban only?

How? Made possible by micro-miniaturization, I guess.

Why? Love of music? I wonder. Are they just counteracting boredom? Sound junkies? *Tune out the world*!

Already Janet was beginning to crystallize her attitude toward portable headsets. She felt it was time to draw out further thoughts through a session of freewriting (30f, p. 380):

essay
34

People looking like space creatures; bugs; glazed eyes. Turtles inside their shells? But be fair: they're getting technically great sound quality. Run longer without boredom, blot out ugly street sounds—well, why not? Sights too; life goes by like a movie. Except here the music *is* the movie, i.e., the main thing, instead of being background. Social danger here? Definitely a *physical* danger: get run over, mugged etc. Maybe it's not so good in less obvious ways, too. Shrinking into yourself: trend of the 80s? These people look peaceful, but what have they got (besides some money for toys)? Another fix that they may not be able to do without. (But this is getting a bit too moralistic, maybe?) Anyway, general problem: technological marvels bring new fun but make us less able to be *really* calm when *really* alone. Also, no improvement in the stuff people want to hear.

Having gone this far, Janet was reasonably sure she would keep her tentative topic, but now she had to decide what *kind* of essay to write:

> Argument or Explanation? What would an argument be—that headsets should be banned? I distrust them, but *that's* too strong. So—no policy issue here. OK, Explanation, but what kind? Maybe cause & effect: show where the fad came from and what it may do to us.

Her next step was therefore to make lists of causes and effects:

> Causes:
>
> > technological advances
> >
> > outgrowth of stereo boxes
> >
> > general conditioning to an electronic environment
> >
> > retreat from public world—cult of privacy?
>
> Effects:
>
> > physical danger? (maybe too trivial)
> >
> > restlessness *without* sets—no real peace
> >
> > more shrinking into oneself
> >
> > less tolerance for disturbance, diversity—just play *your* already known program
> >
> > loss of sympathy with others? political indifference?

essay
34

Looking over these lists, Janet realized two things: that she was much more interested in the effects of stereo headsets than in their causes and that all the effects she had named were negative. Her essay, then, was beginning to take shape as *an explanation of the negative social effects of the headsets*. But now she had to consider her reader, who might regard her as a spoilsport and a fanatic if she took a doomsday approach to a harmless-looking appliance. Thus, as a last exercise before attempting a thesis statement, Janet tried to moderate her stance by listing as many "pluses" as she could find:

Pluses:

    great quality

    soothing

    convenient

    no noise for others—not a nuisance

    tool for learning—e.g. a language

    run farther, skate to rhythm, ski without fear?

She was determined to work at least some of those positive qualities into her essay, preferably at a point early enough to stave off doubts about her open-mindedness.

In her first stab at a thesis statement, Janet came up with this:

essay
34

TRIAL THESIS STATEMENT:

Although we can at least be thankful that portable headphone sets are quiet, they are a perfect symbol of a society that has become dependent on artificial sources of calm, out of touch with reality, and indifferent to other people's problems.

That statement had the degree of complexity Janet needed for a 1000-word paper, but it left her uneasy. The "although" clause seemed like a throwaway remark rather than a real concession; the sweeping condemnation of all American society looked excessive; and there was something awkward about accusing a *society* of being indifferent to *other people's* problems. In a second version Janet scaled down her claims and tried to sound fairer:

REVISED THESIS STATEMENT:

Although portable headphone sets are undoubtedly convenient and plea-surable, they raise disturbing questions about many Americans' de-pendency on artificial sources of calm, decreased contact with reality, and shrinkage of concern for others.

Since the point about "shrinkage of concern" was the one that mat-tered most to Janet, she kept it in the last (most emphatic) position.

Because her essay was to be only a few pages long, Janet thought she could make do with a casual scratch outline (32a, p. 400):

---

1. Introduce headsets as topic.

2. Admit appeal.

3. No immediate threat to anybody.

4. But (thesis here) three disturbing implications (name them).

5. #1: Dependency for calm.

6. #2: Loss of reality.

7. #3: Shrinkage of concern for others.

8. Conclusion: Though more a symptom than a cause of isolation, sets fit all too well with trend of the times.

---

essay
34

As things turned out, Janet found no need to revise this plan. But because she was worried about making her case too one-sided, she devoted two paragraphs instead of one to the positive appeal of the headsets.

At last it was time to draft the essay itself. In its earliest version, this was her opening paragraph (already somewhat revised for conciseness):

```
When I stop to think about technology and the qual-
ity of life, several interesting possibilities come
to mind.  Personal computers, of course, are revo-
lutionizing the world in many ways.  Robots in in-
dustry are giving us more reliable products at the
same time that they are throwing many potential
consumers out of work.  In the field of entertain-
ment, we are deluged with video games and special-
effects extravaganzas from Hollywood.  But if I had
to choose one piece of technology to sum up the
quality of our times--a none too flattering symbol
for the eighties--I think I would take those porta-
ble headsets that one sees everywhere in the street
today.
```

Shown this paragraph, Janet's roommate commented that it would do in a pinch but that she didn't feel particularly motivated to keep reading. Janet had created a classic "funnel opener" (p. 273), but she had also come close to a "deadly opener" (p. 271) as well—the kind that lamely calls an assignment "interesting" instead of showing interest in it. Her revised introduction, Janet decided, would be a "baited opener" (p. 274)—a vivid image of somebody cruising down the sidewalk under earphones (See p. 432 for the final version.)

As for editorial revisions, Janet worked chiefly on problems her instructor had spotted in earlier papers. For example:

essay
34

PROBLEM	ORIGINAL	REVISED
exaggerated language, sarcasm	No doubt it is glorious to be surrounded by one's favorite music (however awful) all day. . . .	No doubt it is pleasant to be surrounded by one's favorite music all day. . . .
comma faults	The quality of sound, as I discovered when I once borrowed a set for thirty seconds is extraordinary.	[add comma after *seconds*; remove comma after *know*]
faulty parallelism	People who should know, claim that the reproduction is as faithful as an expensive home stereo	. . . as faithful as that of an expensive . . .

And since she knew that her main liability was wordiness, Janet worked to tighten her phrasing throughout the essay. For example:

FIRST DRAFT:

essay
34

```
But what worries me the most about the people who wear
headphones is their indifference to other people—an
indifference that probably has some political effects,
too.   Even when he or she is doing something as ac-
tive as running or skiing, the person who is wearing
the speakers has retreated within a cozy space that is
shut off from the real-life situations and needs of
other people.   The same holds true if the headset is
being worn on a city street.   Perhaps the street is
full of old people, or sick people, or crazy people.
It wouldn't matter who they are—workers, people out
```

on strike, immigrants, or whoever. It would be as if
they weren't there at all. For all that the headset
wearer knows or cares, World War III could be starting!

REVISED:

What worries me most about the headphone wearers is
their social--and therefore also political--indiffer-
ence. Even when running or skiing, the person sandwiched between the speakers has retreated within a
cozy space, insulated from the claims of other people
and their problems. That space remains just as private on a city street, where no one--not the old or
the sick or the crazy, not workers or strikers or
immigrants or beggars--can interrupt the programmed
mood. If the city is decaying, if depression or race
war is just around the corner, what does it matter?
One can always raise the volume if the world's troubles approach too near.

essay
34

As for a title, Janet had expected to use either "Personal Convenience versus Social Concern" or "Stereo Headsets: Symbol of the Indifferent Eighties." The second seemed better because it was more
definite, but neither of them sounded especially lively. Reading
through a draft, Janet ran across something more promising, the
phrase "head tripper." What about "The New Head Trippers" for a
title? It might whet the reader's interest, set an informal tone, hint
at Janet's disapproval of the stereo fad, and refer both to headgear
and to portability.

Here is Janet's essay as submitted:

Janet Stein

English 1A, sec. 2

Mr. Peterson

THE NEW HEAD TRIPPERS

Most of us by now have had the experience of
coming across a friend or acquaintance dreamily
tuned in to a stereo headset as she weaves through
a crowd of pedestrians. We are glad to recognize
Sally, as I will call her; we slow down, smile, and
prepare a greeting. But Sally, though she is looking our way, sees nothing at all. She is on automatic pilot, avoiding the other walkers by a kind
of radar that never requires her eyes to focus.
And suddenly we change our mind about saying hello
to her. To take Sally away from her tapes--assum-
ing we could get her attention at all--would be as
intrusive as waking her with a midnight phone call
or dropping in to share her dinner. We pass by,
disappointed and vaguely bothered.

And perhaps vaguely envious as well. For, un-

2

less we happen to have a headset of our own, we can
only imagine how agreeable it must be for Sally to
occupy a movable cocoon of rock music or Beethoven
or language lessons. Sally has missed out on a
small personal encounter, but so what? She has
found a way of turning "nothing" time into pleasure
or learning. Isn't that better than having some
trivial chitchat on the sidewalk?

Let us admit it: those little tape players are
a marvel. The quality of sound, as I discovered
when I once borrowed a set for thirty seconds, is
extraordinary. People who should know claim that
the reproduction is as faithful as that of an expensive home stereo. In fact, if you want sheer
music without distraction or irrelevant noise, you
might do better to play tapes on your headset than
to attend the finest live concert.

Though Sally may risk being run over in the
intersection, she is not threatening or endangering
anyone else. Indeed, she makes a favorable con-

3

trast with the brash kid who climbs aboard a bus
with his giant hand—held stereo box turned all the
way up. He may be looking for trouble; at the very
least he is trying to impose his music on a captive
audience. But Sally is the very picture of some—
body minding her own business. Why, then, is there
something unsettling about watching her electronic
trance?

    I can only answer for myself. For all I know,
I may be the only person in the world to find this
latest wonder of technology a little scary. But
even very enjoyable novelties can have negative
consequences for the society as a whole. Many in—
formed experts now consider television, for all its
obvious benefits, to be such a mixed blessing, and
video games may offer a less debatable example.
Surely there is something a little flabby and weird
about a mass passion for shooting down little fig—
ures of spaceships that appear on idiotically beep—
ing screens. To me, the tiny stereos look like a

4

similar development. In particular, I am worried about three implications of the headset vogue: a growing dependency on artificial means of staying calm, decreased contact with reality, and a corresponding shrinkage of concern for other people.

First, the matter of dependency. No doubt it is pleasant to be surrounded by one's favorite music all day, but I wonder if the experience isn't addictive. To be constantly under the earphones in the midst of other activities seems rather like having to pop "happy pills" to keep one's sanity or good temper. What becomes of the headset junkies when they are stranded without their fix? I suspect that they are left more fidgety than they were before Sony or Sanyo came to their aid. The possibility is worth looking into, anyway.

Second, as you could tell from seeing her glazed expression, Sally is not exactly alert to new experience. In a literal sense she has become a head tripper, tuning out whatever may be fresh or

5

unpredictable in her environment while she strolls
to the beat of tapes that are totally, soothingly
familiar. She is turning life into a movie with
background music—but there is a revealing difference. In the movies, the music builds appropriate
excitement or emotion for a significant action.
For Sally, in contrast, the music is the action;
reality will get through to her only when it is
compatible with her mental Muzak.

But what worries me most about the headphone
wearers is their social—and therefore political—
indifference. Even when running or skiing, the
person sandwiched between the speakers has retreated within a cozy space, insulated from the
claims of other people and their problems. That
space remains just as private on a city street,
where no one—not the old or the sick or the crazy,
not workers or strikers or immigrants or beggars—
can interrupt the programmed mood. If the city is
decaying, if depression or race war is just around

6

the corner, what does it matter? One can always
raise the volume if the world's troubles approach
too near.

Of course I am overdramatizing here; we are
not yet a nation of callous zombies. Furthermore,
for all I know, the movable cocoon may be more a
symptom than a cause of isolation. Let me admit
the point but still insist that even as symbolism,
the image of the musically tranquilized citizen,
aloof from everything except that steady tapping on
the cranium, tells us something unsettling about
the times we live in. Not long ago, the latest toy
was CB radio—a means of communicating, even when
there was nothing much to say. If the Eighties are
to be the self-absorbed era of the head tripper,
those who wear the sets are not the only ones who
will want to put the whole decade out of mind as
soon as it is over.

35 Examination Answers and In-Class Essays

35a Be Prepared for the Special Conditions of an Examination.

Most of the skills you are developing for the writing of essays will serve you well in answering essay questions on exams. At the same time, it is vital to understand the ways in which the exam situation limits your options and calls for a more direct and emphatic style of writing. Here are eleven points of advice, the first of which you can put into operation weeks before the exam.

1. *Try to anticipate questions.* Listen and take notes throughout the term. Attend especially to topics and theories that keep coming up week after week, so that you arrive at the exam with ideas that tie together the assigned material.

2. *Read through all instructions and questions before beginning any answer.* Determine whether you must answer all the questions. If you have a choice, decide which questions you can answer best. Responding to more than the required number may take time from your strong area to answer an unnecessary question in a weaker area, and the grader will usually be under no obligation to count "extra credit" answers.

438

3. *Gauge your available time.* Translate the point value of a question into a time value. A 30-point question in a 50-minute, 100-point exam should not take much more of your time than 15 minutes (30 percent of 50). If you find yourself running over, stop and leave some blank space while you get something written on *all* other questions.

4. *Note the key instruction in each question.* Always pause and study the wording of each question. Be aware that most questions begin with a key word that tells you what to do: *compare, contrast, discuss, analyze, classify, list, define, explain, summarize, describe, justify, outline.* Let that word guide the writing of your answer. If you are asked to *describe* how lasers are used to unblock obstructed arteries, do not waste time *explaining* possible causes of the obstruction. And do not be tempted into writing prepared answers to questions that were not asked. If you are to contrast *X* with *Y*, be sure you are not setting out to give 90 percent of your emphasis to *X*. If you are to state the relationship between *A* and *B*, do not throw in *C* for good measure. And if the question tells you to analyze the content and style of a quoted passage, do not suppose that a double effort on content alone will gain you full credit. Break the question into its parts and attend to all of them.

5. *Plan your answer.* For longer answers, draw up a scratch outline (32b, p. 400), and check the outline against the question to make sure it covers the required ground.

6. *Do not waste time restating the question.* A grader can only be annoyed by a hollow introductory paragraph that merely announces your willingness to address the question. Your grader will already be looking for ideas.

7. *Begin with a clear statement of your thesis in the opening paragraph.* Use your first paragraph to announce your main point and to establish the structure of everything that will follow. Do not fear that your strategy will be made too obvious. There is no such thing as being too obvious about your thesis in an examination answer. The danger, on the contrary, is that a harried grader will miss it.

8. *Highlight your main points.* Remember that your grader will be reading rapidly and will appreciate signals that make the structure of your answer clear. Consider enumerating key points, either with

exam
35a

actual numbers *(1, 2, 3)* or with words *(First, Second, Third);* you can even underline the most essential statements to ensure that they will come to the grader's notice.

9. *Support your generalizations with specific references.* Most essay questions are broad enough to allow for a variety of "right" answers. Give your grader evidence that you have done the reading and have thought about it carefully. Your own ideas, backed by material drawn from the assigned reading, will be much more impressive than unsupported statements taken directly from lectures and textbooks.

10. *Keep to the point.* In an examination answer you have no time for digressions—passages that stray from the case being made. You should not, for example, try to befriend your grader with humorous asides or pleas for sympathy.

11. *Read through your completed answer.* Try to leave time to go over your answer. Read it as if you were the grader, and try to catch inconsistencies, incoherent sentences, illegible scribbles, and unfulfilled predictions about what follows. Do not hesitate to cross out whole paragraphs if necessary or to send your grader, through an inserted arrow and a boldly printed note, to an extra page in the back of the blue book.

A Sample Answer

For a further idea of the way an examination answer typically goes straight to the point and reveals its structure, read this answer to a question on an American history final.

**exam
35a**

Question:
Summarize and explain the importance of Jefferson's reforms in the Virginia Legislature after 1776.

Answer:

Thesis first ⟶ Jefferson's purpose in revising the laws of Virginia was to get rid of all traces of aristocracy and to lay the foundations for a democratic government. There were four key reforms—governing inheritance, education, and religion—that helped to change Virginia from a royal colony to a republican state.

Preview of
supporting ⟶
points

First, the abolition of primogeniture. This ancient practice meant that the first-born son inherited all the father's wealth. The importance of the reform was that wealth could now be distributed among several surviving offspring, thereby breaking down the holdings of large landowners and distributing ownership to a wider number of Virginians.

Second, the repeal of the laws of entail. These laws provided that a landowner who had inherited an entailed estate had to leave it whole to a fixed line of heirs. Jefferson's reform allowed an owner to divide up his property and leave it to whomever he liked. The importance, again, was that the repeal broke the power of a landed aristocracy, a sure threat to a young democracy.

Third, the establishment of a system of general education. Jefferson felt it was the duty of the state to provide education and libraries for the poor. He felt that free education was the only guarantee against tyranny—that only educated people could become useful citizens by participating in the drafting of sound laws, thereby insuring the well-being and happiness of all citizens.

And fourth, the disestablishment of the state church and the guarantee of freedom of conscience. A deist himself, Jefferson supported the ethical teachings of religion but rejected a church/state alliance, which he felt unavoidably led to favoritism and tyranny. He proposed that Virginians be free of statutory taxation in support of a state church. Jefferson's legislation went beyond mere tolerance to guarantee freedom of religion for all by law.

These four reforms broke down a landed aristocracy, educated a democratic citizenry to participate in government, and guaranteed for all a separation of church and state, thereby eradicating all traces of hereditary rank and privilege in Virginia.

Each numbered point receives a paragraph of its own. Each paragraph both summarizes and explains the importance of its point.

A brief concluding paragraph emphasizes that the terms of the question have been met.

exam 35b

35b Modify Your Composing Method to Suit the Conditions of the In-Class Essay.

Nearly all the advice in this book applies to the writing of in-class as well as at-home essays. But an in-class essay resembles an examination (35a) in requiring you to make the "first draft" fully adequate. As in an exam, you must carefully gauge your available time, be absolutely sure you are meeting the terms of the question, and foreshorten your planning and revision.

If you are given an hour to produce an essay, do not feel that you have been directed to write for exactly sixty minutes. Take out about ten minutes for planning, and try to finish in time to read through the whole essay and make emergency corrections. The key period is the beginning: you must not start writing until you have a clear idea of your thesis. If you search for ideas as you go along, your essay will probably show a meandering structure or even a self-contradictory one.

To guide your writing, make a scratch outline (32b, p. 400) indicating the anticipated order of your points. Steer clear of elaborate or highly unusual structures that could turn out to be unworkable. Get your thesis into the first or second paragraph, and then concentrate on backing it with important points of evidence.

Your instructor will make allowances for the time constraint when judging your essay. Remember as you write, however, that it *is* an essay—one that should show such virtues as clear statement, coherent paragraph development, and variety of sentence structure. Do not, then, write like someone who has crammed for a test and who must now hastily spill out page after page of sheer information. The length of your in-class essay will be less crucial than the way it hangs together as a purposeful structure controlled by a thesis.

In your remaining time, check first to see that you have adequately developed your thesis, and insert any needed additions as neatly as you can (see 35a, point 11, p. 440). Then check for legibility and correctness of usage, punctuation, spelling, and diction, making needed changes as you go. Your instructor will not object to a marked-up manuscript if it remains reasonably easy to read.

exam
35b

H THE RESEARCH PAPER

The Research Paper

When assigned a research paper, some students feel they must set aside everything they have learned about writing essays and concentrate instead on showing how much library reading they can do. The result may be a paper crammed with references but lacking a clear point or concern for the reader's patience. A research paper is above all an essay—one that happens to be based in part on library materials (Chapter 36), duly documented (Chapter 37). The advice that follows should be regarded not as a self-sufficient unit but as a supplement to Chapters 30–34. If you are undertaking a research paper and have not gone through those chapters, it would be good to do so now.

Note that Chapter 38 contains two student research papers illustrating different essay modes and documentation styles. Those papers are longer, more polished, and more fully documented than most. Do not regard the sample papers as models to be matched; your instructor will probably expect a more modest effort on your part.

36 Finding and Mastering Sources

A college library is in essence an information retrieval system. As with a computer, the knack of using it successfully consists in knowing the right questions to present it with. Searching through the stacks without any questions at all would be as senseless as trying to browse in the computer's memory bank; you have to be looking for something from the outset. And the more specific your question, the more shortcuts you can take. Experienced researchers do not run through all the ways of seeking information described in this chapter. Rather, they find a few key works as early as possible and then allow those works—especially those containing a **bibliography,** or list of further books and articles on the topic—to suggest how to proceed.

36a Get Acquainted with the Parts of Your Library.

Perhaps your college library strikes you as mysterious or even vaguely threatening. If so, bear in mind that you do not have to understand the whole system—just some procedures for retrieving the books and articles you need. Watch for free library tours and information packets, and do not hesitate to ask a **reference librarian** for help in getting an efficient start on your project.

Although no two libraries are quite alike, your college library probably contains at least seven places to serve essential functions:

1. *Stacks.* These are shelves on which most books and bound periodicals are stored. In the "open stack" system, all users can enter

the stacks, find materials, and take them to a check-out desk. If your library has "closed stacks," access to the stacks is limited by status; see the next item.

2. *Circulation desk*. In a closed-stack library, you can check out a book or bound periodical by submitting a call slip—a card identifying what you need—to the circulation desk, to which a clerk will return either with the book or with an explanation that it is on reserve (see item 4), out to another borrower, or missing. If it is out to another borrower, you can "put a hold" on it—that is, indicate that you want to be notified as soon as the book has been returned. Since you may have to wait as long as two weeks for some items, it is important to begin your research early.

3. *Catalog*. Near the circulation desk you will find cabinets full of alphabetically filed cards, listing all the library's printed holdings (books, periodicals, pamphlets, and items on microfilm, but not manuscripts, records, or tapes). This is the **card catalog**. Its listings are by author, title, and subject. In some libraries the card catalog has been supplemented or replaced by a **microfiche catalog**, consisting of miniaturized photographic entries on plastic cards that can be read when placed in a microfiche reader, available nearby. Your library may even have an **on-line catalog**—that is, a continually updated computer file. If so, you will see computer terminals, accompanied by appropriate instructions, near the circulation desk. Whatever its form, the catalog is your master key to the stacks, for it gives you call numbers enabling you or a clerk to locate the books you need.

4. *Reference room*. In the reference room (or behind the reference desk) are stored sets of encyclopedias, indexes, dictionaries, bibliographies, and similar multipurpose research tools. You cannot check out reference volumes, but you can consult them long enough to get the names of promising-looking books and articles that you *will* be able to get from the main collection. The reference room usually doubles as a reading room, enabling you to do much of your reading near other sources of information.

5. *Reserve desk*. Behind the reserve desk (or in the reserve book room) are kept multiple copies of books that are essential to current

courses. The distinctive feature of reserved books is that they must be returned quickly, usually within either an hour or a day or a week. When you learn that a book is "on reserve," even for a course other than your own, you can be reasonably sure of finding an available copy.

6. *Periodical room.* In the periodical room you can find magazines and journals too recent to have been bound as books. Thus, if you do research on a topic of current interest, you are certain to find yourself applying to the periodical room for up-to-date articles.

7. *Newspaper room.* Take your call slips to this room to get a look at newspaper articles and editorials. Most newspapers are stored on microfilm, which can be read only with a microfilm reader. Ask a clerk to show you how the machine works.

Thus your research is likely to take you back and forth between various sites:

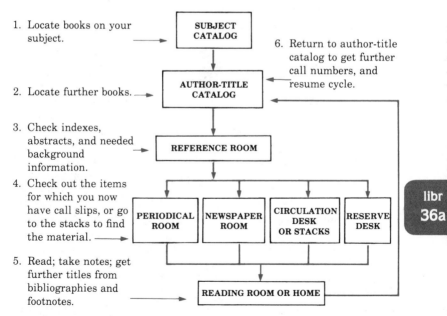

1. Locate books on your subject.

6. Return to author-title catalog to get further call numbers, and resume cycle.

2. Locate further books.

3. Check indexes, abstracts, and needed background information.

4. Check out the items for which you now have call slips, or go to the stacks to find the material.

5. Read; take notes; get further titles from bibliographies and footnotes.

SUBJECT CATALOG

AUTHOR-TITLE CATALOG

REFERENCE ROOM

PERIODICAL ROOM

NEWSPAPER ROOM

CIRCULATION DESK OR STACKS

RESERVE DESK

READING ROOM OR HOME

libr
36a

At some point, obviously, this cycle has to be interrupted; the first draft beckons. But even as you write successive drafts, you may find yourself dipping back into library sources to check new leads and follow up ideas that now look more fruitful than they did at first.

36b Learn the Most Efficient Means of Searching for Books.

Subject Catalogs

If you are searching for a topic within a general subject area, the first thing you want to do is check your library's holdings within that area. You can do so by consulting the **subject catalog,** which is arranged not by authors and titles of books but by fields of knowledge, problems, movements, schools of thought, and so forth. Once you locate an array of relevant titles, you should fill out call slips for the most recent appropriate-looking works. If you get hold of just one recent book that has a bibliography—a list of consulted works—in the back, you may discover that you already have the names of all the further books and articles you will need.

Guide to Subject Headings

But how do you know which headings your subject catalog uses to classify the entries you will want to review? You can try your luck, sampling a number of alternative phrases, or you can take a more systematic and reliable approach. Your subject catalog probably follows the headings adopted by the Library of Congress in Washington, D.C. Ask your reference librarian where a book called *Library of Congress Subject Headings* is to be found. That book is heavily **cross-indexed**; in other words, if you look up a plausible-sounding phrase, you will not only learn whether it constitutes a Library of Congress subject heading, you will also be directed to other phrases that do serve as headings.

Thus the student who wanted to investigate computer crime for his research paper (pp. 500–508) began by going to the *Library of Congress Subject Headings* pages referring to *Computers*. There he found the following valuable listing:

Computer crimes *(Indirect)* *(HV6773)* ———————— 1

2 ——————————— *sa* Computers — Access control
Electronic data processing departments
— Security measures
Privacy, Right of

3 ——————————— *x* Computer fraud
Computers and crime

4 ——————————— *xx* Computers — Access control
Crime and criminals
Privacy, Right of
White collar crimes

Observe in this typical entry:

1. The Library of Congress call number of a key book on the subject—an authoritative government study containing a bibliography.

2. The symbol *sa* ("see also") introduces three related headings that can be consulted to locate titles that may not be covered under the main heading *Computer crimes.*

3. The symbol *x* tells the reader not to bother looking up *Computer fraud* or *Computers and crime;* since these are not Library of Congress headings, they will not be headings in the campus library catalog either.

4. The symbol *xx* introduces four *broader* headings that will cover some works on computer crime. By checking these phrases in the subject catalog the reader can see the chosen problem in several wider perspectives.

Shelf List

Armed with this much information, the student researcher was able to make use of the subject catalog without a single wasted step. And already possessing a key call number, he could also inspect the related cards in his library's **shelf list**—still another catalog, this one arranged in order of call numbers. Since his library followed the Library of Congress system of numbering, and since call numbers in any library are ordered by subject, he could be sure of finding relevant material near card HV6773.

libr
36b

On-Line Catalog

The student was aware, however, that his library had recently begun to compile an **on-line** (computer) catalog which would eventually replace the card catalog. Though this catalog was still fragmentary, he knew it would be more up-to-date than any of the others. Following the instructions listed beside a terminal, he told the computer to retrieve all titles about *Computer crimes* listed in the on-line catalog. Here is what he read on the display and copied out:

Your search for: subject words COMPUTER CRIMES retrieved: 9 books.

1. Bequai, August. COMPUTER CRIME. 1978
2. Deighton, Suzan. THE NEW CRIMINALS: A BIBLIOGRAPHY OF COMPUTER . . . 1978
3. Leibholz, Stephen W. USERS' GUIDE TO COMPUTER CRIME: ITS . . . 1974
4. Lin, Joseph C. COMPUTER CRIME, SECURITY, AND PRIVACY: A SELECTED . . . 1979
5. McKnight, Gerald. COMPUTER CRIME. 1973
6. McKnight, Gerald. COMPUTER CRIME. 1974
7. McNeil, John. THE CONSULTANT: A NOVEL OF COMPUTER CRIME. 1978
8. THE NEW CRIMINALS: A BIBLIOGRAPHY OF COMPUTER RELATED CRIME . . . 1979
9. Parker, Donn B. CRIME BY COMPUTER. 1976

---

libr
36b

Like most examples of computer retrieval, this list contained some obviously false leads. Items 6 and 8 were simply reprints of items 5 and 2, respectively, and item 7 was a work of fiction. But items 1, 2, and 9 turned out to be centrally important; the researcher already had access to more information than he could possibly use in his essay.

Author-Title Catalog

If you know that your essay will deal with a certain author, you can bypass the various subject catalogs and go directly to the **author-**

title catalog, which lists works alphabetically by both author and title and includes subject cards as well (see below). The last entries in your author's listing, after his or her own works, may be useful books of biography, criticism, and commentary. Thus the author-title catalog is itself a kind of subject catalog, with prominent authors as the subjects. Even if you are writing about a general problem, you can pick up likely references by browsing in the author-title catalog under possible key terms (*Computer, Crime,* etc.).

The most important piece of information on any catalog card is the **call number** in the upper left corner; it tells exactly where the book or bound journal is shelved. But you can also get several other kinds of information from a card. Consider, for example, an author card actually encountered by the writer of the UFO research paper on pages 510–521:

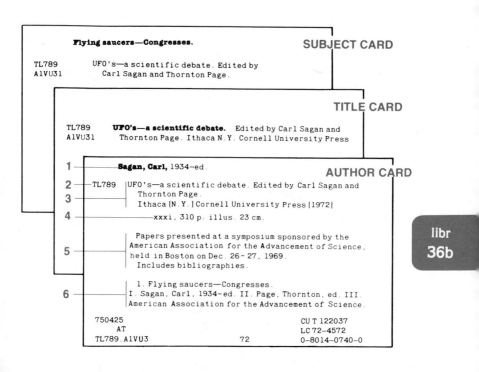

libr
36b

In addition to some coded information chiefly of interest to librarians, this author card conveys six potentially useful kinds of knowledge:

1. The name of one editor of the book.

2. The call number, enabling someone to apply for the book at the circulation desk or to locate it in the stacks.

3. The title of the book, both editors' names, the place of publication, the publisher, and the date of publication. These are facts a researcher would want to get down on a bibliography card (36e, p. 461).

4. Physical features of the book. It consists of 31 pages of prefatory material and 310 pages of main text; it contains illustrations; and it is 23 centimeters in height. The substantial length of this book makes it more worth looking into than, say, a forty-page pamphlet would be.

5. Notes on the context and contents of the book. The A.A.A.S. sponsorship indicates a high standard of quality; the date is recent enough to suggest some historical perspective on the UFO controversy; and the mention of "bibliographies" suggests that this book could lead one to other pertinent materials.

6. A list of all the headings under which this book is filed in the card catalog. By going to "Flying saucers—Congresses," a researcher might find several further cards of related interest. In this manner the card catalog itself can function as a bibliography.

libr
36b

Once in a while you may come across a reference to an apparently indispensable book that is unlisted in your library's catalog. Since there are some sixty thousand new volumes published each year in English alone, no library but the Library of Congress itself could acquire more than a minority of them. You can get essential information about the book's author, title, publisher, and date from the *National Union Catalog,* which reproduces the Library of Congress Catalog and includes titles from other libraries as well. If you cannot visit a library that has the book, you can probably borrow it through interlibrary loan arrangement. The same holds for journals as well.

By consulting the *Union List of Serials in Libraries of the United States and Canada* you can discover which libraries own sets of hard-to-find journals.

36c Learn How to Find Recent Articles and Reviews.

If you have chosen a topic of current interest—the spread and control of a new disease, say, or the changing American family structure—you will want to review the latest available information. You cannot find it in even the most recently published books, which will necessarily be a year or two behind the times. Newspaper articles will be best for following events as they occur. Magazine articles, such as those in *Harper's* or *The Atlantic,* will give you a general perspective that may be just right for the audience and level you have in mind. And in professional journals—specialized scholarly periodicals such as the *New England Journal of Medicine* or the *Bulletin of the Atomic Scientists*—you will get access to detailed knowledge and theory that may not yet have appeared in hard cover. You may also want to check expert reviews of books you hope to use. Digests of reviews (p. 456) can show you how much trust you should place in a given book.

Indexes and Abstracts

Obviously, you would be wasting your time poring over the handiest newspapers, magazines, and journals in the hope of finding relevant items. The efficient thing is to consult indexes and abstracts, which you will find shelved together in your library's reference room. **Indexes** are books, usually with a new volume each year, containing alphabetically ordered references to articles on given subjects. And **abstracts** are summaries of articles, allowing you to tell whether or not a certain article is important enough to your project to be worth tracking down. It is the reference room, then—not the newspaper room or the periodical room—that holds the key to your search for pertinent articles and reviews.

1. *To Newspapers.* The only newspaper index you may ever need to consult is the *New York Times Index* (1913–), which covers a vast array of news and commentary having national or international importance. Since it is issued every two weeks before being bound into

**libr
36c**

annual volumes, you can be sure of staying current with developments in your subject. For coverage of newspapers in Chicago, Los Angeles, New Orleans, and Washington, D.C., try the *Newspaper Index* (1972–). And for international and especially British coverage, consult the *Index to the* [London] *Times* (1906–).

2. *To Magazines.* If you want to find an article in a general-interest magazine, go to the *Reader's Guide to Periodical Literature* (1900–), which covers about 160 magazines on a twice-monthly basis. Indeed, the *Reader's Guide* is so useful for the typical research essay that many students begin their investigation there, saving the subject catalog until they have seen whether their topic has engaged the public lately. Browsing through the headings in the *Reader's Guide* may help you focus your topic better. But if you draw a blank from the *Reader's Guide,* ask yourself whether your topic is too broad, too narrow, too specialized, or too outdated to merit pursuing.

A typical segment of a column in the *Reader's Guide* looks like this:

a ————————————— TYSON, Molly
  Women in outer space. il por WomenSports
    5:20-4+ F '78
b ————————————— —and Durkee, Cutler
  Young lions of golf. il WomenSports 5:56-60
    F '78
c ————————————— TYSON, Richard F. See Tyson, J. H. jt auth

d ————————————— UAL, Inc
  United proposes California-Nevada low fare. L.
    Doty. Aviation W 107:27 N 7 '77
      See also
  Western International Hotels Company
  UFOs
    Center for UFO studies profiled. il Astronomy 6:
      66-7 Mr '78
    Close encounters in New York. T. Clifford. il
      N Y 11:100 F 20 '78
    Data on unidentified flying objects for states.
      specialized agencies. UN Chron 15:47 Ja '78
    Hynek hopes that reported encounters will in-
      crease. J. A. Hynek. por map Sci Digest 83:
      19-21 F '78
    Third coming. M. Gardner. N Y R of Bk 24:21-2
      Ja 26 '78
    2 close encounters of the real kind in Air Force
      files. D. Berliner. Sci Digest 83:21-4 Ap '78
    UFOlogy and Christianity. I. Hexham. Chr To-
      day 22:55 Mr 10 '78
    UFO's. Glamour 76:54 Mr '78
    U.F.O.'s and modern religion. T. Peters. Ameri-
      ca 138:306-8 Ap 15 '78
    UFOs: the next theological challenge? J. A.
      Jennings. il Chr Cent 95:184-9 F 22 '78; Dis-
      cussion. 95:590-2 My 31 '78
    We are all alone. T. Ferris. New Times 10:8
      Ja 9 '78
    We may not be alone. M. Rogers. Roll Stone
      p24 F 9 '78
    We've been asked: is there something to UFO's
      after all? U.S. News 84:56 F 20 '78

e

Here you see:

a. *An entry by author.* Molly Tyson's article, "Women in Outer Space," including an illustration and a portrait, appeared in the February 1978 issue of *WomenSports* (volume 5), on pages 20–24 and some later pages.

b. *An entry by two authors.* In the same issue of *WomenSports,* Molly Tyson wrote another article, this time in collaboration with Cutler Durkee.

c. *A cross-indexed item.* If you are looking for an article by Richard F. Tyson, you are told that you can find it listed under the name of the joint author, J. H. Tyson.

d. *An entry about a corporation.* Here we see that L. Doty, in volume 107 of *Aviation Week* (7 Nov. 1977), page 27, has a brief article about United Air Lines.

e. *Entries about a subject.* Here are references to thirteen articles about Unidentified Flying Objects—the subject of the sample research paper on pages 510–521.

3. *To Journals.* While the *Reader's Guide* gives you good access to such popular magazines as *Time* and *Psychology Today,* it does not cover journals (p. 453) such as *Science* and *Modern Language Quarterly.* Journals are issued less often than magazines and are far more technical in nature. Although you probably want to keep a general-interest focus in your paper, an important piece of information may be accessible to you only in a journal. The key indexes for access to journal articles are the *Humanities Index* (1974–) and the *Social Sciences Index* (1974–). The *Humanities Index* should be your first choice for post-1973 articles in archaeology, area studies, classics, folklore, history, language and literature, literary criticism, performing arts, philosophy, religion, and theology. Use the *Social Sciences Index* for post-1973 articles in anthropology, economics, environmental science, geography, law and criminology, medicine, political science, psychology, public administration, and sociology. For years before 1973, consult the *International Index* (1907–1965) and the *Social Sciences and Humanities Index* (1965–1974); the latter was the parent of the now separate *Humanities Index* and *Social Sciences Index.*

libr
36c

4. *To Book Reviews.* If you want to know how reliable a certain book is, you can quickly learn what some of the book's original reviewers had to say by consulting *Book Review Digest* (1905–   ). Thus, for example, the writer of the research paper on pages 510–521 needed to decide how much trust to place in Philip J. Klass's 1974 book *UFOs Explained.* By looking in *Book Review Digest* in the period following publication, she was able not only to find citations of reviews but also to get a capsule idea of whether the book deserved to be taken seriously:

KLASS, PHILIP J. UFOs explained. 369p pl
$8.95 '74 Random House

001.9 Flying saucers
ISBN 0-394-49215-3   LC 74-9054

The author examines a sampling of UFO cases and seeks to show that when such cases are examined objectively and scientifically rational explanations other than the existence of extraterrestrial spaceships or other phenomena can be found. Index.

———

"The hobby of Mr. Klass, Senior Avionics Editor for Aviation Week & Space Technology, is tracking down and demolishing reports of unidentified flying objects. Sight saucer, sink same is his motto, and he backs it with gingery, well-argued accounts of the process. He demonstrates, among other engaging facts, that flight crews from Venus and environs are infallibly drawn to earthlings who happen to need some quick cash." Phoebe Adams
    Atlantic 235:122 F '75 80w

"[The author] argues in this work that there is no scientific evidence to support belief in the existence of UFOs. He devises ten UFOlogical Principles by means of which he explains the various types of attitudes and beliefs which have developed in the personalities of UFO believers. . . . In thirty-one chapters describing investigations of various categories of UFO reports there appears to be no lack of rigor whatever. The author denies validity of the vast majority of UFO sightings. The description of his investigations is intensely interesting." R. E. O'Brien
    Best Sell 34:537 Mr 1 '75 350w

    Choice 12:863 S '75 200w

"Klass thinks that UFO's can be explained as terrestrial phenomena and not as intelligently guided ships. He is a painstaking investigator and has the technical competence to understand and to be able to explain, for example, a piece of equipment and how it can malfunction. . . . [However] his explanations for UFO's seem thin on occasion. . . . One unfortunate thing is the impression Klass conveys that he alone is right; although irritating, it is a not infrequent attitude in this field. . . . Probably not for small libraries." Robert Molyneux
    Library J 100:491 Mr 1 '75 90w

Reviewed by A. C. Clarke
    N Y Times Bk R p4 Jl 27 '75 500w

"No UFO author has taken such a look at radar as Klass, whose decade of experience in the field as an engineer has been augmented by a later career as a knowing technical reporter covering the aerospace industry. . . . This is a good-sized, meaty, rather contentious work. It treats very successfully many of the classic 'sightings' of the past, making a strong prima facie case of fraud in several of the best-known. . . . There is no more explicit and insightful account of UFO's than this one. . . . The reader can profit a great deal, even though the tone is sometimes rather more indignant than seems wise." Philip Morrison

Scl Am 232:117 My '75 900w

For other guides to book reviews, see *Book Review Index* (1965–   ), *Current Book Review Citations* (1976–   ), and *The New York Times Book Review Index* (1896–1970).

On-Line Searching

In increasing numbers, printed indexes, abstracts, reports, conference proceedings, and government documents are being gathered in the alternative form of **databases**—that is, computer files that can be instantly scanned. If your library has an on-line catalog (36b, p. 450), then that catalog is itself a database. But that is just the beginning. If your library subscribes to such databases as, say, *Pharmaceutical News Index, Population Bibliography,* and *Pollution Abstracts,* you can instruct the computer to retrieve every relevant article from one or more of those sources.

Such "on-line searching" can save time, catch very recent references, and ferret out specific topics that do not constitute subject headings in the index itself. Suppose, for example, you are interested in the connection between child abuse and alcoholism. Instead of asking for all items within each of those large subjects, you can tell the computer to display only those items whose titles refer to *both* problems. The outcome will be a relatively short but highly efficient list, fairly free of "dumb mistakes" on the computer's part.

On-line searching can produce dramatic results if you have a well-defined topic in mind. But there are serious disadvantages as well:

libr
36c

1. You will be charged a fee—possibly a steep one—for the search.

2. You will need the assistance of a trained technician.

3. It is hard to "browse" in computer files; if your chosen keywords do not appear in the title of a relevant article, the computer will probably overlook it.

On the whole, then, for the purposes of a college essay it is better to do your searching in printed sources. But at least you know that on-line searching is available if you should need it. A reference librarian can tell you whether your project is one that lends itself readily to a computer search.

36d Consult Background Sources as Necessary.

The steps we have already covered should be enough to give you all the information you need for a typical research essay. Sometimes, however, you may want an out-of-the-way bit of knowledge or a broad introduction to the field you are going to treat. Where should you turn? Most of the works mentioned below can be found in the reference room.

If you know an author's name but not the title of the book, if you have the title but not the author, or if you want to know when a certain book appeared, try consulting *Books in Print* (1948–), *Cumulative Book Index* (1898–), *Paperbound Books in Print* (1955–), or *Subject Guide to Books in Print* (1957–). The last of these volumes can give you a quick idea of what you could hope to find under a given subject heading of your card catalog. If you see an essential item in the *Subject Guide* that is missing from your catalog, you may be able to send for it through interlibrary loan (36b, p. 452).

Reference works—books that survey a field and tell you how to find materials within that field—are now so numerous that you may need to consult an even more general book that lists reference works and explains their scope. Try, for example, Eugene P. Sheehy, *Guide to Reference Books* (1976), which can lead you to the most appropriate bibliographies and indexes to articles.

For a college research paper, however, you will probably need at the most one survey of your field and one guide to sources. Here is a representative sample of titles to consult:

libr
36d

art
: *Encyclopedia of World Art* (1959–1968)
  Art Index (1929–)

business and economics
: *Dictionary of Economics and Business,* ed. Erwin E. Nemmers (1979)
  Business Periodicals Index (1958–)

drama
: *McGraw-Hill Encyclopedia of World Drama* (1983)
  How to Locate Reviews of Plays and Films, by Gordon Samples (1976)

education
: *A Dictionary of Education,* by Derek Rowntree (1982)
  Resources in Education (1975–)

film
: *International Encyclopedia of the Film* (1972)
  Film Research: A Critical Bibliography, by Peter J. Bukalski (1972)

folklore and mythology
: *Larousse World Mythology* (1968)
  Motif-Index of Folk Literature, by Stith Thompson (1955–1958)

history
: *An Encyclopedia of World History,* ed. William L. Langer (1972)
  The Historian's Handbook, by Helen J. Poulton and Marguerite S. Howland (1972)

literature
: *The Reader's Companion to World Literature,* ed. Lillian H. Hornstein et al. (1973)
  Literary Research Guide, by Margaret C. Patterson (1983)

music
: *The Oxford Companion to Music,* by Kenneth McLeish and Valerie McLeish (1982)
  Music Reference and Research Materials: An Annotated Bibliography, comp. Vincent Harris Duckles (1974)

libr
36d

philosophy	*The Encyclopedia of Philosophy,* ed. Paul Edwards (1973) *A Bibliography of Philosophical Bibliographies,* by Herbert Guerry (1977)
psychology	*Encyclopedia of Psychology,* ed. H. J. Eysenck et al. (1972) *Annual Review of Psychology* (1950–)
religion	*A Reader's Guide to the Great Religions,* ed. Charles J. Adams (1977) *Religion Index One: Periodicals* (1977–)
science and technology	*McGraw-Hill Encyclopedia of Science and Technology* (1982) *Applied Science and Technology Index* (1958–)
social and political science	*International Encyclopedia of the Social Sciences,* ed. David L. Sills (1968–) *Social Sciences Index* (1974–)
women's studies	*Handbook of International Data on Women* (1976) *Women's Studies: A Recommended Core Bibliography,* ed. Esther Stineman (1979)

When you need to chase down a particular fact—the population of a country, an event in someone's life, the origin of an important term, the source of a quotation, etc.—you can go to one of the following sources:

libr
36d

general encyclopedias	*Encyclopaedia Britannica* (1974) *Encyclopedia Americana* (revised annually)
compilations of facts	*Facts on File* (1940–) *The World Almanac and Book of Facts* (1868–)

atlases

National Geographic Atlas of the World (1975)
The New York Times Atlas of the World (1981)

dictionaries
(See 27a, p. 313, for college dictionaries.)

A Comprehensive Etymological Dictionary of the English Language, by Ernest Klein (1979)
A New English Dictionary on Historical Principles (also called *The Oxford English Dictionary*) (1888–1933)

biography

International Who's Who (1935–)
The McGraw-Hill Encyclopedia of World Biography (1973)

quotations

Familiar Quotations, by John Bartlett and E. M. Beck (1968)
The Oxford Dictionary of Quotations (1979)

36e Take Full and Careful Notes from Your Reading.

A typical library book or journal will be available to you for a few hours or days or weeks, depending on its importance to other borrowers. When you try to get it again, you may find that it is on loan to someone else, or sent to the bindery, or even misplaced or stolen. Thus you have to be sure to get everything you need from the work on your first try, and your notes must be clear and full enough to be your direct source when you write. Although it is always a good idea to keep the work before you and recheck it for accurate quotation and fair summary, you should assume that this will not be possible. Your notes should contain all the information necessary for full citations (Chapter 37), and you should make sure your notes are error-free before you let the book or article out of your hands.

libr
36e

Bibliography Cards versus Content Cards

The notes you take from reading will serve two distinct purposes: to keep an accurate list of the works you have consulted and to record key information you have found in them. Sooner or later most researchers understand that these purposes demand different kinds of notecards. To compile a bibliography or list of works consulted, one card per entry is ideal; but content (or informational) notes may run through many cards. To avoid confusion use $3'' \times 5''$ bibliography cards to identify the works you have consulted, and larger (usually $4'' \times 6''$) content cards for quotations, summaries, and miscellaneous comments. Or, if you prefer, use cards of different colors.

You may prefer to jot down ideas on sheets of paper rather than on cards (30h, p. 382). For quoting and summarizing published statements, however, cards are easier to keep track of and to rearrange as the organization of your essay takes shapes.

Observe the following sample cards. (Note that once a separate bibliography card has been prepared, the researcher can give the briefest of references on a content card: *Hynek, p. 225.*)

BIBLIOGRAPHY CARD:

> TL 789
> H 91
>
> Hynek, J. Allen
> The UFO Experience:
> A Scientific Inquiry
> Chicago: Henry Regnery,
> 1972.
> (Hynek's early critique of Condon)

CONTENT CARD:

Hynek, p. 225   *reliability of*
                                 reports

" A great wealth of data, highly variable
in quality, has been gathered over the
past two decades. In its present
form it is much akin to low grade
ore, which must be processed and refined
before it is of value."

        Interesting analogy. But we process
ore only when we have a reasonable
expectation of extracting something
profitable. Does the history of U F O
investigations yield that expectation?

Form Of Notecards

The more systematic you are about note taking, the less likely you
will be to misquote, summarize unfairly, or supply inaccurate references. Here are some tips about form:

1. Use cards of one uniform size or color for all your bibliography notes, and cards or sheets of another uniform size or
   color for all your content notes. This will make for easy
   filing and reshuffling.
2. Write in ink. Penciled notes smudge when pressed against
   other notes.

libr
36e

3. Never put entries from different sources on one card or page, and never write on the reverse side. Otherwise you will probably lose track of some of your work.
4. Include the call number of any book or magazine you have found in the library. You never know when you may want to retrieve it for another look.
5. Quote exactly, including the punctuation marks in the original, and check each quotation as soon as you have copied it.
6. Use quotation marks only when you are actually quoting verbatim, and check to see that the marks begin and end exactly where they should. Use the dots known as ellipses (13m, p. 156) to indicate where you have skipped some material within a quotation.
7. Be attentive to oddities of spelling and punctuation in quoted material. If, for instance, the original text omits a comma that you would have included, you can place a bracketed [*sic*], meaning *this is the way I found it,* at the questionable point in your notes; this will remind you not to improve the quotation illegitimately when reproducing it in your essay. But do not retain the [*sic*] in your paper unless it refers to an obvious blunder.
8. Supply page references for all quotations, paraphrases, and summaries.
9. Do not allow any ambiguities in your system of abbreviations. If two of your symbols mean the same thing, change one of them.
10. Distinguish between your own comments and those of the text you are summarizing. Slashes, brackets, or your initials can be used as signals that the following remarks are yours, not those of the author.
11. When copying a passage that runs from one page to another, mark where the first page ends: *"One other point might be noted, in view of the White / House concern over the military implications of UFOs."* If you finally quote only a portion of the excerpt in your paper, you will want to know where it ended in the original.

12. Use a portion of the card or page to evaluate the material and to remind yourself of possibilities for further study. You might say, for example, *This looks useless—but reconsider chapter 13 if discussing astrology.*

13. Leave some space in the margin or at the top for an indexing symbol.

36f Summarize or Paraphrase Pertinent Material That You Are Not Quoting.

The most accurate way of noting what you have read is to quote it exactly (Chapter 13) or to photocopy it. But in your notes you can only quote a fraction of the important material you have seen, and once you have photocopied many pages you still face the task of drawing from them what is essential to your own purpose. Here is where summary, or brief restatement, and paraphrase, or more ample restatement, can come to your aid.

A **summary** of a text concisely presents the author's key ideas, omitting examples and descriptive detail. Insofar as possible you should use your own language, though some repetition of the author's terms is inevitable. The knack of efficient summary is to strip away everything but the essential content.

ORIGINAL TEXT:

The modern world began on 29 May 1919 when photographs of a solar eclipse, taken on the island of Principe off West Africa and at Sobral in Brazil, confirmed the truth of a new theory of the universe. It had been apparent for half a century that the Newtonian cosmology, based upon the straight lines of Euclidean geometry and Galileo's notions of absolute time, was in need of serious modification. It had stood for more than two hundred years. It was the framework within which the European Enlightenment, the Industrial Revolution, and the vast expansion of human knowledge, freedom and prosperity which characterized the nineteenth century, had taken place. But increasingly powerful telescopes were revealing anomalies. In particular, the motions of the planet Mercury deviated by forty-three seconds of arc a century from its predictable behaviour under Newtonian laws of physics. Why?

libr
36f

In 1905, a twenty-six-year-old German Jew, Albert Einstein, then working in the Swiss patent office in Berne, had published a paper, "On the electrodynamics of moving bodies," which became known as the Special Theory of Relativity. Einstein's observations on the way in which, in certain circumstances, lengths appeared to contract and clocks to slow down, are analogous to the effects of perspective in painting. In fact the discovery that space and time are relative rather than absolute is comparable, in its effect on our perception of the world, to the first use of perspective in art, which occurred in Greece in the two decades *c.* 500–480 B.C.

The originality of Einstein, amounting to a form of genius, and the curious elegance of his lines of argument, which colleagues compared to a kind of art, aroused growing, world-wide interest. In 1907 he published a demonstration that all mass has energy, encapsulated in the equation $E = mc^2$, which a later age saw as the starting point in the race for the A-bomb. Not even the onset of the European war prevented scientists from following his quest for an all-embracing General Theory of Relativity which would cover gravitational fields and provide a comprehensive revision of Newtonian physics. In 1915 news reached London that he had done it. The following spring, as the British were preparing their vast and catastrophic offensive on the Somme, the key paper was smuggled through the Netherlands and reached Cambridge, where it was received by Arthur Eddington, Professor of Astronomy and Secretary of the Royal Astronomical Society.

—PAUL JOHNSON, *Modern Times:*
The World from the Twenties to the Eighties

SUMMARY:

Johnson dates "the modern world" from the solar eclipse observations of 29 May 1919, confirming Albert Einstein's General Theory of Relativity. The world had already shown great interest in Einstein after his 1905 publication of the Special Theory of Relativity, indicating that space and time are relative categories, and his 1907 demonstration that mass possesses energy ($E = mc^2$). The General Theory,

embracing gravitational fields, completed the over-
throw of Newtonian physics, based in its turn on
Euclid's geometry and Galileo's absolute time. The
Einsteinian revolution affected our perception of the
world as radically as the ancient Greek discovery of
perspective in art.

A **paraphrase** is a running restatement of the original passage
in your own words. You should follow the order of the text and include
important detail. Since a paraphrase is closer to the original than a
summary, you must be careful not to repeat the author's wording
without quotation marks; that practice could lead you into accidental
plagiarism (37a, p. 472), or the presentation of someone else's words
(or ideas) as your own.

PARAPHRASE:

Johnson dates "the modern world" from the 29 May 1919
observations of a solar eclipse, taken in Africa and
Brazil, confirming Einsteinian cosmology. For fifty
years the existing Newtonian conception, based on
Euclid's geometry and Galileo's absolute time, had
been in trouble. It had been the set of assumptions
behind the Enlightenment, the Industrial Revolution,
and nineteenth-century progress in learning, democracy, and wealth, but it had been placed in doubt by
unaccountable telescopic data such as the deviated
motion of Mercury.

The new universe began to take shape with Albert
Einstein's 1905 paper, "On the electrodynamics of

libr
36f

moving bodies" (the Special Theory of Relativity),
showing how in some conditions time and space are
variable. This discovery affected our way of seeing
the world as profoundly as did the Greeks' use of
artistic perspective in the fifth century B.C.

In 1907 Einstein proposed that all mass has energy
($E=mc^2$), an idea later seen as having begun the race
to develop the atomic bomb. Not even the outbreak of
World War I could stop scientists from participating in his search for a General Theory of Relativity
that would include gravitational fields. Word of
Einstein's having completed that theory arrived in
London in 1915, and in 1916, at the height of the
awful war, the key paper reached Arthur Eddington,
Secretary of the Royal Astonomical Society, in
Cambridge.

36g Adjust Your Thesis to Match the Evidence You Have Gathered.

Remember that a research paper is essentially an essay with documentation. Like any other essay of explanation or argument, it can
succeed only if its thesis is plausible and strongly backed by evidence
(Chapter 31). Be prepared to change your trial thesis or even your
topic if your reading points in a better direction. The majority of good
research papers take a different approach from the one first intended.

Thus the writer of the UFO paper on pages 510–521, knowing in
a vague way that she doubted the existence of Unidentified Flying
Objects, began by expecting to write about "the UFO cult" as an
expression of mass psychology. As her research advanced, however,
she realized that this "cult" encompassed the majority of her fellow

citizens. If she had gone ahead and treated the UFO issue as already settled, she would have been begging a question (31d, p. 390) that readers might regard as still debatable. She therefore turned her attention to the primary issue of whether or not a belief in UFOs is justified by the present state of knowledge. Instead of writing an explanatory paper, she ended by constructing an argument.

The writer of the paper on computer crime (pp. 500–508), on the other hand, started with an argumentative idea and ended with an explanatory one. Having read a famous *Esquire* article about "phone phreaks" who had discovered how to tap into long-distance telephone connections without being charged, he expected to argue that "ripping off the monopoly" was just as criminal as robbing individuals. But as soon as he saw how little research material was available on that one form of piracy, he turned his attention to electronic crime in general. And at a certain point he decided that an explanatory survey of computer crime—still a fairly unfamiliar matter—would be more engaging than an argument against it.

But if it is inadvisable to press ahead with a project when you are getting no encouragement from standard library resources, it is also a mistake to give up as soon as you have hit one dead end. Even negative results can sometimes be instructive. Thus the writer of the UFO paper began by going to the *Applied Science and Technology Index,* where, to her surprise, she found no references at all to UFOs. Instead of abandoning her topic, she began to grasp a key element of the UFO controversy—namely, that UFOs have thus far left behind no scientifically credible evidence of their existence.

You should also be prepared to reapportion your research time when you have come across decisively important works. The writer on computer crime found that he could hang his paper from two very different hinges: an authoritative government document and a "human interest" case history. As for the UFO project, the student sifted quickly through many books and articles before committing much time to any of them. She was looking for the best representatives of both sides—the authorities who were cited most often by others and who seemed to take the most comprehensive positions. For the pro-UFO side she settled on J. Allen Hynek's *The Hynek UFO Report,* and for the negative, Philip J. Klass's *UFOs Explained.* Instead of continuing to pile up miscellaneous bibliography cards (36e, p. 462)

libr

36g

and rushing between the reference room and the card catalog, she sat down with those two books and made extensive notes comparing their ways of handling evidence and logic. For example:

Hynek — evading the question
Hynek keeps blasting Air Force and Condon for taking UFO reports lightly. Fair enough — but this turns us away from asking the really hard questions. Are there any *good* cases — i.e., ones that are proof against suspicion of fraud or error?

Hynek vs. Klass — rival methods
Note that while Hynek just piles up sightings — implying that they must add up to something — Klass deals with principles of explanation. They're writing at cross-purposes.

Hynek vs. Klass — assumptions required
If Klass is right re UFO's, no extra assumptions
have to be brought in. If Hynek is right, gravity
and gravitation don't seem to affect certain
unique vehicles; we have to believe in time
machines or something; and we have to supply
motives for aliens to travel quadrillions of miles
to visit us - without really introducing themselves!
Note that H. lacks a general hypothesis to cover
sightings. (But he _was_ chief technical consultant
to _Close Encounters_!)

Hynek vs. Klass — dealing w/ objections
Hynek's book comes 3 yrs. after Klass's,
but doesn't refer to it or deal w/ any of
the objections it raises. Interesting! — esp.
since Hynek is a leading character
in Klass's book. See, e.g., the comical
Pascagoula case (K, pp. 347-369). Use?
Anyway, if H. _could_ have replied to K,
why didn't he?

libr
36g

By the time she had finished intensively comparing the books by
Hynek and Klass, the student had a firm point of view and the mak-
ings of a thesis. Then she returned to her other sources with a much
clearer idea of which items to pursue and which to discard.

37 Documenting Sources

37a Learn Where Documentation Is Called For.

If you have done research for a paper, there are several reasons why you should cite your sources, using a standard form of documentation. You want credit for your efforts, and your documentation will help to show a reader that your ideas are consistent with facts and expert judgments that have already appeared in print. In some cases you may even want to pose a challenge to received views, showing that you know what those views are and where they can be found. And documentation is also a courtesy to your readers, who ought to be able to check your sources either to see if you have used them responsibly or to pursue an interest in your topic.

Avoiding Plagiarism

A further reason for providing documentation is to avoid **plagiarism**—the serious ethical violation of presenting other people's words or ideas as your own. Plagiarism does tempt some student writers who feel too rushed or insecure to arrive at their own conclusions. Yet systematic dishonesty is only part of the problem. For every student who buys a term paper or copies a whole article without acknowledgment, there are dozens who indulge in "little" ethical lapses through thoughtlessness, haste, or a momentary sense of opportunity.

Though nearly all of their work is original, they too are plagiarists—just as someone who robs a bank of $2.39 is a bank robber.

Unlike the robber, however, some plagiarists fail to realize what they have done wrong. Students who once copied encyclopedia articles to satisfy school assignments may never have learned the necessity of using quotation marks and citing sources. Others may think that by *paraphrasing* a quotation or *summarizing* an idea (36f, p. 465)—that is, by putting it into their own words—they have turned it into public property. Others acknowledge the source of their idea but fail to indicate that they have borrowed words as well as thoughts. And others plagiarize through sloppy note taking (36e, p. 461). Since their notes do not distinguish adequately between personal observations and the content of a consulted book or article, their papers repeat the oversight. And finally, some students blunder into plagiarism by failing to recognize the difference between fact and opinion. They may think, for example, that a famous critic's opinion about a piece of literature is so authoritative that it belongs to the realm of common facts—and so they paraphrase it without acknowledgment. All these errors are understandable, but none of them constitutes a good excuse for plagiarism.

What to Acknowledge

Consider the following source and three ways that a student might be tempted to make use of it.

SOURCE:

The joker in the European pack was Italy. For a time hopes were entertained of her as a force against Germany, but these disappeared under Mussolini. In 1935 Italy made a belated attempt to participate in the scramble for Africa by invading Ethiopia. It was clearly a breach of the covenant of the League of Nations for one of its members to attack another. France and Great Britain, as great powers, Mediterranean powers, and African colonial powers, were bound to take the lead against Italy at the league. But they did so feebly and half-heartedly because they did not want to alienate a possible ally against Germany. The result was the worst possible: the league failed to check aggression, Ethiopia lost her independence, and Italy was alienated after all.

—J. M. ROBERTS, *History of the World*

**doc
37a**

VERSION A:

Italy, one might say, was the joker in the European
deck.   When she invaded Ethiopia, it was clearly a
breach of the covenant of the League of Nations;
yet the efforts of England and France to take the
lead against her were feeble and half-hearted.   It
appears that those great powers had no wish to alienate a possible ally against Hitler's rearmed
Germany.

Comment: Clearly plagiarism. Though the facts cited are
public knowledge, the stolen phrases are not. Note that the
writer's interweaving of his own words with the source does
not make him innocent of plagiarism.

VERSION B:

Italy was the joker in the European deck.   Under
Mussolini in 1935, she made a belated attempt to
participate in the scramble for Africa by invading
Ethiopia.   As J. M. Roberts points out, this vio-
lated the covenant of the League of Nations (Roberts 845).   But France and Britain, not wanting to
alienate a possible ally against Germany, put up
only feeble and half-hearted opposition to the
Ethiopian adventure.   The outcome, as Roberts observes, was "the worst possible: the league failed
to check aggression, Ethiopia lost her independence, and Italy was alienated after all" (Roberts
845).

**doc
37a**

Comment: Still plagiarism. The two correct citations of Roberts serve as a kind of alibi for the appropriating of other, unacknowledged phrases.

VERSION C:

Much has been written about German rearmament and militarism in the period 1933–1939. But Germany's dominance in Europe was by no means a foregone conclusion. The fact is that the balance of power might have been tipped against Hitler if one or two things had turned out differently. Take Italy's gravitation toward an alliance with Germany, for example. That alliance seemed so very far from inevitable that Britain and France actually muted their criticism of the Ethiopian invasion in the hope of remaining friends with Italy. They opposed the Italians in the League of Nations, as J. M. Roberts observes, "feebly and half-heartedly because they did not want to alienate a possible ally against Germany" (Roberts 845). Suppose Italy, France, and Britain had retained a certain common interest. Would Hitler have been able to get away with his remarkable bluffing and bullying in the later Thirties?

doc 37a

Comment: No plagiarism. The writer has been influenced by the public facts mentioned by Roberts, but he has not tried to pass off Roberts' conclusions as his own. The one clear borrowing is properly acknowledged.

There *is* room for disagreement about what to acknowledge; but precisely because this is so, you ought to make your documentation relatively ample. Provide citations for all direct quotations and paraphrases, borrowed ideas, and facts that do not belong to general knowledge.

Ask yourself, in doubtful cases, whether the point you are borrowing is an opinion or a fact. Opinions are by definition ideas that are not yet taken for granted; document them. As for facts, do not bother to document those that could be found in any commonly used source—for example, the fact that World War II ended in 1945. But give references for less accessible facts, such as the numbers of operational submarines that Nazi Germany still possessed at the end of the war. The harder it would be for readers to come across your fact through their own efforts, the more surely you need to document it.

If you are quoting, paraphrasing, or alluding to statements or literary passages that are not generally familiar, cite the source. A phrase from Lincoln's Gettysburg Address could get by without a citation, but a remark made in a presidential news conference could not.

DO NOT DOCUMENT	DOCUMENT
the population of China	the Chinese balance of payments in 1984
the existence of a disease syndrome called AIDS	a possible connection between AIDS and the virus that carries cat leukemia
the fact that Dickens visited America	the supposed effect of Dickens' American visit on his subsequently written novels
the fact that huge sums are wagered illegally on professional football games	an alleged "fix" of a certain football game
a line from a nursery rhyme	a line from a poem by Elizabeth Bishop

**doc
37a**

37b Observe the Differences between Reference List Style and Footnote/Endnote Style.

In your reading you will encounter many documentation forms, but every version will belong to one of two general styles. In **reference list style**, parenthetical citations in the main text are keyed to a list of "Works Cited" or "Works Consulted," which appears at the end of the article, chapter, or book. In **footnote/endnote style**, raised numbers in the main text—usually at the ends of sentences—are keyed to notes appearing either at the foot of the page or at the end of the whole text. Both styles allow for **supplementary notes** that make comments or mention further references.

REFERENCE LIST STYLE	FOOTNOTE/ENDNOTE STYLE
No note numbers are used (except for supplementary notes).	Raised numbers appear in text.
No notes are used to cite works.	Notes appearing at foot of page or at end of text give citations corresponding to note numbers in text.
All references are made through parenthetical citations within text.	Parenthetical citations within text are used only for "subsequent references" to frequently cited works.
Supplementary notes, if any, appear after main text but before reference list.	Supplementary notes, if any, are integrated into footnotes or endnotes.
A reference list, identifying only works cited or consulted, appears at the end. The listed works match the parenthetical citations in the text.	A bibliography, identifying both works cited and works consulted, may appear after all the notes.

doc
37b

Until recently, reference list style has generally prevailed in the sciences and footnote/endnote style in the humanities. Today, however, reference list style is gaining ground in the humanities as well. It is better suited to handling a large number of citations without distracting a reader from the main text. But since we remain in a transitional period and since some of your college instructors may prefer footnote/endnote style, you should know how both systems work.

In some disciplines—for example, mathematics, chemistry, physics, biology, and engineering—the textual citations in reference list style are Arabic numerals that correspond to numbered items in the reference list. A numbered item may mention any number of works.

SENTENCE IN TEXT:

It appears that female choice is frequently involved in the evolution of the conspicuous acoustic signals that precede mating (2, 3).

ITEMS IN REFERENCE LIST:

2. L. Fairchild, *Science 212,* 950 (1981); R. D. Howard, *Evolution 32,* 850 (1978); M. J. Ryan, *Science 209,* 523 (1980).

3. R. D. Alexander, in *Insects, Science, and Society,* D. Pimentel, Ed. (Academic Press, New York, 1975), p. 35; P. D. Bell, *Can. J. Zool. 58,* 1861 (1980); W. Cade, *Science 190,* 1312 (1975); in *Sexual Selection and Reproductive Competition in Insects,* M. S. Blum and N. A. Blum, Eds. (Academic Press, New York, 1979); D. J. Campbell and E. Shipp, *Z. Tierpsychol. 51,* 260 (1979); A. V. Popov and V. F. Shuvalov, *J. Comp. Physiol. 119,* 111 (1977); S. M. Ulagaraj and T. J. Walker, *Science 182,* 1278 (1973).

   —CHRISTINE R. B. BOAKE and ROBERT R. CAPRANICA, "Aggressive Signal in 'Courtship' Chirps of a Gregarious Cricket"

doc 37b

In other disciplines—for example, botany, geology, zoology, economics, psychology, and sociology—the parenthetical citations include the author(s) and date of publication *(Comstock & Fisher, 1975),* and the reference list is ordered alphabetically. If you are writing for publication in any field, look at a relevant journal and adopt its conventions.

37c   Learn How to Present a Reference List According to MLA Form.

Traditionally, research papers written for composition courses followed the footnote/endnote form of the Modern Language Association of America (MLA). The MLA, however, now endorses a reference list form, spelled out in Joseph Gibaldi and Walter S. Achtert, *MLA Handbook for Writers of Research Papers,* 2nd ed. (New York: MLA, 1984). Unless your instructor indicates otherwise, you can use the following guidelines in documenting your research paper. For a sample result, study the paper appearing on pages 500–508 below.

After your text, including any supplementary notes (37f, p. 497), supply a list of "Works Cited" or, if you are including uncited items, "Works Consulted." Start on a new page, consecutively numbered with the foregoing ones. Space your list like the sample on pages 507–508.

Order your reference list alphabetically by authors' last names or, when no author appears, by the first significant word of the title (omitting *A, An,* and *The*). If the author is an institution—for example, SRI International—list it by the first letter in the corporate name's first significant word (in this case *S*). Within each entry, present information (where relevant) in the following order.

BOOKS	ARTICLES
1. Author's name	1. Author's name
2. Title of part of book	2. Title of article
3. Title of book	3. Name of periodical
4. Name of editor, translator, or compiler	4. Series number or name
5. Edition used	5. Volume number
6. Number of volumes	6. Date of publication
7. Name of series	7. Page numbers
8. Place of publication, shortened name of publisher, date of publication	
9. Page numbers	

doc
37c

DOCUMENTING SOURCES

...are sample entries covering typical works that might appear
...reference list.

Books

A BOOK BY A SINGLE AUTHOR:

Langbaum, Robert. The Modern Spirit: Essays on the
   Continuity of Nineteenth- and Twentieth-Century
   Literature. New York: Oxford UP, 1970.

TWO OR MORE BOOKS BY THE SAME AUTHOR:

Michaels, Leonard. I Would Have Saved Them If I Could.
   New York: Farrar, 1975.
---. The Men's Club. New York: Farrar, 1981.

A BOOK BY TWO AUTHORS:

Liehm, Mira, and Antonin J. Liehm. The Most Important
   Art: Soviet and Eastern European Film after 1945.
   Berkeley: U of California P, 1977.

A BOOK BY THREE AUTHORS:

Burns, James MacGregor, J. W. Peltason, and Thomas E.
   Cronin. Government by the People. 12th ed. En-
   glewood Cliffs, NJ: Prentice-Hall, 1984.

doc
37c

A BOOK BY MORE THAN THREE AUTHORS:

Dickerson, Richard E., et al. Chemical Principles.
   3rd ed. Menlo Park, CA: Benjamin/Cummings, 1979.
      This book was published in several cities, but only the

first-mentioned one need be named. Note that an abbreviated name of the state or country is added for less well-known place names.

A BOOK BY A CORPORATE AUTHOR:

American Society of Hospital Pharmacists. Consumer
   Drug Digest. New York: Facts on File, 1982.

AN ANONYMOUS BOOK:

Chicago Manual of Style. 13th ed. Chicago: U of Chicago P, 1982.

A WORK IN AN ANTHOLOGY:

Collins, William. "Ode to Evening." Norton Anthology
   of English Literature. Ed. M. H. Abrams et al.
   4th ed. 2 vols. New York: Norton, 1979. 2:
   2451–52.

If you are citing more than one work from an anthology, provide an entry for the anthology itself, and cite it within references to the separate works, as follows.

THE ANTHOLOGY ITSELF:

Abrams, M. H., et al., eds. Norton Anthology of English Literature. 4th ed. 2 vols. New York:
   Norton, 1979.

doc
37c

TWO WORKS WITHIN THE CITED ANTHOLOGY:

Collins, William. "Ode to Evening." Abrams et al.
   2: 2451–52.

Owen, Wilfred. "Insensibility." Abrams et al. 2:
1936—37.

A WORK FROM A COLLECTION BY ONE AUTHOR:

Mill, John Stuart. <u>On Liberty</u>. <u>Three Essays: On Lib-</u>
<u>erty, Representative Government, The Subjection of</u>
<u>Women</u>. New York: Oxford UP, 1975. 1—141.

A PREFACE, INTRODUCTION, FOREWORD, OR AFTERWORD:

Scully, Vincent. Preface. <u>The Earth, the Temple, and</u>
<u>the Gods: Greek Sacred Architecture</u>. By Scully.
Rev. ed. New Haven: Yale UP, 1979. xiv—xvi.

Baker, Richard. Introduction. <u>Zen Mind, Beginner's</u>
<u>Mind</u>. By Shunryu Suzuki. New York: Weatherhill,
1970. 13—18.

Note the different handling according to whether the
same author did or did not write the larger work.

THE EDITED WORK OF AN AUTHOR:

Plato. <u>The Collected Dialogues of Plato: Including</u>
<u>the Letters</u>. Ed. Edith Hamilton and Huntington
Cairns. Princeton: Princeton UP, 1961.

doc
37c

A BOOK EDITED BY TWO OR THREE PEOPLE:

White, George Abbott, and Charles Newman, eds. <u>Liter-</u>
<u>ature in Revolution</u>. New York: Holt, 1972.

A BOOK EDITED BY MORE THAN THREE PEOPLE:

Kermode, Frank, et al., eds.   The Oxford Anthology of
   English Literature.   2 vols.   New York: Oxford
   UP, 1973.

A BOOK THAT FORMS PART OF A SERIES:

Kuhn, Thomas S.   The Structure of Scientific Revolu-
   tions.   2nd ed.   International Encyclopedia of
   Unified Science.   2nd series, no. 2.   Chicago:
   U of Chicago P, 1970.

A TRANSLATION:

Kundera, Milan.   The Book of Laughter and Forgetting.
   Trans. Michael Henry Heim.   New York: Knopf,
   1981.

A REPUBLISHED BOOK:

Conroy, Frank.   Stop-time.   1967.   New York: Penguin,
   1977.

A PUBLISHER'S IMPRINT:

Hobbes, Thomas.   Leviathan: Or the Matter, Forme and
   Power of a Commonwealth Ecclesiasticall and
   Civil.   Ed. Michael Oakeshott.   New York: Col-
   lier-Macmillan, 1962.

An "imprint" is the name of a special line of books, in this
case the Collier Classics in the History of Thought. Give
the imprint first and then the publisher: *Anchor–Double-
day, Modern Library–Random House,* etc.

**doc
37c**

Articles in Journals, Magazines, and Newspapers

AN ARTICLE IN A JOURNAL WITH CONTINUOUS PAGINATION:

Cooper, Arnold M.   "Psychoanalysis at One Hundred: Beginnings of Maturity."   Journal of the American
Psychoanalytic Association 32 (1984): 245–67.

AN ARTICLE IN A JOURNAL THAT DOES NOT IDENTIFY THE EXACT DATE OF EACH ISSUE:

Wheeler, Richard P.   "Poetry and Fantasy in Shakespeare's Sonnets 88–96."   Literature and Psychology 22.3 (1972): 151–162.

The article appears in number 3 of volume 22.

AN ARTICLE IN A MAGAZINE WITH SEPARATE PAGINATION FOR EACH ISSUE:

Begiebing, Robert.   "Twelfth Round: An Interview with
Norman Mailer."   Harvard Magazine Mar.–Apr. 1983:
40–50.

A REVIEW:

Schwendener, Peter.   Rev. of Red and Hot: The Fate of
Jazz in the Soviet Union, 1917–1980, by S. Frederick Starr.   American Scholar 53 (1984): 429–30.

doc
37c

AN UNSIGNED MAGAZINE ARTICLE:

"Drugs That Don't Work."   New Republic 29 Jan. 1972:
12–13.

AN UNSIGNED NEWSPAPER ARTICLE OR EDITORIAL:

"The Water Plan." San Francisco Chronicle 20 June

1984, four-star ed.: 52.

> It is sometimes helpful to specify which edition of a newspaper you are citing.

A SIGNED NEWSPAPER ARTICLE:

Weisman, Steven R. "President Assails Soviet in Ad-

dress at Irish College." New York Times 3 June

1984, sec. 1: 1.

> Specify sections only if the pagination of the newspaper begins anew for each section. Here the article is fully contained on page 1 of section 1. If the article were completed on a later page, the reference would say *sec. 1: 1 +*.

Other Written Works

AN ENCYCLOPEDIA ENTRY:

L[ustig], L[awrence]. "Alluvial Fans." Encyclopaedia

Britannica: Macropaedia. 1974.

> The author's initials appear at the end of the entry; they are identified elsewhere. Note that volume and page numbers are unnecessary when items appear in alphabetical order. But since the *Britannica* from 1974 onward has three sets of contents, the note should indicate which one is intended—in this case the "Macropaedia."

doc
37c

A PAMPHLET OR MANUAL:

Kater, David A. Epson FX-80 Printer User's Manual.

Torrance, CA: Epson, 1983.

A DISSERTATION:

Boudin, Henry Morton. "The Ripple Effect in Classroom
Management." Diss. U of Michigan, 1970.

A PUBLIC DOCUMENT:

United States. Dept. of Agriculture. "Shipments and
Unloads of Certain Fruits and Vegetables, 1918–
1923." Statistical Bulletin 7 (Apr. 1925).

A PUBLISHED LETTER:

Allen, Steve. Letter. Popular Photography June 1978:
4.

Dickinson, Emily. "To Joel Warren Norcross." 11 Jan.
1850. Selected Letters. Ed. Thomas H. Johnson.
Cambridge: Harvard UP, 1971. 31–34.

AN UNPUBLISHED LETTER:

Graff, Gerald. Letter to the author. 18 Aug. 1984.

Nonwritten Works

A THEATRICAL PERFORMANCE:

A Moon for the Misbegotten. By Eugene O'Neill. Dir.
David Leveaux. With Kate Nelligan, Ian Bannen,
and Jerome Kilty. Cort Theatre, New York. 23
June 1984.

A FILM:

Star Trek III: The Search for Spock. Dir. Leonard
Nimoy. With William Shatner and DeForest Kelley.
Paramount, 1984.

A RADIO OR TELEVISION PROGRAM:

The World's Worst Air Crash. Narr. Bill Moyers. PBS,
Los Angeles. 27 July 1979.

A RECORDING:

Beethoven, Ludwig van. Symphony no. 8 in F, op. 93.
Cond. Pierre Monteux. Vienna Philharmonic Orch.
Decca, STS 15238, 1964.

A LECTURE:

Hirsch, E. D., Jr. "Frontiers of Critical Theory."
Wyoming Conference on Freshman and Sophomore English, U of Wyoming. Laramie, 9 July 1979.

AN INTERVIEW:

Collier, Peter, and David Horowitz. Personal interview. 5 Nov. 1984.
Sutherland, Jennifer. Telephone interview. 21 June
1984.

doc
37c

COMPUTER SOFTWARE:

The Benchmark. Computer Software. Metasoft, 1984.
IBM DOS, Version 4.0, disk.

37d Learn How to Present Parenthetical Citations according to MLA Form.

The idea behind all parenthetical citations is to give the minimum of information that will send a reader to the correct item in the reference list (37c) and, where applicable, to the cited portion of the work. Look at pages 500–506 below to get a sense of the way such citations are typically used and where they are placed.

If you are referring to a whole work and if the author's name appears in your sentence, you need not supply any further information:

- Cooper's presidential address struck a gloomy note.

But the same sentence would require a parenthetical page reference—without repeating the author's name—if you had in mind only part of the item:

- Cooper's presidential address struck a gloomy note (249–52).

Where the author's name does not appear in your sentence, supply it in the citation:

- One prominent spokesman has expressed serious doubt about the current health of the profession (Cooper 249–52).

The following sample citations cover ways of referring to works showing a variety of features.

Sample Citations

doc 37d

A MULTIVOLUME WORK:

- Sidney shows a healthy distrust of what he calls, in "An Apology for Poetry," "that honey-flowing matron Eloquence" (Abrams et al. 1:503).

A WORK LISTED BY TITLE:

- The name of our planet is usually capitalized only when other bodies in the Solar System are also named (*Chicago Manual* 7.113).

Note the shortened title; compare page 481. No edition number is needed, since the reference list contains only one entry under this name. Note, too, the citing of a section rather than a page of a reference work thus ordered.

A WORK BY A CORPORATE AUTHOR:

- The American Society of Hospital Pharmacists considers methicillin "particularly useful" in treating hospital-acquired infections (89).

  "Corporate" names are usually too long to be inserted into a parenthetical citation without distracting the reader. Make an effort to get the name into the main part of your sentence. Here the remark about methicillin is attributed to page 89 of the book in the reference list named under *American Society of Hospital Pharmacists.*

TWO OR MORE WORKS BY THE SAME AUTHOR:

- "I feel you're feeling anger," says Kramer after his wife has clobbered him with an iron pot (Michaels, *Men's Club* 172).

  The title of the work is included in the citation when two or more works by the same author appear in the reference list (p. 480).

AN INDIRECT SOURCE:

- Writing in *Temps Modernes* in 1957, Woroszylski expressed surprise at "how much political nonsense we allowed ourselves to be talked into" (qtd. in Liehm and Liehm 116).

  If you have no access to the original text, use *qtd. in* to show that your source for the quotation is another work.

A CLASSIC VERSE PLAY OR POEM:

- "I prithee, daughter," begs Lear, "do not make me mad" (II.iv.212).

doc
37d

Cite acts, scenes, and lines instead of pages. The capital and lower-case Roman numerals here help to distinguish the act and scene from the line number; however, *2.4.212* would also be acceptable.

MORE THAN ONE WORK IN A CITATION:

• The standard view of "scientific method" has come under concentrated attack in recent years (Kuhn; Lakatos; Laudan).

But if your parenthetical citation becomes too cumbersome, consider replacing it with a substantive note (37f, p. 497).

37e Observe the Features of Footnote/Endnote Style.

If your instructor prefers a documentation style using footnotes or endnotes (37b, p. 477), you can make use of the "alternative MLA" form illustrated in the research paper on pages 510–521. That paper shows how **endnotes** are customarily handled; they appear in a consecutive series at the end of the paper, article, chapter, or book. **Footnotes**, by contrast, appear at the bottom of the page on which the reference occurs. Prefer endnotes unless your instructor requires footnotes.

Wherever you decide to put your notes, you should follow these rules for handling the note numbers within your text:

---

1. Number all the notes consecutively (1, 2, 3, . . .).
2. Elevate the note numbers slightly, as here.[8]
3. Place the numbers after, not before, the quotations or other information being cited: not x As Rosenhan says,[11] "the evidence is simply not compelling," but As Rosenhan says, "the evidence is simply not compelling."[11]
4. Place the numbers after all punctuation except a dash; even parentheses, colons, and semicolons should precede note numbers.

Endnotes versus Footnotes

Type endnotes on a new page after your main text, but before a bibliography if you are supplying one. Here is the standard form.

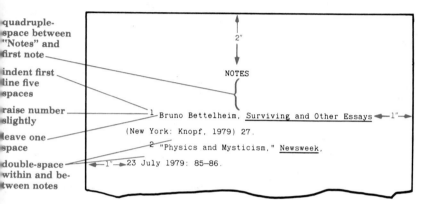

quadruple-space between "Notes" and first note

indent first line five spaces

raise number slightly

leave one space

double-space within and between notes

NOTES

2"

1 Bruno Bettelheim, Surviving and Other Essays ← 1" →
(New York: Knopf, 1979) 27.
2 "Physics and Mysticism," Newsweek,
← 1" → 23 July 1979: 85–86.

when only 1" remains at the bottom of the page, continue notes on a following page

Handle footnotes just like endnotes except for these differences:

1. On each page where you will have notes, stop your main text high enough to leave room for the notes.

2. Quadruple-space between the end of the text and the first note on a page.

3. Single-space within the notes, but double-space between them.

4. If you have to carry a note over to the next page, type a solid line a full line below the last line of text on that new page, quadruple-space, and continue the note. Then continue any new notes.

doc
37e

Thus, footnotes at the bottom of a page look like this.

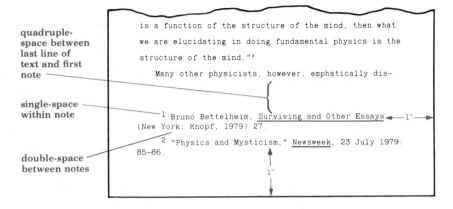

quadruple-
space between
last line of
text and first
note

single-space
within note

double-space
between notes

is a function of the structure of the mind, then what

we are elucidating in doing fundamental physics is the

structure of the mind."²

    Many other physicists, however, emphatically dis—

  ¹ Bruno Bettelheim, <u>Surviving and Other Essays</u>
(New York: Knopf, 1979) 27.

   ² "Physics and Mysticism," <u>Newsweek</u>, 23 July 1979:
85–86.

1"

1"

And here is a footnote carried over from a preceding page.

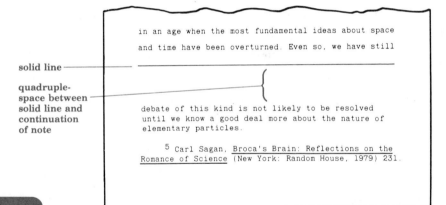

solid line

quadruple-
space between
solid line and
continuation
of note

in an age when the most fundamental ideas about space

and time have been overturned. Even so, we have still

debate of this kind is not likely to be resolved
until we know a good deal more about the nature of
elementary particles.

   ⁵ Carl Sagan, <u>Broca's Brain: Reflections on the
Romance of Science</u> (New York: Random House, 1979) 231.

**doc
37e**

First Notes

To see how notes differ from reference list entries, compare the following sample notes with the corresponding entries on pages 480–
487. Notes 1–21 end with references to specific parts of the cited works.

1 Robert Langbaum, The Modern Spirit: Essays on the Continuity of Nineteenth- and Twentieth-Century Literature (New York: Oxford UP, 1970) 64.

2 Mira Liehm and Antonin J. Liehm, The Most Important Art: Soviet and Eastern European Film after 1945 (Berkeley: U of California P, 1977) 234–45.

3 American Society of Hospital Pharmacists, Consumer Drug Digest (New York: Facts on File, 1982) 107.

4 Chicago Manual of Style, 13th ed. (Chicago: U of Chicago P, 1982) 8.14.

5 Wilfred Owen, "Insensibility," Norton Anthology of English Literature, ed. M. H. Abrams et al., 4th ed., 2 vols. (New York: Norton, 1979) 2: 1936–37.

6 Richard Baker, introduction, Zen Mind, Beginner's Mind, by Shunryu Suzuki (New York: Weatherhill, 1970) 15.

7 Plato, The Collected Dialogues of Plato: Including the Letters, ed. Edith Hamilton and Huntington Cairns (Princeton: Princeton UP, 1961) 327.

8 Frank Kermode et al., eds., The Oxford Anthology of English Literature, 2 vols. (New York: Oxford UP, 1973) 1:209–11.

doc
37e

9 Thomas S. Kuhn, The Structure of Scientific Revolutions, 2nd ed., International Encyclopedia of Uni-

fied Science, 2nd series, no. 2 (Chicago: U of Chicago P, 1970) 179–82.

[10] Milan Kundera, The Book of Laughter and Forgetting, trans. Michael Henry Heim (New York: Knopf, 1981) 54–61.

[11] Frank Conroy, Stop-time (1967; New York: Penguin, 1977) 8.

[12] Thomas Hobbes, Leviathan: Or the Matter, Forme and Power of a Commonwealth Ecclesiasticall and Civil, ed. Michael Oakeshott (New York: Collier-Macmillan, 1962) 348–49.

[13] Arnold M. Cooper, "Psychoanalysis at One Hundred: Beginnings of Maturity," Journal of the American Psychoanalytic Association 32 (1984): 250.

[14] Richard P. Wheeler, "Poetry and Fantasy in Shakespeare's Sonnets 88–96," Literature and Psychology 22.3 (1972): 159.

[15] Peter Schwendener, rev. of Red and Hot: The Fate of Jazz in the Soviet Union, 1917–1980, by S. Frederick Starr, American Scholar 53 (1984): 429.

[16] "Drugs That Don't Work," New Republic 29 Jan. 1972: 13.

[17] Steven R. Weisman, "President Assails Soviet in Address at Irish College," New York Times 3 June 1984, sec. 1: 1.

[18] L[awrence] L[ustig], "Alluvial Fans," Encyclo-

paedia Britannica, 1974, Macropaedia.

   [19] Henry Morton Boudin, "The Ripple Effect in Classroom Management," diss., U of Michigan, 1970, 78–93.

   [20] United States, Dept. of Agriculture, "Shipments and Unloads of Certain Fruits and Vegetables, 1918–1923," Statistical Bulletin 7 (Apr. 1925): 208.

   [21] Steve Allen, letter, Popular Photography June 1978: 4.

   [22] Eugene O'Neill, A Moon for the Misbegotten, dir. David Leveaux, with Kate Nelligan, Ian Bannen, and Jerome Kilty, Cort Theatre, New York, 23 June 1984.

   [23] Star Trek III: The Search for Spock, dir. Leonard Nimoy, with William Shatner and DeForest Kelley, Paramount, 1984.

   [24] The World's Worst Air Crash, narr. Bill Moyers, PBS, Los Angeles, 27 July 1979.

   [25] Ludwig van Beethoven, Symphony no. 8 in F, op. 93, cond. Pierre Monteux, Vienna Philharmonic Orch., Decca, STS 15238, 1964.

   [26] Peter Collier and David Horowitz, personal interview, 5 Nov. 1984.

Subsequent References

After you have provided one full endnote or footnote, you can be brief in citing the same work again:

   [27] Langbaum 197.

doc
37e

If you refer to more than one work by the same author, add a shortened title:

> 28 Michaels, <u>Men's Club</u> 45.
>
> 29 Michaels, <u>I Would Have Saved Them</u> 89–91.

If you cite the same work a third time, do not use the obsolete abbreviations *ibid.* or *op. cit.;* repeat the identifying information given in your first shortened reference. If the title of the whole work is cumbersome, abbreviate it.

FIRST NOTE:

> 30 <u>The McGraw-Hill Encyclopedia of World Biog-</u>
> <u>raphy</u>, 12 vols. (New York: McGraw-Hill, 1973) 6: 563;
> hereafter cited as <u>MEWB</u>.

SUBSEQUENT NOTE:

> 31 <u>MEWB</u> 8: 354.

If the same work comes up repeatedly in your notes, provide one full reference and then shift to parenthetical citations.

FIRST NOTE:

> 32 William Shakespeare, <u>The Merchant of Venice</u>,
> ed. Louis B. Wright and Virginia LaMar (New York: Wash-
> ington Square, 1957) II.iii.43.

doc
37e

SUBSEQUENT PARENTHETICAL REFERENCE:

- Portia tells Nerissa that she will do anything "ere I will be married to a sponge" (I.ii.90–91).

Bibliography

A bibliography is a list of works that you have consulted or that you recommend to your readers for further reference. Research papers, dissertations, and scholarly books that do not follow a reference list style of documentation (37b–37d) typically contain bibliographies at the end. If you are supplying endnotes or footnotes you can decide whether or not to include a bibliography by asking whether your notes have given a sufficient idea of your sources.

For bibliographical form, follow the conventions specified for a reference list of "Works Cited" or "Works Consulted" (37c, p. 479). In practice, the only difference between a bibliography and a "Works Consulted" list is that parenthetical citations are not keyed directly to a bibliography. You will find an example of a bibliography on pages 520–521.

37f Learn the Uses of Supplementary Notes.

If you are using a reference list form of documentation (37b–d), you will not be routinely supplying footnotes or endnotes. But you may nevertheless want to include some notes—usually endnotes, placed between the final paragraph of your main text and the beginning of your reference list—to make substantive comments (**substantive notes**) and to supply more references than you could gracefully fit into one set of parentheses (**bibliographic notes**).

SUBSTANTIVE NOTE:

```
1 According to Jalby, the peasants of Languedoc
dressed lightly on the whole, but on feastdays, regard-
less of the heat, they wore their best winter clothes
over their best summer ones to demonstrate their sense
of luxury (194).
```

doc
37f

BIBLIOGRAPHIC NOTE:

> 2 See also E. R. Dodds, <u>The Greeks and the Irra-</u>
> <u>tional</u> (Berkeley: U of California P, 1951) 145–62;
> Richard Stillwell, "The Siting of Classical Greek Tem-
> ples," <u>Journal of the Society of Architectural Histori-</u>
> <u>ans</u> 13 (1954): 5; and Robert Scranton, "Group Design in
> Greek Architecture," <u>Art Bulletin</u> 31 (1949): 251.

If the works cited in this note appeared in the reference list, the note
could be briefer:

> 2 See also Dodds 145–62; Stillwell 5; Scranton
> 251.

If you have been following a footnote/endnote form, your "supplementary" notes should be integrated with the others. But whichever
form you use, beware of demoting important points from your main
text to your notes. Remember that readers would be annoyed by having to lurch back and forth between text and notes in order to follow
your reasoning.

38 Sample Research Papers

To illustrate the fruits of library research, here are two student papers differing in mode and documentation form.

	COMPUTER CRIME PAPER	UFO PAPER
Mode	Explanation (p. 371)	Argument (p. 371)
Thesis Statement	Not included	Included (p. 394)
Documentation Form	MLA reference list	MLA endnote
List of Sources	"Works Cited" reference list (p. 479)	Bibliography (p. 497)
Sample Handwritten Page	Included (p. 509)	Not included

For information about the two writers' research procedures, see pages 448, 454, 462, 468. The UFO paper has been condensed to approximate the length of a typical effort in a composition course.

Suitable form for paper with no title page, thesis statement, or outline

Barry Lewis

English 101

Mr. Swenson

13 May 1983

Computer Theft: Crime Wave of the Future?

It is hardly a secret these days that computers are quickly becoming an indispensable feature of our lives. The Internal Revenue Service, the Census Bureau, Social Security, banks, insurance companies, corporations, universities, hospitals, small businesses, farmers, families, and students all use computers to maintain files, solve problems, and perform many other vital operations. Our checking accounts, taxes, bills, school registration, and grades are all routinely handled by computer. With personal computer sales for 1982 estimated at 2.8 million units as compared with 724,000 in 1980 ("The Computer Moves In" 14), the age of universal data processing is at hand. It is little wonder that _Time_'s "Man of the Year" for 1982 was no man at all but a machine, the computer ("The Computer Moves In").

The parenthetical citations are keyed to the "Works Cited" list on p. 8.

But if our number one hit is now the computer, its flip side is bound to be computer crime. In the new cybernetic world, just how safe from theft and misuse will our records and money be? How well can access to sensi-

The writer narrows to his topic, computer crime.

2

tive data be controlled? Will computer fraud become, as
The Futurist magazine predicted back in 1976, "the domi-
nant mode of criminal conduct" in America ("Crime in a
Cashless Society" 132)?

The problem of computer crime is such a novelty that
we must still consult experts to learn just what the phenomenon is. We must go, for example, to the U.S. Department of Justice's publication Computer Crime: Criminal
Justice Resource Manual, which divides the field into the
introduction of fraudulent records or data into a computer
system; unauthorized use of computer-related facilities;
the altering or destroying of information or files; and
the stealing of money, financial instruments, property,
services, or valuable data (SRI 5). And if that sounds
too abstract, the manual also gets down to specific capers, including "data diddling," "salami techniques" (such
as rounding down on accounts and depositing the fractions
of a cent in a favored account), and "scavenging" to obtain procedures, codes, and proprietary secrets (SRI 9–
29).

> The writer surveys the various types of computer crime.

Though computer crime is in its infancy, outlaws have
already disabled computers, held them for ransom, de-
stroyed essential files, stolen equipment, pirated programs, created huge insurance frauds, and "borrowed"

> Examples of current and potential crimes make the topic more concrete.

Several items from the "Works Cited" list are combined in one citation.

company time to develop gambling systems (Bartimo; Gomes; Parker; Whiteside). Nevertheless, bigger game may lie ahead. Recent articles have speculated about the advent of electronic terrorism and war, whereby extremists or enemy powers may create riots by crippling the computers that process welfare checks or black out the air traffic control computers across the country. Donn Parker, a Stanford Research Institute computer security expert and the author of <u>Crime by Computer</u>, has outlined several possible battle plans that might cause national or even international computer failures.

Whether or not such scenarios are exaggerated, there is no doubt that computer theft is already lucrative, relatively easy, and on the rise. Donn Parker believes that wrongdoers will find the computer a more and more attractive target. The average computer bank robbery, he points out, nets $500,000 as opposed to $2500 for the conventional version. Estimated annual losses from computer crime already range from $300 million to $5 billion (Ball). Everyone knows, furthermore, that those figures are unrealistically low. "Much chicanery goes undetected, and even when culprits are caught, the victimized company often tries to hush up the scandal and absorb its losses rather than admit to having poor computer security" (Alexander 60).

To indicate the widening scope of the problem, the writer calls on authorities and numerical data.

4

    It is a mistake, furthermore, to think that only a handful of evil geniuses are capable of computer fraud. The robbers, according to one expert's profile,

> tend to be relatively honest and in a position of trust; few would do anything to harm another human, and most do not consider their crime to be truly dishonest. . . . Between the ages of 18 and 30, they are usually bright, eager, highly motivated, adventuresome, and willing to accept technical challenges. Actually, they sound like the type of person managers would like to employ. (Ball 23)

    One typical, if spectacular, case can illustrate how the odds on computer theft presently favor the criminal. On October 25, 1978, Stanley Mark Rifkin, a 32-year-old computer consultant who still phoned his mother every day, managed to steal $10.2 million from Security National Bank in Los Angeles—with three telephone calls and a computer code number. The theft went unnoticed for eight days and was discovered then only because Rifkin's lawyer had revealed it to an unsuspecting agent of the FBI's white-collar crime unit in Los Angeles. Nor did Rifkin have to draw on much of his expertise to carry out the plan. The bank's passwords were reportedly posted on a bulletin board, and Rifkin obtained the code for transferring funds simply by posing as a Federal Reserve Bank consultant (Henderson and Young).

For a prose quotation of more than four typed lines, the writer uses the extracted form, indenting by ten spaces and omitting quotation marks.

One case dramatically illustrates lax computer security.

Form for citing coauthors of a single article

5

The Rifkin story makes it clear that we are still in the horse-and-buggy stage of computer security.[1] Such conventional safeguards as identification cards, keys, badges, code numbers, and passwords would cause little trouble for an alert, strategically placed thief. Moreover, there is a natural tendency for bright, inquisitive people to test their wits against a computer's "electronic fences"--and for the winning secret to be passed around.

A second long example reinforces the writer's point.

In 1981, for example, undergraduates at the University of California at Berkeley found an astonishingly simple way to invade other users' programs within the university's computer network. Luckily, the students had no criminal intent; they planted anonymous messages within the computer explaining its vulnerability (Petit). Not so luckily, the January 11, 1982, issue of *InfoWorld*, a computer trade newsletter, divulged the incident. Appalled officers of the Stanford Research Institute, the Computer and Business Equipment Manufacturers Association, and the National Security Agency only managed to spread the tantalizing news to potential thieves (Kolata).

Substantive footnotes can be combined with reference list documentation.

[1] "Most managers," observes Herman MacDaniel, president of Management Resources International, "have the misconception that the technology is so sophisticated that it doesn't need to be protected. But most of the frauds have been [committed] by people who were not technically [sophisticated]" ("Locking the Electronic File Cabinet" 123).

6

Needless to say, the would-be computer crook will face tougher obstacles in the future. New programs are being developed to trace internal transactions (Levin). Transactions outside banks are now increasingly protected by "encryption," a mathematical scrambling procedure (Meinel). Furthermore, fingerprint identification devices, retina scanners, and "signature dynamics" machines may soon be used to control access to data and equipment (Yulsman).

Having sketched the present situation, the writer turns to recent developments that could make computer crime difficult.

Even with better management and technology, however, the forces of crime prevention will be handicapped until the law itself is brought up to date. As of now, specific legal deterrents to computer fraud exist only at the state level—and in only eleven states (Frenkel). As Alan G. Merten, professor of computer and information systems at the University of Michigan, acknowledges, "There just aren't laws out there yet" ("Locking the Electronic File Cabinet" 124). And though the FBI has established a school to train special agents in investigating computer crime, under current standards of evidence conviction is difficult and sentencing light. "Our legal system," says August Bequai in White-Collar Crime: A Twentieth-Century Crisis, "has fallen behind our technology" (109).

But in one important area— the law—reform has scarcely begun.

It seems safe to predict that in the longer run, neither side will permanently gain the upper hand. This

7

The writer
concludes by
hazarding a
general pre-
diction about
the future of
computer
crime.

struggle, like the nuclear arms race, will be one of moves
and countermoves based on inside knowledge of the other
party's latest advances.   How can we be sure that the
government, the banks, and the corporations will not find
a way to make their systems absolutely crimeproof?   The
answer is that the security devices will be invented, of

The writer has
saved two
striking quota-
tions for the
end of his pa-
per.

course, by computer experts—experts "just like Stan Rifkin" (Henderson and Young 47).   As one analyst has concluded with a sigh, "the only completely secure computer
would be one that nobody could use" (Conniff 94).

8

Works Cited

Alexander, Charles. "Crackdown on Computer Capers." Time
      8 Feb. 1982: 60–61.
Ball, Leslie D. "Computer Crime." Technology Review Apr.
      1982: 21–27 + .
Bartimo, Jim. "Three WP Typists at Ford Named in Betting
      Operation." Computerworld 10 Jan. 1983: 11.
Bequai, August. White–Collar Crime: A Twentieth–Century
      Crisis. Lexington, Mass.: Lexington, 1978.
"The Computer Moves In." Time 3 Jan. 1983: 14–24.
Conniff, Richard. "Computer War." Science Digest Jan.
      1982: 14–15 + .
"Crime in a Cashless Society." The Futurist June 1976:
      132.
Frenkel, Karen A. "Computers in Court." Technology
      Review Apr. 1982: 28–29.
Gomes, Lee. "Secrets of the Software Pirates." Esquire
      Jan. 1982: 58–65.
Henderson, Bruce, and Jeffrey Young. "The Heist."
      Esquire May 1981: 36–40 + .
Kolata, Gina. "Students Discover Computer Threat."
      Science 215 (1982): 1216–17.
Levin, Stephen E. "Security Possible in Communications
      Networks." Computerworld 31 Jan. 1983: 5–10.

9

"Locking the Electronic File Cabinet." <u>Business Week</u> 18
Oct. 1982: 123–24.

Meinel, Carolyn. "Encryption: Can Spies and Thieves Break
It?" <u>Technology Review</u> Nov.–Dec. 1982: 72–74.

Parker, Donn B. <u>Crime by Computer</u>. New York: Scribner's,
1976.

Petit, Charles. "UC Students' Computer Trick Worries
Experts." <u>San Francisco Chronicle</u>, 2 Mar. 1982: 6.

SRI International. <u>Computer Crime: Criminal Justice
Resource Manual</u>. Washington: US Dept. of Justice,
1977.

Whiteside, Thomas. <u>Computer Capers: Tales of Electronic
Thievery, Embezzlement, and Fraud</u>. New York:
Crowell, 1978.

Yulsman, Tom. "Amazing Laser Locks." <u>Science Digest</u> June
1982: 26+.

A Sample Handwritten Page

5

    The Rifkin story makes it clear that we are still in the horse-and-buggy stage of computer security.[1] Such conventional safeguards as identification cards, keys, badges, code numbers, and passwords would cause little trouble for an alert, strategically placed thief. Moreover, there is a natural tendency for bright, inquisitive people to test their wits against a computer's "electronic fences" — and for the winning secret to be passed around.

    In 1981, for example, undergraduates at the University of California at Berkeley found an astonishingly simple way to invade other users' programs within the university's computer network. Luckily, the students had no criminal intent; they planted anonymous messages within the computer explaining its vulnerability (Petit). Not so luckily, the January 11, 1982, issue of *Info World*, a computer trade newsletter, divulged the incident. Appalled officers of the Stanford

---

[1] "Most managers," observes Herman Mac Daniel, president of Management Resources International, "have the misconception that the technology is so sophisticated that it doesn't need to be protected. But most of the frauds have been [committed] by people who were not technically [sophisticated]" ("Locking the Electronic File Cabinet" 123).

38b Note the Features of an Argumentative Research Paper Using MLA Endnote Form.

Kate Englander

Professor Keogh

English 1A

December 13, 1978

The writer forms a full thesis statement (p. 394) by surrounding her thesis with *although* and *because* clauses that remind her to consider the opposing position and to supply evidence.

UFOs: Should Seeing Be Believing?

Thesis statement: Although many private citizens, scientists, and government officials continue to be seriously concerned about Unidentified Flying Objects, belief in UFOs must rest on faith, not science, because no sound reasons for that belief have yet been presented.

Outline

She uses a sentence outline (p. 402) showing the subordination of some ideas to others.

I. The UFO Hypothesis Remains Popular.

    A. Thousands of sightings have been reported over a thirty-year period.

    B. The American public and many astronomers take UFOs seriously.

    C. So do some members of the government.

II. The Quality of the Evidence, Not the Number of Eye-witnesses, Should Decide the Issue.

III. No Sound Reasons for Believing in UFOs Have Yet Been Presented.

Outline 2

A. Decades of investigations have failed to convince officially chosen experts.

B. The case for UFOs rests on reports that are open to challenge.

   1. The reports never provide independent chains of evidence.

   2. The reports do not exclude alternative explanations.

C. The UFO hypothesis is the least likely of available explanations for reported sightings.

   1. Interstellar visitation—the only way of accounting for the alleged flight capabilities of UFOs— is highly improbable.

   2. When a plausible alternative is brought into view, a UFO report typically falls apart.

IV. Belief in UFOs Must Therefore Rest on Faith, Not Science.

UFOs: Should Seeing Be Believing?

The paper be-gins with three para-graphs grant-ing the popularity of the idea it will oppose.

    For more than thirty years now, a controversy has raged over the existence or nonexistence of Unidentified Flying Objects (UFOs). Sightings have been reported con-tinually since the first "flying saucers" caused panic in the 1940s, and in some periods, such as 1965–67 when nearly three thousand reports descended on the Air Force, waves or epidemics of alleged sightings have kept UFOs

The writer has chosen to use endnotes rather than footnotes. See page 490.

near the center of public concern.[1] And the UFO phenome-non shows no signs of letting up. In the past few weeks alone, my morning newspaper has covered sightings in West Virginia, Australia, and the oil fields of Kuwait.[2] To quote the title of one recent article on the subject, "UFO's Just Will Not Go Away."[3]

    The center of controversy is not, of course, whether many people have been alarmed by strange sights in the sky, but whether any of the objects seen should be consid-ered vehicles showing extraordinary, indeed unearthly, propulsion capabilities. By a narrow margin, the American public's answer to that question appears to be yes. A Gallup poll of 1973 showed, for example, that fifty-one percent of the respondents considered UFOs "real,"[4] and by 1978 Gallup found that the percentage of believers had

2

increased to fifty-seven.[5] More strikingly, a 1977 survey
of the American Astronomical Society disclosed that fifty-
three percent of the membership believed that UFOs merited
scientific study. Of the 1,356 members who completed the
survey, sixty-two reported having personally seen UFOs.[6]

In view of such widespread interest, it is not surprising to learn that worry about the reality and significance of UFOs extends to the highest levels of government.
Responding to an increasing flow of UFO reports, the
Presidential science advisor approached the National
Aeronautics and Space Administration in 1977 about the
possibility of a new federal investigation.[7] During the
same period, a special U.N. committee began discussing a
proposal that an agency within the UN be established to
study UFOs.[8]

Although NASA eventually rejected the White House's
request that it begin another study, stating that such an
inquiry would be "wasteful and probably unproductive,"[9]
the idea of UFOs clearly makes some of our leaders uneasy.
Indeed, American concern over UFOs goes straight to the
top--to President Carter, who, one evening in 1969 when he
was Governor of Georgia, looked up and saw a large bright
object which, he reported, "came close, moved away--came
close, then moved away . . . then disappeared."[10] As late

3

as 1976 Mr. Carter maintained in an interview that his experience had proved to him the reality of UFOs.[11]

In the face of so much testimony from varied sources, we might be inclined in advance to favor the UFO hypothesis--the notion that some astonishingly advanced vehicles have veered and vanished in our skies. But UFOs could nevertheless be what one critic calls "the modern myth"--a quasi-religious fantasy rather than a physical actuality.[12] The only way to settle the issue is to appeal to the quality of the evidence that has been produced so far. When we do, we will have to conclude that the present state of our knowledge does not justify a belief in UFOs.

No comparable phenomenon, as it happens, has ever been as thoroughly investigated as have UFOs--and the results have been entirely negative. During the period 1947-1966, when the Air Force was officially responsible for checking UFO reports, not one among thousands of cases was found to be substantial. When the Air Force, under criticism from UFO supporters, handed the investigation over to a group of civilian scientists, the outcome was the same. Edward U. Condon, the civilian project director, stated the group's joint position in these words:

> As indicated by its title [Scientific Study of Unidentified Flying Objects], the emphasis of

Here she pivots from pro-UFO considerations to her own point of view.

From here on, every paragraph will build support for the thesis.

Standard form for an extracted quotation (p. 152)

4

> this study has been on attempting to learn from
> UFO reports anything that could be considered as
> adding to scientific knowledge. Our general
> conclusion is that nothing has come from the
> study of UFOs in the past 21 years that has
> added to scientific knowledge.[13]

Although believers in UFOs have dismissed the Condon
Report as little better than a coverup,[14] even they generally admit that the case for UFOs rests only on unverified
stories, not on physical data that an outsider would have
to consider authentic. When those stories are checked,
furthermore, they never yield the minimum requirement for
proof, namely, what one physicist calls "independent and
multiple chains of evidence, each capable of satisfying a
link-by-link test of meaning."[15] Many people in an area
may think they have seen a UFO, but the alleged flying
object never flies to a second area where its features can
be corroborated or where the intentions of its supposed
occupants can be guessed at.

Unfortunately, a failure to search vigorously for alternative explanations appears to be an inevitable feature
of UFO reports. When people with alien spacecraft on
their minds glimpse something that seems to be flashing
through the sky, they rarely pause to ask themselves
whether they may have seen only a reflection, a meteor, or

5

a bright planet.[16]   And UFO enthusiasts, instead of holding off from crediting a report until doubters have probed
it for mistakes, treat the most plausible-looking new reports as if they corroborated the thousands of previous
ones. The result is a very long, hastily formed chain of
testimony, every link of which is seriously weak.

The neglect of alternative explanations becomes fatal
when we realize that the UFO hypothesis is always the
least likely explanation of a given sighting. When people
state that they have seen a vehicle defy gravity, they are
talking about a technology that must almost certainly have
been devised outside our solar system. If the UFO came to
us from the nearest stellar system, Alpha Centauri, it
must have traveled about 4.3 light-years, or
25,318,400,000,000 miles. If its speed during the journey
had been a million miles per hour, it would have been
launched some twenty-nine centuries ago, at about the time
King David was uniting the tribes of Israel.[17]   The pros-
pect is hard to imagine. It is also quite unnecessary to
consider until less extreme possibilities have been ruled
out.[18]

The writer re-
considers a fa-
mous UFO
case, which
she had delib-
erately used
as "bait" on
page 2.

Now let us return to the celebrated case that made a
believer of Governor Jimmy Carter. The Governor's report
states that the luminous object in the Georgia sky ap-

6

peared to him around 7:15 p.m. on January 6, 1969, at
about 30° elevation in the western sky. At that hour of
that clear evening, the planet Venus was in the west-
southwest at an elevation of 25° and was nearly 100 times
brighter than a first-magnitude star. Venus does not, of
course, advance and retreat or change its size, but whenever it becomes brilliant, hundreds of people think it is
a UFO in motion. Indeed, during World War II U.S. planes
frequently tried to shoot it down, mistaking it for an
enemy aircraft.[19] In view of these facts, how likely is
it that Governor Carter saw a UFO rather than Venus?

Although the idea of UFOs carries a vaguely scientific aura, science clearly offers no encouragement to believers. "We may even have to face the fact," writes the
most knowledgeable spokesman for UFOs, "that the scientific framework, by its very internal logic, excludes certain classes of phenomena, of which UFO's may be one"
(Hynek, UFO Experience 261). But the logic of science is
simply the logic of determining, as best we can, whether
something actually happened or will happen in a specified
way. Hynek's statement thus leads to a drastic conclusion: UFOs make so little empirical sense that we must
choose between believing in them on the one hand and reasoning from available facts on the other.

A parentheti-
cal citation
(p. 496) of a
previously cited
work elimi-
nates the need
for still an-
other note.

7

Notes

For the form
of notes, see
pages 490–495.

1 See David Michael Jacobs, <u>The UFO Controversy in
America</u> (Bloomington: Indiana UP, 1975).

2 <u>San Francisco Chronicle</u> 24 Oct. 1978: 16; 1+; 14
Nov. 1978: 10.

3 See D. Shapley, "UFO's Just Will Not Go Away," <u>Science</u> 198 (1977): 1128.

4 "Is There Something to UFO's after All?" <u>U.S. News
& World Report</u> 20 Feb. 1978: 56.

5 George Gallup, "Most Americans Believe in UFOs,"
<u>San Francisco Chronicle</u> 25 May 1978: 2.

A shortened
citation of a
work already
cited in note 4.

➤ 6 "Is There Something . . . ?" 56.

7 Boyce Rensberger, "U.F.O. Interest Rising, Stirred
by Science Fiction Films," <u>New York Times</u> 9 Dec. 1977,
sec. 2:1.

8 Rensberger 1.

9 "NASA Refuses to Reopen Investigation of U.F.O.'s,"
<u>New York Times</u> 28 Dec. 1977, sec.1: 14.

10 Shapley 1128.

11 Cited in "Is There Something . . . ?" 56.

12 See Donald H. Menzel, "UFO's—the Modern Myth," in
Carl Sagan and Thornton Page, eds., <u>UFO's—a Scientific
Debate</u> (Ithaca: Cornell UP, 1972) 123–82.

8

13 Edward U. Condon, Scientific Study of Unidentified Flying Objects (New York: Bantam, 1969) 1.

14 For the case against the Condon Report, see J. Allen Hynek, The Hynek UFO Report (New York: Dell, 1977).

15 Philip Morrison, "The Nature of Scientific Evidence: A Summary," in Sagan and Page 280.

16 For an understanding of the kinds of events that typically set off UFO reports, see Philip J. Klass, UFOs Explained (1974; New York: Vintage, 1976).

17 These figures can be checked in The Random House Encyclopedia (New York: Random House, 1977) 1900 (Alpha Centauri), 2346 (light-year), and 982 (reign of David).

18 Significantly, the leading proponent of UFOs admitted in 1972 that "after more than twenty years' association with the problem, I still have few answers and no viable hypothesis" (J. Allen Hynek, The UFO Experience: A Scientific Inquiry [New York: Ballantine, 1972] 258).

19 See Robert Sheaffer, "President Carter's 'UFO' Is Identified as the Planet Venus," Humanist July 1977: 46–47; Shapley 1128; "Is There Something . . . ?" 56.

Bibliography

Condon, Edward U. Scientific Study of Unidentified Flying
      Objects. New York: Bantam, 1969.

Emenegger, Robert. UFO's Past, Present, and Future. New
      York: Ballantine, 1974.

Gallup, George. "Most Americans Believe in UFOs." San
      Francisco Chronicle 25 May 1978: 2.

---. "UFO's, Ghosts and True Believers." San Francisco
      Chronicle 15 June 1978: 2.

Hynek, J. Allen. The Hynek UFO Report. New York: Dell,
      1977.

---. The UFO Experience: A Scientific Inquiry. New York:
      Ballantine, 1972.

"Is There Something to UFO's after All?" U.S. News &
      World Report, 20 Feb. 1978: 56.

Jacobs, David Michael. The UFO Controversy in America.
      Bloomington: Indiana UP, 1975.

Klass, Philip J. UFOs Explained. 1974; New York: Vin-
      tage, 1976

---, and J. Allen Hynek. "The Great UFO Debate." Chris-
      tian Science Monitor 24 Aug. 1977: 11—13.

Menzel, Donald H. "UFO's--the Modern Myth." Sagan and
      Page 123—82.

**The right form
for a second
bibliography
entry by the
same author.**

10

"NASA Refuses to Reopen Investigation of U.F.O.'s." <u>New
York Times</u> 28 Dec. 1977: sec. 1: 14.

Rensberger, Boyce. "U.F.O. Interest Rising, Stirred by
Science Fiction Films." <u>New York Times</u> 9 Dec. 1977:
sec. 2: 1.

Sagan, Carl, and Thornton Page, eds. <u>UFO's—a Scientific
Debate</u>. Ithaca: Cornell UP, 1972.

Shapley, D. "UFO's Just Will Not Go Away." <u>Science</u> 198
(1977): 1128.

Sheaffer, Robert. "President Carter's 'UFO' Is Identified
as the Planet Venus." <u>Humanist</u> July 1977: 46—47.

Vallee, Jacques. <u>UFO's in Space: Anatomy of a Phenomenon</u>.
1965; New York: Ballantine, 1977.

I BUSINESS WRITING

Business Writing
Most of the writing skills you are developing in college will serve you beyond the classroom as well. To operate successfully in the larger world, however, you must familiarize yourself with some new conventions. Chapter 39 indicates several standard ways of writing a business letter. Following one of those forms, you can make an impression of competence and confidence as you apply for a job, order merchandise, reply to correspondence, state a claim, or request information. And Chapter 40 gives you a model for the résumé that can show your accomplishments to best advantage when you apply for a job.

39 The Business Letter

To write an effective business letter you must come across as "all business." You can expect a good reception only if your letter shows neatness, accuracy, consistency, courtesy, efficiently concise and unpretentious statement, and adherence to standard form.

39a Master the Standard Features of the Business Letter.

Customary Elements

Examine the business letter on the following page. Here you see:

1. *The heading.* It contains your address and the date of writing. Notice the absence of end punctuation.

2. *The inside address.* Place this address high (or low) enough so that the body of the letter will appear centered on the page. Include the name of the addressee, that person's title or office, the name of the company or institution, and the full address:

```
Joan Lacey, M.D.            Mr. Kenneth Herbert
Pioneer Medical Group       Director of Personnel
45 Arrow Avenue             Cordial Fruit Cooperative
Omaha, NE 68104             636 Plumeria Boulevard
                            Honolulu, HI 96815
```

[MODIFIED BLOCK FORMAT]

2264 N. Cruger Avenue
Milwaukee, WI 53211 ——————— 1. heading
November 22, 1984

Mr. Robert F. Stone
Customer Relations ————————————————— 2. inside address
Kaiser Appliances, Inc.
834 La Salle Street
Chicago, IL 60632

Dear Mr. Stone: ————————————————————— 3. salutation

The Kitchen-Aid dishwasher I purchased in your
store on November 14 was installed yesterday. Unfortunately, the installation was complete before
the plumber and I noticed a large chip on the edge
of the white front panel. Since the panel was
still in its carton when the plumber arrived, it
was probably defective upon delivery. The serial
number of the dishwasher is T53278004; I enclose a
copy of the bill, already paid.

In my phone conversation with you yesterday, I
agreed to put this complaint in writing. I would
like you to send a representative here to replace
the damaged panel. To fix a time, please call me
at home after 5:30 P.M. at (312) 565-9776.

Thank you for your prompt attention to this matter.

4. body

Sincerely, ————— 5. complimentary close

Kevin Oppenheimer ————— 7. signature
Kevin Oppenheimer ——— 6. typed name

KO:sms
enc. ———————————————————————————— 8. special notations

3. *The salutation.* This formal greeting appears two lines lower than the inside address:

```
Dear Dr. Lacey:          Dear Ms. Diaz:
Dear Mr. Herbert:        Dear Reverend Melville:
```

Ms. is now the preferred form for addressing a woman who has no other title such as *Dr.* or *Professor.* Use *Miss* or *Mrs.* only if your correspondent has put that title before her own typed name in a letter to you: *(Mrs.) Estelle Kohut.* And unless you see otherwise, you should assume that a woman wishes to be known by her own first name, not her husband's.

When writing to an institution or a business, you can avoid the possibly offensive *Dear Sir* or *Dear Sirs* by choosing a neutral salutation:

```
Dear Personnel Manager:    Dear Editor:
Dear Sir or Madame:        Dear Macy's:
Dear Bursar:               To Whom It May Concern:
```

Note that business salutations end with a colon. Only if the addressee happens to be a friend should you strike a more informal note: *Dear Estelle, Dear Andy, . . .*

4. *The body.* Use the body of your letter to explain the situation and to make your request or response in a straightforward, concise way. You can write briefer paragraphs than you would use in an essay. Prefer middle-level diction, avoiding both slang and legalese: not ₓ *You really put one over on me* or ₓ *The undersigned was heretofore not apprised of the circumstances cited hereabove* but *I was not aware of the problem.*

Single-space the paragraphs of your letter but leave a double space between one paragraph and the next.

bus
39a

5. *The complimentary close.* Type the complimentary close two lines below the last line of the body. The most common formulas are:

Sincerely,	Yours sincerely,
Sincerely yours,	Very truly yours,
Yours truly,	Cordially,

Of these tags, *Cordially* is the only one that hints at actual feeling.

6. *Your typed name.* Leave four lines between the complimentary close and your typed name as you intend to sign it. If you have a professional title or role that is relevant to the purpose of the letter, add it directly below your name:

Nicole Pinsky	Jackson Marley
Assistant Manager	Lecturer

In general, such titles are appropriate when you are using letterhead stationery.

7. *Your signature.* Always use blue or black ink. Match your signature and your typed name; a briefer signature is a sign of impatience.

8. *Special notations.* Lowest on the page, always flush left, come notations to indicate the following circumstances if they are applicable:

NOTATION	MEANING
cc: A. Pitts F. Adler	"Carbon copies" (probably photocopies) are being simultaneously sent to interested parties Pitts and Adler.
enc.	The mailing contains an enclosure (always mentioned in the body of the letter).
att.	A document has been attached to the letter.
BR:clc *or* BR/clc	The writer (initials *BR*) has used the services of a typist (initials *CLC*).

bus
39a

Alternative Formats

There are three recognized ways of handling the arrangement of a business letter's elements on the page. You can choose any of the three, but they make somewhat different impressions. For extreme impersonality, *block format* works best. A middle style, very commonly used, is *modified block format.* And if you want your business letter to have some of the flavor of a personal letter, *indented format* is available.

Here are the three formats in a nutshell:

	BLOCK FORMAT	**MODIFIED BLOCK FORMAT**	**INDENTED FORMAT**
Heading	Flush left	Toward right margin	Toward right margin
Inside Address	Flush left	Flush left	Flush left
First Lines of Paragraphs	Flush left	Flush left	Indented 5–10 spaces
Complimentary Close, Name, and Signature	Flush left	Toward right margin	Toward right margin
Special Notations	Flush left	Flush left	Flush left

("Flush left" means that the lines begin at the left margin. "Toward right margin" means that the lines should end at or near the right margin.)

These differences may sound complicated, but they are easy to see in examples:

BLOCK FORMAT: p. 531
MODIFIED BLOCK FORMAT: pp. 526, 533
INDENTED FORMAT: p. 534

**bus
39a**

Note that indented format is simply modified block format plus indentions for the first lines of paragraphs.

Form of Envelope

Make the address on your envelope identical to the inside address. In the upper left corner, type your own address as it appears in the heading:

```
Kevin Oppenheimer
2264 N. Cruger Avenue
Milwaukee, WI 53211


                    Mr. Robert F. Stone
                    Customer Relations
                    Kaiser Appliances, Inc.
                    834 La Salle Street
                    Chicago, IL 60632
```

39b Recognize the Main Purposes of the Business Letter.

Asking for Information

Make your inquiry brief, and limit your request to information that can be sent in an available brochure or a brief reply. Be specific, so that there can be no doubt about which facts you need.

Ordering Merchandise

Begin by stating which items you are ordering, using both product names and stock or catalog page numbers. Tell how many units of each item you are ordering, the price per item, and the total price. If you want to receive the shipment at a different address, say so. Mention that you are enclosing payment, ask to be billed, or indicate a credit card number.

bus
39b

[BLOCK FORMAT]

36 Hawthorne Hall
University of the North
Bridgewater, CT 06413
January 15, 1984

NF Systems, Ltd.
P. O. Box 76363
Atlanta, GA 30358

Dear NF Systems:

Please send me the following software items for use on
the IBM Personal Computer, as described on page 40 in the
December 1983 issue of <u>Softalk</u> magazine:

    1 "Household Aids," a group of six
       programs, total package, $49.95
    1 "Check Register," includes 40 ledger/
          budget headings,   39.95

Kindly ship this merchandise to the address shown above.
I enclose my check #186 for $89.90. Since your adver-
tisement does not specify shipping costs, please bill me
for them separately if they are not included in the
prices.

Sincerely yours,

Lily Marks
Lily Marks

Stating a Claim

Take a courteous but firm tone, setting forth the facts so fully and clearly that your reader will be able to act on your letter without having to ask for more information. If you are complaining about a purchase, supply the date of purchase, the model and serial number, and a brief description. If you have been mistakenly billed twice for the same service or product, state what that service or product is, the date of your payment, and the check number if you paid by check. If possible, enclose a photocopy of the canceled check (both sides). In a second paragraph, calmly and fairly state what adjustment you think you are entitled to. (See page 526 for a sample claim letter.)

Making an Application

Tailor your letter to the particular job, grant, or program of study you are applying for. Name the opening precisely. If you are asking to be considered for a job, explain how you heard about it. If a person in authority recommended that you apply, say who it was. Tell how you can be reached, and express your willingness to be interviewed.

When applying for a job, include your résumé (Chapter 40, pp. 535–537) and mention that you have included it. Emphasize those elements in the résumé that qualify you for *this* position. Avoid boasting and false modesty alike. The idea to get across is that the facts of your record make such a strong case for your application that no special pleading is necessary.

The following letters illustrate how an applicant can state qualifications in different ways for different opportunities. Both letters pertain to the résumé appearing on page 537. Notice how each letter brings out "job-related" elements in the writer's background.

**bus
39b**

[MODIFIED BLOCK FORMAT]

137–20 Crescent Street
Flushing, NY 11367
August 17, 1985

F 1384
New York Times
New York, NY 10108

Dear Personnel Manager:

I am applying for the position of "Accounting Aide to CPA firm," which was advertised in yesterday's <u>Times</u>. I have completed my second year at Queens College as an Accounting major and plan to take a year off to supplement my education with relevant work.

From my enclosed résumé, you can see that I have been working in the business offices of Gristede's Food Stores, where I have assisted the bookkeeper in auditing procedures, including applications to computerized systems. My work requires strong mathematics skills and some familiarity with a Texas Instruments calculator.

As a prospective accountant, I am especially interested in spending next year with a CPA firm. I can send you the names of references both at Queens College and at Gristede's and would be grateful for the chance to be interviewed. Please write to me at the above address or call me at (212) 317-1964 after 5:30 P.M.

Sincerely yours,

Janet Madden

Janet Madden

encl.

[INDENTED FORMAT]

137-20 Crescent Street
Flushing, NY 11367
August 17, 1985

Ms. Charlotte DeVico
Rock of Ages Health Related
  Facility
7481 Parsons Boulevard
Flushing, NY 11367

Dear Ms. DeVico:

    Mr. Gene Connelly of the Flushing YMCA has suggested
I write to you about working as a recreation assistant
or bookkeeper in your facility beginning this fall. I am
an Accounting major with a minor in Communications, and I
plan to take a year off from school to supplement my
education with relevant work.

    From my enclosed résumé you can see that, in addi-
tion to a business background, I have experience in working with people. At the Flushing "Y" I have helped stage
the annual talent show, held informal "chat" sessions,
and presented films. I enjoy this work and find the el-
derly full of ideas and a willingness to make themselves
happy.

    Mr. Connelly has offered to write you about my work
at the "Y," and I can also send you the name of my
supervisor at Gristede's. I would be grateful for the
chance to be interviewed. Please write to me at the above
address or call me at (212) 975-1122 between 9:00 A.M.
and 4:30 P.M.

Sincerely yours,

Janet Madden

Janet Madden

encl

40 The Résumé

40a Recognize the Standard Features of the Résumé.

Your résumé is a brief (usually one-page) record of your career and qualifications. Along with your letter of application (39b, p. 532), it can land you a job interview. To that end it should be clear, easy on the eye, and totally favorable in emphasis. Have your résumé typed by a professional if you are unsure of your typing skills.

Divide your résumé into the following sections:

1. *Personal information.* Provide only what is necessary: name, present address, permanent address, phone numbers. Add your age, marital status, and condition of health only if you believe they are relevant to the job you want.

2. *Career objective.* Include a statement of your career goals. Avoid being so specific that you exclude reasonable opportunities or so broad as to be uninformative. Cite two goals if necessary, and mention any geographical limitations.

3. *Education.* Begin with the college you currently attend or have attended most recently, and work backward to high school. (If you have already graduated from college, omit high school.) Give dates of attendance, degrees attained, major and minor areas of study, and memberships in special societies. Briefly explain any outstanding projects or courses. Include your grade-point average only if it happens to be high.

4. *Work experience.* Begin with your current or most recent employment, and list all relevant jobs since high school. Try not to leave suspicious-looking gaps of time. Give the name and address of each employer, the dates of employment, and a brief description of your duties. Include part-time or volunteer work that may be relevant. Remember that you can mention relevant skills learned on a job that seems unrelated. If you are seeking a teaching position, consider beginning this part of your résumé with a section called *Teaching Experience* and following it with another called *Other Work Experience.*

5. *Special skills, activities, and honors.* Include special competencies that make you a desirable candidate, such as proficiency in a foreign language, ability to operate equipment, or skill in unusual procedures or techniques. Mention any honors, travel, or community service.

6. *References.* Supply the address of your college placement office, which will send out your dossier (dáhss-ee-ay) upon request. The dossier is a complete file of your credentials, including all letters of recommendation and transcripts. You may wish to give the names, positions, and addresses of three people you can trust to write strong letters in your behalf. Be sure you have their permission, however.

Further advice:

1. *Keep the format clear and the text concise.* Single-space within each section, and double-space between sections. Try to keep your résumé to one page; do not exceed two pages.

2. *Do not mention the salary you want.* You will be considered for more openings if you stay flexible on this point.

3. *Update your résumé periodically.* Do not hesitate to ask for new letters of recommendation.

4. *Rewrite your résumé for a particular job opening.* Rewriting allows you to highlight those elements of your background that will suit the job you are aiming for.

résumé
40a

JANET MADDEN

Current Address: Permanent Address:
  137-20 Crescent Street   28 Pasteur Drive
  Flushing, NY 11367   Glen Cove, NY 11542
  (212) 317-1964   (516) 676-0620

CAREER   Position as accountant or assistant accoun-
OBJECTIVE: tant in an accounting firm. (Temporary po-
                sition as a recreation assistant or
                bookkeeper in a recreational facility.)

EDUCATION: Queens College (CUNY)
                B.A. expected June 1986
                Majoring in Accounting
                Minoring in Communications

                Pratt High School, Glen Cove, New York
                Received Regents Diploma, June 1982

EXPERIENCE:

  Summer 1984   Assistant bookkeeper, Gristede Brothers
                Food Stores, Bronx, New York

  Summers   Dramatics Counselor, Robin Hill Day Camp,
  1982-83   Glen Cove, New York

  1982-84   Volunteer, Flushing YMCA. Worked with el-
                derly. Assistant director, annual "Y" tal-
                ent show.

SKILLS: Type 65 wpm.
                Use Texas Instruments Calculator.

REFERENCES: Placement Office
                Queens College
                Flushing, NY 11367

Glossary of Terms

The Glossary offers simple definitions of terms used in this book. Words appearing in **boldface** have separate entries which you can consult if the term is unfamiliar. The abbreviation *cf.* means "compare"—that is, note the difference between the term being defined and another. And *e.g.* means "for example."

abbreviation (20g) A shortened word, with the addition of a period to indicate the omission (*Dr.*).

absolute phrase (4f) A **phrase** that, instead of modifying a particular word, acts like an **adverb** to the rest of the **sentence** in which it appears:

> ABS PHRASE
> * *All struggle over*, the troops lay down their arms.

Absolute phrases are not considered mistakes of usage. Cf. **dangling modifier**.

abstract language (28f) Words that make no appeal to the senses: *agree, aspect, comprehensible, enthusiasm, virtuously*, etc. Cf. **concrete language**.

ad hominem **reasoning** (31g) A **fallacy** whereby someone tries to discredit a position by attacking the person, party, or interest that supports that position.

adjective (4a) A **modifier** of a **noun**, **pronoun**, or other **nounlike element**—e.g., *strong* in *a strong contender*. Most adjectives can be compared: *strong, stronger, strongest*. See **degree**. See also **interrogative adjective**.

gl

adverb (4a)   A word modifying either a **verb**, an **adjective**, another adverb, a **preposition**, an **infinitive**, a **participle**, a **phrase**, a **clause**, or a whole **sentence**: *now, clearly, moreover,* etc. Any one-word modifier that is not an adjective or an **article** is sure to be an adverb.

agreement (3b)   In grammar, the correspondence of a **verb** with its **subject** in **number** and **person**. In *I stumble,* e.g., the verb *stumble* "agrees with" the subject *I*; both are singular and first-person in form. Cf. **pronoun reference**.

allusion (37a)   A passing reference to a work or idea, either by directly mentioning it or by borrowing its well-known language. Thus, someone who writes *She took arms against a sea of troubles* is alluding to, but not mentioning, Hamlet's most famous speech. The sentence *He did it with Shakespearean flair* alludes directly to Shakespeare. Quotation through allusion differs from **plagiarism** in that readers are expected to notice the reference.

analogy (30i)   In general, a similarity of features or pattern between two things: *The nearest analogy to human speech may be the songs of whales.*

In **rhetoric**, an analogy is an extended likeness purporting to show that the rule or principle behind one thing also holds for the quite different thing being discussed. Thus, someone who disapproves of people leaving their home towns might devise this analogy: *People, like trees, must find their nourishment in the place where they happen to grow up; to seek it elsewhere is as fatal as removing a tree from its roots.* Like most analogies, this one starts with an obvious resemblance and proceeds to a more debatable one.

analysis (30h)   In a narrow sense, the breaking of something into its parts or functions and showing how those smaller units go to make up the whole. More broadly, analysis is the application of explanatory strategies (30i) to a given problem.

antecedent (6b)   The word for which a **pronoun** stands:

    ANT   PRO
- *Jane* was here yesterday, but today *she* is at school.

anticipatory pattern (26b) A structure, such as *both x and y* or *not x but y*, which gives an early signal of the way it will be completed.

aphorism (26c) A memorably concise sentence conveying a very general assertion: *If wishes were horses, beggars would ride.* Many aphorisms show **balance** in their structure.

appositive (41) A word or group of words whose only function is to identify or restate an immediately preceding **noun, pronoun**, or **nounlike element**:

APP
- Mike *the butcher* is quite a clown.

argument (30a) The **mode** of writing in which a writer tries to convince the reader that a certain position on an issue is well-founded. Cf. **description, explanation, narration**.

article (4a) An indicator or determiner immediately preceding a **noun** or **modifier**. Articles themselves may be considered modifiers, along with **adjectives** and **adverbs**. The *definite article* is *the*; the *indefinite articles* are *a* and *an*.

attributive noun (27c) A **noun** serving as an **adjective**: *beach* in *beach shoes*, or *Massachusetts* in *the Massachusetts way of doing things.*

auxiliary (8b) A **verb** form, usually lacking **inflection**, that combines with other verbs to express possibility, likelihood, necessity, obligation, etc.: *She can succeed*; *He could become jealous.* The commonly recognized auxiliaries are *can, could, dare, do, may, might, must, need, ought, should*, and *would. Is, have*, and their related forms act like auxiliaries in the formation of **tenses**: *He is coming*; *They have gone.*

baited opener (23c) An introductory **paragraph** which, by presenting its early sentences "out of context," teases its reader into taking further interest.

balance (26c) The effect created when a whole **sentence** is controlled by the **matching** of grammatically like elements, as in *He taught us the intricate ways of the city; we taught him the simple ways of nature.* A balanced sentence typically repeats a grammatical pattern and certain words in order to highlight important differences.

gl

base form of verb (15a) An **infinitive** without *to*: *see, think,* etc. Base forms appear with **auxiliaries** (*should see*) and in the formation of present and future **tenses** (*I see, I will see*).

begging the question (31d) The **fallacy** of treating a debatable idea as if it had already been proved. If, in a paper favoring national health insurance, you assert that only the greedy medical lobby could oppose such an obviously needed program, you are begging the question by assuming the rightness of your position instead of establishing it with **evidence**.

bibliographic note (37f) A **supplementary note** directing the reader to further sources of information than the origin of a specific cited passage. Cf. **substantive note**.

bibliography (37e) A list of consulted works presented at the end of a book, article, or **essay**. Also, a whole book devoted to listing works within a certain **subject area**.

bound subordinate element (25b) A modifying word, **phrase**, or subordinate **clause** which, because it is **restrictive**, is not set off by commas. Cf. **free subordinate element**.

case (5a) The **inflectional** form of **nouns** and **pronouns** indicating whether they designate actors (*subjective* case: *I, we, they*), receivers of action (*objective* case: *me, us, them*), or "possessors" of the thing or quality modified (*possessive* case: *his* Toyota, *their* indecision, *Geraldine's* influence). *Personal pronouns* also have "second possessive" forms: *mine, theirs,* etc. Cf. **double possessive**.

choppiness (26e) The undesirable effect produced by a sequence of brief sentences lacking **significant pauses**.

circular thesis (31c) A faulty **thesis** that doubles back on itself, self-evidently saying only what is already implied by some of its own language: x *If we had more good weather in this part of the country, the climate would be much improved.*

circumlocution (28b) Roundabout expression, or one such expression—e.g., *when all is said and done* in place of *finally*.

clause (1c) A cluster of words containing a **subject** and a **predicate**. All clauses are either *subordinate* (dependent) or *independent*.

A subordinate clause cannot stand alone: x *When he was hiding in the closet.* An independent clause, which is considered grammatically complete, can stand alone: *He was hiding in the closet.*

There are three kinds of subordinate clauses.

1. An *adjectival* clause serves the function of an **adjective**:

ADJ CLAUSE
- Marty, *who was extremely frightened*, did not want to make a sound.

The adjectival clause modifies the **noun** *Marty*.

2. An *adverbial* clause serves the function of an **adverb**:

ADV CLAUSE
- Marty held his breath for forty seconds *when he was hiding in the closet.*

The adverbial clause modifies the **verb** *held*.

3. And a *noun* clause serves the function of a **noun**:

NOUN CLAUSE
- *That an intruder might slip through his bedroom window* had never occurred to him.

The noun clause serves as the **subject** of the **verb** *had occurred*.

cliché (28e)   A trite, stereotyped, overused expression: *an open and shut case*; *a miss is as good as a mile*. Most clichés contain **figurative language** that has lost its vividness: *a heart of gold, bring the house down*, etc. When two clichés occur together, the effect is usually **mixed metaphor**.

collective noun (3g)   A **noun** that, though singular in form, designates a group of members: *band, family*, etc.

comma splice (2b)   A **run-on sentence** in which two independent clauses are joined by a comma alone, without the necessary coordinating conjunction: x *It is raining today, I left my umbrella home.* Cf. **fused sentence**.

common gender (27e)   The intended sexual neutrality of **pronouns** used to indicate an indefinite party. Traditionally, *indefinite* (*one*) and masculine *personal pronouns* (*he*) were used, but the masculine ones are now widely regarded as **sexist language**.

complement (1a)   Usually, an element in a **predicate** that identifies or describes the **subject**. A single-word complement is either a *predicate noun* or a *predicate adjective*:

> PRED N
> • He is a *musician*.

> PRED ADJ
> • His skill is *unbelievable*.

In addition, a **direct object** can have a complement, known as an *objective complement*:

> D OBJ   OBJ COMPL
> • They consider *the location desirable*.

Infinitives, too, can have complements:

> INF   COMPL INF
> • They beg him *to be* more *cooperative*.

compound, adj. (3h)   Consisting of more than one word, as in a compound verb (They *rode* and *drove*), a compound noun (*ice cream*), a compound preposition (*in spite of*), a compound subject (*He and she* were there), or a compound modifier (*far-gone*).

concession (31h)   In **argument**, the granting of an opposing point, usually to show that it does not overturn one's own **thesis**.

conciseness (28b)   Economy of expression. Not to be confused with simplicity; conciseness enables a maximum of meaning to be communicated in a minimum of words.

concrete language (28f)   Words describing a thing or quality appealing to the senses: *purple, car, buzz, dusty,* etc. Cf. **abstract language**.

conjunction (2a)   An un**inflected** word that connects other words, **phrases**, or **clauses**: *and, although,* etc.

A *coordinating* conjunction—*and, but, for, nor, or, so, yet*—joins grammatically similar elements without turning one into a **modifier** of the other: *You are sad, but I am cheerful.*

A *subordinating* conjunction joins grammatically dissimilar elements, turning one of them into a modifier and specifying its logical relation to the other—e.g., *Although* in *Although you are sad, I am cheerful.*

Correlative conjunctions are matched pairs with a coordinating or a disjunctive purpose: *either/or, neither/nor*, etc.

connotation (27d)   An association that a word calls up, as opposed to its **denotation** or dictionary meaning. Thus, the word *exile* denotes enforced separation from one's home or country, but it connotes loneliness, homesickness, and any number of other, more private, thoughts and images.

contraction (16u)   The condensing of two words to one, with an apostrophe added to replace the omitted letter or letters: *isn't, don't*, etc. Contractions are used primarily in speech and informal writing.

"contrary" modifier (4p)   A **modifier** that opposes the emphasis of a preceding one:

> "CONTRARY" MOD
> • an attractive, *but finally unworkable*, solution.

The commas surrounding such a modifier are optional.

coordination (2a)   The giving of equal grammatical value to two or more parts of a **sentence**. Those parts are usually joined by a *coordinating conjunction*: *He tried, but he failed; The lifeguard reached for her megaphone and her whistle.* Cf. **subordination**.

cumulative sentence (26i)   A **sentence** that continues to develop after its **main idea** has been stated, adding **clauses** or **phrases** that **modify** or explain that assertion: *She crumpled the letter in her fist, trembling with rage, wondering whether she should answer the accusations or simply say good riddance to the whole affair.* Cf. **suspended sentence**.

dangling modifier (4c)   The **modifier** of a term that has been misplaced or wrongly omitted from the sentence:

> DANGL MOD
> x *Not wishing to be bothered*, the telephone was left off the hook.

The person who did not wish to be bothered goes unmentioned and is thus absurdly replaced by the telephone.

gl

dead metaphor (28g) A **metaphor** that has become so common that it usually does not call to mind an **image**: *a devil of a time, rock-bottom prices*, etc. When overworked, a dead metaphor becomes a **cliché**.

declarative sentence (9b) A **sentence** that makes a statement rather than a question or an **exclamation**: *Lambs are woolly.*

degree (17a) The form of an **adjective** or **adverb** showing its quality, quantity, or intensity. The ordinary, uncompared form of an adjective or adverb is its *positive* degree: *quick, quickly.* The *comparative* degree is intermediate, indicating that the modified term surpasses at least one other member of its group: *quicker, more quickly.* And an adjective or adverb in the *superlative* degree indicates that the modified term surpasses all other members of its group: *quickest, most quickly.*

demonstrative adjective (6e) A *demonstrative pronoun* form serving as a **modifier** e.g., *those* in *those laws.*

denotation (27a) The primary, "dictionary," meanings of a word. Cf. **connotation**.

description (30a) The **mode** of writing in which a writer tries to acquaint the reader with a place, object, character, or group. Cf. **argument**, **explanation**, **narration**.

dialogue (13d) The direct representation of speech between two or more persons. Cf. **indirect discourse**.

diction (p. 312) The choice of words. Diction is commonly divided into three levels: formal (*deranged*), middle (*crazy*), and slang (*nuts*).

digression (21c) A temporary change of topic within a **sentence**, **paragraph**, or whole discourse. In an **essay** an *apparent digression*—one that later turns out to have been pertinent after all—may sometimes serve a good purpose. In general, however, digressions are to be avoided.

direct object (1a) A word naming the item directly acted upon by a **subject** through the activity of a **verb**:

    S   V   D OBJ
- She hit the *jackpot.*

Cf. **indirect object, object of preposition.**

direct paragraph (22a)   A **paragraph** in which the **main sentence** comes at or near the beginning and the remaining sentences support it, sometimes after a **limiting sentence** or two.

disjunctive subject (3i)   A **subject** containing elements that are alternative to one another, as in *Either you or I must back down.*

distinct expression (24a)   The forming of **sentences** in the clearest manner, without causing a reader to guess at the meaning or the relations between elements. Distinct expression is enhanced by effective punctuation, **subordination,** and **conciseness** of phrasing.

double negative (4g)   The nonstandard practice of conveying the same negative meaning twice: x *They don't want no potatoes.*

double possessive (5i)   A possessive form using both *of* and *-'s: an idea of Linda's.*

either-or reasoning (31e)   The depicting of one's own position as the better of an artificially limited and "loaded" pair of alternatives— e.g., x *If we do not raise taxes this year, a worldwide depression is inevitable.*

ellipsis (13m)   The three or four spaced dots used to indicate material omitted from a quotation: *"about the . . . story."* A whole row of dots indicates omission of much more material.

endnote (37e)   A **note** placed in a consecutive series with others at the end of an **essay,** article, chapter, or book.

essay (p. 370)   A fairly brief (usually between two and twenty-five typed pages) piece of nonfiction that tries to make a point in an interesting way. For the essay **modes** see **argument, description, explanation, narration.**

euphemism (27g)   A vague or "nice" expression inadvisedly used in place of a more direct one; e.g., *rehabilitation facility* for *prison,* or *disincentive* for *threat.*

evidence (31h)   Facts and testimony tending to support a **thesis.** One statement can be used as evidence for another only if there is a high likelihood that readers will accept it as true.

exclamation (1b)   An extremely emphatic statement or outburst: *Get out of here! What a scandal!* Cf. **interjection.**

explanation (30a)   The **mode** of writing whereby a writer presents information or analyzes something. Also called **exposition.** Cf. **argument, description, narration.**

expletive   The word *it* or *there* when used only to postpone a **subject** coming after the verb:

    EXPL V   SUBJ
- *There* are many reasons to doubt his story.

extracted quotation (13h)   A quoted passage set apart from the writer's own text. Prose quotations of more than four typed lines and verse quotations of more than two or three lines are customarily extracted. Such passages are **indented** by ten spaces, and quotation marks at the beginning and end are dropped. Also called *block quotation.* Cf. **incorporated quotation.**

fallacy   A formal error or illegitimate shortcut in reasoning. See *ad hominem* **reasoning, circular thesis, begging the question, either-or reasoning, faulty generalization,** *post hoc* **explanation,** and **straw man.**

false start (26g)   A device whereby a **sentence** appears to present its grammatical **subject** first but then breaks off and begins again, thus turning the opening element into an **appositive:** *Elephants, gorillas, pandas—the list of endangered species grows longer every year.* A false start can be a good means of seizing a reader's attention. Cf. **mixed construction.**

faulty generalization (31b)   The **fallacy** of drawing a general conclusion from insufficient **evidence**—e.g., concluding from one year's drought that the world's climate has entered a long period of change.

figurative language (28g)   Language that heightens expressiveness by suggesting an imaginative, not a **literal,** comparison to the thing described—e.g., *a man so emaciated that he looked more like an x-ray than a person.* See **metaphor, simile.** Cf. **literal language.**

footnote (37e)   A **note** at the bottom of a page. Cf. **endnote**.

free subordinate element (25b)   A **modifying** word, **phrase**, or subordinate **clause** that deserves to be set off by commas. Most but not all free elements are **nonrestrictive**; some **restrictive elements** at the beginnings of sentences can be treated as free—that is, without a following comma.

freewriting (30f)   The practice of writing continuously for a fixed period without concern for logic or correctness. In *focused freewriting* the writer begins with a specific **topic**.

funnel opener (23b)   An introductory **paragraph** beginning with a broad assertion and gradually narrowing to a specific **topic**.

fused sentence (2b)   A **run-on sentence** in which two independent **clauses** are joined without either a comma or a coordinating **conjunction**: x *He is a dapper newscaster I love his slightly Canadian accent.*

gender (27e)   The grammatical concept of sexual classification determining the forms of masculine (*he*), feminine (*she*), and neuter (*it*) *personal pronouns* and the feminine forms of certain nouns (*actress*). Cf. **common gender, sexist language**.

gerund (1a)   A form derived from a **verb** but functioning as a **noun**—e.g., *Skiing* in *Skiing is dangerous*. Gerunds take exactly the same form as **participles**, and they are capable of having **subjects** (usually possessive in **case**) as well as **objects**:

SUBJ GER   GER   OBJ GER
• *Elizabeth's making* the *putt* was unexpected.

Cf. **participle**.

governing pronoun (32d)   The prevailing **pronoun** in a piece of writing, helping to establish the writer's point of view.

governing tense (8a)   The prevailing verb **tense** in a piece of writing, establishing a time frame for reported events.

image (28g)   An expression that appeals to the senses. More narrowly, an example of **figurative language**. In both senses the use of images is called *imagery*.

implied subject (1b)   A **subject** not actually present in a **clause** but nevertheless understood: [*You*] *Watch out!* The customary implied subject, as here, is *you*.

incorporated quotation (13b)   A quotation placed within quotation marks and not set off from the writer's own prose. Cf. **extracted quotation**.

indention (13h)   The setting of the first word of a line in from the left margin, as in a new paragraph (5 spaces) or an **extracted quotation** (usually 10 spaces).

index (36c)   A book, usually with a new volume each year, containing alphabetically ordered references to articles (and sometimes books) in a given field. Also, an alphabetical list of subjects and the page numbers where they are treated in a nonfiction book, as on pages 564–591 below.

indirect discourse (8d)   Reporting what was said, as opposed to directly quoting it. Not *She said, "I am tired,"* but *She said she was tired.* Also called *indirect statement.* Cf. **indirect question**.

indirect object (5a)   A word designating the person or thing for whom or which, or to whom or which, the action of a **verb** is performed. An indirect object never appears without a **direct object** occurring in the same clause:

IND OBJ   D OBJ

- She sent *Fernando* a discouraging *letter.*

indirect question (9b)   The reporting of a question without use of the question form—not, e.g., *She asked, "Where should I turn?"* but *She asked where she should turn.* Cf. **indirect discourse**.

infinitive (1a)   The **base form of a verb**, usually but not always preceded by *to*: *to win*; *prove, to prove.*

inflection (1a)   A change in the ending or whole form of a word to show a change in function without creating a new word. Thus *he* can be inflected to *his*, *George* to *George's*, *go* to *went*, etc.

intensifier (28c)   A "fortifying" expression like *absolutely, definitely,* or *very.* Habitual use of intensifiers weakens the force of assertion.

gl

interjection   A word that stands apart from other constructions in order to command attention or show strong feeling: *aha, hey, wow,* etc. Cf. **exclamation.**

interrogative adjective   An interrogative **pronoun** form that combines with a **noun** to introduce a question—e.g., *Whose* in *Whose socks are these?*

interrupting element (4m)   A word or group of words that interrupts the main flow of a sentence:

> INT EL
> • You, *I regret to say*, are not the one.

Interrupting elements (also called *parenthetical elements*) should be set off at both ends by punctuation, usually by commas.

intransitive verb (1a)   A **verb** expressing an action or state without connection to a **direct object** or a **complement**—e.g., *complained* in *They complained.* Cf. **linking verb, transitive verb.**

introductory tag (13j)   A **clause**, such as *He said* or *Agnes asked*, introducing a quotation. A tag may also interrupt or follow a quotation.

irony (32f)   A sharply incongruous or "poetically just" effect—created, for example, when the Secretary of the Treasury has to borrow a coin to make a phone call.

In **rhetoric**, irony is the saying of one thing in order to convey a different or even opposite meaning: *Brutus is an honorable man* [he really isn't]. Irony can be *broad* (obvious) or *subtle*, depending on the writer's purpose. Cf. **sarcasm.**

irregular verb (15b)   A **verb** that forms its past **tense** and its past **participle** in some way other than simply adding -*d* or -*ed*: *go* (*went, gone*), *swim* (*swam, swum*), etc.

jargon (27f)   Technical language used in inappropriate, nontechnical contexts—e.g., *upwardly mobile* for *ambitious, positive reinforcement* for *praise, paranoid* for *upset.*

leading idea (21a)   The "point" of a **paragraph**, to which all other ideas in that paragraph should relate.

limiting sentence (22b)   A **sentence** that addresses a possible limitation, or contrary consideration, to the **leading idea** of a paragraph.

linking verb (1a)   A **verb** connecting its **subject** to an identifying or modifying **complement**. Typical linking verbs are *be, seem, appear, become, feel, sense, grow, taste, look, sound*:

       S   LV   COMPL
- They *were* Mormons.

       S   LV   COMPL
- She *became* calmer.

Cf. **intransitive verb, transitive verb**.

literal language (28g)   Words that factually represent what they describe, without poetic embellishment. Cf. **figurative language**.

main idea (24a)   The core of statement, question, or exclamation in a **sentence**, consisting usually of an independent **clause** and any **bound subordinate elements**. Elements falling outside the main idea are set off by punctuation, usually commas.

main sentence (21a)   The sentence in a paragraph that conveys its **leading idea**. Often called *topic sentence*.

matching (26a)   The placing into related or identical grammatical structures of elements that are related in meaning: *not only eggs but also bacon; days of struggle and nights of terror*. Matching is an act of **coordination**, creating an effect of **parallelism**.

metaphor (28g)   An implied comparison whereby the thing at hand is figuratively asserted to be something else: *His fists were a hurricane of ceaseless assault*. Cf. **simile**.

microfiche catalog (36a)   A listing of a library's printed holdings on sheets of microfilm that can be read only in a special machine known as a microfiche reader.

mixed construction (3a)   The use of two clashing structures within a **sentence**, as in x *Even with a relaxed interviewer asks difficult questions*.

gl

mixed metaphor (28g) **A metaphor** whose elements clash in their implications: *Let's back off for a closer look*; *He is a straight arrow who shoots from the hip.*

mode (30a) A type of writing characterized by its **rhetorical** purpose. The modes recognized in this book are **argument**, **description**, **explanation**, and **narration**. One essay can make use of several modes.

modifier (4a) A word, **phrase**, or **clause** that limits or describes another element:

-   the *gentle* soul
     MOD
-   *When leaving*, turn out the lights *on the porch.*
     MOD   MOD
-   *Before you explain*, I have something to tell you.
     MOD

mood (15d) The manner or attitude that a speaker or writer intends a **verb** to convey, as shown in certain changes of form. Ordinary statements and questions are cast in the *indicative* mood: *Is he ill? He is.* The *imperative* mood is for commands: *Stop! Get out of the way!* And the *subjunctive* mood is used for certain formulas (*as it were*), unlikely or impossible conditions (*had she gone*), *that* clauses expressing requirements or recommendations (*They ask that she comply*), and *lest* clauses (*lest he forget*).

narration (30a) The **mode** of writing in which a writer recounts something that has happened. Cf. **argument, description, explanation**.

nonrestrictive element (4j) A **modifier**, often a **phrase** or **clause**, that does not serve to identify ("restrict") the modified term and is therefore set off by punctuation:

                NONRESTR EL
-   That woman, *whom I met only yesterday*, already understands my problems.

Cf. **restrictive element**.

noun (1b) A word like *house, Jack, Pennsylvania,* or *assessment,* usually denoting a person, place, thing, or idea, capable of being **inflected** for both plural and possessive forms (*houses, house's, houses'*) and of serving a variety of sentence functions.

nounlike element (1b)   A word or group of words having the same function, but not the same **inflectional** features, as a **noun** or **pronoun**—e.g., *what you mean* in *He knows what you mean.* Also called *nominal* or *substantive.*

number (15a)   In grammar, the distinction between *singular* and *plural* form. The distinction applies to **verbs** (she *drives*, they *drive*), **nouns** (*boat*, *boats*), and personal **pronouns** (*I*, *we*).

numeral (20l)   A number expressed as a figure (*6*, *19*) or a group of letters (*VI*, *XIX*) instead of being written out (*six*, *nineteen*).

object (1a)   A **noun, pronoun,** or **nounlike element** representing a receiver of an action or relation. See **direct object, indirect object,** and **object of preposition.** In addition, **infinitives, participles,** and **gerunds** can take objects:

OBJ INF
- to chair the *convention*

OBJ PART
- Chairing the *convention* impartially, she allowed no disorder.

OBJ GER
- Chairing a turbulent *convention* is a thankless task.

object of preposition (5a)   A **noun, pronoun,** or **nounlike element** following a **preposition** and completing the prepositional **phrase**—e.g., *November* in *throughout November*, or *siesta* in *during a long siesta.*

paragraph block (21j)   A group of paragraphs addressing the same part of a **topic**, with strong continuity from one paragraph to the next.

parallelism (7a)   The structure or the effect that results from **matching** two or more parts of a **sentence**—e.g., the words *Utica, Albany,* and *Rye* in the sentence *He went to Utica, Albany, and Rye,* or the three equally weighted **clauses** that begin this sentence: *That he wanted to leave, that permission was denied, and that he then tried to escape—these facts only became known after months of official secrecy.* Cf. **balance, coordination, matching.**

paraphrase (36f)   Sentence-by-sentence restatement, in different words, of the meaning of a passage. Cf. **summary.**

parenthetical citation (37d) A reference to a work, given not in a **footnote** or **endnote** but in parentheses within a main text—e.g., (*Meyers 241–75*).

part of speech Any of the major classes into which words are customarily divided, depending on their dictionary meaning and their syntactic functions in **sentences**. Since many words belong to more than one part of speech, you must analyze the sentence at hand to see which part of speech a given word is occupying. The commonly recognized parts of speech are:

Verb	try, adopts, were allowing
Noun	Cynthia, paper, Manitoba
Pronoun	she, himself, each other, nothing, these, who
Preposition	to, among, according to
Conjunction	and, yet, because, although, if
Adjective	wide, lazier, more fortunate
Adverb	agreeably, seldom, ahead, together, however
Interjection	oh, ouch, gosh
Article	a, an, the
Expletive	it [is], there [were]

participle (1a) An **adjectival** form derived from a **verb**—e.g., *Showing* in *Showing fear, he began to sweat.* Participles can be present (*showing*) or past (*having shown*) and active or passive (*having been shown*). Like other **verbals**, they can have **objects** (*fear* in the sentence above), but unlike other verbals, they do not have **subjects**. Cf. **gerund**.

person (15a) In **grammar**, a characteristic of **pronouns** and **verbs** indicating whether someone is speaking (*first* person: *I go, we go*), being spoken to (*second* person: *you go*), or being spoken about (*third* person: *he, she, it goes; they go*).

phrase (1d) A cluster of words functioning as a single **part of speech** and lacking a **subject-predicate** combination. Cf. **clause**.

A **noun** and its **modifiers** are sometimes called a *noun phrase* (*the faulty billiard balls*), and a **verb** form consisting of more than one word is sometimes called a *verb phrase* (*had been trying*). But the types of phrases most commonly recognized are *prepositional, infinitive, participial, gerund,* and **absolute.**

A *prepositional phrase* consists of a **preposition** and its **object,** along with any **modifiers** of those words:

PREP MOD   MOD   MOD OBJ PREP
- *among her numerous painful regrets*
              PREP PHRASE

An *infinitive phrase* consists of an **infinitive** and its **object** and/or **modifiers:**

              S INF INF MOD MOD   MOD OBJ INF
- They asked *John to hit the almost invisible target.*
                        INF PHRASE

A *participial phrase* consists of a **participle** and its **object** and/or **modifiers:**

MOD   PART   MOD MOD OBJ PART
- *Quickly reaching the correct decision,* he rang the bell.
              PART PHRASE

A *gerund phrase* consists of a **gerund** and its **object** and/or **modifiers,** and it may also include a *subject of the gerund*:

S GER   GER   OBJ GER MOD
- *Their sending Matthew away* was a bad mistake.
       GER PHRASE

An **absolute phrase** may contain an **infinitive** or a **participle,** but it always modifies a whole **main idea.**

pivoting paragraph (22b)   A **paragraph** that begins with one or more **limiting sentences** but then makes a sharp turn to its **main sentence,** which may or may not be followed by **supporting sentences.**

plagiarism (37a)   The taking of others' thoughts or words without due acknowledgment. Cf. **allusion.**

post hoc **explanation** (31f)   A **fallacy** whereby the fact that one event followed another is wrongly taken to prove that the first event caused the later one. (In Latin, *post hoc ergo propter hoc* means "after this, therefore because of it.")

predicate (1a) In a **clause**, the **verb** plus all the words belonging with it:

<u>PRED</u>

• He *had a serious heart attack.*

Cf. **subject**.

predication (24c) The selection of a **predicate** for a given **subject**. The problem of *faulty predication* appears when subjects and predicates are mismatched in meaning: x *The purpose of the film wants to change your beliefs.* **Mixed construction** is a more radical form of faulty predication.

prefix (18j) One or more letters that can be attached before the root or base form of a word to make a new word: *pre-*, *with-*, etc., forming *prearranged*, *withstand*, etc. Cf. **suffix**.

preposition (5a) A function word that introduces a prepositional **phrase**— e.g., *to* in *to the lighthouse.* Cf. **conjunction**. A preposition consisting of more than one word is **compound**: *along with*, *apart from*, etc. See also **object**.

principal parts (15b) The **base** or simple **infinitive** form of a **verb**, its past **tense** form, and its past **participle**: *walk, walked, walked; grow, grew, grown.*

process analysis (30i) The **analysis** of a series of steps constituting a complete activity (cooking a stew, making a candle, testing a product, etc.).

pronoun (5a) One of a small class of words mostly used in place of **nouns** for a variety of purposes:

1. A *demonstrative* pronoun (*this, that, these, those*) singles out what it refers to: <u>*This*</u> *is what we want.*

2. An *indefinite* pronoun (*anybody, each, whoever*, etc.) leaves unspecified the person or things it refers to: <u>*Anyone*</u> *can see that you are right.*

3. An *intensive* pronoun (*myself, yourself, itself, ourselves*, etc.) emphasizes a preceding personal pronoun. *She <u>herself</u> is a vegetarian.*

4. An *interrogative* pronoun (*who, whom, whose, which, what*) introduces a question: <u>Who</u> *will win the election?*

5. A *personal* pronoun (*I, you, he, she, it, we, they*) stands for one or more persons or things and is used in the tense formation of verbs: <u>They</u> *are willing to compromise.* Personal pronouns also have objective (*him, them*) and possessive (*his, their*) forms: *We asked <u>her</u> to recognize <u>our</u> rights.*

6. A *reciprocal* pronoun (*each other, each other's, one another, one another's*) expresses mutual relation: *We recognized <u>each other's</u> differences of outlook.*

7. A *reflexive* pronoun (*myself, yourself, itself, ourselves,* etc.) differs from an intensive pronoun in serving as a **direct** or **indirect object**. The reflexive pronoun shows that the **subject** of the **clause** is the same person or thing acted upon by the **verb**: *He hurt <u>himself</u> on the track.*

8. A *relative* pronoun (*who, whom, that, which*) introduces a relative or adjectival clause: *My uncle, <u>who</u> lives next door, slept through the earthquake.* Some grammarians also recognize an "indefinite relative pronoun" (one lacking an antecedent): *She knows <u>what</u> you mean.* See also **relative clause.**

pronoun reference (6b)   The correspondence of **pronouns** with their **antecedents**, with which they should correspond in **number**, **person**, and **gender**. Thus, in the sentence *When they saw Bill, they gave him a cool welcome,* the pronoun *him* properly refers to the singular, third-person, masculine antecedent *Bill.* Cf. **agreement.**

punctuation marks   (p. 118)   Marks used to bring out the meaning of written **sentences**. They are:

period .	parentheses ( )
question mark ?	brackets [ ]
comma ,	apostrophe '
semicolon ;	hyphen -
colon :	quotation marks " "
dash —	slash /

racist language (27e)   **Diction** that can give offense by using a derogatory name for an ethnic group or by perpetuating a demeaning stereotype: *greaser, dumb Pole*, etc.

rebuttal (30a)   An opposing **argument**, intended to overturn an argument already made. Rebuttals do not always succeed; cf. **refutation**.

redundancy (28b)   The defect of unnecessarily conveying the same meaning more than once. Also, an expression that does so—e.g., *retreat back, ascend up.*

reference list (37c)   A list of "Works Cited" or "Works Consulted," supplied at the end of an **essay**, paper, article, or book, and showing where and when the cited or consulted materials appeared. The **parenthetical citations** within the text refer to items in the reference list.

refutation (30a)   The disproving of an **argument**. By definition, all refutations are successful; cf. **rebuttal**.

relative clause (lc)   In this book, any adjectival **clause**.

restrictive element (4j)   A **modifier**, often a **phrase** or **clause**, that "restricts" (establishes the identity of) the modified term. Unless it comes first in the sentence, a restrictive element is not set off by commas:

> RESTR EL
- The woman *whom I met* has disappeared.
> RESTR EL
- The man *in the black suit* is following you.
> RESTR EL
- *On long ocean voyages*, seasickness is common.

Because it is brief, the restrictive element that begins the last example could also appear without a following comma. Cf. **nonrestrictive element.**

rhetoric (32c)   The strategic placement of ideas and choice of language, as in *His rhetoric was effective* or *His ideas were sound but his rhetoric was addressed to the wrong audience*. Note that *rhetoric* need not mean deception or manipulation.

rhetorical question (26f)   A question posed for effect, without expectation of a reply: *How often have we seen this same pattern of betrayal?*

run-on sentence (2b) A **sentence** in which two or more independent **clauses** are improperly joined. One type of run-on sentence is the **comma splice:** ₓ *She likes candy, she eats it every day.* The other type is the **fused sentence:** ₓ *She likes candy she eats it every day.* Runons are typically corrected either with a semicolon (*She likes candy; she eats it every day*) or with a comma and a coordinating **conjunction** (*She likes candy, and she eats it every day*).

sarcasm (9g) Abusive ridicule of a person, group, or idea, as in *What pretty phrases these killers speak!* Cf. **irony**.

sentence (1a) A grammatically complete unit of expression, usually containing at least one independent **clause**, beginning with a capital letter and ending with a period, question mark, or exclamation point. See also **sentence fragment**.

sentence adverb (2c) An **adverb** that serves to indicate a logical connection between the modified **clause** or whole **sentence** and a previous statement—e.g., *therefore* in *She took the job; therefore, she had to hire someone for child care.* Also called *conjunctive adverb*.

sentence fragment (1d) A set of words punctuated as a **sentence** but lacking one or more of the elements usually considered necessary to a sentence: ₓ *When they last saw her.*

In general, sentence fragments are regarded as blunders. But an *intentional sentence fragment*—one whose context shows that it is a shortened sentence rather than a dislocated piece of a neighboring sentence—can sometimes be effective:

INT FRAG
● How much longer can we resist the enemy? *As long as necessary!*

series (7j) A set of more than two **parallel** items within a **sentence**:

SERIES
● They were upset about *pollution, unemployment, and poverty.*

sexist language (27e) Expressions that can give offense by implying that one sex (almost always male) is superior or that the other sex is restricted to certain traditional roles: *lady doctor, a man-sized job, Every American pursues his own happiness*, etc.

significant pause (26e) A pause, marked by punctuation, that serves to combat **choppiness** in a sequence of **sentences**. The pauses between items in a **series** are not significant, but a pause between **clauses** or **phrases** is: *When she inquired, no one could tell her anything; He tried, along with his weight training, to run at least five miles a day.*

simile (28g)   An explicit or open comparison, whereby the object at hand is **figuratively** asserted to be like something else: *His eyes that morning were like an elephant's.* Cf. **metaphor**. Both similes and metaphors are called *metaphorical* or **figurative language**. See also **analogy, image**.

slash (13g)   The punctuation mark **/**. A slash is used to separate alternatives (*either/or*) and to indicate line endings in **incorporated quotation** of verse. Sometimes called *virgule*.

split infinitive (4e)   An **infinitive** interrupted by at least one **adverb**: *to firmly stand*. Some readers consider every split infinitive an error; others object only to conspicuously awkward ones such as x *Jane wanted to thoroughly and finally settle the matter.*

squinting modifier (4d)   A **modifier** awkwardly trapped between sentence elements, either of which might be regarded as the modified term:

SQ MOD

x Why he collapsed *altogether* puzzles me.

Did he collapse altogether, or is the writer altogether puzzled?

stance (32e)   The **rhetorical** posture a writer adopts toward an audience, establishing a consistent point of view. This book recognizes two stances, *forthright* and *ironical*. A forthright stance implies that the writer's statements are to be taken "straight"; an ironical stance implies that the reader is to "read between the lines" and uncover a different or even opposite meaning.

straw man (31g)   The fallacy of misrepresenting an opponent's position so that it will appear weaker than it actually is. The writer "knocks over a straw man" by attacking and dismissing an irrelevant point.

subject (1b)   The part of a **clause** about which something is **predicated**:

SUBJ

• *Ernest* shot the tiger.

The subject alone is called the *simple subject*. With its **modifiers** included it is called the *complete subject*—e.g., *The only thing to do* in *The only thing to do is compromise.*

Not only **verbs** but also **infinitives**, **gerunds**, and **absolute phrases** can have "subjects":

SUBJ INF   INF
- They wanted *Alexander* to be king.

SUBJ GER   GER
- *Alexander's* refusing upset them.

SUBJ ABS PHRASE
- *The summit conference having ended,* the diplomats went home.
ABS PHRASE

subject area (30c)   A wide range of related concerns within which the **topic** of an **essay** or paper may be found. Cf. **thesis**, **topic**.

subordination (1c)   In general, the giving of minor emphasis to minor elements or ideas. In syntax, subordination entails making one element grammatically dependent on another, so that the subordinate element becomes a **modifier** of the other element, limiting or explaining it. Thus, in *They were relieved when it was over*, the subordinate **clause** *when it was over* limits the time to which the **verb** *were relieved* applies.

substantive note (37f)   A **supplementary note** which, instead of merely giving a reference for a cited passage or idea, makes further comments. Cf. **bibliographic note**.

suffix (18f)   One or more letters that can be added at the end of a word's root or base to make a new word or form: *-ed, -ing, -ship, -ness,* etc., as in *walked, singing, membership, weakness.* Cf. **prefix**.

summary (36f)   A concise recapitulation of a passage. Cf. **paraphrase**.

supplementary note (37f)   A **footnote** or **endnote** which, instead of merely giving a reference for a specific passage or idea, adds further commentary or reference information. See **bibliographic note**, **substantive note**.

supporting sentence (22a)   A **sentence** that restates, elaborates, or provides **evidence** or context for some aspect of a paragraph's **leading idea**.

gl

suspended comparison (7e)   A comparison proposing two possible relations between the compared items, in which the second item is stated only at the end of the construction: *Taco Bell is as good as, if not better than, Pizza Hut.*

suspended paragraph (22c)   A paragraph that builds, without a decisive shift of direction, toward a **main sentence** at or near the end. Cf. **direct paragraph, pivoting paragraph.**

suspended sentence (26j)   A **sentence** that significantly delays completing the statement of its **main idea** while **clauses** and/or **phrases** intervene: *The important thing is not to study all night before the exam, nor to try reading the instructor's mind, nor to butter up the TA, but to keep up with the assignments throughout the term.* Also called *periodic sentence.*

tense (15b)   The time a **verb** expresses: present (*see*), future (*will see*), etc.

thesis (30c)   The point, or one central idea, of an **essay**, paper, article, book, etc. Cf. **subject area, topic.**

thesis statement (31h)   A one-**sentence** statement of the **thesis** or central idea of an **essay** or paper. In this book a thesis statement is considered *full* only if it is complex enough to give organizing guidance.

tone (32d)   The quality of feeling conveyed by something. Words like *factual, sober, fanciful, urgent, tongue-in-cheek, restrained, stern, pleading,* and *exuberant* may begin to suggest the range of tones found in **essays**. Cf. **stance, voice.**

topic (30c)   The specific subject of an **essay** or paper; the ground to be covered or the question to be answered. Cf. **subject area, thesis.**

topic sentence   Replaced in this book by the term **main sentence**, since the key sentence in a paragraph is the one stating the **leading idea**, not the one announcing a "topic."

transitional paragraph (23e)   A whole paragraph devoted to announcing a major shift in focus.

transitional phrase (2c)   A **phrase** having the same function as a

sentence adverb, modifying a whole **clause** or **sentence** while showing its logical connection to a previous statement:

> • She says she simply can't bear to be late for anything; *in other*
> TRANS
> PHRASE
> *words*, she expects the rest of us to show up on time.

transitive verb (1a) A **verb** transmitting an action to a **direct object**:

> TR V
> • They *cast* the dice.

Cf. **intransitive verb**, **linking verb**.

trial thesis (31a) A possible **thesis**, or central idea, considered before a final thesis has been chosen.

understatement (32f) A device of **rhetoric**, often used for **irony**, whereby the writer conveys the importance of something by appearing to take it lightly: *Living near the edge of a runway for jumbo jets is not altogether relaxing.*

verb (1a) A word or words like *goes, saw,* or *was leaving*, serving to convey the action performed by a **subject**, to express the state of that subject, or to connect the subject to a **complement**.

verbal (1a) A form derived from, but different in function from, a **verb**. Verbals are either **infinitives**, **participles**, or **gerunds**. When mistakenly used as verbs, they cause **sentence fragments**:

> VERBAL
> x George *going* to the movies tonight.

voice (15b, 32d) The form of a **verb** indicating whether the **subject** performs the action (*active* voice: *we strike*) or receives the action (*passive* voice: *we are struck*). Also, the "self" projected by a given piece of writing. In the latter sense, this book recognizes two voices, the *personal* and *impersonal*.

weaseling thesis (31c) A **thesis** that fails to take any definite stand: x *People can be found who oppose gun control;* x *Abortion is quite a controversial topic.*

Index

NOTE: The numbers in **boldface** are thumb indexes and indicate where you can find the major discussion of a term or rule. An *italicized* number refers to a definition in the Glossary of Terms.

abbreviation, **20g–k:** 233–238, *538*; appropriateness in main text, **20h:** 234–236; capitalization of, **20i:** 236; in documentation, 231, **20g:** 233–234, 496; in Index of Diction, 341–342; italics vs. roman in, 231–232; Latin, 231; of months, 235; in notes on reading, 464; obsolete, 496; with or without periods, 235, **20j:** 237; of place name, 235, 237, 481; plural of, **16h–i:** 186–187; punctuation of, **9e:** 121, 235, **20j:** 237; sentence ending with, punctuation of, **9e:** 121; spacing of, **20k:** 237–238; in technical prose, 236; after time, 235, **20i:** 236, 238, 240, 343; of title with name, 234–235; of unit of measure, 235, 237, 239; verb derived from, 194; before ZIP code, 237

above, 343

absolute phrase, **4f:** 54–55, *538*

abstract diction, **28f:** 334–335, *538*

abstracts, in library, 453–457

accent, in dictionary entry, 314–315

accept vs. *except*, 200

acknowledgment of sources. *See* documentation

acronym: punctuation of, 235; spacing of, **20k:** 237–238

active voice, **15b:** 170–178; and sentence strength, **24g:** 287–288

A.D., 235, 343

adapt vs. *adopt*, 200

addition, and agreement problems, 43

additive phrase, **3d:** 32–33

address: in business letter, 525–526,
529–530; comma in, 132–133; figures in, 240

ad hominem argument, 393, *538*

adjective, 39, 47, *538*; attributive noun as, 319; capitalization of, **19h:** 223, **19n:** 225; comparison of, **17a, c:** 195–196, 197; demonstrative, 86, 254, 416; derived from name, **19h:** 223, **19n:** 225; indefinite pronoun vs., 39; irregular, 196; placement of, **4b:** 47–48

adverb, 47, *539*; comparison of, **17b–c:** 196–197; irregular, 196; ordinal number as, 242; placement of, **4b:** 47–48. *See also* sentence adverb

advice vs. *advise*, 200

affect vs. *effect*, 200, 343

afraid vs. *frightened, scared*, 354

afterword, cited in reference list, 482

again vs. *back*, 343

agreement, subject-verb, 30–31, *539*; with collective noun, **3g:** 34–35; with *either . . . or* or *neither . . . nor*, **3i:** 36–37; with indefinite pronoun, **3m:** 39–40; in mathematical operations, **3p:** 43; with quantity term, **3l:** 38–39. *See also* subject-verb relations

ain't, 343

album title: capitalization of, 229; cited in reference list, 487

all vs. *all of*, 343

alliteration, 339

all ready vs. *already*, 200

all that, 343

all together vs. *altogether*, 200

allusion, 476, *539*

comma (*cont.*):

separate items in series, **10n:** 132; within items in series, 102; with modifier, **4h–p:** 56–67; in numbers, **10o:** 132–133; omitted after final or only modifier, **10k:** 131; optional after brief independent clause, 26; with paired elements, **10m:** 131; with parentheses, **12i:** 145; after question mark, **9i:** 123; with quotation marks, 150–151; with restrictive and nonrestrictive elements, **4j:** 58–60, 61–63, **10f–h:** 128–130; and run-on sentence, 19–22, **10b:** 125–126; with sentence adverb, **10g:** 129; significant pause marked by, 304–305; spacing with, **14f:** 164; with title or degree, 133; with transitional phrase, **10g:** 129; unnecessary, **3r:** 44–45, **10c:** 126–127. *See also* comma splice

comma splice, 19–21, *542*; acceptable, 27; avoiding, 20–25

command: imperative mood for, 180; implied subject in, 8–9; punctuation of, **9a:** 119, **9c:** 120

commence, 348

common gender, 322–324, *542–543*

comparative degree, **17a:** 195–196, 197, *545*

compare vs. *contrast*, 348

comparison: parallelism in, 90; suspended, **7e:** 95–96, *562*. *See also* degree

comparison and contrast, 385

complement, 6 *)43*; and agreement problems, 41–42; punctuation with, 126

complement vs. *compliment*, 200

complimentary close, in business letter, 526, 528

composing, **30–34:** 371–437; asking reporter's questions in, 383–384; for an audience, 404–405; brainstorming in, **30g:** 381–382; expe-

rience as basis for, **30e:** 379–380; flexibility in process of, **30b:** 373–375; freewriting in, **30f:** 380–381, 383; full thesis statement in, **31h:** 394–396; of in-class essay, **35b:** 441–442; notes used in, **30h:** 382; outlining in, **32b:** 399–404; planning vs. improvising in, **32g:** 411; and revision, 373–375, **33:** 412–423; of sample essay, **34:** 424–431; thesis development in, **31:** 386–396; topic choice in, **30:** 371–385; trial thesis in, **31a:** 386–387; trial topic in, **30i:** 382–385; ways of beginning, 380–383; 411. *See also* essay

compound modifier, *543*; hyphenation of, **18l:** 216–218

compound noun, *543*; hyphenation of, **18k:** 215

compound possessive, **16o:** 189

compound prefix, 215

compound subject, *543*; disjunctive, **3i:** 36–37; verb agreement with, **3h–k:** 35–37

compound verb, hyphenation of, **18k:** 215

comprise vs. *compose*, *constitute*, 348

computer catalog. *See* on-line catalog

computer software, cited in reference list, 487

concept vs. *conception*, *idea*, 348

conceptual revision, **33b:** 413–414

concession, 396, *543*

concise diction, **28b:** 328–330, *543*

conclusion. *See* closing paragraph

concrete diction, **28f:** 334–335, *543*

concur in vs. *concur with*, 349

conditional form of verb, 108–110

condition contrary to fact, subjunctive mood for, 181

conjunction, 9–10, *543–544*; optional in series of independent clauses, 27; after semicolon, **11c:** 135–136; sentence adverb vs., **2c:** 22–25;

ics for emphasis in, **20e:** 232; misspelling within, 160, 464; on notecard, **36e:** 461–465; omission of material within, **13m–o:** 156–159; paraphrase vs., **36f:** 465–468; parenthetical citation following, 151; of poetry, **13b:** 147–148, **13g–h:** 152–154, 158, 163; punctuation of, **13:** 146–160; within a quotation, **13c:** 148; summary vs., **36f:** 465–468; tense problems with, **8c–d:** 110–112; **8f–g:** 114–115

quotation marks: for Bible citation, not used, 230; and extracted quotation, 154; italics vs., **20a:** 229–230; in notes on reading, 464; other punctuation marks with, **13f:** 150–152; for sarcastic effect, 122–123, 160; single, 146, **13c:** 148, 231; spacing with, **14f:** 164,**14i:** 165; for speech of more than one paragraph, **13e:** 149; for title, **20a:** 229–230; for translation, 231; for word presented *as* word, **20d:** 232. *See also* quotation

quotations, dictionaries of, 461
quote, 362

racist diction, **27e:** 321, *558*
rack vs. *wrack*, 202
radio program: capitalization of, 229; cited in reference list, 487
rain vs. *rein, reign*, 202
raise vs. *rise*, 362
rank, capitalization of, **19j:** 223
readability, 267, 301, 331
reading, as source of topic, 379. *See also* notes from reading
real, 362
reason is because, 362
reason vs. *cause*, 347
reasoning: cause and effect, 385, 392; either-or, **31e:** 391, *546*
rebut vs. *refute*, 362
rebuttal, *558*
reckon, 362–363

recording: cited in reference list, 487; italicized title of, 229
redundancy, *558*; avoiding, 329; in comparison of adjective or adverb, **17c:** 197; in restating examination question, 439; in sound pattern, 339–340. *See also* repetition
reference (citation). *See* documentation
reference books, **36d:** 458–461
reference librarian, 445
reference list style of documentation, 488; abbreviations for, **20g:** 233–234; footnote/endnote style vs., **37b:** 477–478; reference list in, **37c:** 479–487, *558*; in sample paper, **38a:** 500–508
reference of pronoun. *See* pronoun reference
reference room, 446–447, 453
refutation, 372, *558*
regular verb, principal parts of, 173
relation vs. *relationship*, 363
relative clause, 9–10, *558*; and agreement problems, **3n:** 40–42
relative pronoun, 9–10, *557*; and reference problems, **3n:** 40–42; antecedent of, **6b–f:** 82–87
relevant, 363
religion reference books, 460
repetition: and balance in sentence, **26c:** 302–303; implied, 254–255; and paragraph continuity, 254–258; of sound patterns, **28h:** 339–340; as transitional signal, 254. *See also* redundancy
replace vs. *substitute*, 364
reporter's questions, for exploring trial topic, 383–384, 425
republished book, cited in reference list, 483
research paper: documentation for, **37:** 472–498; sample, **38:** 499–521; sources for, **36:** 445–471
reserve desk, 446–447
restrictive element, **4j:** 58–60, 61–63, *558*

sentence (*cont.*):
26j: 308–309, *562*; unnecessary *that* or *what* clause in, 24i: 289–290; variety in, 26e–k: 304–310; verb *to be* overused in, 24e: 286; verb to convey action in, 24f: 286–287; within another sentence, capitalization of, 220

sentence adverb, *559*; conjunction vs., 2c: 22–25; as interrupting element, 63; logical relation shown by, 134–135; placement of, 48–49; punctuation with, 25, 4k: 61–62, 10g: 129

sentence fragment, 1: 5–16, *559*; following semicolon, 11b: 135; intentional, 1e: 15–16, 124, 220; recognition of, 13–15; subordinate clause as, 1c: 9–11; verbal as, 7–8; ways of correcting, 1d: 11–15, 9d: 121

sentence outline, 402–403, 510–511

sentence pattern, 26: 298–310; and balance, 26c: 302–303; *540*; cumulative sentence, 26i: 308, *544*; and false start, 12c: 142, 307, *547*; and matching, 26a–d: 298–304; and paragraph continuity, 21h: 256–258; suspended sentence, 26j: 308–309. *See also* limiting sentence, main sentence, supporting sentence

serial numbers, hyphens in, 132

series, *559*; climax in, 26d: 303–304; consistency in, 26d: 303–304; defined, 90; of independent clauses, conjunctions optional in, 27; and parallelism problems, 7j–l: 100–102; punctuation of, 7j–l: 100–102, 11d: 136

series, book in, cited in reference list, 483

sexist diction, *559*; avoiding, 82, 27e: 321–324, 527; and common gender, 322–324

shall, 172

shelf list, in library, 449

ship, italicized name of, 20c: 231–232

[*sic*], 160, 234, 464

signals of transition, 21f: 252–255

signature, in business letter, 526–528

significant pause, 26e: 304–305, 309–310, *559–560*

similar, 363

simile, *560*; extended, 337; metaphor vs., 336

since, 363

single quotation marks: for quotation within quotation, 13c: 148; with translation, 231

sit vs. *set*, 363

slang, 317, 327, 341, 527; middle diction vs., 327

slash (virgule), *560*; form and functions of, 146–147, 13g: 152; in notecard, 464; in quotation of poetry, 13g: 152; in correcting final copy, 422; spacing with, 14d: 163; with time, 147, 163

social science reference books, 460

some, 363

somebody vs. *some body*, 344

something, 363

some time vs. *sometime, sometimes*, 202

somewheres, 364

sort of vs. *kind of, type of*, 357–358

sound patterns, 28h: 339–340; alliteration in, 339; Latinate diction in, 340; prepositions in, 340; rhyme in, 339–340

spacing: of abbreviation or acronym, 20k: 237–238; of business letter, 527–530; of endnote or footnote, 490–491; of essay lines, 422; of extracted quotation, 13h: 152–154, 422, 514; of punctuation marks, 14d–k: 163–166; of reference list, 479. *See also* indention; margin

specially vs. *special, especially*, 352

spelling, 18: 198–219; common errors

About the Authors

Frederick Crews, Professor of English at the University of California, Berkeley, received the Ph.D. from Princeton University. Throughout a distinguished career he has attained many honors, including a Guggenheim Fellowship, appointment as a Fulbright Lecturer in Italy, and recognition from the National Endowment for the Arts for his essay "Norman O. Brown: The World Dissolves." His writings include the widely used *Random House Handbook* as well as highly regarded books on Henry James, E. M. Forster, and Nathaniel Hawthorne, the best-selling satire *The Pooh Perplex,* and a volume of his own essays entitled *Out of My System.* Professor Crews has published numerous articles in *Partisan Review, New York Review of Books, Commentary, Tri-Quarterly,* and other important journals. He has twice been Chairman of Freshman Composition in the English Department at Berkeley.

Sandra Schor is Assistant Professor of English at Queens College (City University of New York), where she teaches writing to students at all levels of experience and has served as director of the writing program. She is the coauthor, with Judith Fishman, of the *Random House Guide to Writing;* her essays and reviews on the theory of composition and the teaching of writing have been collected in *The Writer's Mind, What Makes Writing Good, Linguistics, Stylistics, and the Teaching of Composition,* and appear in *College Composition and Communication* and other national publications. She has received a Mellon Fellowship in composition studies as well as a grant from the Fund for the Improvement of Postsecondary Education. In 1981, in recognition of her contributions as a teacher of writing, the City University of New York named her a Master Teacher in the retraining of faculty to teach writing. Professor Schor's fiction and poems appear frequently in such literary journals as *Prairie Schooner, Shenandoah, Centennial Review,* and *Ploughshares.*

A Note on the Type

The text of this book was set on the Linotron 606 in Century School-book, one of the several variations of Century Roman to appear within a decade of its creation. The original face was cut by Linn Boyd Benton in 1895 in response to a request by Theodore Low DeVinne for an attractive, easy-to-read type to fit in the narrow columns of his *Century* magazine.

Century Schoolbook was drawn especially for textbooks used by pupils in primary grades, but because of its easy legibility, it quickly gained popularity in varied applications. The Century family remains the only American typeface cut before 1910 still widely in use today.

This book was composed by TCI, Chicopee, Mass., and was printed and bound by Rand McNally, Indianapolis, Ind.

Symbols for Comment and Revision

When commenting on your written work, your instructor may use some of the following marks. If a mark calls for revision, consult the chapter or section of the *Handbook* printed in boldface type.

√	Excellent point; well said	div	Faulty word division (hyphenation), **18i–m**
√arg	Effective argument		
√concr	Good use of concrete language	dm	Dangling modifier, **4c**
		doc	Faulty documentation form, **37**
√det	Effective supporting detail		
√dev	Effective development of the point	emph	Weak or inappropriate sentence emphasis, **26a–d**
√fig	Apt figure of speech	exag	Exaggeration; overstated claim, **31b**
√ //	Effective parallelism		
√p	Effective choice of punctuation	fig	Inappropriate figure of speech, **28g**
√trans	Good transition	frag	Sentence fragment, **1**
√word	Effective word choice	fs	Fused sentence, **2b**
		gl	Look up this expression in the Glossary of Terms, **538**
abbr	Faulty abbreviation, **20g–k**	ital	Underline (italicize), **20a–f**
		jarg	Jargon, **27f**
ad	Faulty comparison of adjective or adverb, **17**	lc	Do not capitalize (leave in lower case), **19**
agr	Faulty subject-verb agreement, **3**	livel	Stale language; rewrite for liveliness, **28**
awk	Awkward expression		
cap	Capitalize this letter, **19**	log	Faulty logic, **31c–g**
case	Wrong pronoun case, **5**	mixed	Mixed construction, **3a**
chop	Choppy sequence of sentences, **26e**	ms	Faulty manuscript form, **33f**
		no ¶	Do not begin a new paragraph here, **22d**
cl	Cliché, **28e**		
coh	Coherence lacking, **24**	num	Inappropriate form for a number, **20l–n**
colloq	Colloquial expression, **28a**		
comp	Faulty comparison, **7a, 7e**	p	Faulty punctuation, **9–13**
cs	Comma splice, **2b**	pass	Inappropriate use of passive voice, **24g**
d	Inappropriate diction (word choice), **27–29**	p/form	Faulty form or spacing of punctuation mark, **14**